FSA George Wallis

A Catalogue of Manufactures, Decorations and Designs

The Work of the Students of the Schools of Art in Great Britain and Ireland, in

Connection with the Science and Art Department, South Kensington

FSA George Wallis

A Catalogue of Manufactures, Decorations and Designs
The Work of the Students of the Schools of Art in Great Britain and Ireland, in Connection with the Science and Art Department, South Kensington

ISBN/EAN: 9783742809902

Manufactured in Europe, USA, Canada, Australia, Japa

Cover: Foto ©Thomas Meinert / pixelio.de

Manufactured and distributed by brebook publishing software (www.brebook.com)

FSA George Wallis

A Catalogue of Manufactures, Decorations and Designs

International Health Exhibition,

LONDON 1884

SECTION II.—EDUCATION.

A

CATALOGUE

OF

MANUFACTURES, DECORATIONS, AND DESIGNS,

THE WORK OF THE STUDENTS OF THE SCHOOLS OF ART
IN GREAT BRITAIN AND IRELAND, IN CONNECTION
WITH THE SCIENCE AND ART DEPARTMENT,
SOUTH KENSINGTON,

WITH AN INTRODUCTION

By GEORGE WALLIS, F.S.A.,

KEEPER OF THE ART COLLECTIONS, SOUTH KENSINGTON MUSEUM.

LONDON:
WILLIAM CLOWES AND SONS, LIMITED,
1884.

Lord President, LORD CARLINGFORD, K.P.
Vice President, RT. HON. A. J. MUNDELLA, M.P.
Secretary, Col. DONNELLY, R.E.

IIBITION TO ILLUSTRATE THE OPERATIONS AND INFLUENCE OF
SCHOOLS OF ART.

SCHOOL STUDIES.

KS OF ORNAMENTAL AND DECORATIVE ART PRODUCED FROM DESIGNS BY STUDENTS IN
SCHOOLS OF ART.

KS OF ORNAMENTAL AND DECORATIVE ART, WOODCUTS, LITHOGRAPHS, AND ETCHINGS DESIGNED
OR EXECUTED BY THOSE WHO HAVE BEEN STUDENTS IN SCHOOLS OF ART.

1. My Lords consider that it will be of advantage to the Art Education of
country if an Exhibition of Works of Art Manufacture, designed and
:uted by Students of Schools of Art, be held during the present year, in
1ection with and forming part of the International Exhibition at South
sington.

2. The works will consist of Carvings in all materials, Furniture, Decora-
s, Metal working of all kinds, Jewellery, Goldsmiths' work, Pottery, Glass,
ven and Printed Fabrics, &c.

3. All articles exhibited must be the work of past or present Students of
ools of Art, or executed from designs by such Students, the works them-
es having been executed since the year 1862. The articles must be certified
the manufacturers, by the Master of the School of Art in which the Student
received instruction, or by the Student himself. The name of the Manu-
irer, of the School of Art, and of the Student will be published.

4. The decision as to the acceptance of any work for exhibition will rest
rely with the Committee of Selection.

5. The works must be sent to the Department on or before 31st March.
' must be addressed to the Secretary and accompanied by a note (written

A 2

only on the first and third pages) describing them as they are meant to be inserted in the Catalogue. The note should also state the names of the Manufacturers, the Designers, and the Artizans; the names of the Schools of Art attended by any of them; and the periods for which they attended. The prices of each article may be given if it be desired.

6. Every possible care will be taken of the works sent for exhibition, but the responsibility for loss or damage in transit and during the period of the Exhibition will rest with the Exhibitor.

SCIENCE AND ART DEPARTMENT,
SOUTH KENSINGTON,
31st *December,* 1883.

CIRCULAR LETTER TO SCHOOLS OF ART.

EXHIBITION TO ILLUSTRATE THE OPERATIONS AND INFLUENCE OF SCHOOLS OF ART.

SIR,

I am directed to request your attention to the enclosed announcement of the intention of My Lords to organize a Special Exhibition of Works of Ornamental and Decorative Art designed and executed by Students of Schools of Art, or executed from designs by Students, to be held in connection with the International Exhibition which will be opened in May next.

A similar Special Exhibition was held in the South Kensington Museum in 1858, and the evidence then produced of the effect of the instruction imparted in the Schools on some of the more important branches of industrial art was of a very satisfactory character, and My Lords consider that it will be to the advantage of the future action of the Schools that such an exhibition should be held in 1884.

In order to make the illustration of the results of the instruction imparted in Schools of Art as complete and successful as possible, the earnest co-operation of the Committees and Masters is essential, and I am instructed to request that you will bring the matter before your Committee at as early a date as possible, and also that you will obtain all the information in your power as to works which have been manufactured from designs by Students, or executed by them, within the period named in the Circular, viz., since the year 1862, and supply this Department with lists of such manufactures and students, with a brief statement of the articles so produced.

The regulations for sending the various objects, and for their receipt by the Department, with all necessary information respecting transmission, will be forwarded to you in due course on receipt of the information now asked for as preliminary.

As this Exhibition will form an integral part of the Health and Education International Exhibition, the works exhibited will be eligible for consideration by the Juries, and such examples as may be found of sufficient excellence in design and manufacture may be distinguished by the award of medals, &c.

I am, Sir,
Your obedient Servant,
J. F. D. DONNELLY,
Colonel R.E., Secretary.

January, 1884.

INTRODUCTION TO THE CATALOGUE.

THE practical results of the instruction imparted in the Schools of Art now so generally established throughout Great Britain and Ireland, and in the subsidiary art classes in connection with them, cannot fail to be interesting to all who care for national progress in matters of taste; and who desire to enquire how far these institutions are fitting our manufacturers and art workmen to meet the competition of foreign rivals in the markets of the world.

The position of these schools in their relation to manufactures, was fairly illustrated, in spite of the obvious difficulties of the task, by an exhibition of works of art, manufactured, designed or executed by students of the schools, in the summer of 1858, held in the then temporary galleries of the South Kensington Museum. The operations and results of 24 schools were shown on that occasion; this having been the first attempt to illustrate the practical value of the instruction imparted since the foundation of those institutions in 1837.

More than a quarter of a century has elapsed since this effort was made to demonstrate the importance of the work which had fallen into the hands of the Science and Art Department, and to impress the public mind with the primary purpose of these schools. It has therefore appeared expedient to take advantage of the present opportunity to show some of the results of the Technical Teaching in Art Schools, as well as to ascertain as fully as possible the true position of affairs, in order that the workers of the future may have the benefit, at least, of knowing distinctly what were the real shortcomings of the past. The operations of 78 Schools of Art or Art Classes are more or less illustrated on this occasion, but it must be remembered that of the 177 Schools now existing a considerable number are in towns having no special Art Industry, and have been there established with a view to general Art Education, and as a means of stimulating a demand for a higher class of design as applied to objects of domestic use.

Undoubtedly the short period of time allowed for organising the Exhibition has been a drawback in many ways, inasmuch as it not only gave no opportunity for special preparation, but inconveniently limited the time for getting together such existing illustrations as could legitimately come within the range of the period fixed upon, that is, since 1862; the date of the last great International Exhibition in London. On the other hand, the limited time allowed for collecting the illustrations had its advantages in insuring that the works had been produced in the ordinary course of instruction, so far as the schools were concerned, and that the articles of manufacture were only those which had been supplied in the ordinary course of trade, and might thus be considered to fairly represent the current products of the day, as influenced by the schools.

It is, however, very questionable if in every instance the best productions have been shown, owing to the hesitation on the part of many manufacturers to give the full credit properly due to the designer. This hesitation is at once unwise and unfair. The unwisdom is shown in the determination on the part of employers or managers to alter designs in accordance with some workshop tradition or supposed adaptation to the market. This is frequently evident enough to the educated ornamentist, inasmuch as he sees that the incongruity of some detail with the original style of the design is such as no educated student of ornament would for a moment tolerate, but is perpetrated with the greatest self-confidence by the traditional deviser in order to meet what he believes to be the exigencies of the mode of manufacture and the demands of the market. The first is of course paramount, but in many instances alteration is not needed, and the change is not an improvement but an impertinence. The second is based entirely upon an assumption of a knowledge of public demand, and is sought to be justified by the subsequent sale the article has met with, not so much because the consumer really admired the design, but because he must take it or get nothing.

The success of Schools of Art in relation to their original and primary purpose has been most seriously interfered with by this suppression of the designer, the want of that public recognition of his position as an artist which exists in France, Germany, and Belgium, almost invariably driving the ablest and most original into the practice of pictorial and sculptural art, and inducing a public opinion in the schools themselves that if a student is to rise he should rather avoid the study of ornament than seek to make himself master of it, since the result will only be to make him the not overpaid, but the very subordinate servant of the manufacturer, or the caterer to the markets for decorative works. Thus it is that students frequently only tolerate the study of ornamental design rather than enter into its varied phases with scholar-like aptitude, enjoying, as the best ornamentists of the past have always done, its infinite adaptation to the refinement of every-day life, and the production of works of elegance and beauty for the home and the fireside.

It is no uncommon thing to find students who give great promise of excellence in this direction declaring that they would have gone on with their practice of ornamental design if they could have been properly appreciated and fairly remunerated ; but, above all, have been free from the dictation of those who really had no knowledge of the principles of decorative art, and whose only notions of style and beauty arose out of a foregone conclusion of what would *sell.*

The result has been that whilst many resorted to pictorial art and teaching, others have gone abroad, chiefly to the United States, others to Canada and the Australian Colonies. The Chief Medallist of the United States Mint at Philadelphia, Mr. George Morgan, who contributes to this Exhibition, and the Managing

Director of the Gorham Silver Plate Manufacturing Company, Providence, Rhode Island, Mr. George Wilkinson, were both former students of the Birmingham School of Art. The latter, an able designer and die sinker for silver plate, was dissatisfied with the work he was called upon to execute in this country. A more recent case may be quoted. Mr. John Watkins entered the Birmingham School some years ago, a comparatively poor boy, having to work his own way as best he might. He distinguished himself, and ultimately came to the South Kensington Schools as a national scholar (1873 to 1875). Here he devoted himself to ornamental design so successfully, that in 1878 a design he had executed for a shield, which obtained the prize of £50 from the Goldsmiths' Company, was purchased for £50 by the Department, on the recommendation of Mr. E. J. Poynter, R.A., then Art Director; and subsequently Messrs. Elkington & Co., obtaining the loan of the work, decided to execute it in silver. Both design and unfinished shield are shown in this Exhibition. For some time before going to Paris, Mr. Watkins was employed by the proprietors of "*L'Art,*" to make drawings for that publication, and subsequently, after his removal to Paris, to design titles and other decorative details for that journal and other works. Recently, a commission was offered to Mr. Watkins, to execute certain decorative designs in the Science and Art Department. It is best to give his reply in his own words.

"Paris, *April* 4, 1884.

"I should have been glad to undertake the commission at an earlier period, but have now entered on a new course of study, quite different to anything I have ever done before, and entirely at my own expense. I find that it demands my whole attention, and that any return to decoration would be very prejudicial to my progress.

"I have relinquished ornamental art, and would rather be excused from undertaking the design."

This is a clear and distinct illustration of the want of timely encouragement on the part of those for whose assistance students have been trained in our Schools of Art to the practice of ornamental design. Instances, though of a less marked character, are constantly occurring. Complaints have been made by past students, invited to contribute to this Exhibition, of the interference of Trades Unions with their employment as decorators, and the consequent necessity for their falling back on pictorial art, as copyists, &c.

Can it be wondered at, then, that students do not enter freely upon a course of study, if it only yields such results?

If the Technical Colleges and Schools now so energetically advocated are to result in an equal ignoring of the men trained therein, because the science they would bring to bear upon industry is not in conformity with the foregone conclusions of manufacturers, managers, foremen and trades unions, these institutions will only prove to be training grounds for the future assistants of our foreign rivals, who will appreciate that knowledge which our own people do not care to make use of.

Happily there is an aspect of this question which, forming an exception, also proves the rule. Whenever the sons of manufacturers have availed themselves earnestly of the instruction given in these Schools of Art, or when students have afterwards become manufacturers and managers, and have been true to their training, they have invariably improved the designs of the industry they have engaged in, and in spite of the buyer for the market and the salesman, carried these improvements before the public.

Again, when the manufacturer has resolved to use the school as the handmaid of the workshop, and to utilise the ability developed in its teaching, the results have invariably been of a satisfactory character, alike to manufacturer, student and the public. No better evidence of this can be afforded than in the remarkable rise and progress of the well-known Doulton ware: beginning, little more than fifteen years ago, by the employment of the students of the Lambeth School of Art. This has grown into a successful art industry, belonging more to the present certainly than to the past, asserting itself for its own day and the wants of our own time.

Nottingham, again, is another illustration of the wise use of the School of Art to a comparatively new industry, that of furniture lace. Here the ingenious machinery applicable to the production of those fabrics is made subservient to the designer, by giving him perfect mastery over the means at his disposal; and even if it modifies, and to a certain extent possibly limits the elaboration of his forms, it yet exercises a restraining power which is more healthy than otherwise, preventing the almost licentious use of the loom in the production of designs utterly inconsistent alike with the material in which the fabric is produced and the use to which it is to be devoted.

The honourable position attained by Singer's Art Workshops at Frome may also be cited as an instance of success largely due to the benefits derived from the art teaching of the department, two of the junior members of the firm having been trained at South Kensington, and its subordinate workers being prepared by receiving instruction in a School of Art at Frome, which has grown up with the manufactory.

Letheren's Art Manufactory and Construction Iron Works, Cheltenham, is another example of the same kind.

It is to be regretted that some important centres of art manufacture are not by any means adequately represented in this Exhibition. In some instances manufacturers were willing to acknowledge the value of the instruction imparted in the Schools of Art in the education of their designers, but hesitated to allow the names of the designers to appear in this illustration of the action of the schools. It must, however, be perfectly clear that the Department of Science and Art could not consent to the suppression of the names of the designers in a collective illustration of the operations and influence of the schools. The Exhibition must of necessity be a student's and designer's Exhibition, and not a manufacturer's, although it was gratifying to find that some manufacturers heartily concurred in taking this opportunity for encouraging native design. It was therefore better for the integrity of the demonstration that when the names of the designers could not be given, no exhibition of results should take place.

One very satisfactory feature of this Exhibition, as a contrast to that of 1858, is the readiness with which former students, who have taken positions which render them independent of the manufacturer, have come forward to prove their capacity, and to show that they appreciate their former connection with the schools. In 1858 this candour was by no means general, and indeed the manufacturer then rather exceeded the designer in readiness to exhibit.

Those manufacturers who have come forward on this occasion have done so in a genuine and liberal spirit, seeking to give credit to those to whom credit is due.

One fact may be unhesitatingly recorded. It is that at least eighty per cent. of the objects of industrial art here exhibited would have been impossible of production, thirty or even twenty-five years ago, for the very best possible reasons; the men who made the designs were uneducated for the purpose, as the workmen to carry out the designs when made, would have been difficult to find; and the probability is that the manufacturer would not have dared to produce them, without the permission of his dictator, the buyer or salesman, who of course would not believe they would *sell.*

It may be readily granted that concurrent forces were at work in the efforts of individuals seeking to influence public taste, and thus to create a demand in a higher direction; but even they had to take advantage of the elementary training gained in the schools, and certainly they were not free from the influences around them, either for better or worse.

If, however, any one supposes that this Exhibition is a full and complete illustration of all that has been done by and through Schools of Art since 1862, he forgets what has been going on throughout the whole country. After all, it simply shows little more than the outer margin of the ground which has been more or less covered.

As a matter of course the influence of the schools upon the thousands of workmen who have gone through the classes during the period from the extension of the schools to the provinces, say 1843-4, to the present time, cannot be in any way fully illustrated. The improvement of handicraft through the study of the elements of drawing alone, has been proved over and over again to those coming in contact with workmen who had availed themselves of the instruction; the proof being seen in the work done—an utterly unappreciated phase of the action of the schools.

The influence of the Central Museum at South Kensington which has been recognised all over Europe, can scarcely have been inoperative in Great Britain. The public has had the opportunity of studying fine works of art, bought because they were fine, not from any fancied adaptation to this or that means of imitation; thus making industrial capital out of them. Taste has been raised by the sight of such objects and a feeling gradually created which demands something of a higher order than had been supplied before, and the producer finds himself face to face with an advancing knowledge and discovers that there is a market for objects appealing to an art perception higher than that to which he had been before called upon to minister, to which he himself has hitherto been a stranger. The branches of the Museum, and the many allied

institutions to which from time to time it has circulated collections on loan
have widened and strengthened this influence.

The question of the artizan and art workman has, however, a good deal to
do with this matter. What was the argument of the manufacturer prior to
the establishment of these schools, and for some years after, until their influences
began to be felt? It was, that even if we got good designs, they were spoiled
by the want of art—skill in the workman in carrying them out! This was
the origin of the demand for skilled Frenchmen who could not only design,
but realise their own designs—Emile Jeannest, Protat, Carrier, Willms, and
others.

The change in this point is in itself an illustration. Even twenty-five years
ago it was no uncommon thing with those actively at work in the schools to
find workmen who had passed through them complain of the designs which
they were compelled to execute, because the exigencies of the market necessitated
their production. Later on, those who took the trouble to converse with art
workmen on the character of designs they were producing, might be shocked,
but not much astonished, at the strong language with which they denounced the
things in hand. The fact is that the intelligent art workman, who from boy-
hood to early manhood has studied in these Schools of Art, is far in advance of
the employer, in point of critical acumen and art knowledge, to say nothing of
the manager or foreman, whose notions he has to tolerate; or of that conventional
arbiter of public taste, the man who only buys an object to *sell*, and of course
makes it sell, however objectionable it may be to the educated taste of the
consumer.

One feature of the view which the seller adopts is shown in the fact that
the best designs in textile fabrics are frequently offered as French. Specimens
in this Exhibition have been labelled " French " in the shop windows, and
attempts have been made to obtain the withdrawal of examples exhibited,
because the seller objected to the real origin of the design and fabric being
made known to the public.

Those who can look back to the state of the arts of design as applied to the
various industries illustrated, say a quarter of a century ago, to say nothing of
the period at which Schools of Design were first founded, cannot fail to see that
the progress has been enormous. This is the only true test of the results, and
not the mere comparison with what has been growing up before our eyes from
year to year, influenced by the Schools and their teaching. Those who cannot
go back thus far, and therefore have no means of comparison, may be none the
worse for being reminded that the standard according to which they form their
opinions now, and in reliance on which they very legitimately, as they think,
sit in judgment, is the absolute product of the very progress in the arts which
some of them fancy themselves privileged to deny.

The assumption that the course pursued has been wrong, is simply an
assumption without proof. That the course has been perfect, or in any
way complete, possibly no one will maintain. But when honestly, earnestly,
and energetically worked out, it has done more than any system existing
at this moment in Europe, and the best witnesses in its favour are our

Continental neighbours themselves, who seek, with some modifications, no doubt, to adapt it to their own wants.

Finally, it may be well to record the fact, that the early promoters of the Art Education of the people through these schools held very distinctly the opinion, that it would take at least a generation, possibly nearer two, before any very marked results could possibly arise, and that, moreover, without taking into account the apathy and opposition which subsequently arose from the impatience of some, and the self-satisfaction of others.

In all the contributions to the Exhibition the greatest care has been taken to have evidence of the connection of the exhibitor with the school or schools in which he or she studied; and, when necessary, to require a certificate that the work is that of the student in whose name it is exhibited, together with a record of the period or periods at which attendance was given in the school.

May, 1884.   GEORGE WALLIS.

CLASSIFICATION

OF THE

EXHIBITION TO ILLUSTRATE THE OPERATIONS AND INFLUENCE OF SCHOOLS OF ART.

CATALOGUE.

DIVISION II.—EDUCATION.

SECTION I.

chool Studies in Stages of Instruction. Designs and Models executed by the Students of the Schools.

The latter are classed with the section to which they belong.]

1. Five School Studies. *Stages* 1 C, 1 D, E, 2 B, 3 B.
    By James Clarke, *South Kensington.*

2. Geometrical Studies. *Stage* 1 A.
    By H. G. Massey, *South Kensington.*

3. Architectural Studies. *Stage* 1 D.
    By Miss M. A. Heath, *Gloucester.*

4. Study in Sepia. *Stage* 5 A.
    By H. G. Massey, *South Kensington.*

5. Study in Chalk from the Cast. *Stage* 5 B.
    By A. Palmer, *York.*

6. Study in Chalk from the Cast. *Stage* 5 B.
    By James Clarke, *South Kensington.*

7. Study in Chalk from the Cast. *Stage* 4 B.
    By Miss Mary C. Lock, *Dorchester.*

8. Study in Chalk from Life. *Stage* 8 C.
    By A. E. Pearce, *Lambeth.*

9. Study from the Cast in Chalk. *Stage* 8 B².
    By W. A. Mulligan, *South Kensington.*

10. Study in Chalk from the Cast. *Stage* 8 B².
    By Miss Florence Reason, *Bloomsbury.*

11. Study in Chalk from Life. *Stage* 8 C¹.
    By Miss C. M. D. Hammond, *Lambeth.*

12. Study in Chalk from the Cast. *Stage* 8 B².
    By George Bathgate, *Edinburgh.*

13. Study in Chalk from the Cast. *Stage* 8 B².
    By Miss Florence Reason, *Bloomsbury.*

14. Sketch in Chalk. *Stage* 23 D.
    By Alfred Hitchins, *South Kensington.*

15. Study in Chalk from Life. *Stage* 8 C².
    By Miss Edith Savill, *Lambeth.*

16. Two Anatomical Studies. *Stage* 9 A.
    By George Morton, *South Kensington.*

17. Two School Sketches. *Stage* 23 D.
    By Miss Agnes Webster, *South Kensington.*

18. Chalk Study from the Life. *Stage* 8 C¹.
    By A. E. Pearce, *Lambeth.*

19. Study from the Cast in Sepia. *Stage* 16 A.
    By W. H. Webb, *West London.*

20. Outline Study from Nature. *Stage* 10 A.
    By J. J. Trego, *Coventry.*

21. Outline Study from Nature. *Stage* 10 A.
    By J. Gardner, *Coventry.*

22. Study of Flowers in Water Colours. *Stage* 13 A.
    By Miss A. M. Bailey, *South Kensington.*

23. Pencil Study from Nature. *Stage* 10 B.
    By G. W. Rhead, *South Kensington.*

24. Water Colour Study from Nature. *Stage* 14 A.
    By W. P. Watson, *South Kensington.*

25. Water Colour Study from Nature. *Stage* 14 A.
    By Miss Jessie Betts, *Weymouth.*

26. Flower Studies from Nature. *Stage* 14 A.
    By H. J. Whiteside, *Birkenhead.*

27. Water Colour Studies of Flowers. *Stage.* 14 A.
    By Miss Laura Dawe, *Plymouth.*

28. Water Colour Study from Nature. *Stage* 14 A.
    By C. T. Howard, *Boston.*

29. Study of Flowers in Tempera. *Stage* 14 A.
    By Miss Rosa Wallis, *South Kensington.*

30. Study in Oil from Nature. *Stage* 14 A.
    By A. Fisher, *Torquay.*

31. Study in Monochrome. *Stage* 12 A.
    By W. P. Watson, *South Kensington.*

32. Water-colour Group. *Stage* 15 B.
    By Miss E. C. Nisbet, *Bloomsbury.*
    (Lent by Mrs. Brightwen.)

33. Study of Drapery. *Stage* 15 A.
    By E. O. Cooke, *Nottingham.*

34. Landscape (copy) in Oils. *Stage* 13 B.
    By W. P. Watson, *South Kensington.*

35. Group in Oils. *Stage* 15 A.
    By S. H. Llewellyn, *South Kensington.*

36. Study of Flowers in Oils. *Stage* 15 A.
    By Miss Lydia B. King, *Bloomsbury.*

37. Study in Oils (copy). *Stage* 17 A.
    By Mrs. Finney. *South Kensington.*

38. Study in Oil (copy). *Stage* 17 A.
    By George Morton, *South Kensington.*

39. Study in Oils, Group. *Stage* 15 A.
    By George Morton, *South Kensington.*

40. Study in Sepia. *Stage* 16 B¹.
    By E. S. Heise, *Birkenhead.*

41. Group in Oils. *Stage* 15 A.
    By E. O. Cooke, *Nottingham*

42. Group in Oils. *Stage* 15 A.
    By Miss E. Slater, *Gloucester.*

43. Study in Oils from Life. *Stage* 17 B.
    By Miss A. Parnell, *Dublin.*

44. Study in Oils from life. *Stage* 17 B.
    By George Hare, *South Kensington.*

45. Study in Water Colour from Life *Stage* 17 C.
    By A. G. Morrow, *South Kensington.*

46. Group in Monochrome. *Stage* 15 C.
    By G. Homan, *West London.*

47. Study in Oils from Life. *Stage* 17 B.
    By George Hare, *South Kensington.*

48. Study in Oils from Life. *Stage* 17 B.
    By Miss Evans, *South Kensington.*

49. Four Life Studies in Oil. *Stage* 3-17 B and 1-17 C.
    By Alfred Hitchins, *South Kensington.*

50. Two Studies in Chalk, monthly competition.
    By A. G. Morrow, *South Kensington.*

51. Study from Life in Water Colour. *Stage* 17 B.
    By Miss F. Reason, *Bloomsbury.*
    (Lent by the Duchess of Edinburgh.)

52. Study of Flowers in Oils. *Stage* 15 A.
    By Miss Isabel Hancock, *Bloomsbury.*
    (Lent by the Duchess of Edinburgh.)

53. Study of Fruit in Water Colours. *Stage* 14 A.
    By E. L. Varley, *Bloomsbury.*

54. Study of Stop and Safety Valves. *Stage* 23 A.
    By J. H. Robertson, *Dundee.*

55. Study of Stop and Safety Valves *Stage* 23 A.
    By Wm. Adamson, *Dundee.*

56. Two Studies of 70-ton Crane. *Stage* 23 A.
    By Robert Witts, *Dundee.*

57. Study of the High Girders, Tay Bridge. *age* 23 A.
> *By* J. McInroy, *Dundee.*

58. Sixteen Frames, containing Time designs rked out in six or eight hours by Students, follows :—

Painted Wall Tiles.
> *By* Misses E. Small, M. Butterton, E. Lupton, and Mr. G. H. Tabor, *Lambeth.*

Table Top, inlaid.
> *By* P. Hall, J. O. Poole, G. Ward, and W. F. White, *South Kensington.*

Silver Vase.
> *By* J. Bradburn, J. Gater, and H. Tomlins, *South Kensington.*

Silver Cup.
> *By* C. Dodd, W. Mulligan, H. Rider, and J. Ward, *South Kensington.*

Earthenware Vase.
> *By* F. Abrahams, G. Henney, and H. Tomlins, *South Kensington.*

Wrought-iron Grill.
> *By* J. Bradburn, J. Gater, G. Henney, and F. Leighton, *South Kensington.*

Clock Case.
> *By* P. Hall, J. Poole, J. Ward, and W. White, *South Kensington.*

Brussels Carpet.
> *By* J. Bradburn, F. Penson, R. Rhodes, and H. Tomlins, *South Kensington.*

Terra Cotta Columns.
> *By* G. Bradburn, J. Henney, and R. Rhodes, *South Kensington.*

Various Designs.
> *By* F. Leighton, G. Henney, and J. Bradburn, *South Kensington.*

59. Illustrations for a method of Studies in ater Colours. 1881. *Stage* 15 B.
> *By* F. Suddars, *Bradford.* Age 16.

60. Study of Still Life in Water Colours, used on the above. 1881. *Stage* 15 B.
> *By* F. Suddars, *Bradford.* Age 16.

61. Drawing in Tempera. *Stage* 14 A.
> *By* W. W. Morrison, *South Kensington.*

62. Study of Palm. *Stage* 14 A.
> *By* C. Humphries, *South Kensington.*

63. Study in Tempera. *Stage* 14 A.
> *By* E. A. Slocombe, *South Kensington.*

SECTION II.

Ceramic Manufactures, Porcelain, Earthenware, Stoneware, Terra Cotta, &c.

EXHIBITED BY MESSRS. DOULTON, LAMBETH, AS A COLLECTIVE ILLUSTRATION OF THE INFLUENCE OF THE LAMBETH SCHOOL OF ART.

A central pavilion with four stands around. The pavilion is in the form of a dome and tympanum 30 ft. high and 30 ft. square, supported on Doulton ware columns backed by wood pilasters. The roof is of parti-coloured glazed tiles with ribs of Doulton ware, and bulls' eyes in each alternate division. The dome rests upon a cornice carried on 16 pilasters, between which are panels of pottery, mosaic, and painted glass alternating. The lower part forms a square with four entrances, over which are Doulton arches, and between which are large hand-painted subject tiles, arranged four on each side, representing :—

> Science, Commerce, Western Art, Eastern Art.
> Old Lambeth, New Lambeth, The Bishop's Palace, High Street.
> Throwing, Lathing, Tile Making, Kiln Work.
> Palissy, Della Robbia, Wedgwood, Shonsui of Tse.

The interior of dome is of special construction, being of semi-circular arches intersecting each other, the spaces thus formed being filled in with faience tiles, divided by ribs of Doulton ware, and a gallery of Doulton ware balusters above. Within the pavilion are exhibited mantel-pieces, and patented fire-places of pottery with art ware, &c., representing : *Drawing-room, Dining-room, Boudoir and Study.* The stands around are placed at each corner of the space occupied, and are also ornamented with Doulton ware and faience, the front being an open arcade with balusters. In these stands are exhibited : *Bath Room complete, Open and Close Stoves, Filters and General Stoneware, Queen's ware, Brass work,* and *Sanitary Appliances in action.*

The following are the names of some of the artists engaged in the work, nearly all of them having been students of the Lambeth School of Art :—

Constructional design and details . . . }	A. E. Pearce.
Stained glass . . .	do.
Mosaic panels. . . .	do.
Doulton columns . . {	A. E. Pearce and F. A. Butler.
Doulton balusters and Modelling . . . }	J. Broad.
Doulton Caps and Friezes	H. Ellis.

Faience tile panels designed by J. Eyre.

B

The following have also taken part in the execution of various portions of the work :—

J. W. Nunn.	Miss E. Lewis.
Cruickshank.	Miss E. Roberts.
J. H. McLellan.	Miss Vargas.

together with about 120 others who likewise assisted in carrying out the details.

64. Vase, dark blue ground, yellow flowers.
   Designed by Miss Margaret Challis, Lambeth.
   Manufactured by Messrs. Doulton.

65. Vase, brown, ornamented with flowers.
   Designed by Miss Louisa Davis, Lambeth.
   Manufactured by Messrs. Doulton.

66. Vase, light green ground, and ornamented with scroll pattern and figure.
   Designed by Jas. R. Cruikshank, Lambeth.
   Manufactured by Messrs. Doulton.

67. Vase, silicon ware.
   Designed by Miss Eliza Simmance, Lambeth.
   Manufactured by Messrs. Doulton.

68. Vase, floral decoration, with birds on green ground.
   Designed by Miss Isabel Lewis, Lambeth.
   Manufactured by Messrs. Doulton.

69. Small Vase.
   Designed by U. A. Larcher, Lambeth.
   Manufactured by Messrs. Doulton.

70. Vase, salt glaze.
   Designed by Miss Ada Dennis, Lambeth.
   Manufactured by Messrs. Doulton.

71. Small Vase for Flowers.
   Designed by Miss Emma Roberts, Lambeth.
   Manufactured by Messrs. Doulton.

72. Bowl, decorated silicon.
   Designed by Miss Edith H. Ball, Lambeth.
   Manufactured by Messrs. Doulton.

73. Vase, floral ornament, parcel gilt.
   Designed by Miss B. M. Durtnall, Lambeth.
   Manufactured by Messrs. Doulton.

74. Vase, Champlevé ware.
   Designed by Miss Edith M. Coleman, Lambeth.
   Manufactured by Messrs. Doulton.

75. Bowl, Champlevé ware.
   Designed by Miss A. Horne, Lambeth.
   Manufactured by Messrs. Doulton.

76. Vase, floral decoration.
   Designed by Miss Fanny Elliott, Lambeth.
   Manufactured by Messrs. Doulton.

77. Vase, floral ornament.
   Designed by Miss K. B. Smallfield, Lambeth.
   Manufactured by Messrs. Doulton.

78. Bowl, stone ware.
   Designed by Miss L. Wakely, Lambeth.
   Manufactured by Messrs. Doulton.

79. Small Vase, salt glaze.
   Designed by Miss Elizabeth French, Lambeth.
   Manufactured by Messrs. Doulton.

80. Jug, parcel gilt.
   Designed by Miss A. Campbell, Lambeth.
   Manufactured by Messrs. Doulton.

81. Vase, grey silicon ware.
   Designed by Miss L. Stuart, Lambeth.
   Manufactured by Messrs. Doulton.

82. Flower Vase, stone ware.
   Designed by Miss E. A. London, Lambeth.
   Manufactured by Messrs. Doulton.

83. Vase, Champlevé ware.
   Designed by Miss A. M. Barker, Lambeth.
   Manufactured by Messrs. Doulton.

84. Decorated Plaque.
   Designed by Walter Nunn, Lambeth.
   Manufactured by Messrs. Doulton.

85. Vase, Champlevé ware.
   Designed by Miss E. Chandler, Lambeth.
   Manufactured by Messrs. Doulton.

86. Bottle, Champlevé ware.
   Designed by Miss Alice Eckenstein, Lambeth.
   Manufactured by Messrs. Doulton.

87. Vase, Champlevé ware.
   Designed by Miss A. Herapath, Lambeth.
   Manufactured by Messrs. Doulton.

88. Vase.
    Designed by Miss Mary Capes, Lambeth.
    Manufactured by Messrs. Doulton.

89. Flower Pot, salt glaze stone ware.
    Designed by Miss Martha M. Rogers, Lambeth.
    Manufactured by Messrs. Doulton.

90. Vase, Champlevé ware.
    Designed by Miss M. Canty, Lambeth.
    Manufactured by Messrs. Doulton.

91. Vase, salt glaze, stone ware.
    Designed by E. L. Rumble, Lambeth.
    Manufactured by Messrs. Doulton.

92. Green Vase, floral ornament.
    Designed by Miss Mary Capes, Lambeth.
    Manufactured by Messrs. Doulton.

93. Flower Vase.
    Designed by Miss E. A. Forsey, Lambeth.
    Manufactured by Messrs. Doulton.

94. Jug, stone ware.
    Designed by Miss B. J. Youatt, Lambeth.
    Manufactured by Messrs. Doulton.

95. Vase, Champlevé ware.
    Designed by Miss Jessie Gandy, Lambeth.
    Manufactured by Messrs. Doulton.

96. Vase, green ground with floral decoration.
    Designed by Miss Florence Lewis, Lambeth.
    Manufactured by Messrs. Doulton.

97. Vase, with floral decoration.
    Designed by Miss A. L. Green, Lambeth.
    Manufactured by Messrs. Doulton.

98. Vase, salt glaze stone ware.
    With Etchings by Miss Barlow, Lambeth.
    Manufactured by Messrs. Doulton.

99. Vase, salt glaze ware.
    Designed by Miss A. L. Burlton, Lambeth.
    Manufactured by Messrs. Doulton.

100. Vase, floral ornament.
    Designed by Miss Florence Lewis, Lambeth.
    Manufactured by Messrs. Doulton.

101. Vase, Champlevé ware.
    Designed by Miss Florence C. Roberts, Lambeth.
    Manufactured by Messrs. Doulton.

102. Flower Bowl.
    Designed by Miss Mina Crawley, Lambeth.
    Manufactured by Messrs. Doulton.

103. Bowl, salt glaze.
    Designed by Miss L. E. Edwards, Lambeth.
    Manufactured by Messrs. Doulton.

104. Bowl, floral decoration.
    Designed by Miss Matilda S. Adams, Lambeth.
    Manufactured by Messrs. Doulton.

105. Bottle, salt glaze.
    Designed by Miss Clara S. Barker, Lambeth.
    Manufactured by Messrs. Doulton.

106. Vase.
    Designed by Miss A. Beck, Lambeth.
    Manufactured by Messrs. Doulton.

107. Plaque.
    Designed by Miss Kate Sturgeon, Lambeth.
    Manufactured by Messrs. Doulton.

108. Vase, stone ware.
    Designed by Miss H. E. Lee, Lambeth.
    Manufactured by Messrs. Doulton.

109. Vase, stone ware.
    Designed by Miss Gathercole, Lambeth.
    Manufactured by Messrs. Doulton.

110. Bottle.
    Designed by Miss L. Waters, Lambeth.
    Manufactured by Messrs. Doulton.

111. Flower Bowl, Champlevé ware.
    Designed by Miss E. Rogers, Lambeth.
    Manufactured by Messrs. Doulton.

112. Vase, stone ware.
    Designed by Miss Ellen Garbett, Lambeth.
    Manufactured by Messrs. Doulton.

113. Vase, light brown ground with Cupids.
    Designed by Miss I. M. Rogers, Lambeth.
    Manufactured by Messrs. Doulton.

B 2

114. Vase, stone ware.
Designed by Miss E. Rumbol, *Lambeth.*
Manufactured by Messrs. Doulton.

115. Vase, Impasto ware.
Designed by Miss F. J. Allen, *Lambeth.*
Manufactured by Messrs. Doulton.

116. Vase, Impasto ware.
Designed by Miss Rosa Keen, *Lambeth.*
Manufactured by Messrs. Doulton.

117. Vase, salt glaze stone ware.
Designed by Miss J. Newnham, *Lambeth.*
Manufactured by Messrs. Doulton.

118. Jar and Cover.
Designed by Miss A. Hays, *Lambeth.*
Manufactured by Messrs. Doulton.

119. Vase, stone ware.
Designed by Miss Mary Davis, *Lambeth.*
Manufactured by Messrs. Doulton.

120. Vase, stone ware.
Designed by Miss Hawkesley, *Lambeth.*
Manufactured by Messrs. Doulton.

121. Biscuit Box, inlaid ware.
Designed by Miss B. Evans, *Lambeth.*
Manufactured by Messrs. Doulton.

122. Vase, stone ware.
Designed by Miss M. Aitken, *Lambeth.*
Manufactured by Messrs. Doulton.

123. Vase, salt glaze.
Etchings by Miss Barlow, *Lambeth.*
Manufactured by Messrs. Doulton.

124. Flower Pot.
Designed by Miss A. E. Budden, *Lambeth.*
Manufactured by Messrs. Doulton.

125. Vase.
Designed by Miss E. F. Bowen, *Lambeth.*
Manufactured by Messrs. Doulton.

126. Jar and Cover.
Designed by Miss Isabella Miller, *Lambeth.*
Manufactured by Messrs. Doulton.

127. Small Vase.
Designed by Miss Catherine Hughes, *Lambeth.*
Manufactured by Messrs. Doulton.

128. Mug.
Designed by M. G. Thompson, *Lambeth.*
Manufactured by Messrs. Doulton.

129. Ewer, salt glaze.
Designed by Miss Elizabeth Fisher, *Lambeth.*
Manufactured by Messrs. Doulton.

130. Vase.
Designed by Miss Mary Butters, *Lambeth.*
Manufactured by Messrs. Doulton.

131. Vase, Champlevé ware.
Designed by Miss Alice Groome, *Lambeth.*
Manufactured by Messrs. Doulton.

132. Vase, Impasto ware.
Designed by Miss Lizzie Haughton, *Lambeth.*
Manufactured by Messrs. Doulton.

133. Vase, stone ware.
Designed by Miss Sarah Mary Harey, *Lambeth.*
Manufactured by Messrs. Doulton.

134. Vase.
Designed by Miss Elizabeth Emerton, *Lambeth.*
Manufactured by Messrs. Doulton.

135. Vase, Repoussé ware.
Designed by William Parker, *Lambeth.*
Manufactured by Messrs. Doulton.

136. Pot, clay, with fishes worked with two coloured clays, and glazed.
Designed by William Baron, *Lambeth.*
Manufactured by Messrs. Doulton.

137. Ewer, stone ware.
Designed by Miss Elizabeth Hollis, *Lambeth.*
Manufactured by Messrs. Doulton.

138. Vase, floral decoration.
Designed by Miss Gertrude Smith, *Lambeth.*
Manufactured by Messrs. Doulton.

139. Vase.
Designed by Miss Lillian Goldsack, *Lambeth.*
Manufactured by Messrs. Doulton.

140. Vase, Champlevé ware.
Designed by Miss Lulu Durtnall, *Lambeth.*
Manufactured by Messrs. Doulton.

141. Vase, Impasto ware.
Designed by Miss Kate Rogers, *Lambeth.*
Manufactured by Messrs. Doulton.

142. Bowl, with floral ornament, parcel gilt.
Designed by M. Arding, *Lambeth.*
Manufactured by Messrs. Doulton.

143. Vase, salt glaze.
Designed by Miss Frances E. Lee, *Lambeth.*
Manufactured by Messrs. Doulton.

144. Vase, floral decoration.
Designed by Miss Helen A. Arding, *Lambeth.*
Manufactured by Messrs. Doulton.

145. Vase, silicon ware.
Designed by Miss Jessie Hinchliff, *Lambeth.*
Manufactured by Messrs. Doulton.

146. Vase, floral ornament.
Designed by Miss Lizzie Shettleworth, *Lambeth.*
Manufactured by Messrs. Doulton.

147. Flower Pot.
Designed by Miss Florence E. Barlow, *Lambeth.*
Manufactured by Messrs. Doulton.

148. Vase, Champlevé ware.
Designed by Miss Louisa Russell, *Lambeth.*
Manufactured by Messrs. Doulton.

149. Vase, conventional ornament.
Designed by Miss Mary Denley, *Westminster and Lambeth.*
Manufactured by Messrs. Doulton.

150. Vase, stone ware.
Designed by Miss Emily E. Storwer, *Lambeth.*
Manufactured by Messrs. Doulton.

151. Vase, floral ornament.
Designed by Miss Euphania Thatcher, *Lambeth.*
Manufactured by Messrs. Doulton.

152. Vase, stone ware.
Designed by Miss Elizabeth M. Small, *Lambeth.*
Manufactured by Messrs. Doulton.

153. Vase, stone ware.
Designed by Miss Georgina D. Burr, *Lambeth.*
Manufactured by Messrs. Doulton.

154. Vase, Florentine decoration.
Designed by Miss Josephine A. Durtnall, *Lambeth.*
Manufactured by Messrs. Doulton.

155. Flower Pot, Champlevé ware.
Designed by A. Miss Lillian Curtis, *Lambeth.*
Manufactured by Messrs. Doulton.

156. Flower Pot, Champlevé ware.
Designed by E. B. Smith, *Lambeth.*
Manufactured by Messrs. Doulton.

157. Bowl.
Designed by Miss Amy Georgina Moore, *Lambeth.*
Manufactured by Messrs. Doulton.

158. Vase, Champlevé ware.
Designed by Miss Edith D. Lupton, *Lambeth.*
Manufactured by Messrs. Doulton.

159. Large Vase, floral decoration.
Designed by Miss Florence Lewis, *Lambeth.*
Manufactured by Messrs. Doulton.

160. Large stone ware Vase.
Designed by Frank Butler, *Lambeth.*
Manufactured by Messrs. Doulton.

161. Large Vase, floral ornament.
Designed by Miss Mary Butterton, *Lambeth.*
Manufactured by Messrs. Doulton.

162. Terra Cotta Panel, "The Sons of Cydippe."
Designed and executed by Geo. Tinworth, *Lambeth.*

163. Terra Cotta Panel, "Meeting of Joseph and Jacob"
Designed and executed by Geo. Tinworth, *Lambeth.*

164. Terra Cotta Group, " Hercules and Antæus."
 　　Designed and executed by Geo. Tin-worth, Lambeth.

165. Terra Cotta Group, " Football."
 　　Designed and executed by Geo. Tin-worth, Lambeth.

166. Terra Cotta Panel, " Peter's Denial."
 　　Designed and executed by Geo. Tin-worth, Lambeth.

167. Terra Cotta Panel, " The Four Lepers.'
 　　Designed and executed by Geo. Tin-worth, Lambeth.

168. Terra Cotta Panel, " Finding of Jesus in the Temple."
 　　Designed and executed by Geo. Tin-worth, Lambeth.

169. Terra Cotta Panel, " The Tribute Money."
 　　Designed and executed by Geo. Tin-worth, Lambeth.

170. Terra Cotta Panel, " The Box of Oint-ment."
 　　Designed and executed by Geo. Tin-worth, Lambeth.

171. Terra Cotta Panel, " The Slaughter of the Innocents."
 　　Designed and executed by Geo. Tin-worth, Lambeth.

172. Jardinière, blue and coloured clays.
 　　Designed by Alexander Fisher.
 　　Executed by Torquay Terra Cotta Co.

173. Twelve Specimens of Jugs, Tazzas, Vases, &c.
 　　Designed by Arthur J. Davey.
 　　Executed by The Watcombe Terra Cotta Co., Torquay.

174. Dark Red Lustre Majolica Plateau.
 　　Designed by James Gamble, Sheffield.
 　　(Lent by H.R.H. The Duke of Edinburgh.)

175. Eight Specimens of Salisbury Pottery.
 　　Designed and manufactured by Ella Jacob, The Close, Salisbury.

176. Dessert Plate with pierced border.
 　　Designed, pierced, and coloured by Miss Lucy Worth.
 　　Manufactured by Linthorpe Pottery Co., Middlesborough.

177. Large Plate.
 　　Designed by Miss Lucy Worth, Not-tingham.
 　　Manufactured by Linthorpe Pottery Co., Middlesborough.

178. Six Small Specimens of Linthorpe Ware.
 　　Designed by Miss Worth, Nottingham.
 　　Manufactured by Linthorpe Pottery Co., Middlesborough.

179. Nine Specimens of Linthorpe Pottery (8 Vases and 1 Ewer).
 　　Designed by Wm. Patey, Ryde, Isle of Wight.
 　　Manufactured by Linthorpe Pottery Co., Middlesborough.

180. Vase, light green.
 　　Designed by Sheldon Longbottom, Darlington.
 　　Manufactured by Linthorpe Pottery Co., Middlesborough.

181. Pair of Vases.
 　　Designed by Arthur P. Shorter, Mid-dlesborough.
 　　Manufactured by Linthorpe Pottery Co., Middlesborough.

182. Pair Vases.
 　　Designed by Sheldon Longbottom, Darlington.
 　　Manufactured by Linthorpe Pottery Co., Middlesborough.

183. Jug Incised Ornament.
 　　Designed by Francis Scheibner, Stour-bridge.

184. Plate.
 　　Designed by Sheldon Longbottom, Darlington.
 　　Manufactured by Linthorpe Pottery Co., Middlesborough.

185. Vase.
 　　Designed by Sheldon Longbottom, Darlington.
 　　Manufactured by Linthorpe Pottery Co., Middlesborough.

186. Vase, floral decoration, blue ground.
 　　Designed by Sheldon Longbottom, Darlington.
 　　Manufactured by Linthorpe Pottery Co., Middlesborough.

187. Vase, light brown with fishes, &c.
 　　Designed by Sheldon Longbottom, Darlington.
 　　Manufactured by Linthorpe Pottery Co., Middlesborough.

188. Salad Bowl, Knife and Fork.
Designed and executed by J. A. Rhodes, Sheffield.

189. Plate, floral decoration.
Designed by Sheldon Longbottom, Darlington.
Manufactured by Linthorpe Pottery Co., Middlesborough.

190. Large Plaque.
Designed by F. Gibbons, Cirencester.
Manufactured by W. Allen, Coalbrookdale.

191. Yellow Glazed Plaque.
Designed by F. Gibbons, Cirencester.
Manufactured by W. Allen, Coalbrookdale.

192. Plate.
Designed and manufactured by J. E. A. Brown, Cirencester.

193. Vase, olive green.
Vase, brown, incised ornament.
Bottle, olive green.
Vase, blue.
Tazza, yellow, incised ornament.
Large Vase, incised ornament.
Two Plates, incised ornament.
Majolica Fire-place.
Designed by J. B. Fidler, Sheffield.
Manufactured by Messrs. Maw & Co., Coalbrookdale.

194. Spiral Vase.
Designed and modelled by J. Hadley, decorated by J. Callowhill, Worcester.
Manufactured by The Royal Porcelain Works, Worcester.

195. Nautilus Vase.
Designed and modelled by J. Hadley.
Decorated by J. Callowhill, Worcester.
Manufactured by The Royal Porcelain Works, Worcester.

196. Renaissance Vase.
Designed and modelled by J. Hadley.
Decorated by J. Callowhill, Worcester.
Manufactured by The Royal Porcelain Works, Worcester.

197. Vases, Pair of, blue ground, gold ornaments.
Designed and executed by James Callowhill, Worcester.
Manufactured by James Callowhill, The Nunnery, Worcester.

198. Vases, Pair of, decorated with ferns in gold.
Designed and executed by James Callowhill, Worcester.
Manufactured by James Callowhill, The Nunnery, Worcester.

199. Pair of Vases, decorated with gold.
By James and Sydney Callowhill, Worcester.
Manufactured by James Callowhill, The Nunnery, Worcester.

200. Four Plates, blue ground, decorated with gold.
By Clarence and Sydney Callowhill, Worcester.
Manufactured by James Callowhill, The Nunnery, Worcester.

201. Plate, olive green ground, decorated with gold.
Designed and executed by J. Callowhill.
Manufactured by James Callowhill, The Nunnery, Worcester.

202. One Dozen Plates, white ground with floral ornaments decorated with gold.
By James Callowhill, Worcester.
Manufactured by James Callowhill, The Nunnery, Worcester.

203. Plate, white ground.
With etching by James Callowhill, Worcester.
Manufactured by James Callowhill, The Nunnery, Worcester.

204. Plate, decorated with gold.
By James Callowhill, Worcester.
Manufactured by James Callowhill, The Nunnery, Worcester.

205. Jardinière. Japanese Ornament.
Designed by David Bates, Worcester.
Manufactured by The Royal Porcelain Works, Worcester.

206. Shell Vase.
Designed and modelled by T. Hadley.
Manufactured by The Royal Porcelain Works, Worcester.

207. Jardinière floral decoration on white ground.
By James Bradley, Worcester.
Manufactured by The Royal Porcelain Works, Worcester.

208. Pair of Vases. floral decoration.
     Designed by A. Tatler, *Burslem.*
     Manufactured by Messrs. Doulton,
     Burslem.

209. Pair of Vases.
     Designed by D. Dewsbery, *Burslem.*
     Manufactured by Messrs. Doulton,
     Burslem.

210. Pair of Vases.
     Designed by John Bratt, *Burslem.*
     Manufactured by Messrs. Doulton,
     Burslem.

211. Dessert Plate.
     Designed by F. Wood, *Burslem.*
     Manufactured by Messrs. Doulton,
     Burslem.

212. Dessert Plate.
     Designed by A. R. Kelsall, *Burslem.*
     Manufactured by Messrs. Doulton,
     Burslem.

213. Dessert Plate,
     Designed by William Boardman,
     Burslem.
     Manufactured by Messrs. Doulton,
     Burslem.

214. Dessert Plate
     Designed by John Bratt, *Burslem.*
     Manufactured by Messrs. Doulton,
     Burslem.

215. Dessert Plate.
     Designed by Miss Jane Oakes, *Burslem.*
     Manufactured by Messrs. Doulton,
     Burslem.

216. Ewer and Basin.
     Designed by T. Moorcroft, *Burslem.*
     Manufactured by E. J. D. Bodley,
     Burslem.

217. Oyster Plate.
     Designed by William Wright, *Burslem.*
     Manufactured by E. J. D. Bodley,
     Burslem.

218. Biscuit Box.
     Designed by William Wright, *Burslem.*
     Manufactured by E. J. D. Bodley,
     Burslem.

219. Dessert Plate, light blue ground, floral ornament.
     Designed by William Wright, *Burslem.*
     Manufactured by E. J. D. Bodley,
     Burslem

220. Dessert Plate.
     Designed by H. Cartwright, *Burslem.*
     Manufactured by E. J. D. Bodley,
     Burslem.

221. Dinner Plate.
     Designed by H. Cartwright, *Burslem.*
     Manufactured by E. J. D. Bodley,
     Burslem.

222. Dessert Plate, pink ground, decorated with gold.
     Designed by F. Poole, *Burslein.*
     Manufactured by E. J. D. Bodley,
     Burslem.

223. Dessert Plate.
     Designed by F. Poole, *Burslem.*
     Manufactured by E. J. D. Bodley,
     Burslem.

224. Dessert Plate.
     Designed by H. Cartwright, *Burslem.*
     Manufactured by E. J. D. Bodley,
     Burslem.

225. Dinner Plate.
     Designed by T. Moorcroft, *Burslem.*
     Manufactured by E. J. D. Bodley,
     Burslem.

226. Oyster Plate.
     Designed by F. Poole, *Burslem.*
     Manufactured by E. J. D. Bodley,
     Burslem.

227. Portion of Déjeuner Service.
     Designed by T. Moorcroft, *Burslem.*
     Manufactured by E. J. D. Bodley,
     Burslem.

228. Ewer and Basin.
     Designed by C. J. Beaupré, *West London.*
     Manufactured by Furnival & Son.

229. Fruit Dish, white and gold.
     Designed by James F. Marsh, *Burslem.*
     Manufactured by Messrs. Davenport.

230. Design for a Porcelain Dessert Plate, cobalt blue ground, gold ornament framing, a centre picture of a scene in Derbyshire, and panels with flowers: also panels with the raised gold letters " W. E. G." being the initials of The Right Hon. W. E. Gladstone, M.P.
     A Dessert Service, consisting of 18 plates, 4 tall and 4 low Comports of this pattern, was presented to Mr. Gladstone on December 22nd, 1883, by the Liberal working men of Derby.

Designed by Richard Lunn, *Sheffield.*
The Landscape *painted by* James Platts, student of the Derby School of Art.
The *Flowers by* James Rouse, sen.
The *Gilding by* Charles Rouse.
Manufactured by the Derby Crown Porcelain Co.

231. Dinner Plate and a Dish and Cover, earthenware. Engraved pattern printed upon the biscuit in peacock green.
Designed by Richard Lunn, *Sheffield.*
Manufactured by the Derby Crown Porcelain Co.

232. Set for Boudoir mantel-piece, painted in due black, overglaze, earthenware and porcelain, consisting of one clock stand. The decoration illustrates the old adage of "Early to bed, and early to rise, makes a man healthy, wealthy and wise." The clock face is enamelled copper.
Also 2 vases; subjects "Jack and Gill," and 'A little bird told me."
Also 2 flower pots; subjects, "Four stages of life."
Also 2 candlesticks; subjects, "Four varieties of illuminators, viz., Sun, Moon, Stars and Lightning."
The whole of these articles were *designed and painted by* Richard Lunn, *Sheffield*, except the candlesticks; these were *painted by* Charles Wright, student in the Derby School of Art, and apprentice at the Derby Crown Porcelain Co.'s Works.
The 2 two-handled vases were *made by* Messrs. Maw, of *Broseley*.
The clock stand and 2 flower pots were *modelled by* Richard Lunn, and *made by* Messrs. McIntyre, of *Burslem*.
The two candlesticks were *made by* the Derby Crown Porcelain Co., and are porcelain.
The whole were designed and made for Sir P. Cunliffe Owen, K.C.M.G., C.B., C.I.E.
Lent by Sir P. Cunliffe Owen. K.C.M.G., C.B., C.I.E.

233. Vase, Etruscan.
      Designed by H. Williams, *Coalbrookdale.*
      Manufactured by W. Allen, *Coalbrookdale.*

234. Large Flower Vase.
      Designed and executed by G. F. Lambert, *Derby.*

235. Large Vase.
      Designed by Owen Gibbons, *Cirencester.*
      Manufactured by W. Allen, *Coalbrookdale.*

236. Dessert Plate.
      Designed by G. F. Lambert, *Derby.*
      Manufactured by Crown Porcelain Works, *Derby.*

237. Dessert Plate.
      Designed and executed by G. F. Lambert, *Derby.*

238. Dessert Plate.
      Designed by G. F. Lambert, *Derby.*
      Manufactured by Crown Porcelain Works, *Derby.*

239. Four Cups and Saucers.
      Designed by G. F. Lambert, *Derby.*
      Manufactured by Crown Porcelain Works, *Derby.*

240. Plaque, decoration in gold.
      Designed and executed by G. F. Lambert, *Derby.*

241. Plate, brown and white.
      Designed by H. Williams, *Coalbrookdale.*
      Manufactured by W. Allen, *Coalbrookdale.*

242. Plate.
      Designed by H. Williams, *Coalbrookdale.*
      Manufactured by W. Allen, *Coalbrookdale.*

243. Cup and Saucer.
      Designed and executed by Mrs. Windass, *York.*

244. Cup and Saucer.
      Designed and executed by C. L. Smith, *Selby.*

245. Pair of Vases.
      Designed by Louis Bilton, *Stoke-on-Trent.*
      Manufactured by Messrs. Minton, *Stoke-on-Trent.*

246. Pair of Vases.
      Designed by Louis Bilton, *Stoke-on-Trent.*
      Manufactured by Messrs. Minton, *Stoke-on-Trent.*

247. Pair of Vases, dark blue ground with flowers.
      Designed by William Hodgkinson, *Stoke on-Trent.*
      Manufactured by Messrs. Minton, *Stoke-on-Trent.*

248. Jardinière, Majolica.
Designed by J. Henk, *Stoke-on-Trent.*
Manufactured by Messrs. Minton,
Stoke-on-Trent.

249. Pair of Vases, with decorative medallions of games, &c.
Designed by George Fernyhough,
Stoke-on-Trent.
Manufactured by Messrs. Minton,
Stoke-on-Trent.

250. Flower Holder, dark blue, decoration in gold.
Designed by J. Henk, *Stoke-on-Trent.*
Manufactured by Messrs. Minton,
Stoke-on-Trent.

251. Dessert Plate.
Designed by William Hodgkinson,
Stoke-on-Trent.
Manufactured by Messrs. Minton,
Stoke-on-Trent.

252. Dessert Plate, " Dead Game."
Designed by G. Fernyhough, *Stoke-on-Trent.*
Manufactured by Messrs. Minton,
Stoke-on-Trent.

253. Flower Holder.
Designed by J. Henk, *Stoke-on-Trent.*
Manufactured by Messrs. Minton,
Stoke-on-Trent.

254. Oval Tray.
Designed by W. H. Pilsbury, *Stoke-on-Trent.*
Manufactured by Messrs. Minton,
Stoke-on-Trent.

255. Pin Tray.
Designed by Albert Naylor, *Stoke-on-Trent.*
Manufactured by Messrs. Minton,
Stoke-on-Trent.

256. Salt Cellar.
Designed by E. Parry, *Stoke-on-Trent.*
Manufactured by Messrs. Minton,
Stoke-on-Trent.

257. Tray, Two Cups and Saucers, Sugar Basin, Milk Jug and Tea Pot and Tazza.
Designed by William Hodgkinson,
Stoke-on-Trent.
Manufactured by Messrs. Minton,
Stoke-on-Trent.

258. Vase.
Designed by William Hodgkinson,
Stoke-on-Trent.
Manufactured by Messrs. Minton,
Stoke-on-Trent.

259. Plate, imitation of Limoges enamel.
Designed and executed by G. W. Rhead, *Hanley and Stoke-on-Trent.*

260. Three Porcelain Plaques, ornamented with figures of Cupids, &c.
Designed by J. Cope, *Hanley.*
Manufactured by Messrs. Minton, Hollins, & Co., *Stoke-on-Trent.*

261. Ewer and Basin.
Designed by F. Poole, *Burslem.*
Manufactured by E. J. D. Bodley, *Burslem.*

262. Dark Blue Vase, decorated with gold.
Designed by T. Moorcroft, *Burslem and Hanley.*
Manufactured by E. J. D. Bodley, *Burslem.*

263. Ewer and Basin.
Designed by H. Cartwright, *Burslem.*
Manufactured by E. J. D. Bodley, *Burslem.*

264. Dessert Plate.
Designed by H. Cartwright, *Burslem.*
Manufactured by E. J. D. Bodley, *Burslem.*

265. Butter Dish.
Designed by F. Poole, *Burslem.*
Manufactured by E. J. D. Bodley, *Burslem.*

266. Dessert Plate.
Designed by F. Poole, *Burslem.*
Manufactured by E. J. D. Bodley, *Burslem.*

267. Cup and Saucer.
Designed by T. Moorcroft, *Burslem.*
Manufactured by E. J. D. Bodley, *Burslem.*

268. Dessert Plate, dark blue and gold.
Designed by A. J. Capey, *Burslem.*
Manufactured by E. J. D. Bodley, *Burslem.*

269. Vegetable Dish and Dinner Plate, cream colour, dark blue and gold.
Designed by T. Moorcroft, *Burslem.*
Manufactured by E. J. D. Bodley, *Burslem.*

270. Coffee Cup and Saucer.
    Designed by H. Cartwright, *Burslem.*
    Manufactured by E. J. D. Bodley,
    Burslem.

271. Plate.
    Designed by A. J. Capey, *Burslem.*
    Manufactured by E. J. D. Bodley,
    Burslem.

272. Jug, ornamented with gold.
    Designed by William Wright, *Hanley.*
    Manufactured by E. J. D. Bodley,
    Burslem.

273. Dessert Plate.
    Designed by F. Poole, *Burslem.*
    Manufactured by E. J. D. Bodley,
    Burslem.

274. Jug and Dinner Plate.
    Designed by F. Poole, *Burslem.*
    Manufactured by E. J. D. Bodley,
    Burslem.

275. Plate, blue and white.
    Designed by T. Moorcroft, *Hanley.*
    Manufactured by E. J. D. Bodley,
    Burslem.

276. Jug, white and gold.
    Designed by H. Cartwright, *Burslem.*
    Manufactured by E. J. D. Bodley,
    Burslem.

277. Dinner Plate.
    Designed by T. Moorcroft, *Burslem.*
    Manufactured by E. J. D. Bodley,
    Burslem.

278. Tea Pot.
    Designed by Stephen Hartley, *Burslem.*
    Manufactured by E. J. D. Bodley,
    Burslem.

279. Plate.
    Designed by A. J. Capey, *Burslem.*
    Manufactured by E. J. D. Bodley,
    Burslem.

280. Coffee Pot.
    Designed by Stephen Hartley, *Burslem.*
    Manufactured by E. J. D. Bodley,
    Burslem.

281. Tea Pot, Coffee Pot, and Biscuit Box.
    Designed by Stephen Hartley, *Burslem.*
    Manufactured by E. J. D. Bodley,
    Burslem.

282. Fruit Dish, gold and pink ground.
    Designed by William Wright, *Hanley.*
    Manufactured by E. J. D. Bodley,
    Burslem.

283. Dessert Plate.
    Designed by H. Cartwright, *Burslem.*
    Manufactured by E. J. D. Bodley,
    Burslem.

284. Dessert Plate.
    Designed by A. J. Capey, *Burslem.*
    Manufactured by E J. D. Bodley,
    Burslem.

285. Toilet Ewer and Basin.
    Designed by William Wright, *Burslem.*
    Manufactured by E. J. D. Bodley.

286. Breakfast Service and Tray, white and
gold.
    Designed by A. J. Capey, *Burslem.*
    Manufactured by E. J. D. Bodley,
    Burslem.

287. Dessert Plate.
    Designed by J. Micklewright, *Hanley.*
    Manufactured by E. J. D. Bodley,
    Burslem.

288. Breakfast Service on Tray.
    Designed by T. Moorcroft, *Hanley.*
    Manufactured by E. J. D. Bodley,
    Burslem.

289. Coffee Service on Tray, light green
and gold.
    Designed by H. Cartwright, *Burslem.*
    Manufactured by E. J. D. Bodley,
    Burslem.

290. Dessert and Tea Services, Plates, Cups
and Saucers, Portion of Dinner Service, Ewers
and Basins, mostly floral decoration.
    Designed by H. Overton Jones, *South
    Kensington.*
    Manufactured by George Jones &
    Sons, *Stoke-on-Trent.*

291. Vase, gold ground and floral decoration
in dark blue.
    Designed by D. Dewsbery, *Burslem.*
    Manufactured by Messrs. Doulton,
    Burslem.

292. Vase, floral decoration.
    Designed by A. Wright, *Hanley.*
    Manufactured by Messrs. Doulton,
    Burslem.

293. Pair of Vases, studies of apples.
Designed by D. Dewsbery, Burslem.
Manufactured by Messrs. Doulton,
Burslem.

294. Large Vase, floral decoration in gold.
Designed by D. Dewsbery, Burslem.
Manufactured by Messrs. Doulton,
Burslem.

295. Pair of Vases.
Designed by Robert Seadon, Hanley.
Manufactured by Messrs. Doulton,
Burslem.

296. Pair of Flower Vases.
Designed by D. Dewsbery, Burslem.
Manufactured by Messrs. Doulton,
Burslem.

297. Pair of Jugs.
Designed by D. Dewsbery, Burslem.
Manufactured by Messrs. Doulton,
Burslem.

298. Vase, dark blue and gold ornament.
Designed by D. Dewsbery, Burslem.
Manufactured by Messrs. Doulton,
Burslem.

299. Pair of Globular Vases, gold ground
with floral ornament.
Designed by W. Roberts, Stoke-on-
Trent.
Manufactured by Messrs. Doulton,
Burslem.

300. Ewer, dark brown ground, floral orna-
ment.
Designed by James Wooton, Burslem. .
Manufactured by Messrs. Doulton,
Burslem.

301. Flower Bowl.
Designed by Robert Seaton, Hanley.
Manufactured by Messrs. Doulton,
Burslem.

302. Pair of Flower Bowls.
Designed by Robert Allen, Burslem.
Manufactured by Messrs. Doulton,
Burslem.

303. Vase, dark blue and gold ornament.
Designed by W. Johnson, Stoke-on-
Trent.
Manufactured by Messrs. Doulton,
Burslem.

304. Flower Bowl, ornamented with flowers
in dark blue.
Designed by James Wooton, Burslem.
Manufactured by Messrs. Doulton
Burslem.

305. Flower Bowl, floral decoration in gold.
Designed by Leonard Langley, Burs-
lem.
Manufactured by Messrs. Doulton
Burslem.

306. Salad Bowl.
Designed by John Hughes, Burslem.
Manufactured by Brownhill Pottery
Co., Tunstall.

307. Tray Mounted in Silver, Tea Pot, Milk
Jug, and Sugar Basin, olive green ground
ornamented in gold.
Designed by John Hughes, Burslem.
Manufactured by Brownhill Pottery
Co., Tunstall.

308. Biscuit Box, cream coloured ground, gold
ornament.
Designed by Richard Ford, Burslem.
Manufactured by Brownhill Pottery
Co., Tunstall.

309. Breakfast Cruet Stand.
Designed by Richard Ford, Burslem.
Manufactured by Brownhill Pottery
Co., Tunstall.

310. Box, containing Pepper Boxes and Salt
Cellars, various designs.
Designed by Joseph Parr, Burslem.
Manufactured by Brownhill Pottery
Co., Tunstall.

311. Box, containing 6 Handles for Salad
Forks, various designs.
Designed by Joseph Parr, Burslem.
Manufactured by Brownhill Pottery
Co., Tunstall.

312. Ewer and Stand, Florentine decoration
in white on red ground.
Designed by Joseph Parr, Burslem.
Manufactured by Brownhill Pottery
Co., Tunstall.

313. Box, containing Pepper Castors and
Mustard Pots.
Designed by Joseph Parr, Burslem.
Manufactured by Brownhill Pottery
Co., Tunstall.

314. Biscuit Box, salmon coloured ground, corated in gold.
Designed by Joseph Parr, *Burslem.*
Manufactured by Brownhill Pottery Co., *Tunstall.*

315. Biscuit Box, olive green ground.
Designed by Joseph Parr, *Burslem.*
Manufactured by Brownhill Pottery Co., *Tunstall.*

316. Pair of Vases, white ground, floral decoration in gold.
Designed by Richard Ford, *Burslem.*
Manufactured by Brownhill Pottery Co., *Tunstall.*

317. Ewer and Basin.
Designed by J. Parr, *Burslem.*
Manufactured by Brownhill Pottery Co., *Tunstall.*

318. Ewer and Basin.
Designed by J. F. Marsh, *Burslem and Stoke.*
Manufactured by Messrs. Davenport, *Longton.*

319. Jug, terra cotta.
Designed by J. F. Marsh, *Burslem and Stoke-on-Trent.*
Manufactured by Messrs. Davenport, *Longton.*

20. Flower Vase, terra cotta.
Designed by J. F. Marsh, *Burslem and Stoke-on-Trent.*
Manufactured by Messrs. Davenport, *Longton.*

21. Ewer and Basin.
Designed by J. F. Marsh, *Burslem and Stoke-on-Trent.*
Manufactured by Messrs. Davenport, *Longton.*

22. Cup and Saucer.
Designed by J. F. Marsh, *Burslem and Stoke-on-Trent.*
Manufactured by Messrs. Davenport, *Longton.*

23. Pair Large Ornamental Flower Bowls.
Designed by Louis Bilton, *Stoke-on-Trent.*
Manufactured by Messrs. Minton, *Stoke-on-Trent.*

24. Pair Large Ornamental Flower Bowls.
Designed by Louis Bilton, *Stoke-on-Trent.*
Manufactured by Messrs. Minton, *Stoke-on-Trent.*

325. Large Flower Holder on Stand.
Designed and modelled by John Henk, *Stoke-on-Trent.*
Manufactured by Messrs. Minton, *Stoke-on-Trent.*

326. Two Flower Bowls and Jardinière.
Designed by Owen Gibbons, *Cirencester and South Kensington.*
Manufactured by Messrs. Maw & Co., *Coalbrookdale.*

327. Design for Plate.
By Mary Brett, *Dublin.*
Manufactured by Wedgewood & Sons.

328. Design for Majolica Plaque.
By J. O. Poole, *South Kensington.*

329. Design for Painted Tazza.
By William Davis, *Coalbrookdale.*

330. Design for Tea Pot, Cups, and Saucers.
By Miss Frances Brett, *Dublin.*

331. Design for Plate.
By Miss Emily Mitchell, *West London.*

332. Design for Salver and Pilgrim Bottle.
By Miss Marianne Mansell, *Lambeth.*

333. Design for Salad Bowl and Vase.
By E. Rogers, *Westminster and Lambeth.*

334. Design for China Plaque.
By Miss Mary Denley, *Westminster and Lambeth.*

335. Design for Candlesticks and Vase.
By Miss Martha M. Rogers, *Westminster and Lambeth.*

336. Design for China Plaque.
By Miss Mary Denley, *Westminster and Lambeth.*

337. Designs for Cups and Saucers.
By George Lambert, *Derby.*

338. Designs for Cups and Saucers.
By Miss Martha Rogers, *Westminster and Lambeth.*

339. Original Designs for Cups, Early English and Japanese.
By Albert Binns, *Worcester.*

340. **Design for Painted Tazza.**
By Frederick Leighton, *Coalbrookdale.*

341. **Design for Cups and Saucers.**
By Miss Gertrude Ginn, *East Herts.*

342. **Designs for Door Plates.**
By Miss Mary Rogers, *Westminster and Lambeth.*

343. **Design for Plates.**
By G. F. Lambert, *Derby.*

344. **Design for Dessert & Tea Services.**
By Henry Hill, *Boston.*

345. **Design for Vase and Dish.**
By Miss Mary Moore, *Preston.*

346. **Design for Cups and Saucers.**
By Miss Mary Moore, *Preston.*

347. **Design for Painted Tiles, &c.**
By Miss Martha Rogers, *Westminster and Lambeth.*

348. **Design for Dessert Plates.**
By G. F. Lambert, *Derby.*

349. **Design for Dessert Plates.**
By G. F. Lambert, *Worcester.*

350. **Design for Plate.**
By James Boyle, *Dublin.*

351. **Design for Dinner Service.**
By Frederick Leighton, *Coalbrookdale.*

352. **Design for Plates.**
By Miss Mary Cox, *Worcester.*

353. **Design for Plates.**
By G. F. Lambert, *Worcester.*

354. **Design for Parian Plate.**
By H. J. Hadley, *Worcester.*

355. **Design for Cups and Saucers.**
By Miss Mary Holmes, *Great Yarmouth.*

356. **Design for Persian Vase.**
By Louis Hadley, *Worcester.*

357. **Design for Water Bottle.**
By Miss Mary Moore, *Preston.*

358. **Design for Tiles.**
By John Briggs, *Edinburgh.*

359. **Design for Porcelain Vase.**
By J. C. Callowhill, *Worcester.*

360. **Design for Borders and Cups and Saucers.**
By J. C. Callowhill, *Worcester.*

361. **Design for Painted Panel.**
By W. Gandy, *Lambeth.*

362. **Design for Panel.**
By Miss Mary Denley, *Westminster and Lambeth.*

363. **Design for Tiles.**
By Miss Mary Denley, *Westminster and Lambeth.*

364. **Design for Tiles.**
By E. Hammond, *West London and Lambeth.*

365. **Design for Tiles.**
By Thomas Smith, *Coalbrookdale.*

366. **Design for Encaustic Tiles.**
By J. C. Gibbs, *Worcester.*

367. **Design for Tiles.**
By Miss Mary Denley, *Westminster and Lambeth.*

368. **Design for Dessert Plates.**
By Mrs. Eassie, *Gloucester.*

369. **Design for Tiles.**
By William H. Woodall, *West London.*

370. **Design for Fireplace.**
By Miss Mary Denley, *Westminster and Lambeth.*

371. **Photographs of Designs for Tiles.**
By Mrs. C. A. Sparkes, *Lambeth.*

372. **Design for Freize.**
By Edward Hammond, *West London and Lambeth.*

373. Two Frames of Tiles (Panels).
Designed by T. Emery, Stoke-on-Trent.
Manufactured by Minton, Hollins &
Sons, *Stoke-on-Trent.*

374. Two Frames of Tiles (Panels).
Designed and executed by W. H.
Dixon, *Broseley.*
Manufactured by Minton, Hollins &
Sons, *Stoke-on-Trent.*

375. Three Decorative Tiles.
Designed and executed by F. Abraham, *West London.*

376. Tiles.
Designed and executed by Anna
Baker, *Cork.*

377. Three Decorative Panels.
Designed by William Simpson, *South
Kensington.*
Manufactured by Minton, Hollins &
Sons, *Stoke-on-Trent.*

378. Decorative Panel.
Designed by A. Wright, *Stoke-on-
Trent.*
Manufactured by Minton, Hollins &
Sons, *Stoke-on-Trent.*

379. Panel, Decorative Tiles.
By A. Slater, *Stoke-on-Trent.*
Manufactured by Minton, Hollins &
Sons.

380. Decorative Panel.
Designed by S. Buxton, *Stoke-on-Trent.*
Manufactured by Minton, Hollins &
Sons.

381. Decorative Panel.
Designed by Miss Sarah Bradley.
Manufactured by Minton, Hollins &
Sons.

382. Tile.
Designed and executed by Miss Anne
Baker, *Cork.*

383. Tiles.
Designed by W. Bradburn, *Coalbrookdale.*
Manufactured by Maw & Co., *Coalbrookdale.*

384. Frame, containing Tiles.
Designed by R. A. Ledward, *Burslem.*
Manufactured by Craven, Dunhill &
Co., *Ironbridge, Salop.*

385. Panel.
Designed and executed by R. A.
Ledward, *Burslem.*
(Lent by Sir Philip Cunliffe-Owen, K.C.M.G.,
C.B., C.I.E.)

386. Design for Tiles.
By Miss Margaret Hill, *Cork.*

387. Two Frames of Tiles.
Designed by F. Leighton, *Coalbrook-
dale.*
Manufactured by Craven Dunhill
& Co.

388. Decorative Panel.
Designed by Owen Gibbons, *Cirencester and South Kensington.*
Manufactured by Maw & Co., *Coalbrookdale.*

389. Decorative Panel.
Designed by Carl Almquist, *West
London.*
Manufactured by Shrigley & Hunt.

390. Decorative Panel.
Designed by Owen Gibbons, *Cirencester and South Kensington.*
Manufactured by Maw & Co., *Coalbrookdale.*

391. Decorative Panel.
Designed by Joseph Baugham, *Coalbrookdale.*

392. Decorative Panel.
Designed by Owen Gibbons, *Ciren-
cester and South Kensington.*
Executed by Maw & Co., *Coalbrookdale.*

393. Decorative Panel, white glaze tiles.
Designed by Owen Gibbons, *Cirencester and South Kensington.*
Manufactured by Maw & Co., *Coalbrookdale.*

394. Decorative Panel.
Designed by Owen Gibbons, *Cirencester and South Kensington.*
Manufactured by Maw & Co., *Coalbrookdale.*

395. Decorative Panel.
Designed by Owen Gibbons, *Cirencester and South Kensington.*
Manufactured by Maw & Co., *Coalbrookdale.*

396. Decorative Panel.
Designed by Owen Gibbons, *Cirencester and South Kensington.*
Manufactured by Maw & Co., *Coalbrookdale.*

397. Decorative Panel.
Designed by Owen Gibbons, *Cirencester and South Kensington.*
Manufactured by Maw & Co., *Coalbrookdale.*

398. Decorative Panel.
Designed by Owen Gibbons, *Cirencester and South Kensington.*
Manufactured by Maw & Co., *Coalbrookdale.*

399. Decorative Panel, white glaze tiles.
Designed by Owen Gibbons, *Cirencester and South Kensington.*
Manufactured by Maw & Co., *Coalbrookdale.*

400. Decorative Panel.
Designed by Owen Gibbons, *Cirencester and South Kensington.*
Manufactured by Maw & Co., *Coalbrookdale.*

401. Decorative Panel.
Designed by Owen Gibbons, *Cirencester and South Kensington.*
Manufactured by Maw & Co., *Coalbrookdale.*

402. Decorative Panel.
Designed by Owen Gibbons, *Cirencester and South Kensington.*
Manufactured by Maw & Co., *Coalbrookdale.*

403. Decorative Panel.
Designed by Owen Gibbons, *Cirencester and South Kensington.*
Manufactured by Maw & Co., *Coalbrookdale.*

404. Decorative Panel.
Designed by Owen Gibbons, *Cirencester and South Kensington.*
Manufactured by Maw & Co., *Coalbrookdale.*

405. Decorative Panel.
Designed and executed by Miss Margaret Hill, *Cork.*

406. Design for Mosaic Floor.
By James Thomas, *Westminster.*

407. Two Mosaic Pavements.
Designed by Owen Gibbons, *Cirencester.*
Manufactured by Maw & Co., *Coalbrookdale.*

408. Pair of Decorative Panels.
Designed by Owen Gibbons, *Cirencester.*
Manufactured by Maw & Co., *Coalbrookdale.*

409. Two Designs for Roman Mosaic Pavements.
By Edwin Jarratt, *Coalbrookdale.*

410. Design for Tiles.
By John Briggs, *Edinburgh.*

411. Frame of Tiles.
Designed by Owen Gibbons, *Cirencester.*
Manufactured by Maw & Co., *Coalbrookdale.*

412. Design for Mosaic Floor.
By O. R. Albrow, *Great Yarmouth.*

413. Frame of Tiles.
Designed and executed by Charles Campbell, *Lambeth and West London.*

414. Design for Hearth Tiles.
Designed by Owen Gibbons, *Cirencester.*
Manufactured by Maw & Co., *Coalbrookdale.*

415. Design for Hearth Tiles.
By Owen Gibbons, *Cirencester.*
Manufactured by Maw & Co., *Coalbrookdale.*

416. Decorative Panel, Persian Pattern.
Designed and executed by Andrew Childe, *Coalbrookdale.*

417. Floor Tiles, imitation Mosaic.
Designed by Owen Gibbons, *Cirencester.*
Manufactured by Maw & Co., *Coalbrookdale.*

418. Frame of Tiles.
Designed by Owen Gibbons, *Cirencester.*
Manufactured by Maw & Co., *Coalbrookdale.*

419. Floor Tiles, imitation Mosaic.
Designed by Owen Gibbons, Cirencester.
Manufactured by Maw & Co., Coalbrookdale.

420. Decorative Panel.
Designed by Owen Gibbons, Cirencester.
Manufactured by Maw & Co., Coalbrookdale.

421. Decorative Tiles.
Designed by Owen Gibbons, Cirencester.
Manufactured by Maw & Co., Coalbrookdale.

422. Decorative Tiles.
Designed by Owen Gibbons, Cirencester.
Manufactured by Maw & Co., Coalbrookdale.

423. Decorative Tiles.
Designed by Owen Gibbons, Cirencester.
Manufactured by Maw & Co., Coalbrookdale.

424. Decorative Tiles.
Designed by Owen Gibbons, Cirencester.
Manufactured by Maw & Co., Coalbrookdale.

425. Pair of Small Panels. Decorative Tiles.
Designed and executed by Charles Campbell, Lambeth and West London.

426. Imitation Persian Tiles.
Designed by Owen Gibbons, Cirencester.
Manufactured by Maw & Co., Coalbrookdale.

427. Decorative Tiles.
Designed by Owen Gibbons, Cirencester.
Manufactured by Maw & Co., Coalbrookdale.

428. Frame containing 12 Tiles, historical subjects and nursery rhymes.
Designed by Moyr Smith, Glasgow and Kensington.

429. Frame containing 6 Tiles.
Designed and Executed by Moyr Smith, Glasgow and Kensington.

430. Frame containing 12 Tiles.
Designed and Executed by Moyr Smith, Glasgow and Kensington.

431. Frames containing Decorative Tiles, illustrating Sir Walter Scott's Poems.
Designed and Executed by Moyr Smith, Glasgow and Kensington.

432. Frame containing 4 Tiles.
Designed by W. H. Pilsbury, Stoke-on-Trent.
Two designed by Louis Bilton, Stoke-on-Trent.
One designed by Edward Berks, Stoke-on-Trent.
Manufactured by Messrs. Minton, Stoke-on-Trent.

433. Two Frames containing · Decorative Panels in Terra Cotta.
Designed and Executed by R. J. Morris, South Kensington.

434. Decorative Tiles for Fire-grate, impasto ware.
Designed and executed by F. Lewis, Lambeth.
Manufactured by Messrs. Doulton & Co.

435. Decorative Tiles, pomegranate,
Designed and executed by E. Roberts, Lambeth.
Manufactured by Messrs. Doulton & Co.

436. Decorative Tiles, wild flowers.
Designed and executed by F. Lewis, Lambeth.
Manufactured by Messrs. Doulton & Co.

437. Decorative Tiles, lilies.
Designed and executed by Mrs. Hall, Lambeth.
Manufactured by Messrs Doulton & Co.

438. Four Tiles, female heads.
Designed and executed by Miss Philpot, Lambeth.
Manufactured by Messrs. Doulton & Co.

439. Decorative Tiles for Fireplace.
Designed by Owen Gibbons, Cirencester.
Manufactured by Maw & Co., Coalbrookdale.

C

440. Four Terra Cotta Panels.
Designed and executed by John Broad, Lambeth.
Manufactured by Messrs. Doulton.

SECTION III.

Glass — Cut, Engraved, Flashed, Pressed, &c.; Stained and Painted Glass in windows or panels.

441 Glass Vase, cameo cut, with floral decoration.

442. Glass Lamp, cameo cut, rod and ivory floral decoration.

443. Glass Vase, amber pattern.

444. Glass Vase, cameo cut, with dented sides.

445. Two Glass Vases, gold ground, with ruby fruit and gold leaves.

446. Glass Scent Bottle, ruby on dull white.

447. Glass Scent Bottle, opal on green, cameo cut.

448. Glass Scent Bottle, opal on brown, cameo cut.

449. Glass Vase, opal on green, cameo cut.

450. Glass Bowl, topaz and red, perforated, cameo cut.

451. Glass Vase, cameo cut, brown with white decoration.

452. Glass Scent Bottle, red on lemon, cameo cut.

453. Glass Pilgrim Bottle, brown decoration, in white, tinted in yellow, cameo cut.

454. Two-Handled Glass Vase, brown body, decoration in white, cameo cut.

455. Glass Vase, green, cameo cut.

456. Two-handle Bottle, red on ivory, cameo cut.

457. Glass Finger Bowl, white on pink ground, cameo cut.
Designed and executed by Thomas Woodall, Stourbridge.
Manufactured by Thomas Webb & Sons, Stourbridge.

458. Glass Bowl and Plate, cameo cut.
Designed and executed by Thomas Woodall, Stourbridge.
Manufactured by Thomas Webb & Sons, Stourbridge.
(Lent by Lady Cunliffe-Owen.)

459. Glass Vase, white, with decoration in yellow, cameo cut.

460. Glass Vase, light brown, with decoration in white, cameo cut.

461. Glass Bowl, amber, with decoration in red, cameo cut.

462. Glass Vase, amber body, decoration in red, cameo cut.

463. Glass Vase, white and yellow, cameo cut.

464. Glass Vase, yellow and red ornament, cameo cut.

465. Glass Scent Bottle, blue and white ornament, cameo cut.

466. Glass Toilet Bottle, blue and white, Russian design, cameo cut.

467. Glass Bowl, amber, with decorations in white, cameo cut, Russian design.

468. Glass Vase, blue, with dragons in white, cameo cut.

469. Glass Vase, yellow body with decorations in red, cameo cut.

470. Hock Glass, topaz bowl, with decorations in rod. Leg and foot of flint glass.

471. Glass Vase, amber, with decoration in white, cameo cut.
Designed and executed by Jabez Facer, Stourbridge.
Manufactured by Messrs. T. Webb & Sons, Stourbridge.

472. Glass Gourd-shaped Vase, ivory on ruby ground, Indian design.

473. Glass Bowl with raised stem, carved in the jade style.

474. Glass Scent Bottle, alabaster, with decoration in blue, cameo cut.

475. Glass Scent Bottle, pink ground, with white decoration, cameo cut.

476. Glass Scent Bottle, beeswax ground, with opal decoration, cameo cut.
Designed by T. Woodall, Stourbridge.
Executed by Francis Smith, Stourbridge.
Manufactured by Thomas Webb & Sons, Stourbridge.

477. Glass Vase, cameo cut, white on brown ground.

478. Cameo Plaque: "Blind Man's Buff," brown body, with figures and flowers in white.

479. Glass Scent Bottle, green, with white decoration, cameo cut.

480. Four Glass Panels, black ground, with decoration in white, cameo cut.

481. Glass Cameo Plaque, dark brown ground with white figures—" Dancing Girls."

482. Pair of Glass Vases, ruby, with white decoration, cameo cut.

483. Glass Finger Bowl, turquoise and opal, cameo cut.

484. Two Glass Scent Bottles, red and white, " Cupids,' cameo cut.

Designed by George Woodall, Stour-bridge.
Manufactured by Thomas Webb & Sons, Stourbridge.

485. Three Glass Scent Bottles, and one Vase, decorations in white on various coloured grounds, cameo cut.

Designed by T. Woodall, Stourbridge.
Executed by J. Hodgetts, Stourbridge.
Manufactured by Thomas Webb & Sons, Stourbridge.

486. Three Glass Scent Bottles various colours, cameo cut.

Glass Vase, slate-coloured ground, decorations in white, cameo cut.

Designed by T. Woodall, Stourbridge.
Executed by Benjamin Hollis, Dudley.
Manufactured by Thomas Webb & Sons, Stourbridge.

487. Glass Vase, bronze on green ground, cameo cut.

488. Glass Dessert Plate, brown, with white decorations, Russian style.

489. Glass Dessert Plate, lemon ground, with ruby decorations.

Designed by T. Woodall, Stourbridge.
Executed by William Hill, Stourbridge.
Manufactured by Thomas Webb & Sons, Stourbridge.

490. Glass Bowl, engraved in the Rock Crystal Style.

Designed by T. Woodall, Stourbridge.
Executed by Theodore Kny, Stour-bridge.
Manufactured by Thomas Webb & Sons, Stourbridge.

491. Glass Cameo Vase, with white and pink decoration, Chinese style.

492. Glass Cameo Vase, blue, pink and white decoration.

Designed by T. Woodall, Stourbridge.
Executed by H. A. Davis, Stourbridge.
Manufactured by Thomas Webb & Sons, Stourbridge.

493. Glass Vase, lemon ground, with green decorations.

494. Glass Vase, cameo cut, amber ground.

495. Glass Vase, blue and red, on ivory ground, cameo cut.

496. Glass Vase, opal on red, cameo cut.

497. Glass Vase, cameo cut.

498. Glass Vase, amber, with white decoration.

499. Glass Vase, yellow and red decoration.

Designed by T. Woodall, Stourbridge.
Executed by J. T. Fereday, Dudley.
Manufactured by Thomas Webb & Sons, Stourbridge.

500. Decorated Glass Bowl, ruby and gold.

Designed and executed by E. Goodyear, Dudley.
Manufactured by Thomas Webb & Sons, Stourbridge.

501. Glass Vase, cameo cut, ivory on red, " Orchids."

502. Glass Vase, cameo cut, amber body, with white flowers and green leaves.

Designed by T. Woodall.
Executed by W. H. Richardson, Stourbridge.
Manufactured by Thomas Webb & Sons, Stourbridge.

503. Flint Glass Water Set, richly cut and embossed.

Designed and executed by William Adey, Stourbridge.
Manufactured by Thomas Webb & Sons, Stourbridge.

504. Cut Glass Decanter.

Designed by Frederick Carder, Stour-bridge.
Executed by Charles Swayne, Stour-bridge.
Manufactured by Messrs. Stevens & Williams, Brierley Hill Glass Works.

505. Two Orange-cased Hock Glasses.

Designed by John Northwood.
Executed by Charles Swayne.
Manufactured by Messrs. Stevens & Williams, Brierley Hill Glass Works.

506. Flint Glass Claret Jug and two Wine Glasses.

Designed and executed by Frank Scheibner, Stourbridge. Price £5.
Manufactured by Messrs. Stevens & Williams, Brierley Hill Glass Works.

507. Flint Glass Bowl, imitation of rock crystal.
  Designed by J. Northwood.
  Executed by Frank Scheibner, Stourbridge.
  Manufactured by Messrs. Stevens & Williams, Brierley Hill Glass Works.

508. Engraved Sorbet Cup and Saucer, in ruby and flint glass.
  Designed by Frederick Carder, Stourbridge.
  Executed by J. Orchard, Stourbridge.
  Manufactured by Messrs. Stevens & Williams, Brierley Hill Glass Works.

509. Decanter and Wine Glass, engraved imitation of rock crystal.
  Designed by Frederick Carder, Stourbridge.
  Executed by J. Orchard, Stourbridge.
  Manufactured by Messrs. Stevens & Williams, Brierley Hill Glass Works.

510. Glass Cameo Vase, pink ground-decoration in white. Price £15 15s.

511. Two Small Cameo Plaques: The Head of Shakespeare (Price £6 6s.) and Convolvuli.

512. Seven Wine Glasses.
  Designed and executed by William Northwood, Stourbridge.
  Manufactured by Messrs. Stevens & Williams, Brierley Hill Glass Works.

513. Two Cameo Cut Vases.
  Designed and executed by Charles Northwood, Stourbridge.
  Manufactured by Messrs. Stevens & Williams, Brierley Hill Glass Works.

514. Cameo Carved Column for Lamp, in amber and white glass.
  Designed by J. Hill, Stourbridge.
  Executed by Daniel Beach, Stourbridge.
  Manufactured by Messrs. Stevens & Williams, Brierley Hill Glass Works.

515. Opal and Pink Glass Fruit Dish.
  Designed by John Northwood, Stourbridge.
  Manufactured by Messrs. Stevens & Williams, Brierley Hill Glass Works.

516. Nine Wine Glasses.
  Designed and etched by James Hill, Stourbridge.
  Manufactured by Messrs. Stevens & Williams, Brierley Hill Glass Works.

517. Wine Glass, rock crystal.
  Designed and executed by E. Hammond, Stourbridge.
  Manufactured by Messrs. Stevens & Williams, Brierley Hill Glass Works.

518. Two frames of Designs for Wine Glasses and Tazzas.
  By James Hill, Stourbridge.

519. Designs for Wine Glasses.
  By Marian Mansell, Lambeth.

520. Design for Claret Jug.
  By Ellen M. Ayers, Great Yarmouth.

521. Design for Claret Jug.
  By E. K. Cracknell, Great Yarmouth.

522. Two Paintings, Portraits of Tennyson and Carlyle. Painted on glass.
  Designed by Thomas Wilson, Edinburgh.
  Manufactured by Messrs. Ballantyne & Sons, Edinburgh.

523. Ornamental Panel, stained glass.
  Designed by William Savage, Manchester.
  Manufactured by R. B. Edmundson & Sons, Manchester.

524. Figure Panel in stained glass.
  By Thomas Jenkinson, Manchester.
  Manufactured by R. B. Edmundson & Sons, Manchester.

525. Panel in Stained Glass.
  Designed and executed by Robert Purcell, Manchester.
  Manufactured by R. B. Edmundson & Sons, Manchester.

526. Stained Glass Panel and three Designs for Stained Glass Windows.
  Designed and executed by William Boss, Edinburgh.

527. Stained Glass Panel and Design for Stained Glass Window.
  Designed and executed by George Charles Haité, Croydon.

528. Seven Designs for Stained Glass Windows.
  Designed and executed by F. G. Smith, Lambeth.

529. Three Drawings of Stained Glass Windows.
  By Jane J. Collis, Salisbury.

530. Frame of Designs for Stained Glass Windows for Public Buildings.
2 Frames of Designs for Ecclesiastical Windows.
Cartoon, Merlin's Tower, Camelot, for execution in stained glass,
Designed by T. W. Camm, *Birmingham.*

531. Design for Stained Glass Window.
By Sarah Ann Bradley, *Bloomsbury.*

532. Design for Stained Glass Window.
By Carl Almquist, *West London.* .
Manufactured by Messrs. Shrigley & Hunt, *Bedford Row, W.C.*

533. Two Frames of Designs for Stained Glass Windows.
Designed by E. Hammond, *Lambeth and West London.*
Manufactured by Campbell, Smith & Campbell.

534. Design for Stained Glass Window.
By W. J. Morgan, *South Kensington.*

535. Design for Stained Glass Window.
By H. Rossiter, *South Kensington.*

536. Design for Stained Glass Window.
By C. Hardgrave, *South Kensington.*

537. Two Panels, stained glass, Romeo and Juliet and Taming of the Shrew, and Panel Renaissance Ornament.
Designed and executed by Edward Frampton, *West London.*

538. Four Cartoons for stained glass windows, illustrating music and dancing.

539. Eight Frames, containing designs for stained glass windows and mural decoration.

By Edward Frampton, *West London.*

540. Cartoon designed for stained glass.
By Miss Emily G. Thompson, *Manchester.*

541. Design for stained glass window. ·
By Wm. G. Boss, *Edinburgh.*

542. Design for stained glass windows.
By Moyr Smith, *Glasgow and South Kensington.*

SECTION IV.

Enamels on Metal, Cloisonné, Champlevé, &c.

543. Three studies in enamel on copper, viz.:—(1) Plaque in the manner of old Limoges enamel.
(2) Head of a lady, drapery in translucent enamel.
(3) Rhododendrons, study from nature.
Painted by Miss Rosa Wallis, *South Kensington.*

544. Plaque enamel on copper, in the manner of old Limoges.
Designed by George Wallis, F.S.A., *Somerset House.*
Painted by Miss Rosa Wallis, *South Kensington*

545. Pair of Vases, cloisonné enamel.
Designed by E. Duffield, *Birmingham.*
Executed by Messrs. Elkington, *Birmingham.*

546. Pair of Vases, cloisonné enamel.
Designed by E. Duffield, *Birmingham.*
Executed by Messrs. Elkington, *Birmingham.*

547. Vase, champlevé enamel.
Designed by E. Duffield, *Birmingham.*
Executed by Messrs. Elkington, *Birmingham.*

548. Large Vase, cloisonné enamel, on gilt metal base.
Designed by E. Duffield, *Birmingham.*
Executed by Messrs. Elkington, *Birmingham.*

549. Plate, cloisonné enamel.
Designed by E. Duffield, *Birmingham.*
Executed by Messrs. Elkington, *Birmingham.*

550. Design for an enamelled casket.
By Miss Marianne Mansell, *Lambeth.*

SECTION V.

Ornamental Metal - work. — Bronze, Brass, Iron cast or wrought. Drawings and Photographs of such works as may have been executed.

551. 15 Salvers, Alms Dishes, &c.
Designed by W. H. Singer and E. R. Singer, *Frome and South Kensington.*
Manufactured by Messrs. J. W. Singer & Sons, *Frome.*

552. Door Plates, Lock, Door-handles, Crucifix, Bolts, &c., in wrought iron.
Designed by Thomas T. Freeman, *Manchester.*
Manufactured by Freeman & Collier, *Manchester.*

553. Hinge, Bell-pull, Door-handle, Fingerplates, Gas Brackets, Candle Bracket, in polished brass.
Designed by Thomas T. Freeman, *Manchester.*
Manufactured by Freeman & Collier, *Manchester.*

554. Bronze Gas Bracket and Candelabra.
Designed by Thomas T. Freeman, *Manchester.*
Manufactured by Freeman & Collier, *Manchester.*

555. Door Handle, brass, nickel plated.
Designed by Thomas T. Freeman, *Manchester.*
Manufactured by Freeman & Collier, *Manchester.*

556. Decorative Cast Iron Panel.
Decorative Cast Brass Panel.
Decorative Pewter Panel, used as pattern for bronze castings.
Designed and executed by C. H. Jessop, *Sheffield and Derby.*

557. Small Copper Panel, repoussé scroll work.
Designed and executed by James Booth, *Sheffield.*

558. Two Designs for Metal Panels in wax.
Designed by John Fisher, *Sheffield and South Kensington.*

559. Wrought and Polished Iron Candlestick.
Designed and executed by William Letheren (Senior), *Cheltenham.*

560. Bronze Loving Cup.
Designed and modelled by Henry Archer, *Sheffield.*

561. Eagle Lectern in Polished Brass.
Designed by W. H. and E. R. Singer, *Frome and South Kensington.*
Manufactured by J. W. Singer & Sons, *Frome.*

562. Three Cast Iron Panels, for stove grates.
Designed by G. A. Illston, *Rotherham and Sheffield.*
Manufactured by Corbitt & Co., *Rotherham.*

563. Flower Stand.
Designed by H. P. Hodkinson, *Coventry.*

564. Four Lamp Brackets and Lamps, wrought iron and polished brass.
Designed by W. H. and E. R. Singer, *Frome and South Kensington.*
Manufactured by J. W. Singer & Sons, *Frome.*

565. Wrought-iron Screen, copper panel in centre.
Designed by W. H. and E. R. Singer, *Frome and South Kensington.*
Manufactured by J. W. Singer & Sons, *Frome.*

566. Portion of Balustrade, wrought-iron.
Designed by J. D. Sedding.
Manufactured by Longden & Co., *Sheffield.*

567. Wrought-iron Grille.
Designed and executed by W. Letheren, *Cheltenham.*
Lent by the South Kensington Museum.

568. Hammered-iron Window Grille.
Designed and executed by Samuel Hobbs, *Young Men's Christian Institute, Long Acre.*

569. Wrought-iron Cabinet.
Designed by H. Faulks, *Birmingham.*
Manufactured by A. Newman, *London.*

570. Gate and Railings, cast-iron.
Designed by George W. Shepherd, *Coalbrookdale.*
Manufactured by The Coalbrookdale Iron Co., *Salop.*

571. Pediment of Gates in wrought iron.
Designed and made by W. H. Letheren, *Cheltenham.*

572. Grate, cast iron.
Designed by Joseph Kershaw, *Coal-
brookdale.*
Manufactured by The Coalbrookdale
Co., *Salop.*

573. Grate.
Designed by G. A. Illston, *Sheffield.*
Manufactured by W. Corbitt & Co.,
Rotherham.

574. Three Grates and Two Fenders.
Designed and modelled by F. C. Jessop,
Rotherham.
Manufactured by F. C. Jessop, *Rother-
ham.*

575. Bronze Dining-room Grate.
Designed by J. Lawson, *Sheffield.*
Manufactured by Watson, Moorwood
& Co., *Sheffield.*

576. Cast-iron Grate Front.
Designed by G. W. Shepherd, *Coal-
-brookdale and South Kensington.*
Manufactured by The Coalbrookdale
Co., *Salop.*

577. Cast-iron Chimney-piece and two Cast-
iron Garden Seats.
Designed by John Moses.
Manufactured by The Coalbrookdale
Co., *Salop.*

578. Grate with Tiles.
Designed by William Turner, *Edin-
burgh.*
Manufactured by Scott, Morton & Co.,
Edinburgh.

579. Three Polished Brass Chandeliers

580. Three Gas Brackets, polished brass.

581. One Fender, polished brass, with Fire
Dogs surmounted by brass rosettes.

Designed by Henry Poynton, *Coventry.*
Manufactured by Richardson, Ellson
& Co., *Coventry.*

582. Statuette in Bronze : " Cimabue."
Designed and modelled by Emily
Selous (Mrs. Fenessy), *Bloomsbury.*
Executed by C. Delpech.
(Lent by the Art Union of London.)

583. Door Knocker in wrought iron.

584. Letter Box in wrought iron.

585. Piece of Holly in wrought iron.

586. Mirror Frame in wrought iron.
Designed and executed by Charles
Letheren, *Cheltenham.*

587. Nickle-plated Gas Bracket.

588. Bronze Gas Bracket.

589. Three Brass Chandeliers.

590. Fire Iron Rests, black and brass, and
all brass.

591. Brass Fire Iron Standard.
Designed by Thomas C. Smart,
Dudley.
Manufactured by T. Smart, *Dudley.*

592. Three Polished Brass Fenders.
Fire Brasses, Rests, and Stops.
Designed by Samuel Thompson,
Sheffield.
Manufactured by Thomas Hague,
Sheffield.

593. Two Polished Brass Chandeliers.

594. Polished Brass Library Light, for
candles or gas.
Designed by T. W. Maddox, *Birming-
ham.*
Manufactured by Thomas Ford &
Sons, *Birmingham.*

595. Polished Brass Fender, Fire Brasses,
Fire Dogs.
Designed by T. W. Maddox, *Birming-
ham.*
Manufactured by Crofts & Assinder,
Birmingham.

596. Polished Brass Bracket.
Designed by T. W. Maddox, *Bir-
mingham.*
Manufactured by W. Whitehouse &
Co., *Birmingham.*

597. Two Polished Brass Chandeliers.
Designed by T. W. Maddox, *Bir-
mingham.*
Manufactured by James Barwell, Son
& Co., *London and Birmingham.*

598. Six Fire-iron Heads.
Designed by George V. Parkin,
Dudley.
Manufactured by T. Smart, *Dudley.*

599. Oval Brass Mirror with Girandoles.
Designed by J. Challen Beattie, Birmingham and Stoke-on-Trent.
Manufactured by W. Tonks & Sons, Birmingham.

600. Polished Brass Chandelier.
Designed by H. P. Hodkinson, Coventry.
Manufactured by H. Hodkinson, Coventry.

601. Lacquered Brass Frame.
Designed and executed by Edwin Fox, Birmingham and South Kensington.

602. Polished Brass Pendant Lamps, Candlesticks, Sconces, Candelabra, Gas Brackets and Door Knockers, Repoussé Copper Panel, with Candle Brackets, wrought-iron Pendant Lamps, Lamp Stands and Chains.
Designed by W. H. & E. R. Singer, Frome and South Kensington.
Manufactured by Messrs. J. W. Singer & Sons, Frome.

603. Polished Cast Brass Clocks, Candelabra, Candlesticks, Inkstands, Vases, Mirror, Girandoles, &c.
Designed by Herbert Mason, Birmingham and South Kensington.
Manufactured by Herbert Mason & Co., Birmingham.
Lent by Messrs. Mappin & Webb.

604. Designs for Iron Gates and Chancel Standard.
By Theodore J. Dalgleish, Coventry.

605. Design for Iron Gates.
By G. W. Shepherd, Coalbrookdale.

606. Design for Wrought-iron Reredos. Design for Wrought-iron Gates, four Brass Standard Lamps.
By John J. Trego, Coventry.

607. Designs for Wrought-iron Railing, Balcony, Grille.
By Miss Sydney Thompson, Belfast.

608. Design for Wrought-iron Lodge Gates.
By F. C. Jessop, Rotherham.

609. Designs for four Wrought-iron Grilles and Wrought-Iron Gates.
By O. R. Albrow, Great Yarmouth.

610. Design for Metal Screen.
By P. S. Perkins, Leicester.

611. Design for Balustrade with Lamp and Bronze Fire Dogs.
By Stuart Thorpe, Sheffield.

612. Design for Wrought-iron Gates.
By M. Garbutt, West London.

613. Design for Cast-iron Centre Lamp.
By C. E. Wilson, Sheffield.

614. Design for Entrance Gates.
By Charles Letheren, Cheltenham.

615. Design for Wrought-iron Gates.
By J. Mayston, Great Yarmouth.

616. Design for Wrought-iron Gates.
By W. J. Newman, South Kensington.

617. Design for Metal Chancel Screen.
By H. Chattaway, Coventry.

618. Design for Wrought-iron Entrance Gate.
By R. Ayling, Westminster.

619. Design for Wrought-iron Gates, Burlington House.
By H. Poynton, Coventry.
Manufactured by Richardson, Ellson & Co., Coventry.

620. Design for Park Gates, wrought-iron.
By J. McCulloch, Belfast.

621. Design for Wrought-iron Gates.
By H. S. Bridgewater, Dudley.

622. Design for Wrought-iron Gates and Screen.
By Frank Marshall, Nottingham.

623. Design for Wrought-iron Gates.
By Mary Cox, Worcester.

624. Design for Cast-iron Hat and Umbrella Stand.
By H. S. Tomlins, Worcester.

625. Design for Polished Brass Pendants for electric light.
By G. W. Maddox, Birmingham.

626. Two Photographs, cast-iron centre lamps.
Designed by Charles Wilson, Sheffield.

627. Design for Brass Chandeliers and Lamps.

By G. E. Tucker, *West London*.

628. Seven Frames of Photographs of Lecerns, Lamp Standards, Crosses, Alms Dishes, &c.

Designed by W. H. & E. R. Singer, *Frome and South Kensington*.
Manufactured by W. J. Singer & Sons, *Frome*.

629. Photographs—Lodge Gates, Lamp Standards, Tomb Railings, and Monumental Iron Work.

Designed by W. Letheren, *Cheltenham*.
Manufactured by W. Letheren, *Cheltenham*.

630. Two Brass Dog Grates, with Engraved Brass Work, Fire Irons and Fender.

Designed by H. Longden & F. Fidler. *Sheffield*.
Manufactured by Longden & Co., *Sheffield*.

631. Two Perforated Copper Panels, Repoussé work.

Designed by H. Longden & F. Fidler, *Sheffield*.
Executed by W. Bullas, *Sheffield*.

632. Design for Brass Chandelier.

By George Illston, *Sheffield*.

633. Five designs for decoration of japanned iron trays.

By H. T. Tomlins, *Worcester*.

SECTION VI.

Silver and Gold Plate, Plated Wares, Electro Deposits, including models for silver and gold work. Drawings and Photographs of such works as may have been executed.

634. Candelabra, electro-plate, £52 10s.

635. Breakfast Service, consisting of coffee, tea, sugar, cream and kettle and stand, electro-plate, £22 13s.

636. Claret Jug, electro-plate, £6 6s.

637. Stand for Rosewater Dish, electro-plate, £66 3s.

638. Centre Piece, electro-plate, £105.

639. Liquor Frame, electro-plate, £13 5s.

640. Sugar and Cream Stand, electro-plate, £3 6s. 6d.

641. Sugar and Cream Stand, electro-plate, £4 8s. 6d.; and Cruet Stand, £8 6s.

642. Sugar and Cream Stand, electro-plate, £4 15s.

643. Claret Jug, electro-plate, £5 5s.

644. Cup, electro-plate, £6 12s. 6d.

645. Flower Stand, electro-plate, £7 17s. 6d.

646. Flower Stand, electro-plate, £6 11s. 6d.

647. Flower Stand, electro-plate, £4.

648. Cruet Frame, electro-plate, £6 11s. 6d.

649. Ice-water Jug, electro-plate, £8 2s. 6d.

650. Claret Jug, silver, £18 18s.

Designed by George Allen, *Birmingham*.
Manufactured by Messrs. Elkington & Co.

651. Centre Piece, china-mounted, in metal gilt, £30.

652. Two End Pieces, china mounted in metal gilt, £10 each.

653. Punch Bowl, silver, £100.

654. Pair 3-Light Candelabra, china, mounted in metal gilt.

655. Sugar and Cream Stand, electro-plate, £2 2s.

656. Egg Frame, electro-plate, £5 15s. 6d.

657. Marmalade Jar, electro-plate, £2 12s. 6d.

658. Butter Dish, electro-plate, £1 17s. 6d.

659. Tea, Sugar and Cream electro-plate, "Fluted," £10 2s. 6d.

660. Two Pairs Salts, electro-plate, 19s. per pair.

661. Cruet Frame, electro-plate, £6 12s. 6d.

662. Liquor Frame, electro-plate, £7 17s. 6d.

663. Liquor Frame, electro-plate, £13 5s.

664. Biscuit Box, electro-plate, £4 4s.

665. Coffee, Tea, Sugar and Cream, electro-plate, £23.

666. Tea Tray, electro-plate, £13.

667. Turnover Hash-dish, electro - plate, £12 12s, and Cruet Frame, £6 16s. 6d.

668. Claret Jug, electro-plate, £10.

669. Sugar Basket, glass mounted, £2.

670. Sugar-basket, glass mounted, £2 7s. 6d.

671. Strawberry Stand, £6 12s. 6d.

672. Table Candlesticks, £5 10s.

673. Table Candlesticks, £6.

674. Strawberry Stand, £4.

675. Cake Basket, £4 4s.

Designed by H. Fellows, *Birmingham*.
Manufactured by Messrs. Elkington & Co., *Birmingham*.

676. Athletic Shield of heraldic form, small repoussé panels, £5. 5s.

677. Athletic Shield of heraldic form, small repoussé panels, £5 5s.

678. Centre Piece, electro-plate, £47 5s.

679. Oval End Piece, electro-plate, £16 16s. each.

680. Four Compotiers, electro-plate, £7 7s. each.

681. Coffee, Tea, Sugar and Cream Set, electro-plate, £21 15s.

682. Tray, electro-plate, £23 2s.

683. Cruet, electro-plate, £6.

684. Cruet, electro-plate, £7.

685. Butter Dish, electro-plate, £2 10s. 6d.

686. 6 Salts, electro-plate, 12s 6d. each.

687. Heart-shaped Tea, Sugar and Cream Set, silver-gilt, £35.

688. Oblong Tray, silver-gilt, £40.

689. Biscuit Box, silver, £25.

690. Bouquet Holder, silver, £7 7s.

691. Silver Cradle, Centre Piece.
Designed by Challen Beattie, *Birmingham.*
Manufactured by Messrs. Elkington.

692. Reduction of Panel by Donatello, in repoussé silver.

693. Top of Lady's Handkerchief-Box, in repoussé silver.

694. Reduction of Figure by Scopas in repoussé silver.

695. Three Plaques, repoussé, "Jephthah's daughter going out to meet her father," "Boy and Eagle," and "Birds fighting."
Executed by Thomas Spall, *Birmingham.*
Manufactured by Messrs. Elkington.

695. Two Silver Panels, repoussé work.
Designed and executed by F. Harper, *Birmingham.*
Manufactured by Messrs. Elkington & Co., *Birmingham.*

697. Silver Gilt Tazza, engraved and chased.
Designed by Frank Jackson, *Birmingham.*
Manufactured by Messrs. Elkington & Co., *Birmingham.*

698. Vase, with Cover and Handles, Silver, Italian Renaissance style.
The body of the Vase is divided architecturally into four panels, two of which are occupied by Limoges Enamel, representing the triumph of Poseidon, and the birth of Aphrodite; the other two smaller ones are filled in with ornamental details in repoussé.
On the lower part of the calyx of the Vase are Limoges enamel medallions, containing nautical and other emblems. The handles are composed of rich scrolls, on the top of which are seated youthful winged figures supporting the lip of the Vase, from the termination of the scrolls depend festoons of shells and sea-weed.
The cover is decorated with shell and pearl and surmounted by a knob composed of foliated figures holding up a vase-like form.
The whole is supported by an architectural stem decorated with figures.
Designed by Frank G. Jackson, *Birmingham.*
Figures modelled by Challen Beattie, *Stoke-upon-Trent and South Kensington.*
Limoges Enamel Plaques, &c., painted by Miss Rosa Wallis, *South Kensington.*
Manufactured by Messrs. Elkington & Co., *Birmingham.*

699. Silver Mounted Claret Jug. Six Silver Coffee Spoons, Sugar Tongs. Silver Mounted Sugar and Cream Stand. Two Fruit Spoons and Sugar Sifter. Marmalade Dish and Spoon. Silver Mounted Salad Bowl. Card Basket. Cream Jug. Silver Mounted Tray and Silver Salt Cellars. Milk Jug and Sugar Bowl, Wedgewood, silver mounted. Tea Kettle and Spirit Lamp. Cake Basket, Fish Knives and Forks, Salt Spoons, Caddy Spoons, Grape Cutters, and Dinner Forks. Silver Gilt Jewel Box. Silver Breakfast Cruets, Silver Fish Servers, with ivory handles, Silver Fish Servers, and Silver Gilt Fruit Spoons.
Designed and manufactured by Jehoiada Rhodes, *Sheffield.*

700. Silver Gilt Dessert Service, seven pieces.
Designed by Sir Noel Paton, R.S.A., Illustrative of Shakespeare's play of the "Tempest."
Modelled by Alexander Crichton, 22 Great Sutton-street, Clerkenwell, Edinburgh (School of Art).
Manufactured by Messrs. Mackay and Cunningham, *Edinburgh* (lent by John Polson, Esq.).

701. Silver Tea Pot.
Sugar Basin.
Cream Ewer, in form of nautilus shell.
£35.

702. Four Light Branch Candelabra, Silver Gilt, £120.

703. One Centre Piece for fruit and flowers £50.

704. Two Dishes for fruit, £32 each.

705. Four Dishes for fruit, £16 each.
Designed and modelled by J. Crichton, Edinburgh.
Manufactured by Mackay & Chisholm, 57 Princes Street, Edinburgh.

706. Silver Tea Pot.
Designed by Richard Lunn, Sheffield.
Manufactured by Jehoiada Rhodes, Sheffield.

707. Three sets of Fruit Spoons and Sugar Sifters, silver and silver gilt; three sets of Salt Cellars and Spoons, silver and silver gilt; two pairs of Fish Servers.
Designed and manufactured by Nicholas Bray, Sheffield.

708. Apostle Toast Rack.
Designed by Henry Pearce, Hull.
Manufactured by Henry Pearce, Huddersfield.

709. Copper Gilt Flagon with Cover.
Designed and executed by E. W. Clayton, Sheffield.
Lent by Sir Philip Cunliffe Owen, K.C.M.G., &c., &c

710. Pair of Buffalo Horns, mounted in silver, with silver gilt receptacle for holding flowers, £120.
Designed by Thomas Holiday, Edinburgh.
Manufactured by Messrs. Mackay & Chisholm, Edinburgh.

711. Case containing Silver and Silver-Gilt Fish Carvers, Fish-Eaters, Dessert Knives and Fruit Spoons.
Designed and manufactured by E. L. Thompson, Sheffield.

712. Scotch Ram's Head, silver mounted, as Snuff and Cigar Box, set with Scotch Cairngorms.
Designed by Henry B. Kirkwood, Edinburgh.
Manufactured by Henry B. Kirkwood, Edinburgh.

713. Two Silver Cups in repoussé work, Salver in repoussé work, Jewel Box, with Bronze Panels in repoussé; Silver Coffee Canister, chased; Silver Bell, engraved.
Designed and executed by George Norton, Sheffield.

714. Rose Water Dish and Ewer in Plaster. Illustrative of the Ancient Mariner.
Designed by H. W. Hogg, Derby.

715. Modelled Design for a Loving Cup and Cover, silver panel gilt. The property of the Clothworkers' Company.
The whole *designed, modelled and cast by Richard Lunn, Derby and South Kensington.*
Lent by the South Kensington Museum.

716. Model for Salver.
Designed by Richard Lunn, Sheffield and South Kensington.

717. Model in plaster for Plaque.
Designed by A. Austin, Derby.

718. Model in plaster of Casket.

719. Model in wax for card tray.
Designed and modelled by W. Marshall, Sheffield and South Kensington.

720. Model of Silver Cup.
Designed and modelled by E. Thickett, Sheffield.

721. Silver Panel, chased and engraved.
Designed by R. Price, Charterhouse.

722. Silver Tankard, repoussé work.
Designed by T. T. Freeman, Manchester.
Manufactured by Freeman & Collier, Manchester.

723. Engraved Waiter, Renaissance style.
Designed by James Menses, Edinburgh.
Manufactured by Hamilton, Crichton & Co., Edinburgh.

724. Photograph of Gold Key.
Designed by Edwin Seward, R.C.A., Cardiff.

725. Presentation Inkstand, in silver. Presented to General Lord Wolseley.
Designed and executed by G. M. Kirtland, South Kensington.
Manufactured by Messrs. J. & H. Garrard, Haymarket, London.
Lent by General Lord Wolseley.

726. Group of Figures, in silver, representing Don Quixote and Sancho Panza, the "Steward's Cup," Goodwood.

727. Silver Group, modelled from life, representing mare and foal, with two panels. Lent by Sir John Astley.
Designed by G. A. Carter, Lambeth.
Manufactured by Hunt & Roskell, Bond Street.

728. Group of Figures, in silver, representing King John signing Magna Charta.
Designed by G. A. Carter, Lambeth.
Manufactured by Hunt & Roskell, Bond Street.
Lent by J. D'Aguilar Samuda, Esq.

729. Silver Vase.
Designed by T. Swaffield Brown, Finsbury.
Manufactured by Messrs. Hunt & Roskell, Bond Street.

730. Testimonial, in silver (four pieces). Presented to Thomas Hawksley, Esq., C.E., F.R.S.
Designed by T. Swaffield Brown, Finsbury.
Manufactured by Messrs. Hunt & Roskell.
Lent by Thomas Hawksley, Esq., C.E., F.R.S.

731. Claret Jug, mounted in silver gilt.
Designed by Miss Ellen K. Cracknell, Yarmouth.
Manufactured by Messrs. Hunt & Roskell.

732. Metal Gilt Clock, representing the death of King Arthur.
Designed by C. P. Slocombe, Spital-fields and Somerset House.
Manufactured by E. White.

733. The Magdala Trophy, silver and silver gilt.
Designed by C. P. Slocombe, Spital-fields and Somerset House.
Manufactured by Messrs. Elkington, Birmingham.
Lent by the Officers of the 1st Battalion of the King's Own Royal Regiment.

734. Silver Shield, repoussé.
The design is illustrative of a description of a shield in Virgil's Æneid, Book VIII.
The centre represents the Naval Battle of Actium, encircled by a border of Deities favourable to the opposing forces, surrounding which are twelve panels illustrating the following incidents :—
  1. Romulus and Remus, with the Tiber in the foreground.
  2. The Rape of the Sabines.
  3. The Sabine War.
  4. The Treaty with the Sabines.
  5. The Death of Nictius.
  6. Horatius Cocles defending the Bridge.
  7. Manlius defending the Capitol against the Gauls.
  8. A Sabine Procession.

  9. The Lower Regions.
  10. Triumph of Cæsar.
  11-12. The Conquered Nations brought to Rome.
Designed by John Watkins, Birmingham and South Kensington.
Chased by Thomas Spall, Birmingham.
Manufactured by Messrs. Elkington & Co., Birmingham.

735. Original design and drawing of the above shield *designed and executed by John Watkins, Birmingham and South Kensington.*
Lent by the South Kensington Museum.

736. Design for Five-light Silver Candlestick.
By A. Winterbottom, Sheffield.

737. Design for Five-branch Candlestick.
By J. Mackenzie, Belfast.

738. Design for Five-light Candlestick and Seven-light Candlestick.
By John Bradburn, Coalbrookdale.

739. Design for Silver Fruit Dish and Tankard.
By Edwin Jarratt, Coalbrookdale.

740. Design for Silver Tea Kettle and Stand, and Silver Salad Bowl.
By Robert Needham, Sheffield.

741. Design for Flagon, in gold and silver.
742. Design for Chalice, in gold and silver.
By Stuart Thorpe, Sheffield.

743. Four Frames, Design for Centre Pieces, Tazzas, &c.
By W. F. Randall, Stroud and Gloucester.

744. Design for Centre Piece and Tea Kettle.
By Thomas Smith, Coalbrookdale.

745. Design for The Republic Shield.
By Henry Tidmarsh, West London.

746. Design for Loving Cup, Dagger Handle and Sheaths.
By Frederick Fidler, Sheffield.

747. Design for Loving Cup.
By Wm. McGowan, Belfast.

748. Design for Soup Tureen and Dinner Dish.
    By Richard Lunn, *Sheffield.*

749. Design for Loving Cup, presented to Alderman Hadley.
    By G. E. Tucker, *West London.*

750. Design for Salt Cellars.
    By A. A. Peace, *Sheffield.*

751. Designs for two Candelabra, Tea Kettle, Tankard, Claret Jug, and Mirror Frames.
    By J. A. Sherlock, *Warrington and South Kensington.*

752. Design for Silver Salt Cellar and Spoons.
    By O. R. Albrow, *Great Yarmouth.*

753. Design for Clock and Candlesticks.
    By W. H. Banks, *Rotherham.*

754. Design for Silver Scissors and Sheaths.
    By G. Mackenzie, *Sheffield.*

755. Photographs of Silver Cups.
    Designed by Henry Archer, *Sheffield.*

756. Design for Silver Salad Bowl.
    By J. Thomas, *Westminster.*

757. Design for Gold Casket.
    By T. Walter Wilson, for H.R.H. The Prince of Wales.
    Manufactured by Messrs. Garrard & Co.

758. Design for Gold and Jewelled Casket.
    By T. Walter Wilson, presented to H.I.M. The Emperor of Russia.
    Manufactured by Benson & Son, *Ludgate Hill.*

759. Plaster Model of Shield.
    Designed and modelled by Owen Gibbons, *South Kensington and Cirencester.*

SECTION VII.

Jewelry and Personal Ornaments. Gold, Silver, Plated, or in any suitable Materials. Medals, Seals, and Fans.

760. Gold Bouquet Holder, presented to H.R.H. the Princess of Wales, by the Mayor of Swansea, in October, 1881 enamelled and jewelled. Decoration entirely composed of emblematic and nautical devices; red dragon of Wales at sides, with arms of Princess.
    Designed by J. W. Tonks, *Birmingham.*
    Manufactured by Messrs. T. & J. Bragg, *Birmingham.*
    (Lent by H.R.H. the Princess of Wales.)

761. Gold Chatelaine, presented to H.R.H. the Princess of Wales, by the Swansea Harbour Trust, on the ceremony of naming the new Dock, October, 1881. Set with diamonds, rubies, pearls and turquoises. All decoration and appliances designed in reference to the occasion.
    Designed by J. W. Tonks, *Birmingham.*
    Manufactured by Messrs. T. & J. Bragg, *Birmingham.*
    (Lent by H.R.H. the Princess of Wales.)

762. Spade, silver and ivory, enamelled and parcel-gilt. Presented by the ladies of Leicester to H.R.H. the Princess of Wales, on planting a tree in the Abbey Park. 29 May, 1882.
    Designed by J. W. Tonks, *Birmingham.*
    Manufactured by S. Blanckensee & Son, *Birmingham*
    (Lent by H.R.H. the Princess of Wales.)

763. Gold Key, Gothic style, presented to H.R.H. the Prince of Wales, on the occasion of his opening the Abbey Park, Leicester, with enamelled Arms of Prince and of Borough, oak device, King Charles' Day, 1882.
    Designed by J. W. Tonks, *Birmingham.*
    Manufactured by S. Blanckensee and Son, *Birmingham.*
    (Lent by H.R.H. the Prince of Wales, K.G.)

764. Suite of Jewellery, 22-carat gold. Collarette containing fifteen repoussée plaques, illustrating the arts of drawing and design, Italian foliated borders, pendant illustrating sculpture, bracelet and earrings indicating painting and music.
    Designed by J. W. Tonks, *Birmingham.*
    Manufactured by Messrs. T. and J. Bragg, *Birmingham.*
    (Lent by Mrs. Thos. Dix Perkin.)

764a. Brooch and Silver Gilt Muffineer.
    Designed and executed by Harry Stapleton, *St. Martin's.*

765. Silver Mace, presented to West Bromwich Corporation, by Mr. Alderman R. Farley, First Mayor, with heraldic and civic decoration.
> *Designed by J. W. Tonks, Birmingham.*
> *Manufactured by Messrs. T. and J. Bragg, Birmingham.*
(Lent by the Corporation of West Bromwich.)

766. Mayoral Gold Chain and Badge, Stoke-upon-Trent, enamelled Arms of Borough, Crest, Moth and Civic Devices. Presented to the Borough by Mr. Colin Minton Campbell, J.P. in 1875.
> *Designed by J. W. Tonks, Birmingham.*
> *Manufactured by Messrs. T. & J. Bragg, Birmingham.*
(Lent by the Corporation of Stoke-upon-Trent.

767. Mayoral Chain and Badge, Rotherham, 18-carat gold. Badge entirely wrought and carved gold work, various enamelled shields, emblems, and local references. Arms of Earl of Effingham, Lord of Manor, on centre link. Heraldic bearings of successive mayors and borough devices on side links of chain, initial letter of borough forming connection.
> *Designed by J. W. Tonks, Birmingham.*
> *Manufactured by Messrs. T. & J. Bragg, Birmingham.*
(Lent by the Corporation of Rotherham.)

768. Silver Key with Gold and Enamelled Arms, presented to Rt. Hon. John Bright, M.P., on opening "Cobden" Coffee House, Birmingham, August, 1883. Style Gothic, column, enriched capital, head trefoil form, crocketed. Arms of Birmingham, surmounted by civic crown.
> *Designed by J. W. Tonks, Birmingham.*
> *Manufactured by Messrs. T. & J. Bragg, Birmingham.*
(Lent by the Rt. Hon. John Bright, M.P.)

769. Gold Belt—subject: "The 12 Months," a story of the year. The belt is composed of a series of plaques chased in repoussé, and between each plaque a flower characteristic of the month which it follows.
> *Designed and executed by G. A. Carter, Lambeth.*
> *Manufactured by Messrs. Hunt & Roskell, New Bond Street.*

770. Sword of Honour, presented to Sir Archibald Alison, K.C.B., &c.
> *Designed by W. J. Milwain, Glasgow.*
> *Manufactured by G. Edwards & Sons, Glasgow.*
(Lent by Sir Archibald Alison, K.C.B.)

771. Seals for City of Bangor, and Boroughs of Accrington and Bacup, arranged for wax and paper respectively. Accrington, vesica shaped. Bangor City Seal in quatrefoil design. Bacup two modes of treatment, bold for wax impression, other in low relief for paper.
> *Designed by J. W. Tonks, Birmingham.*

772. Pierced and Engraved Silver-mounted Dirk, with Cairngorm handle, Sgian-Dhu to match, Sporran to match.

773. Pierced and Engraved Silver-mounted Dirk, Celtic ornament with fine brown Cairngorm handles, Brooch and Sporran to match, Waistbelt with pierced silver bosses and centre plate.

774. Antique Dirk, engraved silver mountings, gold bosses. Antique Sporran of Otter Skin, with engraved silver mountings, tooled leather front, gold bosses, and plaited leather tassels.

775. Pierced and Engraved Silver-Mounted Dirk, Celtic ornament, antique carved ivory handles, gold studs.

776. Pierced and Engraved Silver-Mounted Sporran, of ermine, with silver tassels and pierced silver-covered crystal bosses.

777. Pierced and Engraved Silver-Mounted Sgian-Dhu, with buckhorn handle. topaz in top.

778. Pierced and Engraved Silver-Mounted Sgian Dhu, with Cairngorm handle.
> *Designed and executed by H. B. Kirkwood, Edinburgh.*

779. Gold-Mounted Fob and Seal.
> *Designed and executed by Henry Pearce, Sheffield.*

780. Six Gold Watch Cases.
> *Designed by Walter Scott, Thomas Baker, C. H. Everington, James Friday, Coventry.*
> *Engraved by B. A. Hall, Coventry.*
> *Manufactured by Messrs. Rotherham.*

781. Frame containing Six Medals.
1. David Roberts, R.A. Bronze.
2. Reverse of No. 1. Bronze.
3. Thomas Carlyle. In commemoration of his 80th birthday. Bronze.
4. Captain Francis Fowke, R.E. Bronze.
5. Reverse of No. 4. Bronze.
6. Henry Bessemer. Bronze.

Frame containing Fifteen Medals.
1. David Cox. Bronze.
2. Reverse of No. 1. Bronze.
3. Rutherford B. Hayes, 1875. Bronze.
4. Rutherford B. Hayes, 1877. Bronze.
5. First Prize Army Division, United States, for marksmanship. Bronze.
6. Art Treasures and Industrial Exhibition of North Wales. Bronze.
7. Madam Parepa-Rosa.
8. Rutherford B. Hayes (oval). Bronze.
9. Medal given by the Assay Commission of the United States Mint, Philadelphia. Bronze.
0. National Exposition of Railway Appliances, Chicago. Bronze.
1. Joseph E. Temple. Lead.
2. Reverse of No. 11. White metal.
3. Coin. Copper.
4. Reverse of No. 13. Copper.
5. James A. Garfield. White metal.
> *Designed and executed by* George T. Morgan, *Chief Medallist United States Mint, Birmingham and South Kensington.*

782. Necklace and Pendant, gold, set with wels.
> *Designed by* T. Walter Wilson, *South Kensington.*
> *Manufactured by* Messrs. Garrard for H.R.H. the Prince of Wales.

783. Design for Necklace and Pendant, in ld, enamelled and jewelled, with cameos presenting Apollo and the Muses.
> *Designed by* T. Walter Wilson, *South Kensington.*

784. Design for Watch Cases.
> *By* John Frost, *Coventry.*

785. Design for Watch Cases.
> *By* James Friday, *Coventry.*

786. Frame of Designs for Watch Cases.
> *By* H. Baynton, *Coventry.*

787. Frame of Designs for Watch Cases.
> *By* Walter Scott, *Coventry.*

788. Frame of Designs for Watch Cases.
> *By* John J. Trego, *Coventry.*

789. Frame of Design of Jewellery.
> *By* Miss Marianne Mansell, *Lambeth*

790. Six Frames of Photographs of Mayor's ins of office of the Corporations of Stockport, crington, Neath, Swansea, Kidderminster, lsall,
> *Designed by* J. William Tonks, *Birmingham.*
> *Manufactured by* Messrs. H. and J. Bragg, *Birmingham.*

791. Two Frames of Designs of Mayors' Chains of Office of the Corporations of Swansea and Rochester.
> *Designed by* T. William Tonks, *Birmingham.*
> *Manufactured by* Messrs. H. and J. Bragg, *Birmingham.*

792. Design for Album Cover.
> *By* T. W. Tonks, *Birmingham.*
> *Manufactured by* Messrs. H. and J. Bragg, *Birmingham.*

793. Design for Fan, painted on Silk, Apple Blossoms and Cupids.
> *Designed and executed by* Ethel C. Nisbet, *Bloomsbury.*
(Lent by H.R.H. The Duchess of Albany.)

794. Design for Fan, water colours on vellum, "The Feast."
> *By* Henrietta Montalba, *South Kensington.*
(Lent by South Kensington Museum.)

795. Design for Fan, water colour on vellum, "La Grace."
> *By* Hilda Montalba, *South Kensington.*
(Lent by South Kensington Museum.)

796. Design for Fan.
> *By* Mrs. Eassie, *Gloucester.*

797. Design for Fan, painting on Silk.
> *By* A. L. West, *Bloomsbury.*

797a. Frame of Designs for Jewellery.
> *By* J. J. Oxer, *Lambeth.*

SECTION VIII.

Furniture and Wood Carving. Inlaid Wood. Parqueterie. Papier Maché Ware, etc.

798. Box, carved oak.
> *Designed and executed by* Henry Archer, *Sheffield.*

799. Carved Coin Cabinet, in imitation of 16th Century Work.
> *Designed and Carved by* George Norton, *Sheffield.*

800. Richly Carved Sideboard in Italian Walnut, 16th Century Style.
> *Designed and Carved by* William Allwright, *West London.*
> *Manufactured by* Messrs. Holland.
(Lent by Sir Richard Wallace, Bart.)

801. Carved Oak Hall Seat, seat and back covered with embossed leather.
    Designed by Thomas Finchett, *Manchester.*
    Manufactured by Messrs. Kendal Milne & Co., *Manchester.*
    (Lent by John Lomax, Esq.)

802. Sideboard, with carved panels, mouldings, &c.
    Designed by Richard Pinches, *Chester.*
    Manufactured by Messrs. W. & F. Brown & Co., *Chester.*

803. Four Specimens of Wood Mosaics for Floors. No curved lines can be used and the choice of colours is limited to those afforded by the natural shades of the woods.
    Designs by Richard Pinches, *Chester.*
    Manufactured by Messrs. W. & F. Brown & Co., *Chester.*

804. Table Top, inlaid wood.
    Designed by F. J. Millward, *Kendal.*
    Manufactured by A. J. Millward.

805. Solid Spanish Mahogany Sideboard, relieved by black moulding.

806. Octagonal Table Top, Parqueterie.

807. Solid Walnut Cabinet, with black moulding, with bevelled glass panels to door.
    Designed and executed by Gunston Tite, *South Kensington.*

808. Elizabethan Coffer with draw in base.
    Designed and executed by Frank Boucher, *Kensington.*

809. Cabinet, Coal Scuttle, Small Table, and Waste Paper Box.
    Designed and executed by J. E. A. Brown, *Cirencester.*

810. Two Cabinets made of unstained oak.
    Designed by W. Alderton, *Brighton.*
    Manufactured by H. Alderton, *Brighton.*

811. American Walnut Wardrobe.

812. Commode and Chair.

813. Mahogany Sideboard with mirror back.

814. Mahogany Wardrobe with mirror front.

815. Mahogany Dressing Table, with bevelled mirror.

816. Mahogany Washstand with marble top.

817. Two Mahogany Chairs, stamped leather.
    Designed by Thomas Dewson.
    Manufactured by E. Goodall & Co., *Manchester.*

818. Cabinet Side-Board, Carved Oak.
    Designed and executed by Nathaniel Long, *Cork.*

819. Carved Oak Chair.
    Designed and executed by E. Moody, *Huddersfield.*

820. American Walnut Music and China Cabinet.
    Designed by Sydney Haward, *South Kensington.*
    Manufactured by J. A. Haward, *Darlington.*

821. Screen Fourfold, Painted Tapestry.
    Designed and executed by Frank Horsman, *Leeds.*

822. Portion of Carved Teak Wood Mantelpiece, Fruit and Leaves, Carved Circular Panel in Sycamore Wood.
    Designed and executed by Miss Girardot, *Farnham.*

823. Two Panels of Lime Wood, carved in high relief.
    Executed by James Minns, *Norwich.*
    (Lent by B. E. Fletcher, Esq., Norwich.)

824. Copy of Eighteenth Century Carved Mantelpiece (English). The original in the South Kensington Museum. Price £55.
    Executed by the Students of the School of Art Wood Carving, *Albert Hall.*
    The Grate and Fittings by Messrs. Longden.
    The Marble Slips by Mr. Sinclair.

825. Carved Oak Frame. Copy of Italian Frame in the South Kensington Museum. Price £5 5s.
    Executed by D. Chisholm, *School of Art Wood Carving, Albert Hall.*

826. Three Pairs of Carved Walnut Sconces. Price £4, £5, £6.
    Executed by Miss M. E. Reeks. *Assisted by* Signor Bulletti and Miss Rowe, *School of Art Wood Carving, Albert Hall.*

827. Bellows, Carved in Italian Walnut. Original in the South Kensington Museum. Price £10 10s.
    Executed by Miss M. E. Reeks, *School of Art Wood Carving, Royal Albert Hall.*

828. Bellows, Carved in Italian Walnut.
Copied from a pair in the South Kensington
Museum. Price £12.
> *Executed by Miss H. E. Wahab, School
> of Art Wood Carving, Royal Albert
> Hall.*

829. Carved Panel.
> *Executed by C. H. Walton, School of
> Art Wood Carving, Royal Albert
> Hall.*

830. Carved Panel.
> *Executed by Miss Smith, School of
> Art Wood Carving, Royal Albert
> Hall*

831. Carved Panel.
> *Executed by W. Page, School of Art
> Wood Carving, Royal Albert Hall.*

832. Panel in American Walnut, copied from
a Flemish panel now in the South Kensington
Museum. Price £6 6s.
> *Executed by Miss Henrietta E. Wahab,
> School of Art Wood Carving, Royal
> Albert Hall.*

833. Large Carved Panel.
> *Executed by the Students of the School
> of Art Wood Carving, Royal Albert
> Hall.*

834. Architectural Moulding.
> *Executed by Horace L. Montford,
> School of Art Wood Carving, Royal
> Albert Hall.*

835. Copy of 18th century Moulding.
> *Executed by Miss J. C. Holt, School
> of Art Wood Carving, Royal Albert
> Hall.*

836. Copy of 18th century Moulding.
> *Executed by Miss Smith, School of
> Art Wood Carving, Royal Albert
> Hall.*

837. Sample Mouldings of Picture Frame
carved and gilded.
> *Executed by the Students of the School
> of Art Wood Carving, Royal Albert
> Hall.*

838. Carved Hall Seat in American Walnut.
> *Executed by Wm. Page, Miss M. L.
> Irwin, and Miss M. E. Reeks.
> Price £18. School of Art Wood
> Carving, Royal Albert Hall.*

839. Carved Wooden Box.
> *Designed and executed by Miss A.
> Howitt, Sheffield.*

840. Two carved Oak Panels, and Flowers
on Stand.
> *Designed and executed by William
> Martin, Edinburgh.*

841. Carved Walnut Panel.
> *Executed by E M. Moore, Southampton.*

842. Carved Panel.
> *Executed by Robert Smith, Inverness.*

843. Carved Panel.
> *Executed by J. W. Bush, Bath.*

844. Carved Bracket.
> *Executed by J. T. Ogleby, Sunderland,*
> Price £10 10s.

845. Small Circular Panel.
> *Executed by E. Lock, Bath.*

846. Specimen of Carved Oak.
> *Executed by H. Frith, Gloucester.*

847. Picture Moulding, carved and gilt.
> *Executed by Miss B. Alcock, Man-
> chester.*

848. Painted Girandole and Panel.
> *Designed and executed by W. J.
> Tatham, West London.*

849. 2 Blotting Books.
> *Designed and executed by J. E. A.
> Brown, Cirencester.*

850. Tea Caddy, inlaid with different coloured
woods.
> *Designed and executed by Gunston
> Tite, South Kensington.*

851. Two American Walnut Wood Panels.
> *Executed by J. J. Clów, Exeter and
> Barnstaple.*

852. Panel of Madonna and Child.
> *Executed by Miss Jane Biram, Shef-
> field.*

853. Carved Oak Panel.
> *Executed by Miss S. E. M. Cook,
> Sheffield.*

D

854. Carved Mantelpiece.
Designed by H. Longden, *Sheffield.*
Manufactured by Messrs. Longden, *Sheffield.*

855. Design for Bay of Music Room.
By John Briggs, *Edinburgh.*

856. Design for Fireplace and over mantel.
By W. H. Banks, *Rotherham.*

857. Design for Cabinet.
By W. Scott Morton, *Glasgow and South Kensington.*

858. Design for Side of Small Dining Room, Sideboard, Chairs, &c.
Library with Wall, Panelling, &c.
By W. F. Randall.
Manufactured by Messrs. Howard & Sons, *London.*

859. Design for Cabinet.
In pen and ink by E. P. Milne, *Lancaster.*

860. Coloured Photograph of Oak Cabinet.
Designed by E. P. Milne, *Lancaster.*
Executed by Messrs. Appleyard & Sons, *Sheffield.*

861. Design for Cabinet.
By George Ilston, *Sheffield.*

862. Photographs of Tables, Screens, and Chairs.
Designed by Frederick Muntzer, *South Kensington.*
Manufactured by Messrs. Cowtan & Sons, *Oxford Street.*

863. Design for Sideboard.
By F. Leighton, *Coalbrookdale.*

864. Design for Carved Oak Sideboard.
By A. D. McCormick, *Belfast.*

865. Design for Inlaid Cabinet.
By E. P. Milne, *Lancaster.*

866. Two Designs for Cabinets.
By John Knight, *Nottingham.*

867. Three Photographs of Cabinets and Sideboard.
Designed by E. P. Milne.
Executed by Messrs. Milne & Sons, *Lancaster.*

868. Tinted Photograph of Mirror Frame and Piano.
Designed by Frederick Müntzer, *South Kensington.*
Manufactured by Cowtan & Sons, *Oxford Street.*

869. Coloured Drawing of Sideboard.
Designed by E. P. Milne, *Lancaster.*

870. Cabinet.
Designed by Frederick Müntzer, *South Kensington.*
Manufactured by Cowtan & Sons, *Oxford Street.*

871. Design for Cabinet.
By F. Müntzer, *South Kensington.*

872. Cabinet with Divan Seat and Wall Decorations.
Designed by W. F. Randall, *Stroud and South Kensington.*
Manufactured by Howard & Sons.

873. Design for Rosewood Cabinet and Rosewood Mantelpiece.
By W. F. Randall, *Stroud and South Kensington.*
Manufactured by Howard & Sons.

874. Photograph of Side board in English Oak.
Designed by George Read, *Leeds.*
Executed by Roodhouse & Sons, *Leeds.*

875. Two Designs for Sideboards.
By John Knight, *Nottingham.*

876. Four Designs for Sideboards.
By C. J. Beaupré, *West London.*
Manufactured by Lilley & Wood.

877. Designs for Sideboard, Dado, and Chairs.
By Robert Walker, *Edinburgh.*

878. Photograph of Chimney Nook.
Designed by W. F. Randall, *Stroud and South Kensington.*
Manufactured by Howard & Sons.

879. Two Photographs of Mantel and over Mantel in Oak.
Designed by R. G. Robertson, *Kilmarnock.*
Manufactured by R. C. Robertson, *Kilmarnock.*

880. Water Colour Drawing of Fire Place, Mantel and over Mantel, and Wall Decoration.
　　Designed by A. Weatherstone, *West London.*
　　Manufactured by Howard & Sons.

881. Design for Mantel and over Mantel.
　　By James Heron, *Edinburgh.*

882. Design for Mantel and over Mantel. Design for Buffet.
　　By W. F. Randall, *Stroud and South Kensington.*
　　Manufactured by Howard & Sons.

883. Photograph of Rosewood Cabinet.
　　Designed by W. F. Randall, *Stroud and South Kensington.*
　　Manufactured by Howard & Sons.

884. Design for Oak Sideboard and Oak Panelling.
　　By W. F. Randall, *Stroud and South Kensington.*
　　Manufactured by Howard & Sons.

885. Design for Buffet.
　　By W. F. Randall, *Stroud and South Kensington.*

886. Design for Sideboard.
　　By C. C. Allen, *West London.*

887. Design for Mantel and over Mantel.
　　By W. F. Randall, *Stroud and South Kensington.*

888. Design for inlaid Table Top.
　　By Ella Jacob, *Salisbury.*

889. Design for Fireplace with over Mantel.
　　By Thomas Smith, *Coalbrookdale.*

890. Design for Mantel, over Mantel, and Dado.
　　By Alfred Carpenter, *West London.*

891. Design for Inlaid Box.
　　By Miss Edith E. Rogers, *Westminster and Lambeth.*

892. Design for side of Library.
　　By E. P. Milne, *Lancaster.*

893. Design for Mantel, over Mantel, and Bookcase.
　　By W. F. Randall, *Stroud and South Kensington.*
　　Manufactured by Howard & Sons.

894. Design for Mantel and over Mantel.
　　By C. A. Allom, *West London.*

895. Design for Panel.
　　By W. S. Watson, *South Kensington.*

896. Design for Inlaid Mirror.
　　By J. F. Boyle, *Dublin.*

897. Design for Mantel, over Mantel, and Wall Decoration.
　　By H. Thornton Garner, *West London.*

898. Photograph of Mantel and over Mantel in Library.
　　Designed by E. Page Turner, *Sheffield.*

899. Design for Mantel and over Mantel.
　　By G. Tucker, *West London.*

900. Design for Billiard Table.
　　By G. Tucker, *West London.*

901. Design for Rosewood inlaid Bedroom Suite.
　　By F. C. Norris, *Bath.*

902. Design for Franklin Testimonial.
　　By W. F. Randall, *Stroud and South Kensington.*
　　Manufactured by Howard & Sons.

903. Design for Chimney Nook.
　　By W. F. Randall, *Stroud and South Kensington.*
　　Manufactured by Howard & Sons.

904. Design for Ingle Nook in Dining Room.
　　By W. F. Randall, *Stroud and South Kensington.*
　　Manufactured by Howard & Sons.

905. Design for Doorway.
　　By Austin Winterbottom, *Sheffield,*

906. Two Designs for Staircases.
　　By J. G. Edwards, *Sheffield.*

907. Design for Fireplace and over Mantel.
　　By Walter Platt, *Great Yarmouth.*

908. Design for Fireplace and over Mantel.
　　By J. Rowley, *West London.*

909. Design for Inlaid Border.
　　By P. K. Symes, *Dublin.*

D 2

910. Design for Inlaid Work.
By W. B. Cockrill, *Great Yarmouth.*

911. Design for Inlaid Border.
By O. R. Albrow, *Great Yarmouth.*

912. Design for Inlaid Border.
By Mary Lloyd, *Dublin.*

913. Design for Inlaid Border.
By T. C. Bergins, *Dublin.*

SECTION IX.

Decorative Carvings in Stone or Marble, and Plastic Decorations, &c.

914. Decorative Panel in Plaster
By S. R. Canton, *Bloomsbury.*

915. Large Panel in Plaster. Figure subject.
Designed and executed by S. R. Canton, *Bloomsbury.*

916. Plaster Cantilever.
Designed and executed by Mark Rogers, *Lambeth.*

917. Figure of Warrior.
Designed and modelled by W. B. Rhind, *Edinburgh.*

918. Figure in Plaster.
Designed and modelled by W. B. Rhind, *Edinburgh.*

919. Design for Cantilever in Plaster.
By John A. Evans, *Gloucester.*

920. Support for side of Fireplace.
Designed and modelled by Mark Rogers, *Lambeth.*

921. Panel Design, in plaster.
Designed and modelled by John Fisher, *South Kensington.*

922. The Dead Christ.
Designed and modelled by W. B. Rhind, *Edinburgh.*

923. Frieze.
Designed and modelled by A. W. Bowcher, *South Kensington.*

924. Panel.
Designed and modelled by H. Tyzack, *Sheffield.*

925. Decorative Panel.
Designed and modelled by A. J. Davey, *Torquay.*

926. Group in plaster, "Jacob wrestling with the Angel."
Designed and modelled by O. Junck, *West London.*

927. Panel, "Blacksmith at Work."
Designed and modelled by A. W. Bowcher, *South Kensington.*

928. Panel, "Christ before Pilate."
Designed and modelled by W. B. Rhind, *Edinburgh.*

929. Design for a doorway, &c.
Designed and modelled by R. Rhodes, *South Kensington.*

930. Design for a doorway, &c.
Designed and modelled by A. Whitehead, *South Kensington.*

931. Design for a Fountain.
Designed and modelled by A. W. Bowcher, *South Kensington.*

932. Panel, after Albert Dürer.
Modelled by George Morgan, *South Kensington.*

933. Decorative Panel, and in plaster.
Designed and modelled by John E. Taylorson, *Lambeth.*

934. Head.
Modelled by Mark Rogers, *Lambeth.*

935. Panel.
Designed and modelled by Richard Ferris, *Westminster.*

936. Figure of a Warrior.
Designed and modelled by T. S. Burnett, *Edinburgh.*

937. Figure of a Warrior.
Designed and modelled by T. S. Burnett, *Edinburgh.*

938. Christ in the Temple.
Designed and executed in stone by J. J. Millson, *Manchester.*

939. Design for Bay of Music Room.
By Margaret A. Heath, Gloucester.

940. Design for Bay of Music Room.
By G. W. Shepherd, Coalbrookdale.

941. Model in plaster of frieze for a Fireplace, renaissance.
Designed and modelled by G. Wilson, Westminster.

942. Three Frames, containing Photographs of Sculpture.
Designed and executed by S. Ruddock, Marlborough House and South Kensington.

943. Two Frames, containing Photographs of portions of Terra-Cotta columns.
Designed and executed by Godfrey Sykes, South Kensington.

944. Three Frames, containing Photographs of Panels, for The Wedgewood Institute.
Designed and modelled by R. J. Morris, South Kensington.

945. Model of a Tomb.
Designed and executed by Wm. Firth, Lambeth.

946. Group in plaster, "Boadicea."
Designed and modelled by Wm. Firth, Lambeth.

947. Photograph of an Altar-piece.
By Samuel Ruddock, Marlborough House and South Kensington.

948. Photograph of Stone Carving.
Designed and executed by H. Bates.

949. Frame, containing autotypes of designs in plaster.
By G. Bedford, Torquay; R. Lane, Glasgow; F. Gibbons, Cirencester; and W. Marshall, Kensington

SECTION X.

Lace. — Point, Pillow, and Machine made Lace. Drawings and Photographs of such as may have been executed.

950. Five Lace Curtains.
Designed by Wm. Coates, Nottingham. Manufactured by Heymann & Alexander, Nottingham.

951. Lace Bed Cover.
Designed by Wm. Coates, Nottingham. Manufactured by Heymann & Alexander, Nottingham.

952. Lace Bed Cover and Curtain.
Designed by Samuel W. Oscroft, Nottingham. Manufactured by Heymann & Alexander, Nottingham.

953. Six Lace Curtains.
Designed by Samuel W. Oscroft, Nottingham. Manufactured by Heymann & Alexander, Nottingham.

954. Lace Curtain.
Designed by Gavin Morton, Kilmarnock. Manufactured by Messrs. Morton & Co., Darwell.

955. Two Lace Curtains.
Designed by Arthur Jennings, Nottingham. Manufactured by Hamel & Wright, Nottingham.

956. Two Lace Curtains.
Designed by Geo. E. Drake, Halifax. Manufactured by Carey & Sons, Nottingham.

957. Two pairs of Lace Curtains.
Designed by George Broadhead Nottingham.

958. Two Lace Curtains.
Designed by Thomas W. Hammoud, Nottingham. Manufactured by Hamel & Wright, Nottingham.

959. Machine-made Lace Curtain.
Designed by W. R. S. Hancock, Nottingham. Manufactured by M. Jacoby & Co., Stoney St., Nottingham.

960. Six specimens of Irish Crochet Work.
Designed by Michael Holland, Lough Road, Cork.

961. Design for Irish Crochet Work.
By Michael Holland, Lough Road, Cork.

962. Specimen of Lace.
From Dublin Museum of Science and Art.

963. Two designs and three executed specimens of Irish Crochet.
By Miss Ellen Hayes, Industrial School, Ursuline Convent, Cork.

964. Two designs and three executed specimens of Irish Crochet.
By Miss Eliza Meade, Industrial School, Ursuline Convent, Cork.

965. Design for Lace Curtain.
By Thomas Meldrum, Nottingham.

966. Two designs for Honiton Point Lace.
By Miss M. Joyce, Dover.

967. Three designs for Lace Curtains.
By W. R. Walton, Nottingham.

968. Two frames of photographs of designs for Lace.
By George Lees, Kidderminster.

969. Three Designs for Lace.
By Miss Marianne Mansell, Lambeth.

970. Design for Lace Curtain.
By William Hardy, Nottingham.

971. Design for Lace Curtain.
By William Hardy, Nottingham.

972. Design for Lace Curtain.
By Thomas William Hammond, Nottingham.

973. Design for Lace Curtain.
By Thomas William Hammond, Nottingham.

974. Three Designs for Lace.
By Miss A. Dickeson, Dover.

975. Design for Lace Curtain.
By Thomas F. Travell, Nottingham.

976. Design for Lace Curtain.
By William J. Spooner, Nottingham.

977. Design for Lace Curtain.
By John Clews, Nottingham.

978. Design for Lace Curtain.
By George Woollatt, Nottingham.

979. Two Designs for Lace Curtains.
By Miss Marion Elwood, Nottingham.

980. Design for Lace Curtain.
By George F. Turton, Nottingham.

981. Design for Lace Curtain.
By A. J. Sewell, Nottingham.

982. Design for Lace Curtain.
By William J. Spooner, Nottingham.

983. Design for Lace Curtain.
By W. R. S. Hancock, Nottingham.

984. Design for a Lace Curtain.
By Francis B. Heald, Nottingham.

985. Design for a Lace Curtain.
By Frederick H. Dobbs, Nottingham.

986. Design for a Lace Curtain.
By William Bucknall, Nottingham.

987. Design for a Lace Set.
By Miss Agnes Dickeson, Dover.

988. Design for a Swiss Store.
By James Butler, Nottingham.

989. Design for Lace Curtain.
By Miss Blanche Story, Nottingham.

990. Design for a Swiss Hand-made Lace Curtain.
By Thomas W. Hammond, Nottingham.

991. Designs for Lace Flouncings.
By Miss Emily S. Heise, Birkenhead.

992. Design for Lace Curtain.
By Thomas Kirk, Nottingham.

993. Design for Lace Curtain.
By Robert H. Bishop, Nottingham.

994. Design for Lace Curtain.
By John M. Carr, Nottingham.

995. Design for Lace Curtain.
By Thomas Dutton, Nottingham.

996. Design for a Lace Set.
By Miss M. Joyce, Dover.

997. Design for a Lace Curtain.
By George Stafford, Nottingham.

998. Design for a Lace Curtain.
By Miss Helen Goodyer, *Nottingham.*

999. Design for a Lace Curtain.
By John M. Carr, *Nottingham.*

1000. Design for Lace Collar, Cuffs, and Handkerchief.
By George H. Holmes, *Nottingham.*

1001. Design for a Lace Handkerchief.
By Miss Marion Browning, *Salisbury.*

1002. Design for a Lace Cape.
By Miss Jessie Hallam, *Exeter.*

1003. Design for a Lace Set.
By William Harding, *Nottingham.*

1004. Design for a Lace Set.
By Louis Bircumshaw, *Nottingham.*

1005. Design for Lace Flouncing.
By Miss Marcella Irwin, *Dublin.*

1006. Design for Lace Flouncing.
By Miss Jessie Hallam, *Exeter.*

1007. Design for a Lace Rotonde.
By Edwin Doughty, *Nottingham.*

1008. Design for Lace Window Valance.
By William J. Spooner, *Nottingham.*

1009. Design for Lace Flouncing.
By Miss Frances L. Jordan, *Dublin.*

1010. Design for Lace Flouncing.
By Miss Elizabeth Irwin, *Dublin.*

1011. Design for Lace Flouncing.
By Miss Anne Twigge, *Exeter.*

1012. Two Designs for Lace Curtains.
By J. W. Wood, *Nottingham.*

1013. Design for a Lace Collar.
By Miss Maud Kingdon, *Exeter.*

1014. Design for Lace Flouncing.
By Miss Jessie Hallam, *Exeter.*

1015. Design for Lace Shawl.
By Henry Horsefield, *Nottingham.*

1016. Design for Lace Neckerchief.
By Miss Marion Browning, *Salisbury.*

1017. Design for Lace Fan.
By Miss Caroline Maltby, *Bloomsbury.*

1018. Design for Lace Curtain.
By J. G. Mackenzie, *Belfast.*

1019. Design for Lace Flouncing.
By Miss Louise Wheaton, *Exeter.*

1020. Design for a Lace Flounce.
By Miss Charlotte G. Trower, *East Herts.*

1021. Design for Lace Flouncing.
By Miss Marcella Irwin, *Dublin.*

1022. Design for Lace Handkerchief.
By Miss Agnes Dickeson, *Dover.*

1023. Design for Lace Parasol Cover.
By Miss Adeline King, *Salisbury.*

1024. Design for Lace Flouncing.
By Miss Adeline King, *Salisbury.*

1025. Design for Lace Fan.
By Miss Marion Browning, *Salisbury.*

1026. Design for Lace Collarette.
By Miss Maud Kingdon, *Exeter.*

1027. Design for Lace Flouncing.
By Miss Marian Moore, *Dublin.*

1028. Design for Lace Curtain.
By Miss Alice Bailey, *Dublin Metropolitan.*

1029. Design for Lace Flounce and Edging.
By Miss Marianne Mansell, *Lambeth.*

1030. Design for Lace Handkerchief Border.
By Miss Charlotte G. Trower, *East Herts.*

1031. Design for Lace Curtain.
By William McGowan, *Belfast.*

1032. Design for Lace Flounce.
By Miss Susan Ball, *Dublin.*

1033. Design for Damask Table Cloth.
By John G. Mackenzie, *Belfast.*

1034. Six Specimens of Lace Edging.
By F. J. Staynes, Nottingham.
Manufactured by Thos. B. Cutts,
Nottingham.

1035. Design for Lace Flouncing.
By Miss Anne Twigge, Exeter.

1036. Design for Lace Curtain.
By William Hardy, *Nottingham.*

1037. Design for Lace Cape.
By George Sheldon, *Nottingham.*

1038. Five Specimens of Lace Edging.
By Arthur Foster, Nottingham.
Manufactured by Thornley & Clark,
Nottingham.

1039. Four Specimens of Lace Edging.
By Arthur Foster, Nottingham.
Manufactured by Thornley & Clark,
Nottingham.

1040. Eight Specimens of Lace Edging.
By Arthur Foster, Nottingham.
Manufactured by Thornley & Clark,
Nottingham.

1041. Nine Specimens of Lace Edging.
By John Cutts, *Nottingham.*
Manufactured by Thos. B. Cutts,
Nottingham.

1042. Four Specimens of Lace Edging.
By Charles J. Atkey, Nottingham.
Manufactured by Thomas B. Cutts.
Nottingham.

1043. Seven Specimens of Lace Edging.
By Arthur Foster, Nottingham.
Manufactured by Thornley & Clark,
Nottingham.

SECTION XI.

Woven Damasks in Linen and Cotton,
plain or in colours.

1044. Six White Damask Table-cloths.
Designed by John Guthrie Mackenzie,
Belfast.
Manufactured by Hamilton, Hill, &
Co., *Belfast.*

1045. Two Damask Table-cloths, one bleached,
one unbleached.
Designed by J. Spence Ingall, Barnsley.
Manufactured by Messrs. Richardson
& Co., *Barnsley.*

1046. White Damask Table-cloth.
Designed by William Jones, *Manchester.*
Manufactured by Oliver & Atcherley,
Manchester.

1047. Twelve Damask Table-napkins.
Designed by William Jones, *Manchester.*
Manufactured by Oliver & Atcherley,
Manchester.

1048. Damask Table-cloth.
Designed by Miss Susan Ball, Dublin.
Manufactured by The Bessborough
Co., *Newry.*

1049. Damask Table-cloth.
Designed by James Ward, Belfast and
South Kensington.
Manufactured by Messrs. Magee &
Co., *Belfast.*

SECTION XII.

Silks, Ribbons, Trimmings, etc., including Furniture and Dress Fabrics.
Embroidery in Silk.

1050. Silk Hanging, designed for the decoration of H.M. State Throne and Ball-room at
Buckingham Palace.
By William Folliott, *Spitalfields.*
Manufactured by W. Walters & Sons,
Newgate Street, E.C.

1051. Damasked Silk Hanging; blue floral
design on "old gold" satin ground.
Designed by William Folliott, *Spitalfields.*
Manufactured by W. Walters & Sons,
Newgate Street, E.C.

1052. Tissue Silk Hanging, floral design in
Louis XIII. style, in red on black satin ground.
Designed by William Folliott, *Spitalfields.*
Manufactured by W. Walters & Sons,
Newgate Street, E.C.

1053. Tissue Silk Hanging, floral design in coral and gold, on bronze green satin ground.
Designed by William Folliott, *Spitalfields.*
Manufactured by W. Walters & Sons, *Newgate Street, E.C.*

1054. Damasked Silk Hanging, arbutus design in shot black on old gold, satin ground.
Designed by William Folliott, *Spitalfields.*
Manufactured by W. Walters & Sons, *Newgate Street, E.C.*

1055. Damasked Silk Hanging; trophies of musical instruments, in the early French style, in brown on buff satin ground.
Designed by William Folliott, *Spitalfields.*
Manufactured by W. Walters & Sons, *Newgate Street, E.C.*

1056. Silk Hanging with decoration of conventional cornflowers and leaves, in colours on black satin ground.
Designed by William Folliott, *Spitalfields.*
Manufactured by W. Walters & Sons, *Newgate Street, E.C.*

1057. Damasked Silkhanging, conventional Greek design in brown on buff satin ground.
Designed by William Folliott, *Spitalfields.*
Manufactured by W. Walters & Sons, *Newgate Street, E.C.*

1058. Silk Hanging; decoration of Oleander with peacocks and butterflies, illuminated in proper colours, on black satin ground.
Designed by William Folliott, *Spitalfields.*
Manufactured by W. Walters & Sons, *Newgate Street, E.C.*

1059. Damasked Silk Hanging; decoration of conventional oleanders.
Designed by William Folliott, *Spitalfields.*
Manufactured by W. Walters & Sons, *Newgate Street, E.C.*

1060. Brocatelle Hanging; conventional floral design in colours on buff ground.
Designed by William Folliott, *Spitalfields.*
Manufactured by W. Walters & Sons, *Newgate Street, E.C.*

1061. Damasked Silk Hanging; floral design interspersed with birds in " shot black " on yellow ground.
Designed by William Folliott, *Spitalfields.*
Manufactured by W. Walters & Sons, *Newgate Street, E.C.*

1062. Brocaded Silk Hanging; design in early French style of birds and fruits, in colours on dead ivory ground.
Designed by William Folliott, *Spitalfields.*
Manufactured by W. Walters & Sons, *Newgate Street, E.C.*

1063. Silk Hanging, richly brocaded; design of seaweeds and shells, in natural colours on green satin ground.
Designed by William Folliott, *Spitalfields.*
Manufactured by W. Walters & Sons, *Newgate Street, E.C.*

1064. Silk Hanging, richly brocaded; design of seaweeds and shells, in natural colours, on ivory satin ground.
Designed by William Folliott, *Spitalfields.*
Manufactured by W. Walters & Sons, *Newgate Street, E.C.*

1065. Piece of Brocaded Satin Damask.
Designed by G. C. Haité, *Croydon.*
Manufactured by Messrs. Cowlishaw, Nicol, and Co., 23, *Portland-street, Manchester.*

1066. Piece of Brocaded Satin Damask.
Designed by J. J. Black, *Manchester.*
Manufactured by Messrs. Cowlishaw, Nicol, and Co., *Manchester.*

1067. Piece of Brocaded Silk Damask.
Designed by J. J. Black, *Manchester.*
Manufactured by Messrs. Cowlishaw, Nicol, and Co., *Manchester.*

1068. Piece of Brocaded Satin Damask.
Designed by J. J. Black, *Manchester.*
Manufactured by Messrs. Cowlishaw, Nicol, and Co., *Manchester.*

1069. Piece of Brocaded Satin Damask.
Designed by G. C. Haité, *Croydon.*
Manufactured by Messrs. Cowlishaw, Nicol, and Co., *Manchester.*

1070. Table Cover, Silk Damask.
Designed by T. W. Hay, Edinburgh.
Manufactured by Cowlishaw, Nicol,
and Co., Manchester.

1071. Piece of Brocaded Satin Damask.
Designed by J. J. Black, Manchester.
Manufactured by Messrs. Cowlishaw,
Nicol, and Co., Manchester.

1072. Piece of Brocaded Satin Damask.
Designed by J. J. Black, Manchester.
Manufactured by Messrs. Cowlishaw,
Nicol, and Co., Manchester.

1073. Piece of Satin Damask.
Designed by J. J. Black, Manchester.
Manufactured by Messrs. Cowlishaw,
Nicol, and Co., Manchester.

1074. Piece of Satin Damask.
Designed by J. J. Black, Manchester.
Manufactured by Messrs. Cowlishaw,
Nicol, and Co., Manchester.

1075. Piece of Brocaded Satin Damask.
Designed by J. J. Black, Manchester.
Manufactured by Messrs. Cowlishaw,
Nicol, and Co., Manchester.

1076. A Collection of Specimens of Silk
Manufacture.
Designed by James Adams, Coventry
and Manchester; James Hoggins,
Coventry and Macclesfield; Frank
E. Adams, Macclesfield; J. O.
Nicholson, Macclesfield.
Manufactured by J. O. Nicholson,
Macclesfield.

1077. Silk Hanging. Chinese design.
Designed by John Sheldon, Maccles-
field.
Manufactured by John Birchenough
& Sons, Macclesfield.

1078. Satin Damask Handkerchief.
Designed by John Sheldon, Maccles-
field.
Manufactured by John Birchenough
& Sons, Macclesfield.

1079. Silk and Metal Brocade.
Designed by John Sheldon, Maccles-
field.
Manufactured by John Birchenough
& Sons, Macclesfield.

1080. Broché Satin Muffler or Wrap.
Designed by John Sheldon, Maccles-
field.
Manufactured by John Birchenough
& Sons, Macclesfield.

1081. Silk Hanging, design reproduced from
old stuff.
Designed by John Sheldon, Maccles-
field.
Manufactured by John Birchenough
& Sons, Macclesfield.

1082. Figured Silk Muffler or Wrap.
Designed by J. H. Wild, Macclesfield.
Manufactured by John Birchenough
& Sons, Macclesfield.

1083. Silk Muffler or Wrap.
Designed by J. H. Wild, Macclesfield.
Manufactured by John Birchenough
& Sons, Macclesfield.

1084. Figured Satin Dress Piece.
Designed by J. H. Wild, Macclesfield.
Manufactured by John Birchenough
& Sons, Macclesfield.

1085. Figured Silk, reproduction of a "Moyen-
Age" design.
Designed by J. H. Wild, Macclesfield.
Manufactured by John Birchenough
& Sons, Macclesfield.

1086. Silk Muffler or Wrap.
Designed by J. H. Wild, Macclesfield.
Manufactured by John Birchenough
& Sons, Macclesfield.

1087. Figured Satin Dress Fabric.
Designed by Arthur Cartwright,
Macclesfield.
Manufactured by John Birchenough
& Sons, Macclesfield.

1088. Brocaded Handkerchief.
Designed by Arthur Cartwright,
Macclesfield.
Manufactured by John Birchenough
& Sons, Macclesfield.

1089. Brocaded Handkerchief.
Designed by Arthur Cartwright,
Macclesfield.
Manufactured by John Birchenough
& Sons, Macclesfield.

1090. Satin Damask Dress Piece.
Designed by F. W. Sheldon, Maccles-
field.
Manufactured by John Birchenough
& Sons, Macclesfield.

1091. Silk and Metal Brocade for garments.
Designed by F. W. Sheldon, Maccles-
field.
Manufactured by John Birchenough
& Sons, Macclesfield.

1092. Silk Damask Handkerchief.
Designed by F. W. Sheldon, Macclesfield.
Manufactured by John Birchenough & Sons, Macclesfield.

1093. Figured Silk Muffler or Wrap.
Designed by F. W. Sheldon, Macclesfield.
Manufactured by John Birchenough & Sons, Macclesfield.

1094. Satin Damask Handkerchief.
Designed by F. W. Sheldon, Macclesfield.
Manufactured by John Birchenough & Sons, Macclesfield.

1095. Two Brocaded Silk Handkerchiefs.
Designed by Thomas Kerr, Macclesfield.
Manufactured by John Birchenough & Sons, Macclesfield.

1096. A Series of Five Designs in Silk for Furniture Coverings.
Designed by George Edward Drake, Halifax.
Manufactured by Messrs. W. Walters & Sons, Newgate Street, E.C.

1097. Four Specimens of Furniture Silk Damasks.
Designed by Miss Susan P. Ball, Dublin.
Manufactured by Messrs. Pym Bros., South Gt. George's Street, Dublin.

1098. Specimen of Silk Furniture Damask.
Designed by Miss Mary Cameron, Dublin.

1099. Specimen of Silk Furniture Damask.
Designed by Miss Isabella C. Bergin, Dublin.

1100. Specimen of Furniture Tapestry.
Designed by Joseph Kavanagh, Dublin.
Manufactured by Messrs. Fry & Co., Westmoreland Street, Dublin.

1101. Design for Furniture Damask, and Specimen of same.
Designed by Miss Anna F. Ruxton, Dublin.
Manufactured by Messrs. Fry & Co., Westmoreland Street, Dublin.

1102. Three Specimens of Silk Furniture Damasks.
Manufactured by Messrs. Fry & Co., Westmoreland Street, Dublin.

1103. Specimen of Silk Furniture Damask.
Designed by T. Thomas, Dublin.

1104. Design for Silk Damask.
By W. J. Clulow, Macclesfield.

1105. Design for Silk Handkerchief.
By W. J. Clulow, Macclesfield.

1106. Two Designs for Printed Silk Hangings.
By Frank E. Adams, Macclesfield.

1107. Design for Furniture Silk.
By H. Riseley, Macclesfield.

1108. Design for Furniture Silk.
By J. T. Robinson, Macclesfield.

1109. Design for Silk Handkerchief.
By Thomas E. Doran, Macclesfield.

1110. Design for Printed Silk Handkerchief.
By J. E. Dawson, Macclesfield.

1111. Two Designs for Silk Handkerchiefs.
By Hugh Grimshaw, Macclesfield.

1112. Design for Embroidered Silk Cover.
By T. J. Donohue, Macclesfield.

1113. Design for Embroidered Silk Cover.
By John Booth, Macclesfield.

1114. Design for Silk Hanging.
By Miss Charlotte F. Shelton, Cheltenham.

1115. Design for Damask Table-Cover.
By John Quiller Lane, Belfast and South Kensington.

1116. Design for Damask Table-Cover.
By Miss Frances Brett, Dublin.

1117. Design for Damask Table-Cover.
By Miss Mary A. Mayee, Dublin.

1118. Two Bed Quilts, embroidered in coloured silks.
Designed by James Hoggins, Coventry and Macclesfield.
The colouring by J. O. Nicholson.
Executed in the Macclesfield Embroidery School.

1119. Sofa Back, embroidered in coloured silks.
> *Designed by* Frank E. Adams, *Coventry.*
> *Executed at the Macclesfield Embroidery School.*

1120. Screen, embroidered with "Lahore Scroll" pattern in coloured silks.
> *Designed by* James Hoggins, *Coventry and Macclesfield.*
> *The colouring by* J. O. Nicholson.
> *Executed at the Macclesfield Embroidery School.*

1121. Silk Handkerchief.
> *Designed by* James Hoggins, *Coventry and Macclesfield.*
> *Manufactured by* J. O. Nicholson, *Macclesfield.*

1122. Design for Furniture, silk brocade.
> *From the School of Art, Dublin.*

1123. Design for silk damask.
> *By* Elizabeth E. Irwin, *Dublin.*

SECTION XIII.

Mixed Woven Fabrics for Dresses, Shawls, Scarfs, etc.

1124. Damasks, mixed fabrics, awarded the Gold Medal of the Yorkshire Union of Mechanics' Institutes.
> *Designed by* Jonathan Foster, *Halifax School and Bradford Technical College.*

1125. Damasks, mixed fabrics.
> *Designed by* Joseph Midgley, *Halifax School and Bradford Technical College.*

1126. Fancy Fabrics and Damasks, mixed fabrics, awarded the Cloth-workers' Gold Medal at the Bradford Industrial Exhibition, 1882.
> *Designed by* James T. Lushman, *Halifax School and Bradford Technical College.*

SECTION XIV.

Printed Fabrics.

1127. Four designs for Muslins.
> *By* Frances L. Jordan, *Dublin.*

1128. Four designs for Muslins.
> *By* Miss Eleanor Kerr, *Dublin.*

1129. Four designs for Muslins.
> *By* Miss Marcella Irwin, *Dublin.*

1130. Five designs for Muslins.
> *By* Mary Baumgartner, *Great Yarmouth.*

1131. Five designs for Muslins.
> *By* Rosetta C. Burgess, *Great Yarmouth.*

1132. Four designs for Muslins.
> *By* Gertrude L. Brown, *Great Yarmouth.*

1133. Specimens of Printed Cotton Fabrics.
> *Designed by* Joseph Waterhouse, *Manchester.*
> *Manufactured by* Thomas Hoyle & Sons, *Manchester.*

1134. Two specimens of Cretonnes.
> *Designed by* Charles A. Brindley, *Kidderminster and South Kensington.*

1135. Two specimens of Cretonnes.
> *Designed by* Charles A. Brindley, *Kidderminster and South Kensington.*

1136. Specimens of Cretonnes and Printed Fabrics for Dresses.
> *Designed by* W. J. Muckley, *Stourbridge, Birmingham, Somerset House, and Marlborough House, assisted by* W. R. & A. F. Muckley, *Manchester.*
> *Manufactured by* E. C. Potter & Co., *Manchester.*

1137. Designs for Cretonnes.
> *By* Henry Gibson, *South Kensington.*

1138. Designs for Cretonnes.
> *By* James Rowley, *West London.*

1139. Designs for Chintz.
> *By* Miss Louisa Aumonier, *St. Martin's.*

SECTION XV.

Carpets and Tapestry. Curtains, Table Covers, &c.

1140. Pattern of Carpet, "Gobelins Axminster."
Designed by Peter Adam, *Kidderminster and South Kensington.*
Manufactured by Tomkinson & Adam, *Church Street, Kidderminster.*

1141. Pattern of Carpet, "Victorian Axminster."
Designed by Peter Adam, *Kidderminster and South Kensington.*
Manufactured by Tomkinson & Adam, *Church Street, Kidderminster.*

1142. Pattern of Carpet, "Victorian Axminster."
Designed by Peter Adam, *Kidderminster and South Kensington.*
Manufactured by Tomkinson & Adam, *Church Street, Kidderminster.*

1143. Pattern of Carpet, "Victorian Axminster."
Designed by Peter Adam, *Kidderminster and South Kensington.*
Manufactured by Tomkinson & Adam, *Church Street, Kidderminster.*

1144. Pattern of Brussels Carpet, with border.
Designed by David Campbell, *Glasgow and Halifax.*
Manufactured by J. W. & C. Ward, *Halifax.*

1145. Pattern of Brussels Carpet.
Designed by Herbert Robinson, *Halifax.*
Manufactured by Messrs. J. Crossley & Co., *Halifax.*

1146. "Mecca" Rug.
Designed by Peter Adam, *Kidderminster and South Kensington.*
Manufactured by Messrs. Tomkinson & Adam, *Church Street, Kidderminster.*

1147. "Mecca" Rug.
Designed by Peter Adam, *Kidderminster and South Kensington.*
Manufactured by Messrs. Tomkinson & Adam, *Church Street, Kidderminster.*

1148. "Mecca" Rug.
Designed by Peter Adam, *Kidderminster and South Kensington.*
Manufactured by Messrs. Tomkinson & Adam, *Church Street Kidderminster.*

1149. "Mecca" Rug.
Designed by Peter Adam, *Kidderminster and South Kensington.*
Manufactured by Messrs. Tomkinson & Adam, *Church Street, Kidderminster,*

1150. "Mecca" Rug.
Designed by Peter Adam, *Kidderminster and South Kensington.*
Manufactured by Messrs. Tomkinson & Adam, *Church Street, Kidderminster.*

1151. "Mecca" Rug.
Designed by Peter Adam, *Kidderminster and South Kensington.*
Manufactured by Messrs. Tomkinson & Adam, *Church Street, Kidderminster.*

1152. Pattern of Brussels Carpet.
Designed by P. Morrison, *Kidderminster.*
Manufactured by Messrs. R. Smith & Sons, *Kidderminster.*

1153. Pattern of Wilton Carpet.
Designed by Daniel Duck & J. H. Park, *Coventry and Kidderminster.*
Manufactured by Whittall & Co., *Kidderminster.*

1154. Pattern of Brussels Carpet.
Designed by J. B. Smith, *Halifax.*
Manufactured by Messrs. J. W & C. Ward, *Ellen Royd Mills, Halifax.*

1155. Pattern of Brussels Carpet, with border.
Designed by David Campbell, *Glasgow and Halifax.*
Manufactured by J. W. & C. Ward, *Halifax.*

1156. Pattern of Brussels Carpet.
Designed by Herbert Robinson, *Halifax.*
Manufactured by Messrs. John Crossley & Co., *Halifax.*

1157. Pattern of Brussels Carpet.
Designed by J. B. Smith, *Halifax.*
Manufactured by J. W. & C. Ward, *Halifax.*

1158. Small Tapestry Carpet.

1159. Pattern of Wilton Pile Carpet.
Designed by William Winbury, *Kidderminster.*
Manufactured by Messrs. Morton & Sons, *Kidderminster.*

1160. Pattern of Brussels Carpet.
Designed by P. Morrison, *Kidderminster.*
Manufactured by Messrs. Smith & Sons, *Kidderminster.*

1161. Pattern of Brussels Carpet.
Designed by Herbert Robinson, *Halifax.*
Manufactured by John Crossley & Co., *Halifax.*

1162. Pattern of Brussels Carpet, with border.
Designed by William Winbury, *Kidderminster.*
Manufactured by Morton & Sons, *Kidderminster.*

1163. Pattern of Carpet, Indian design.
Designed by Daniel Duck, *and* John H. Park, *Kidderminster and Coventry.*
Manufactured by Charles Harrison, *Stourport.*

1164. Pattern of Brussels Carpet.
Designed by Herbert Robinson, *Halifax.*
Manufactured by Messrs. John Crossley & Co., *Halifax.*

1165. Pattern of Brussels Carpet, with border.
Designed by F. Crossley, *Halifax.*
Manufactured by J. W. & C. Ward, *Halifax.*

1166. "Royal Wilton" Carpet.
Designed by Micah Chambers, *Durham.*
Manufactured by Messrs. Henderson & Co., *Durham,* price £10 17s. 6d.
(Lent by Messrs. Treloar & Sons, London.)

1167. Henderson's "Patent Durham Axminster."
Designed by Micah Chambers, *Durham.*
Manufactured by Messrs. Henderson & Co., *Durham,* price £10 14s. 6d.
(Lent by Messrs. Treloar & Sons, London.)

1168. Pattern of Royal Axminster Carpet.
Designed by George Kingman, *Bath, Kidderminster, and South Kensington.*
Manufactured by Messrs. H. J. Dixon & Sons, *Kidderminster.*

1169. Pattern of Best Wilton Carpet.
Designed by George Kingman, *Bath, Kidderminster, and South Kensington.*
Manufactured by Messrs. H. J. Dixon & Sons, *Kidderminster.*

1170. Pattern of Best Wilton Carpet.
Designed by George Kingman, *Bath, Kidderminster, and South Kensington.*
Manufactured by Messrs. H. J. Dixon & Sons, *Kidderminster.*

1171. Pattern of Best Brussels Carpet.
Designed by George Kingman, *Bath, Kidderminster, and South Kensington.*
Manufactured by Messrs. H. J. Dixon & Sons, *Kidderminster.*

1172. Pattern of Best Wilton Carpet.
Designed by George Kingman, *Bath, Kidderminster, and South Kensington.*
Manufactured by Messrs. H. J. Dixon & Sons, *Kidderminster.*

1173. Pattern of Royal Axminster Carpet.
Designed by George Kingman, *Bath, Kidderminster, and South Kensington.*
Manufactured by Messrs. H. J. Dixon & Sons, *Kidderminster.*

1174. Pattern of Royal Axminster Carpet.
Designed by George Kingman, *Bath, Kidderminster, and South Kensington.*
Manufactured by Messrs. H. J. Dixon & Sons, *Kidderminster.*

1175. Pattern of Wilton Carpet, with border.
Designed by James Rowley, *West London.*
Manufactured by R. Hellbronner, 300 *Oxford Street, W.*

1176. Pattern of Brussels Carpet.
Designed by Herbert Robinson, *Halifax.*
Manufactured by Messrs. John Crossley and Co., *Halifax.*

1177. Pattern of Brussels Carpet, with border.
Designed by F. Crossley, *Halifax.*
Manufactured by J. W. and C. Ward, *Halifax.*

1178. Pattern of Tapestry Hanging.
Designed and manufactured by John Thomas, *Halifax.*

1179. Carriage Tapestry.
Designed by W. Jones, *Manchester.*
Manufactured by Messrs. Cowlishaw, Nicol, and Co., *Manchester.*

1180. Two Patterns of Tapestry.
Designed by J. J. Black, *Manchester.*
Manufactured by Messrs. Cowlishaw, Nicol, and Co., *Manchester.*

1181. Pattern of Tapestry Hanging.
Designed by W. H. Webster, *Halifax.*
Manufactured by Messrs. J. W. and C. Ward, *Halifax.*

1182. Pattern of Tapestry Hanging.
Designed by John Thomas, *Halifax.*
Manufactured by Messrs. J. W. and C. Ward, *Halifax.*

1183. Tapestry Hanging.
Designed by J. W. Riley, *Halifax.*
Manufactured by H. C. McCrea and Co., *Harrison Road, Halifax.*

1184. Tapestry Hanging.
Designed by J. W. Riley, *Halifax.*
Manufactured by H. C. McCrea and Co., *Harrison Road, Halifax.*

1185. Tapestry Hanging.
Designed by J. W. Riley, *Halifax.*
Manufactured by H. C. McCrea and Co., *Harrison Road, Halifax.*

1186. Pattern of Tapestry Hanging.
Designed and manufactured by John Thomas, *Halifax.*

1187. Specimen of Tapestry Hanging.
Designed by W. Jones, *Manchester.*
Manufactured by Messrs. Cowlishaw, Nicol, and Co., *Manchester.*

1188. One Specimen of Tapestry.
Designed by J. J. Black, *Manchester.*
Manufactured by Messrs. Cowlishaw, Nicol, and Co., *Manchester.*

1189. Specimen of Tapestry.
Designed by J. J. Black, *Manchester.*
Manufactured by Messrs. Cowlishaw, Nicol, and Co., *Manchester.*

1190. Specimen of Tapestry.
Designed by J. Alexander, *Manchester.*
Manufactured by Messrs. Cowlishaw, Nicol, and Co., *Manchester.*

1191. Specimen of Tapestry.
Designed by J. J. Black, *Manchester.*
Manufactured by Messrs. Cowlishaw, Nicol, and Co., *Manchester.*

1192. Tapestry Table Cover.
Designed by J. Thomas, *Halifax.*
Manufactured by Messrs. J. W. & C. Ward, *Halifax.*

1193. Pattern of Carpet.
Designed by J. Alexander, *Manchester.*
Manufactured by Messrs. Cowlishaw, Nicol, & Co., *Manchester.*

1194. Patent Oriental Reversible Curtain of Noil Silk, with section of another curtain showing the colours of plain filling.
Designed by E. F. Adams, *Kidderminster.*
Manufactured by Messrs. Barbour, Anderson, & Lawson, *Park View Works, Evanhaugh, Glasgow.*

1195. Red Plush Curtain, with tapestry border.
Designed by John Thomas, *Halifax.*
Manufactured by H. Eastwood & Co., *Moll Spring Works, Netherton, near Huddersfield.*

1196. Green Plush Curtain, with tapestry border.
Designed by John Thomas, *Halifax.*
Manufactured by H. Eastwood & Co., *Moll Spring Works, Netherton, near Huddersfield.*

1197. Muslin-Crete Curtain.
Designed by William Tannahill, *Kilmarnock.*
Manufactured by Messrs. Barbour & Anderson, *Glasgow.*

1198. Muslin-Crete Curtain.
Designed by William Tannahill, *Kilmarnock.*
Manufactured by Messrs. Barbour & Anderson, *Glasgow.*

1199. Silk and Wool Tapestry Hanging, buttercup pattern.
Designed by James Rowley, *West London.*
Manufactured by R. Hellbronner, *300 Oxford Street, W.C.*

1200. Silk Tapestry Curtain.
Designed by William Jones, *Manchester School.*
Manufactured by Messrs. Cowlishaw, Nicol & Co., *Manchester.*

1201. Tapestry Curtain.
Designed by William Jones, *Manchester School*
Manufactured by Messrs. Cowlishaw, Nicol & Co., *Manchester.*

1202. Pair of Patent Oriental Reversible Curtains, made of "Noil silk."
Designed by W. A. Lawson, *Glasgow.*
Manufactured by Messrs. Barbour, Anderson, & Co., *Glasgow.*

1203. Pair of Patent Oriental Reversible Curtains, made of spun silk.
Designed by John Brown, *Glasgow.*
Manufactured by Messrs. Barbour, Anderson, & Co., *Glasgow.*

1204. Curtain, mixed fabric.
Designed by J. W. Riley, *Halifax.*
Manufactured by Messrs. H. C. McCrea & Co., *Halifax.*

1205. Two Specimens of Tapestry.

1206. Design in Tapestry Curtain.
Designed and Manufactured by W. Scott Morton & Co., *Edinburgh.*

1207. Two Designs for Tapestry Curtains.
By Miss Mary Denley, *Lambeth and Westminster.*

1208. Design for a Carpet.
By Marcella Irwin, *Dublin.*

1209. Design for Axminster Carpet.
By Frank Porter, *Stourbridge.*

1210. Three Designs for Brussels Carpet.
By H. A. J. Budd, *Lambeth.*

1211. Design for Brussels Carpet.
By E. J. Milward, *Kendal.*

1212. A Series of Drawings, illustrative of a Technical Course, for Carpet Designers, as developed in the Kidderminster School of Art, by Wm. Tucker, Head Master, consisting of:—
Outline from copy.
By John Cantrell, *Kidderminster*
Painting from copy in one colour.
By George Harriss, *Kidderminster.*

Outline from nature.
By John Cantrell, *Kidderminster.*
Analysis of plant form in outline.
By Frederick Mountford, *Kidderminster.*
Analysis of plant form in colour.
By George Barker, *Kidderminster.*
Painting in tempera from nature.
By C. J. Carter, *Kidderminster.*
Designs to fill spaces in one colour.
By George Randall, *Kidderminster.*
Designs to fill spaces in colours.
W. H. Thatcher, *Kidderminster.*

1213. Design for a Brussels Carpet.
By J. H. Hussey, *Kidderminster.*

1214. Design for an Axminster Rug.
By J. Holgate, *Halifax.*

1215. Design for a Floorcloth.
By William Foster, *Salisbury.*

1216. Design for a Carpet.
By A. Nowell, *Salisbury.*

1217. Designs for Brussels Carpet.
By G. Kingman, *Kidderminster.*

1218. Design for Carpet.
By Miss Mary Denley, *Lambeth and Westminster.*

1219. Design for Carpet.
By W. Chrippes, *West London.*

1220. Design for Carpet.
By G. Barker, *Kidderminster.*

1221. Design for a Carpet.
By Gideon M. Fidler, *Salisbury.*

1222. Designs for Royal Axminster Carpet.
By G. Kingman, *Kidderminster.*

1223. Design for Patent Axminster Carpet.
By Alexander Park, *Glasgow.*

1224. Design for Carpet.
By Miss Mary Denley, *Lambeth and Westminster.*

1225. Design for Carpet.
By William H. Murray, *Dublin.*

1226. Design for Axminster Carpet.
By G. Kingman, *Kidderminster.*

1227. Design for Carpet.
By M. Harding, *Salisbury.*

1228. Design for Brussels Carpet.
By C. A. Brindley, *Kidderminster and South Kensington.*

1229. Design for Carpet.
By J. H. Park, *Coventry.*

1230. Design for Royal Axminster Carpet.
By G. Kingman, *Kidderminster.*

1231. Photographs of Designs for Carpets.
By George Lees, *Kidderminster.*

1232. Design for Brussels Carpet.
By F. Porter, *Stourbridge.*

1233. Designs for Brussels Carpet.
By George Kingman, *Kidderminster.*

1234. Designs for Brussels Carpet.
By George Kingman, *Kidderminster.*

1235. Design for Carpet.
By Miss Mary Denley, *Lambeth and Westminster.*

1236. Design for Brussels Carpet.
By F. Porter, *Stourbridge.*

1237. Design for Brussels Carpet.
By F. Porter, *Stourbridge.*

1238. Design for Patent Axminster Carpet.
By Alexander Park, *Glasgow.*

1239. Design for Wilton Carpet.
By J. J. Brownsword, *Derby Central School.*

1240. Design for Carpet.
By P. Yates, *Salisbury.*

1241. Design for Axminster Rug.
By John Thomas, *Halifax.*

1242. Design for Wilton Carpet.
By Miss Amy Straton.

1243. Design for Rug.
By J. H. Park, *Coventry.*

1244. Design for Patent Axminster Carpet.
By J. Brown, *Glasgow.*

1245. Design for Carpet.
By James Fletcher, *Glasgow.*

1246. Designs for Floor Decorations.
By F. Mountford, *Kidderminster.*

SECTION XVI.

Painted Decorations, Wall Papers, &c.

1247. Frieze.
Designed and Manufactured by Scott, Morton & Co., *Edinburgh.*

1248. Decorative Panel, portion of.
Painted in the Keims Process by J. W. E. Page, *Lambeth and South Kensington.*

1249. Decorative Panel.
Executed by W. M. Palin, *South Kensington.*

1250. Design for Decorative Panel.
By H. Bour, *Lambeth.*

1251. Design for portion of Frieze.
By E. Hammond, *West London.*

1252. Frieze.
Designed and executed by J. Rhind and W. Turner, *Edinburgh.*

1253. Portion of Decorative Screen.
Executed by Louis Davis, *South Kensington.*

1254. Four frames of Decorative Designs.
By Leonard Wyburd, *West London.*

1255. Design for Frieze for Music Room.
By J W. E. Page, *South Kensington.*

1256. Design for Frieze.
By E. Hammond, *Lambeth and West London.*

1257. Design for Wall Decoration, painting on canvas.
By Miss Julianna Lloyd, *West London.*

1258. Wall Paper, Dado Decoration.
Designed by G. C. Haité, *Croydon.*
Manufactured by William Woollams & Co., *London.*

E

1259. Set of four Friezes, wall paper.
Designed by Reuben Bennett, *Manchester.*
Manufactured by William Woollams & Co., *London.*

1260. Design for Wall Paper.
By O. W. Davis, *West London.*
Manufactured by William Woollams & Co., *London.*

1261. Wall Paper, Dado Decoration.
Designed by Owen W. Davis, *West London.*
Manufactured by Wm. Woollams & Co., *London.*

1262. Wall Paper, Dado Decoration (Italian style).
Designed by H. Noble, *West London.*
Manufactured by Messrs. Woollams & Co., *London.*

1263. Wall Decoration.
Designed by J. Holgate, *Westminster.*
Manufactured by F. Walton & Co., *London.*

1264. Design for Interior Decoration.
By E. Page Turner, *Sheffield.*

1265. Decorative Panel in Oils.
By G. C. Haité, *Croydon.*

1266. Wall Paper, Dado Decoration.
Designed by A. Silver, *Reading.*
Manufactured by Messrs. Woollams & Co., *London.*

1267. Wall Paper, Dado Decoration.
Designed by Miss Louisa Aumonier, *St. Martin's.*
Manufactured by Messrs. Woollams, *London.*

1268. Wall Paper, Dado Decoration.
Designed by R. O. Rickatson, *West London.*
Manufactured by William Woollams & Co., *London.*

1269. Wall Paper and Frieze.
Designed by W. Mückley, *Marlborough House and Manchester.*
Manufactured by Messrs. Jeffrey & Co., *London.*

1270. Two Friezes.
Designed by T W. Hay, *Edinburgh.*
Manufactured by Messrs. Woollams & Co., *London.*

1271. Two Designs for Friezes.
By T. W. Hay, *Edinburgh.*
Manufactured by Messrs. Woollams & Co., *London.*

1272. Design for Frieze.
By A. J. Tatham, *West London.*
Manufactured by Messrs. Woollams & Co., *London.*

1273. Wall Paper.
By G. C. Haité, *Croydon.*
Manufactured by Messrs. Woollams & Co., *London.*

1274. Wall Paper, Dado Decoration.
Designed by O. W. Davis, *West London.*
Manufactured by Messrs. Woollams & Co., *London.*

1275. Wall Paper, Dado Decoration.
By A. Silver, *Reading.*
Manufactured by Messrs. Woollams & Co., *London.*

1276. Wall Paper, Dado Decoration.
Designed by G. C. Haité, *Croydon.*
Manufactured by Messrs. Woollams.

1277. Wall Paper, Dado Decoration.
Designed by Henry Noble, *West London.*
Manufactured by Messrs. Woollams.

1278. Wall Paper, Dado Decoration.
Designed by G. C. Haité, *Croydon.*
Manufactured by Messrs. Woollams.

1279. Specimens of Wall and Dado Decoration in Lincrusta Walton.
Designed by C. J Beaupré, *West London.*
Manufactured by Messrs. Walton & Co., *London.*

1280. Frieze and Wall Decoration, Tynecastle Tapestry.
Designed and executed by Scott, Morton, & Co., *Edinburgh.*

1281. Design for Painted Frieze.
By E. Page Turner, *Sheffield.*

1282. Designs and working Drawings to scale for the decorations of the ceilings of the billiard-room at Wortley Hall, near Sheffield, the seat of the Earl of Wharncliffe.
The billiard-room comprises a central portion lighted by a lantern containing five windows on

each side and three at each end, which is surmounted by a cove and ceiling and two wings, each lighted by a skylight above a cove. The designs in the ceiling above the lantern and in the friezes in the central portion and wings are in relief, those in the coves and on the architraves and mouldings are flat, the coves being treated to imitate relief. The designs throughout, whether flat or in relief, are silver and gold, and the ground either blue, green, or purple. The treatment combines a fretwork of a Chinese character, with classical festoons and scrolls; birds, flowers, baskets of fruit, &c., being introduced.

The Chinese fret is carried through every feature of the decoration, and form the basis of the ornamental treatment.

Designed by Edward John Poynter, R.A., *Somerset House.*

1283. Two Chalk Drawings for Fresco Decoration of the Martyrdom of St. Stephen.
By E. J. Poynter, R.A., *Somerset House.*

1284. A Series of Twelve Designs illustrating the Months, for the interior decoration of the Grill Room, South Kensington Museum.
By E. J. Poynter, R.A., *Somerset House.*

1285. Design for the Decoration of the soffit of the Lecture Theatre, South Kensington Museum.
By E. J. Poynter, R.A., *Somerset House.*

1286. Four Frames of Designs for ceilings, Dado, lunette, and wall decorations.
Designed by A. Morgan, *S. Kensington.*

1287. Design for Wall Decoration.
By John Lamb, *West London.*

1288. Design for Wall Decoration.
By James Ward, *Belfast.*

1289. Design for Panel Decoration.
By C. Campbell *and* F. G. Smith, *Lambeth and West London.*

1290. Decorative Panel.
Designed and executed by W. Jones, *Manchester.*

1291. Design for decoration of the chapel, Haileybury College.
Also design for wall decoration, St. Thomas Church, Clapton.
By C. Campbell *and* F. G. Smith, *Lambeth and West London.*

1292. Panel and Door Decoration.
Designed by Alfred Morgan, *Norwich and South Kensington.*

1293. Design for Decorative Panel.
By E. Page Turner, *Sheffield.*

1294. Design for Side of a Room. Painted Majolica Tiles.
By T. Smith, *Coalbrookdale.*

1295. Design for Wall and Lunette Decoration; also Decoration of Chimney Corner of billiard room.
By E. Page Turner, *Sheffield.*

1296. Design for Staircase and Wall Decoration.
By Charles Campbell, *Lambeth and West London.*
Executed by Campbell, Smith & Campbell.

1297. Design for Wall Decoration.
By James Ward, *Belfast.*

1298. Two frames of Designs for Wall Papers.
By George E. Drake, *Halifax.*
Manufactured by Scott, Cuthbertson & Co., *Chelsea.*

1299. Wall Paper.
Designed by Miss Louisa Aumonier, *St. Martin's.*
Manufactured by Woollams & Co.

1300. Design for Wall Paper.
By Louis Bircumshaw, *Nottingham.*

1301. Two Wall Papers.
Designed by G. E. Drake, *Halifax.*
Manufactured by Scott, Cuthbertson & Co., *Chelsea.*

1302. Design for Wall Paper.
By J. Dunlop, *Kilmarnock.*

1303. Wall Paper and Border.
Designed by G. F. Drake, *Halifax.*
Manufactured by Scott, Cuthbertson & Co., *Chelsea.*

1304. Wall Paper,
Designed by G. E. Drake, *Halifax.*
Manufactured by Scott, Cuthbertson & Co., *Chelsea.*

1305. Wall Paper,
Designed by R. O. Rickatson, *West London.*
Manufactured by Messrs. Woollams.

1306. Wall Paper,
Designed by G. C. Haité, Croydon.
Manufactured by Messrs. Woollams.

1307. Design for Wall Paper,
By F. E. Adams, Macclesfield.

1308. Design for Wall Paper,
By C. J. Beaupré, West London.

1309. Design for Wall Paper,
By G. P. Churcher, South Kensington.

1310. Design for Wall Paper.
By A. J. Budd, Lambeth.

1311. Twenty-four Frames containing specimens of Wall Paper,
Designed by H. W. Ellis, Cambridge; T. W. Hay, Edinburgh; A. Silver; Reading; G. C. Haité, Croydon; Jane Tarver, Northampton; A. Mannoch, West London; O. W. Davis, West London; Louisa Aumonier, St. Martin's; Allan Ramsey, West London; R. O. Rickatson, West London; A. J. Tatham, West London; B. A. Lillie, West London; H. Noble, West London.
Manufactured by Messrs. Woollams & Co., London.

1312. Two Wall Papers,
Designed by Allan Ramsey, West London.

1313. Two Designs for Wall Papers,
By John J. Allen, Nottingham.

1314. Design for Wall Paper.
By S. L. Chadbourne, Nottingham.

1315. Design for Wall Paper.
By Miss Frances Brett, Dublin.

1316. Design for Wall Paper.
By H. J. Tomlins, Worcester.

1317. Wall Paper.
Designed by G. C. Haité.
Manufactured by Woollams, Croydon.

1318. Design for Wall Paper.
By H. King, Nottingham.

1319. Design for Wall Decoration.
By Miss Alice Bailey, London.

1320. Wall-Paper.
Designed by T. W. Hay, Edinburgh.
Manufactured by Messrs. Woollams.

1321. Design for Wall Paper.
By Miss Beatrice Alcock, Manchester.

1322. Design for Frieze and design for Decorative Panel.
By E. Page Turner, Sheffield.

1323. Design for the decoration of the Billiard Room at Stoke Court, Bucks.
By Charles Campbell, Lambeth and West London.

1324. Design for the side of a Room, in painted tiles and majolica, with stained glass windows.
By Frederick Leighton, Coalbrookdale.

1325. Design for a Ceiling, suitable for a synagogue.
By John W. Bradburn, Coalbrookdale.

1326. Design for Panel.
By J. C. Callowhill, Worcester.

1327. Design for Frieze.
By A. McCormick, Belfast.

SECTION XVII.

Lithographs, Chromolithographs, &c.

1328. Sheet of Calendars, Invitation Cards, &c.
Designed by W. S. Black, Edinburgh.
Chromolithographed by Messrs. G. Waterston & Sons, Edinburgh.

1329. Sheets of Designs for the Backs of Ball Programmes, &c.
By Miss Lilian Young, Bloomsbury.

1330. Sheet of Designs for the Illustration of Children's Picture Books.
By W. S. Black, Edinburgh.
Chromolithographed by Messrs. G. Waterston & Sons, Edinburgh.

1331. Sheet of Designs for the Illustration of Children's Picture Books.
By W. S. Black, Edinburgh.
Chromolithographed by Messrs. G. Waterston & Sons, Edinburgh.

1332. Sheet of Designs for the Backs of Playing Cards and Catalogue Covers.
By J. N. Fletcher, Nottingham.

1333. Fan.
Designed by a Student of the Bloomsbury School.
Chromolithographed by the Students of the Female Chromolithographic Studio, 33 Red Lion Square.

1334. Sheet of Book Covers, &c.
Designed by Miss Elizabeth Gulland, Edinburgh.
Chromolithographed by Messrs. T A. Constable & Co., Edinburgh.

1335. Sheet of New Year Cards.
Designed by H. Maurice Page, Croydon.
Chromolithographed by Messrs. Hildesheimer & Faulkener, London.

1336. Sheet of Christmas and New Year Cards.
Designed by Eleanor Manley, Bloomsbury.
Chromolithographed by Messrs. Hildesheimer & Faulkner, London.

1337. Christmas and other Cards.
Designed by Mrs. T. W. Grey, St. Martin's.

1338. Two Sheets of Christmas, Easter, and other Cards.
Designed by W. J. Muckley, Stourbridge, Birmingham, Somerset House, and Marlborough House; assisted by W. R. & A. F. Muckley, Manchester.
Chromolithographed by Messrs. Hildesheimer & Faulkener, Jewin Street, London.

1339. Sheet of Birthday and other Cards.
Designed by Miss Maud Ashley West, Bloomsbury.
Chromolithographed by Messrs. T. De la Rue & Co., London.

1340. Sheet of Birthday and other Cards.
Designed by Charlotte James, Bloomsbury.
Chromolithographed by Messrs. Raphael Tuck & Sons, London.

1341. Sheet of Christmas and other Cards.
Designed by Miss Mary Agnes Lewis, Lambeth.

1342. Two designs for Christmas Cards.
Designed by Frederick Leighton, Coalbrookdale.

1343. Sheet of Christmas and other Cards.
Designed by Miss Alice L. West, Bloomsbury.
Chromolithographed by Messrs. T. De la Rue & Co., London.

1344. Chromolithograph of a Chinese Cloisonné Vase, from a drawing. By W. J. Muckley, Manchester.
Executed by George Moore, Manchester.
Printed by Messrs. J. J. Sale & Sons, Manchester.

1345. Sheet of Menu and other Cards.
Designed by Wm. S. Black, Edinburgh.
Chromolithographed by Messrs. T. A Constable & Co., Edinburgh,

1346. Four Lithograhic Plates from drawings on Stone by John Hawkins.
Executed for C. Spence Bate, Esq., F.R.S., for his report of the Macrurous Crustacea of H.M.S. " Challenger."
Lithographed by Messrs. Brendon & Sons, Plymouth.

1347. Chromo of a Foxglove, copied from the original water-colour drawing from nature.
By Miss Lilian Young.
Purchased by the Science and Art Department.
Chromolithographed by Mr. Griggs.

1348. Chromolithograph of H.R.H. the Prince of Wales.
By the Students of the Female Chromolithographic Studio, under the direction of Mons. Faustin, 33 Red Lion Square, London.

1349. Chromolithograph of H.M. the Queen.
By the Students of the Female Chromolithographic Studio, under the direction of Mons. Faustin, 33 Red Lion Square, London.

1350. Chromo of a Sunflower, from the original drawing from nature.
By Miss Emily Lucy Varley, Bloomsbury.
Chromolithographed by Mr. Griggs, Peckham.

SECTION XVIII.

Illuminations, Illuminated Addresses, Title Pages of Books, Bookbindings, &c.

1351. Examination Certificate.
Designed by James Gamble, Sheffield.
Lithographed by C. Mateaux.

1352. Certificate for the University of Cambridge.
Designed by F. W. Andrew, South Kensington.
Lithographed by Dalziel Bros.

1353. Science Diploma, Ireland.
Designed by W. H. Wise.
Lithographed by H. Harrel, Dublin.

1354. Science Certificate.
Designed by R. Townroe, Sheffield.

1355. Ornamental Alphabet.
Designed by Godfrey Sykes, Sheffield.

1356. Two Title Pages.
Designed by John Watkins, Birmingham and South Kensington.
Lithographed by Petit.

1357. Six sheets of Ornamental Borders, Title-pages, &c., for "L'Art."
Designed by John Watkins, Birmingham and South Kensington.

1358. Two designs for Book Covers and design for Jewel Casket Lid.
By J. H. Fletcher, Nottingham.

SECTION XIX.

Etchings, Engravings on Wood, and Drawings for Engravings.

1359. Portrait of Oliver Cromwell, wood engraving.
By Charles Roberts, Lambeth and South Kensington.

1360. The Industrial Arts applied to War, from the cartoon.
By Sir Fredk. Leighton, P.R.A., in the South Kensington Museum.
Engraved on wood by C. Roberts.

1361. Drawing in black and white, Child Playing Violin.
By L. Wain, West London.

1362. Chalk Drawing, Illustration for "The Frost Queen."
By Florence Reason, Bloomsbury.

1363. Type of Beauty.
By Sir F. Leighton, P.R.A.
Engraved on Wood by C. Roberts.

1364. The Dead Christ.
Painted by Phillippe de Champaigne.
Engraved on steel by W. A. Cox, after Rosells, under the direction of Mr. John Ballin.

1365. Crossing the Sarda, an incident of the tour in India of H.R.H. the Prince of Wales.
By Herbert Johnson, St. Martin's.

1366. The Illuminations at Calcutta in honour of H.R.H. the Prince of Wales.
By Herbert Johnson, St. Martin's.

1367. Portrait.
By C. Roberts, Lambeth and South Kensington.

1368. Ascending a Pyramid, drawing in black and white.
By Herbert Johnson, St. Martin's.

1369. Sheet of drawings in black and white.
By Charles O. Murray, Edinburgh.

1370. An Incident in the Bombardment of Alexandria, drawing in black and white.
By Alfred Pearse, West London.

1371. Types of the Mahdi's Followers.
By Alfred Pearse, West London.

1372. The Shell.
By Davidson Knowles, West London.

1373. The Birth-day Tree, drawing in black and white.
By Davidson Knowles, West London.

1374. "Cavalry Fight at the Battle of Maiwand."
By Alfred Pearse, West London.

1375. "Breaking the News," drawing in black and white.
By Alfred Pearse, West London.

1376. "The Nordenfeldt Gun in Action," drawing in black and white.
By Alfred Pearse, *West London*.

1377. "Christmas Eve," drawing in black and white.
By William S. Black, *Edinburgh*.

1378. "H.R.H. The Prince of Wales and Staff crossing a Nullah," original water-colour drawing.
By Herbert Johnson, *St. Martin's*.

1379. "The Spring of Civilization," drawing in black and white.
By J. Moyr Smith, *Glasgow and South Kensington*.

1380. "The Tambourine Player."
Designed and lithographed for "Decoration," by J. Moyr Smith, *Glasgow and South Kensington*.

1381. "The Magadis Player."
Designed and lithographed for "Decoration."
By J. Moyr Smith, *Glasgow and South Kensington*

1382. Portrait of Mon. de Lesseps, drawing in black and white.
By T. Walter Wilson, *South Kensington*.
(Lent by the Proprietors of the *Graphic*.)

1383. Five Frames of Portraits for the "Dramatic Notes."
Executed by T. Walter Wilson, *South Kensington*.
Published by David Bogue, *London*.

1384. The Dutch Admiral, De Ruyter, after the picture by Franz Hals.
Etched by C. P. Slocombe, *Spitalfields and Somerset House*.
(Lent by R. Dunthorne, Vigo Street.)

1385. "Child and Geese," etching.
Executed by C. O. Murray, *Edinburgh*.

1386. "Homo," after the picture by S. E. Waller.
Etched by F. A. Slocombe, *South Kensington*.
(Lent by the Fine Art Society, Bond Street.)

1387. "Sir Rupert Kettle," after the picture by Frank Holl, R.A.
Etched by C. P. Slocombe, *Spitalfields and Somerset House*.
(Lent by R. Dunthorne, Vigo Street.)

1388. "Stoke Pogis Church."
Etched by F. A. Slocombe, *South Kensington*.
(Lent by the Fine Art Society, Bond Street.)

1389. "Major-General Sir Henry Rawlinson, K.C.B.," after the picture by Frank Holl, R.A.
Etched by C. P. Slocombe, *Spitalfields, Somerset House*.
(Lent by R. Dunthorne, Vigo Street.)

1390. "Her Grace."
After the picture by John Pettie, R.A.
Etched by C. P. Slocombe, *Spitalfields and Somerset House*.
(Lent by R. Dunthorne, Vigo Street.)

1391. A Sylvan Road.
Etched by F. A. Slocombe, *South Kensington*.
(Lent by the Fine Art Society, Bond Street.)

1392. A Pleasant Shady Lane.
Etched by F. A. Slocombe, *South Kensington*.
(Lent by the Fine Art Society, Bond Street.)

1393. A Series of Views in the South Kensington and Bethnal Green Museums.
Etched by John Watkins, *Birmingham and South Kensington*.

1394. "Lazy Moments."
By John Sargeant Noble, *West London*.
Etched by V. Lhuillier.

1395. "Returned from Sport."
By John Sargeant Noble, *West London*.
Etched by C. O. Murray, *Edinburgh*.

1396. "Left Lonely."
An original etching by Charles O. Murray, *Edinburgh*.

1397. "Quiet Pets."
An etching after Alma Tadema, R.A.
By Charles O. Murray, *Edinburgh*.

1398. "The Cornfield."
An etching by Frank McFadden, *Southampton and South Kensington*.

1399. Water Colour Drawings of portions of the contents of a Viking's Grave, opened in the Isle of Colonsay, time 1812.

> *Executed as Illustrations for Publication in the "Archæologia," by the Society of Antiquaries of London.*
> *Painted by Miss Rosa Wallis, South Kensington.*
> Lent by the Council of the Society of Antiquaries, London.

1400. "Karlavagn."

> *An original Drawing by J. Moyr Smith, Glasgow and South Kensington.*
> *Engraved in "Decoration."*

1,01. Head of a Girl. Study in Chalk.

> *By Miss Ida Lovering, Bloomsbury.*
> (Lent by Her Majesty The Queen.)

1402. Three Pen and Ink Drawings.

> *By J. Moyr Smith, Glasgow and South Kensington.*

SECTION XX.

Painted Photographs of Objects of Decorative Art.

1403. Painted Photograph of Triptych. Limoges Enamel on copper. By Nardon Penicaud. French. 1499-1513. Original in the South Kensington Museum.

1404. Painted Photograph of Dagger and Sheath, mounted with jewelled gold; rows of loose pearls in blade. Original in the Prince of Wales's Indian Collection.

1405. Painted Photograph of Shield; Rhinoceros hide, enamelled, and mounted with jewelled gold. Original in the Prince of Wales's Indian Collection.

1406. Painted Photograph of Limoges Enamel dish. Subject: Apollo and the Muses. By Martial Courtois. 16th century. Original belonging to Sir Richard Wallace, Bart., K.C.B.

1407. Painted Photograph of back of dish. Limoges Enamel. By Martial Courtois. 16th century. Original belonging to Sir Richard Wallace, Bart., M.P.

1408. Painted Photograph of Letter Case. Gold embroidery, jewelled Original in the Prince of Wales's Indian Collection.

1409. Painted Photograph of Scent Bottle and Stand. Gold enamelled and jewelled. Jeypore. Original in the Prince of Wales's Indian Collection.

1410. Painted Photograph of Shield. Steel, enamelled and set with diamonds, with jewelled silk pendants. Original in the Prince of Wales's Indian Collection.

1411. Painted Photographs of Sèvres porcelain vase, made to the order of the Empress Catharine II. of Russia as a present to King Gustavus III. of Sweden in 1780. Original in the Jones Collection, South Kensington Museum.

1412. Painted Photograph of French Cabinet. Japanese lacquer and ormolu. Late Louis XIV. period. Original in the Jones Collection, South Kensington Museum.

1413. Painted Photograph of Corner Table. Boule work with ormolu mounts. French. Period of Louis XIV. Original in the Jones Collection, South Kensington Museum.

1414. Painted Photograph of Sécrétaire of kingwood marquetry, with Sèvres panels and ormolu mounts. French. Period of Louis XIV. Original in Jones Collection, South Kensington Museum.

1415. Painted Photograph of Porcelain Clock, with Gouthière ormolu mounts. Made for Queen Marie Antoinette. French. About 1780. Original in the Jones Collection, South Kensington Museum.

1416. Painted Photograph of Boule Table. Probably designed by Bérain. French. Period of Louis XIV. Original in the Jones Collection, South Kensington Museum.

> *Painted by J. I. Williamson, South Kensington.*
> (Lent by the South Kensington Museum.)

1417. Painted Photograph of Triptych, champlevé enamel. German. 13th century. Original in the South Kensington Museum.

1418. Painted Photograph of Shrine or Reliquary. Gilt Copper, with enamelled details and ivory carvings. Rhenish-Byzantine. About 1150. Original in the South Kensington Museum.

1419. Painted Photograph of Triptych or Retable Gilt Metal, enamelled and jewelled. German. 12th century. Original in the South Kensington Museum.

1420. Painted Photograph of Chalice, silver gilt. German. Middle of 15th century. Original in the South Kensington Museum.

1421. Painted Photograph of Triptych, carved ivory. The Virgin and Saints. Venetian. 14th century. Original in the South Kensington Museum.

1422. Painted Photograph of Casket, carved ivory. Byzantine. 12th or 13th century. Original in the South Kensington Museum.

1423. Painted Photograph of Jug, stoneware, mounted in silver. German. 16th century. Original in the South Kensington Museum.

1424. Painted Photograph of Cup, rock crystal, silver-gilt mounting. Engraved with figures of Neptune, Amalthæa, and a phœnix. Italian. About 1600. Original in the South Kensington Museum.

1425. Painted Photograph of Navette, or Incense Holder. Crystal, set in silver, jewelled and gilt. Spanish? About 1540-50. Original in the South Kensington Museum.

1426. Painted Photograph of Cup. Cocoa-nut, mounted in silver, chased and gilt. German. Dated 1615. Original in the South Kensington Museum.

1427. Painted Photograph of Casket. Ivory, mounted in chased silver of 17th century. Spanish? 10th or 11th century. Original in the South Kensington Museum.

1428. Painted Photograph of the "Veroli Casket." Carved ivory. Byzantine. 10th or 11th century. Original in the South Kensington Museum.

1429. Painted Photograph of Reliquary. Gilt copper, jewelled, set with plaques of enamels and niello. French? 14th century. Original in the South Kensington Museum.

Painted by J. Randall, South Kensington.
(Lent by the South Kensington Museum.)

1430. Painted Photographs of Limoges Enamel Dish. The triumph of Galatea, after Raphael. French. 16th century. Original belonging to Sir Richard Wallace, Bart., K.C.B.
Painted by T. Walter Wilson, South Kensington.
(Lent by the South Kensington Museum.)

1431. Painted Photograph of Embroidered Cope. Spanish. 13th century. Original formerly in the College of Daroca, Aragon, but now in the National Archæological Museum, Madrid.

1432. Painted Photograph of Tapestry from St. Mary's Hall, Coventry. Flemish. Late 15th or early 16th century.

1433. Painted Photograph of Hood of a Cope. Original formerly in the Royal Convent of the Escurial, but now in the Royal Palace Madrid.

Painted by Miss Harriett Skidmore, Stourbridge and South Kensington.
(Lent by the South Kensington Museum.)

1434. Painted Photograph of Orphrey of Cope. Spanish. 13th century. Original formerly in the College of Daroca, Aragon, but now in the National Archæological Museum, Madrid.
Painted by Miss Rosa Wallis, South Kensington.
(Lent by the South Kensington Museum.)

1435. Painted Photograph of the Upper Cover of a Book of the Gospels, the property of the Earl of Ashburnham.

1436. Painted Photograph of the Under Cover of a Book of the Gospels, the property of the Earl of Ashburnham. Painted for the Council of the Society of Antiquaries, London, for reproduction with the above in Chromolithography as illustrative to the "Monumenta Vetusta."
Painted by Miss Rosa Wallis, South Kensington.
(Lent by the Council of the Society of Antiquaries, London.)

SECTION XXI.

Architectural Drawings, Designs, and Models of Buildings, &c.

1437. Residence, erected near Pontypridd by H. I. Grover, Esq.
Designed by Edwin Seward, R.C.A., Cardiff.

1438. Preparatory School, Royal Masonic Institution for Boys, Wood-green.
Designed by A. W. Cross, Hastings and St. Leonards.

1439. Original Design of the Cardiff Free Library, Schools for Science and Art and Museum.
By Edwin Seward, R.C.A., Cardiff.

1440. Longitudinal and Transverse Sections, West and South Elevations, and Perspective Views of the Hastings Infirmary.
Designed by A. W. Cross, Hastings and St. Leonards.

1441. Exterior View of the New Church of the Oratory, South Kensington.
Designed by Herbert A. Gribble, Plymouth and South Kensington.

1442. Interior View of the New Church of the Oratory, South Kensington.
Designed by Herbert A. Gribble, Plymouth and South Kensington.

1443. View of the Sanctuary of the New Church of the Oratory, South Kensington.
Designed by Herbert A. Gribble, Plymouth and South Kensington.

1444. View of the Altar in the Chapel of St. Philip Neri, in the New Church of the Oratory, South Kensington.
Designed by Herbert A. Gribble, Plymouth and South Kensington.

1445. Design for Roman Catholic Cathedral.
    By Herbert A. Gribble, *Plymouth and South Kensington.*

1446. Design for a Country Residence, front elevation.
    By W. P. Watson, *South Kensington.*

1447. Design for a Country Residence, front elevation.
    By W. P. Watson, *South Kensington.*

1448. Design for a Country Residence, section.
    By W. P. Watson, *South Kensington.*

1449. Design for a Collegiate School, east elevation.
    By F. W. Woodhouse, *South Kensington.*

1450. East Door of St. Paul's Cathedral.
    By W. P. Watson, *South Kensington.*

1451. Two Bays of Nave of Durham Cathedral.
    By Philip Hall, *Durham.*

1452. Design for Cathedral.
    By H. J. Smith, *Nottingham.*

1453. Photograph of West Doorway of St. Giles's Cathedral, Edinburgh.
    By W. Birnie Rhind, *Edinburgh.*

SECTION XXII.

Miscellaneous Articles not included in any other Section.

1454. Series of Published Books on Plant Form.
    By F. E. Hulme.
    The Illustrations designed and executed by F. E. Hulme, South Kensington.

1455. Specimen of Book-Binding.
    Designed by E. Seward, R.C.A., *Cardiff.*

1456. Lessons in Figure Painting.
    By Misses B. McArthur and Jennie Moore, *Bloomsbury.*

1457. Six Specimens of backs of playing cards.
    Designed by H. Lyndon, *West London.*

1458. Study of Flowers.
    By William Suthers, *South Kensington.*

The following artists were engaged upon the decoration of "Old London," erected by Messrs. Campbell, Smith, and Campbell:
    J. Simkin, *Lambeth and West London.*
    A. Finlayson, *Glasgow.*
    M. Southall, *Bishopsgate.*
    J. McDonald, *West London.*
    J. Pontis, *South Kensington.*
    J. E. Campbell, *Lambeth and West London.*

PRIVATE CONTRIBUTORS

OF WORKS DESIGNED OR EXECUTED BY STUDENTS.

HER MOST GRACIOUS MAJESTY THE QUEEN, 1401.

HIS ROYAL HIGHNESS THE PRINCE OF WALES, K.G., 763.

HER ROYAL HIGHNESS THE PRINCESS OF WALES, 760, 761, 762.

HIS ROYAL HIGHNESS THE DUKE OF EDINBURGH, K.G., 174.

HER IMPERIAL AND ROYAL HIGHNESS THE DUCHESS OF EDINBURGH, 51, 52.

HER ROYAL HIGHNESS THE DUCHESS OF ALBANY, 793.

GENERAL LORD WOLSELEY, G.C.B., G.C.M.G., 725.

GENERAL SIR ARCHIBALD ALISON, BART., K.C.B., 770.

SIR RICHARD WALLACE, BART., M.P., 800.

THE RIGHT HON. JOHN BRIGHT, M.P., 768.

SIR P. CUNLIFFE-OWEN, K.C.M.G., C.B., C.I.E., 232, 385, 709.

LADY CUNLIFFE-OWEN, 458.

SIR JOHN ASTLEY, BART., 727.

OFFICERS COMMANDING FIRST BAT-TALION 4TH KING'S OWN ROYAL LANCASHIRE REGIMENT, 733.

THE MAYOR AND CORPORATION OF WEST BROMWICH, 765.

THE MAYOR AND CORPORATION OF STOKE-UPON-TRENT, 766.

THE MAYOR AND CORPORATION OF ROTHERHAM, 767.

THE COUNCIL OF THE SOCIETY OF ANTIQUARIES OF LONDON, 1399, 1435, 1436.

THE ART UNION OF LONDON, 582.

THE PROPRIETORS OF "THE GRA-PHIC," 1382.

A. W. BAILEY, ESQ., 22.

MRS. BRIGHTWYN, Stanmore, 32.

B. E. FLETCHER, ESQ., Marlingford Hall, Norwich, 823.

THOMAS HAWKSLEY, ESQ., C.E., F.R.S., 730.

JOHN LOMAX, ESQ., Manchester, 801.

MRS. T. DIX PERKIN, Harrow, 764.

JOHN POLSON, ESQ., Paisley, 700.

J. D'AGUILAR SAMUDA, ESQ., M.P., 728.

STUART SAMUEL, ESQ., 569.

MANUFACTURERS who contribute objects designed by Students of Schools of Art of the United Kingdom to the Science and Art Department Exhibition, to illustrate the operations and the influence of Schools of Art, 1884.

ALPHABETICAL LIST OF FIRMS.

AGNEW, THOMAS, & SONS, Manchester; & London.
Gilt Picture Frame. Sec. VIII.

ALDERTON, H., Brighton.
Furniture. Sec. VIII.

ALLEN, W., Coalbrookdale.
Keramic Ware. Sec. II.

APPLEYARD, MESSRS. & SONS, Sheffield.
Furniture. Sec. VIII.

BALLANTINE & SONS, Edinburgh.
Glass. Sec. III.

BARBOUR, ANDERSON & CO., Glasgow.
Carpets. Sec. XV.

BARWELL, J., & CO., Birmingham.
Metal Work. Sec. V.

BENSON & SON, Ludgate Hill.
Gold and Jewelled Casket. Sec. VI.

BESSBOROUGH CO., Newry, Ireland.
Damasks. Sec XI.

BIRCHENOUGH, J., & SONS, Macclesfield.
Furniture and Dress Fabrics. Silk. Sec. XII.

BLANCKENSEE & SONS, Birmingham.
Gold Key. Sec. VII.

BODLEY, E. J. D., Burslem.
Keramic Ware. Sec. II.

BOGUE, DAVID, London.
Engravings. Sec. XIX.

BRAGG, T. & J., Birmingham.
Jewellery and Plate. Secs. VI., VII.

BRAY, NICHOLAS, Sheffield.
Silver and Plated Ware. Sec. VI.

BRENDON & SONS, Plymouth.
Lithographs. Sec. XVII.

BROADHEAD, GEORGE, Nottingham.
Lace. Sec. X.

BROWNHILL POTTERY CO., Tunstall.
Keramic Ware. Sec. II.

BROWN, W. & F., & CO., Chester.
Furniture. Sec. VIII.

CAMPBELL, SMITH, & CAMPBELL, Oxford Street, W.C.
Stained Glass. Sec. III.
Decoration. Sec. XVI.

CAREY & SONS, Nottingham.
Lace. Sec. X.

COALBROOKDALE IRON CO., Shropshire.
Metal Work. Sec. V.

CONSTABLE, T. A., & CO., Edinburgh.
Ornamental Stationery. Sec. XXII.

COPE, J., Stoke-on-Trent.
Keramic Ware. Sec. II.

CORBITT, W., & CO., Rotherham.
Metal Work. Sec. V.

COWLISHAW, NICOL, & CO., Manchester.
Furniture and Carpet Fabrics. Secs. XII., XV.

COWTAN & SONS, London.
Furniture. Sec. VIII.

CRAVEN, DUNNILL & CO., Jackfield, Shropshire.
Tiles.

CROFTS & ASSINDER, Birmingham.
Metal Work. Sec. V.

CROSSLEY, J., & CO., Halifax.
Carpets. Sec. XV.

CUTTS, THOMAS B., Nottingham.
Lace Edgings. Sec. X.

DALZIEL BROTHERS, London.
Lithographed Certificate. Sec. XVIII.

DAVENPORT, MESSRS., Longton.
Porcelain and Pottery. Sec. II.

DE LA RUE & CO., Bunhill Row, E.C.
Lithographs. Sec. XVII.

DERBY CROWN PORCELAIN CO.,
Derby.
Porcelain. Sec. II.

DIXON, H. J., & SONS, Kidderminster.
Carpets. Sec. XV.

DOULTON & CO., High Street, Lambeth; and Nile Street, Burslem.
Pottery and Porcelain. Sec. II.

DUNTHORNE, R., Vigo Street, W.
Engravings. Sec. XIX.

EASTWOOD, H., & CO., Huddersfield.
Carpets. Sec. XV.

EDMUNDSON, R. B., & SON, Manchester.
Glass. Sec. III.

EDWARDS, G., & SON, Glasgow.
Plate. Sec. VI.

ELKINGTON & CO., Regent Street, W.
Ornamental Metal Work and Plate.
Secs. IV., V., VI.

EYRE & SPOTTISWOODE, Great
New Street, W.C.
Lithographs. Sec. XVII.

FINE ART SOCIETY, New Bond
Street, W.
Etchings. Sec. XIX.

FORD, T. & CO., Birmingham.
Metal work. Sec. V.

FRAMPTON, E., Buckingham Palace
Road, S.W.
Stained glass. Sec. III.

FREEMAN & COLLIER, Manchester.
Metal Work. Sec. V.
Silver Plate. Sec. VI.

FRY & CO., Dublin.
Furniture Damasks. Sec. XI.
Furniture. Sec. VIII.

FURNIVAL, T., & SON, Stafford.
Pottery. Sec. II.

GARRARD, R. & S., Haymarket, W.
Silver Plate. Sec. VI.

GOODALL, E., & CO., Manchester.
Furniture. Secs. VIII., XVI.

GRIGGS, W., Peckham.
Chromo-lithographs. Sec. XVII.

HAGUE & CO., Sheffield.
Metal Work. Sec. V.

HAMEL & WRIGHT, Nottingham.
Lace. Sec. X.

HAMILTON, CRICHTON, & CO.,
Edinburgh.
Presentation Salver. Sec. VI.

HAMILTON, HILL, & CO., Belfast.
Damasks. Sec. XI.

HARRISON, C., Stourport.
Carpets. Sec. XV.

HAYWARD, J. A., Darlington.
Furniture. Sec. VIII.

HELBRONNER, R., Oxford Street, W.
Embroidery. Sec. XII.
Carpets. Sec. XV.

HENDERSON & CO., Durham.
Carpets. Sec. XV.

HEYMAN & ALEXANDER, Nottingham.
Lace. Sec. X.

HILDESHEIMER & FALKNER,
Jewin Street, E.C.
Lithographs. Sec. XVII.

HODKINSON, H. P., Art Metal
Works, Coventry.
Metal Work. Sec. V

HOLLAND & SONS, Mount Street, W.
Furniture. Sec. VIII.

HOLLINS MINTON.
See MINTON, HOLLINS.

HOWARD & SONS., Newman Street,
W.C.
Furniture. Sec. VIII.

HOYLE, THOMAS, & SONS, Manchester.
Printed Cotton Fabrics. Sec. XIV.

HUNT & ROSKELL, New Bond Street,
W.
Silver Plate. Sec. VI.

JACOBY, M., & CO., Nottingham.
Lace. Sec. X.

JEFFREY & CO., Essex Road, N.
Wall Papers. Sec. XVI.

JESSOP, C. H., Sheffield.
Metal Work. Sec. V.

JONES, G., AND SONS, Stoke-on-Trent.
Pottery and Porcelain. Sec. II.

KENDAL, MILNE, & CO., Manchester.
Furniture. Sec. VIII.

KIRKWOOD, R. & H. B., Edinburgh.
Silver Metal Work, &c. Secs. VI., VII.

LETHERAN, W., & SONS, Cheltenham.
Metal Work. Sec. V.

LILEY & WOOD, Radnor House, Gloucester Square, W.
Furniture. Sec. VIII.

LINTHORPE POTTERY CO., Middlesborough.
Pottery and Porcelain. Sec. II.

LONGDEN & CO., Sheffield.
Metal Work. Sec V.
Furniture. Sec. VIII.

McCREA & CO., Halifax.
Carpots and Hangings. Sec. XV.

MACKAY & CHISHOLM, Edinburgh.
Silver Plate. Sec. VI.

MACKAY & CUNNINGHAM, Edinburgh.
Silver Plate. Sec. VI.

MAGEE & CO., Belfast.
Decoration. Sec. XVI.
Damasks. Sec. XI.

MASON, HERBERT, & CO., Birmingham.
Metal Work. Sec. V.

MAW & CO., Benthall, Broseley.
Tiles, &c. Sec. II.

MILNE & SON, Lancaster.
Furniture. Sec. VIII.

MILLWARD, A. J., Kendal.
Furniture. Sec. VIII.

MINNS, JOHN, Norwich.
Furniture. Sec. VIII.

MINTON, HOLLINS, & SONS., Stoke-on-Trent.
Pottery and Porcelain. Sec. II.

MINTONS, LIMITED, Stoke-on-Trent
Pottery and Porcelain. Sec. II.

MORTON & CO., Darwell.
Lace Curtain. Sec. X.

MORTON, W., SCOTT, & CO., Edinburgh.
Secs. V., XV., XVI.

MORTON & SONS, Kidderminster.
Carpets. Sec. XV.

NICHOLSON, J. O., Macclesfield.
Embroidery. Sec. XII.
Silks. Sec. XI.

NORTON, GEORGE, Sheffield.
Silver Plate. Sec. VI.

OLIVER & ATCHERLEY, Manchester.
Damasks. Sec. XI.

PEARCE, HENRY, 4 New Street, Huddersfield.
Silver Plate. Goldsmith's Work.
Secs. VI., VII.

POTTER, E. C., & CO., Manchester.
Fabrics; prints. Sec. XIV.

PYM BROTHERS, Dublin.
Silk Fabrics. Sec. XII.

RHIND, WILLIAM BERNIE, Edinburgh.
Statue Models. Sec. XIX.

RHODES, JEHOIADA, Sheffield.
Silver Plate. Sec. VI.

RICHARDSON & CO., Barnsley.
Damasks. Sec. XI.

RICHARDSON, ELLSON, & CO., Coventry.
Metal Work. Sec. V.

ROBERTSON, R. C., & SONS, Kilmarnock.
Furniture. Sec. VIII.

ROODHOUSE & SONS, Leeds.
Furniture. Sec. VIII.

ROTHERHAM & SONS, Coventry.
Engraved Watch Cases, Gold and Silver.
Sec. VII.

SALE, J. J., & SONS, Manchester.
Chromo-lithographs. Sec. XVII.

SCOTT, CUTHBERTSON, & CO., Chelsea.
Wall Papers. Sec. XVI.

SHRIGLEY & HUNT, John Street, W.C.
Tiles. Sec. II.

SINGER, JOHN W., & SONS, Frome.
Art Metal Work. Sec. V.

SMART, THOMAS, Dudley.
Metal Work. Sec. V.

SMITH, R., & SONS, Kidderminster.
Carpets. Sec. XV.

STAPLETON & SON, Poland Street, W.
Jewellery Sec. VII.

STEVENS & WILLIAMS, Brierly Hill, Stourbridge.
Glass. Sec. III.

THOMAS, JOHN, Halifax.
Tapestry Hangings. Sec. XV.

THOMPSON, E. L., Sheffield.
Silver Work. Sec. VI.

TOMKINSON & ADAM, Kidderminster.
Carpets. Sec. XV.

TONKS, WILLIAM, & SONS, Birmingham.
Metal Work. Sec. V.

TORQUAY TERRA COTTA CO., Torquay.
Terra Cotta. Sec. II.

TUCK, RAPHAEL, & SONS, London.
Christmas and Birthday Cards.
Sec. XVII.

WALTON, F. & CO., Berners Street, W.C.
"Walton" Decorations. Sec. XVI.

WALTERS, D., & SON, Newgate Street, E.C.
Silks, &c. Sec. XII.

WARD, J. W., & CO., Halifax.
Carpets. Sec. XV.

WATCOMBE TERRA COTTA CO., Torquay.
Terra Cotta. Sec. II.

WATERSTON, G., & SONS, Edinburgh.
Illuminations, &c. Sec. XVIII.
Chromo-lithographs. Sec. XVII.

WATSON, MOORWOOD, & CO., Sheffield.
Metal Work. Sec. V.

WEBB, THOMAS, & SONS, Stourbridge.
Glass. Sec. III.

WHITTALL & CO., Kidderminster.
Carpets. Sec. XV.

WHITE, EDWARD, Cockspur Street, W.
Gilt Metal Clock. Sec. VI.

WOOLLAMS, WILLIAM, & CO., High Street, Marylebone.
Wall Papers. Sec. XVI.

WORCESTER ROYAL PORCELAIN WORKS.
Pottery and Porcelain. Sec. II.

INDEX TO STUDENT EXHIBITORS,

THE NUMBER OF THEIR EXHIBITS, PERIODS OF STUDY, AND THE SCHOOLS WHICH THEY ATTENDED.

NDREW, F. W., 1352.
Attended 1842 to 1848, 1852 to 1855,
1857 to 1858.
Somerset House, Marl-
borough, and South Ken-
sington.

RCHER, HENRY, 560, 755, 798.
Attended 1850 to 1884.
Sheffield.

RDING, HELEN ALICE, 144.
Attended 1874 to 1878.
Lambeth.

RDING, MARY M., 142.
Attended 1880 to 1883.
Lambeth.

TKEY, CHARLES J., 1042.
Attended 1873 to 1880, 1884.
Nottingham.

UMONIER, LOUISA, 1139, 1267, 1299, 1311.
Attended 1860 to 1864.
S. Martin's, W.C.

USTIN, A., 717.
Attended 1879 to 1884.
Derby.

YERS, ELLEN M., 520.
Attended 1871 to 1879.
Yarmouth.

LING, R., 618.
Attended 1880 to 1883.
Westminster.

AILEY, A. M., 22. (*See* 1319, 1028.)
Attended?
South Kensington.

AILEY, ALICE, 1319.
Attended?
London.

AILEY, ALICE, 1028.
Attended 1878 to 1884.
Dublin Metropolitan.

KER, ANNE, 376, 382.
Attended 1862 to 1876.
Cork.

KER, THOS., 780.
Attended 1864 to 1869.
Coventry.

BALL, EDITH H., 72.
Attended 1880 to 1884.
Lambeth.

BALL, SUSAN, 1032, 1048, 1097.
Attended 1866 to 1870.
Dublin Metropolitan.

BANKS, W. H., 753, 856.
Attended 1872 to 1884.
Rotherham.

BARKER, ALICE M., 83.
Attended 1881 to 1884.
Lambeth.

BARKER, CLARA S., 105.
Attended 1876 to 1878.
Lambeth.

BARKER, GEORGE, 1212, 1220.
Attended 1870 to 1873.
Kidderminster.

BARLOW, FLORENCE E., 147.
Attended 1873 to 1881.
Lambeth and City of Guilds
Institute.

BARLOW, MISS, 98, 123.
Attended?
Lambeth.

BARON, WILLIAM, 136.
Attended?
Lambeth and South Ken-
sington.

BATES, DAVID, 205.
Attended 1856 to 1864, 1872.
Worcester.

BATHGATE, GEORGE, 12.
Attended 1875 to 1879.
Edinburgh.

BANGHAM, JOSEPH, 391.
Attended?
Coalbrookdale.

BAUMGARTNER, MARY, 1130.
Attended 1879 to 1884.
Great Yarmouth.

BAYNTON, H., 786.
Attended 1873 to 1884.
Coventry.

F

BEATTIE, CHALLEN, 599, 676 to 691, 698.
Attended 1859 to 1860.
Birmingham.

BEAUPRÉ, C. J., 228, 876, 1279, 1308.
Attended 6 years, 1882 to 1883.
West London and South
Kensington.

BECK, ACIDALIA, 106.
Attended 1881 to 1884.
Lambeth.

BEDFORD, GEORGE, 949.
Attended 1866 to 1877.
Torquay.

BEECH, DANIEL, 514.
Attended 1872 to 1875.
Stourbridge.

BENNETT, REUBEN, 1259.
Attended 1869 to 1870.
Manchester.

BERGIN, ISABELLA C., 913, 1099.
Attended 1868 to 1881.
Dublin.

BERKS, EDWARD, 432.
Attended ?
Stoke-on-Trent.

BETTS, JESSIE, 25.
Attended 1877 to 1884.
Weymouth.

BILTON, LOUIS, 245, 246, 323, 324, 432.
Attended 1873 to 1884.
Stoke-on-Trent and Fenton.

BINNS, ALBERT, 339.
Attended 1879 to 1882.
Worcester.

BIRAM, MISS JANE, 852.
Attended 1858 to 1884.
Sheffield.

BIRCUMSHAW, LOUIS, 1004, 1300.
Attended 1877 to 1844.
Nottingham.

BISHOP, ROBERT H., 993.
Attended 1869.
Nottingham.

BLACK, J. J., 1066, 1067, 1068, 1071, 1072, 1073, 1074, 1075, 1180, 1188, 1189, 1191.
Attended 1844 to 1851.
Manchester.

BLACK, WILLIAM S., 1328, 1330, 1331, 1345, 1377.
Attended 1870 to 1879.
Edinburgh.

BOARDMAN, WILLIAM, 213.
Attended 1884.
Burslem.

BONE, HERBERT, 1250.
Attended 1870 to 1876.
Lambeth.

BOOTH, JAMES, 557.
Attended 1869 to 1881.
Sheffield.

BOOTH, JOHN, 1113.
Attended 1877 to 1884.
Macclesfield.

BOSS, WM. G., 526, 541.
Attended 1867 to 1872 and 1876 to 188
Edinburgh.

BOWCHER, A. W., 923, 927, 931.
Attended 1878 to 1883.
South Kensington.

BOWCHER, FRANK, 808.
Attended 1881 to 1884.
South Kensington.

BOWEN, ELIZA F., 125.
Attended 1878 to 1884.
Lambeth.

BOYLE, J. F., 350, 896.
Attended 1867 to 1878.
Dublin.

BRADBURN, W., 383.
Attended ?
Coalbrookdale.

BRADBURN, JOHN, 58, 738, 1325.
Attended 1872 to 1883 and 1883 to 18
Coalbrookdale and Sou
Kensington.

BRADLEY, JAMES, 207.
Attended 1862 to 1877.
Worcester.

CHILDE, ANDREW, 416.
Attended 1879 to 1884.
Coalbrookdale.

CHISHOLM, D., 825.
Attended 1869 or 1870.
South Kensington.

CHRIPPES, WALTER, 1219.
Attended 6 years.
West London.

CHURCHER, G. P., 1309.
Attended ?
South Kensington.

CLARKE, JAMES, 1, 6.
Attended ?
South Kensington.

CLAYTON, E. W., 709.
Attended ?
Sheffield.

CLEWS, JOHN, 977.
Attended 1875 to 1882.
Nottingham.

CLOW, J. J., 851.
Attended 1879.
Exeter.

CLULOW, W. J., 1104, 1105.
Attended ?
Macclesfield.

COATES, WILLIAM, 950, 951.
Attended 1870 to 1878.
Nottingham.

COCKRILL, W. B., 910.
Attended 1867 to 1877.
Yarmouth.

COLEMAN, EDITH M., 74.
Attended 1881 to 1884.
Lambeth.

COLLIS, JANE J., 529.
Attended 1874 to 1883.
Salisbury.

COOK, MISS L. E. M., 853.
Attended 1881 to 1884.
Sheffield.

COOKE, ERNEST O., 33, 41.
Attended 1879 to 1884.
Nottingham.

COPE, J., 260.
Attended 1869.
Stoke-on-Trent.
Attended 1870 to 1871.
South Kensington.

COX, MARY, 352, 623.
Attended 1870 to 1880.
Worcester.

COX, W., 1364.
Attended ?
School ?

CRACKNELL, ELLEN K., 521, 731.
Attended 1877 to 1881.
Yarmouth.

CRAWLEY, MINA, 102.
Attended 1874 to 1880.
Lambeth.

CRICHTON, ALEX., 700.
Attended 1861 to 1866.
Edinburgh.

CRICHTON, JOHN, 701 to 705.
Attended 1860 to 1864.
Edinburgh.

CROSS, ALFRED W., 1438, 1440.
Attended ?
Hastings and St. Leonards.

CROSSLEY, FREDERICK, 1 65, 1177.
Attended 1872 to 1876.
Halifax.

CURTIS, A. LILLIAN, 155.
Attended 1881 to 1883.

CUTTS, JOHN, 1041.
Attended 1870 to 1872.
Nottingham.

DALGLEISH, T. J., 604.
Attended 1870 to 1874.
Coventry.

DAVEY, ARTHUR J., 173, 295.
Attended 1873 to 1884.
Torquay.

KENSTEIN, ALICE, 86.
Attended 1880 to 1884.
Lambeth.

WARDS, LOUISA E., 103.
Attended 1876 to 1883.
Lambeth.

WARDS, T. G., 906.
Attended 1871 to 1879.
Sheffield.

LIOTT, FANNY, 76.
Attended 1875 to 1879.
Lambeth.

LIS, H. W., 1311.
Attended 1867 to 1870.
Cambridge.

WOOD, MARION, 979.
Attended 1876 to 1884.
Nottingham.

ERTON, ELIZABETH, 134.
Attended 17 months.
Lambeth.

ERY, T., 373.
Attended ?
Stoke-on-Trent.

RINGTON, C. H., 780.
Attended 1865 to 1873.
Coventry.

ANS, BERTHA, 121.
Attended 1877 to 1881, 1884.
Lambeth.

ANS, JOHN A., 919.
Attended 1878 to 1883.
Gloucester.

ANS, MISS, 48.
Attended ?
South Kensington.

CER, JABEZ, 459 to 471.
Attended 1860 to 1866.
Stourbridge.

LKS, HENRY, 569.
Attended 1879 to 1881.
Birmingham.

LLOWS, II., 651 to 675.
Attended 1858 to 1859.
Birmingham.

FEMALE CHROMOLITHOGRAPHIC STUDIOS, STUDENTS OF, Royal Albert Hall and Red Lion Square, 1333, 1348, 1349.

FENNESY, MRS. (Emily Selous), 582.
Attended 1868 to 1873.
Bloomsbury.

FEREDAY, JOHN T., 493 to 499.
Attended 1867 to 1868.
Dudley.

FERNYHOUGH, GEORGE, 249, 252.
Attended 1870 to 1884.
Stoke-on-Trent.

FIDLER, F., 193, 630, 631, 746.
Attended 1867 to 1884.
Sheffield.

FIDLER, GIDEON M., 1221.
Attended 1873 to 1882.
Salisbury.

FINCHETT, THOS., 801.
Attended 1877 to 1884.
Manchester.

FINLAYSON, A., 1459.
Attended
Glasgow.

FINNEY, MRS. V. L., 37.
Attended 1882 to 1883.
South Kensington.

FIRTH, WILLIAM, 946, 947.
Attended ?
Lambeth.

FISHER, ALEXANDER, 30, 172.
Attended ?
Torquay.

FISHER, JOHN, 558, 921.
Attended 1875 to 1883, and 1883 to 1884.
Sheffield and South Kensington.

FISHER, ELIZABETH, 129.
Attended 1874 to 1877.
Lambeth.

FLETCHER, JAMES, 1245.
Attended 1881 to 1884.
Glasgow.

FLETCHER, J. H., 1332, 1358.
Attended 1873 to 1884.
Nottingham.

FOLLIOTT, WILLIAM, 1050 to 1064.
Attended 1851 to 1857.
Spitalfields.

FORD, RICHARD, 308, 309, 316.
Attended 1878 to 1881.
Burslem.

FORSEY, EMILY A., 93.
Attended 1881 to 1884.
Lambeth.

FOSTER, ARTHUR, 1038, 1039, 1040, 1043.
Attended 1874 to 1878.
Nottingham.

FOSTER, JONATHAN, 1124.
Attended 1877, 1883.
Halifax and Bradford.

FOSTER, WILLIAM, 1215.
Attended 1879 to 1884.
Salisbury.

FOX, EDWIN, 601.
Attended 1855, and 1865 to 1866.
Birmingham and South Ken-
sington.

FRAMPTON, EDWARD, 537, 538, 539.
Attended 1865 to 1868.
West London.

FREEMAN, THOS. F., 552 to 555, 722.
Attended 1874 to 1877.
Manchester.

FRENCH, ELIZABETH, 79.
Attended 1879 to 1882.
Lambeth.

FRIDAY, JAMES, 780, 785.
Attended 1863 to 1875.
Coventry.

FRITH, HENRY, 846.
Attended 1861 to 1863.
Gloucester.

FRITH, WILLIAM, (*See* Firth, William).

FROST, JOHN, 784.
Attended 1862 to 1869 and 1870 to
1873.
Coventry.

GAMBLE, JAMES, 174, 1351.
Attended 1852 to 1860.
Sheffield.

GANDY, JESSIE, 95.
Attended 1881 to 1884.
Lambeth.

GANDY, WALTER, 361.
Attended?
Lambeth.

GARBETT, ELLEN, 112.
Attended 1877 to 1880.
Lambeth.

GARBUTT, M., 612.
Attended 18 months.
West London.

GARDNER, JOHN, 21.
Attended 1874 to 1878.
Coventry.

GATER, J., 58.
Attended 1878 to 1882, 1882 to 1884.
Newcastle-under-Lyme and
South Kensington.

GATHERCOLE, ELLEN, 109.
Attended 1882 to 1884.
Lambeth.

GIBBONS, FRANCIS, 190, 191, 949.
Attended 1869 to 1879, 1879 to 1881,
1881 to 1882.
Cirencester, South Kensington, Coalbrookdale.

GIBBONS, OWEN, 235, 326, 388, 390, 392,
393, 394, 395, 396, 397, 398, 399, 400, 401,
402, 403, 404, 407, 408, 411, 414, 415, 417,
418, 419, 420, 421, 422, 423, 424, 426, 427,
439, 759.
Attended 1860 to 1867 and 1867 to
1873.
Cirencester and South Kensington.

GIBBS, JAMES C., 366
Attended 1874 to 1884.
Worcester.

GIBSON, HENRY, 1137.
Attended?
South Kensington.

GINN, GERTRUDE, 341.
Attended 1879 to 1884.
Bloomsbury and East Herts.

GIRARDOT, MISS, 822.
Attended 1880 to 1883.
Farnham.

GOODYEAR, E., 500.
Attended 1878 to 1884.
Dudley.

GOODYER, HELEN, 998.
Attended 1875 to 1884.
Nottingham.

GOLDSACK, LILIAN, 139.
Attended 1883, 1884.
Lambeth.

GREEN, ALBERTA L., 97.
Attended 1879 to 1883.
Lambeth.

GREY, JANE WILLIS, 1337.
Attended 3 years.
S. Martin's, W.C.

GRIBBLE, HERBERT A., 1441, 1442, 1443, 1444, 1445.
Attended 1862 to 1866, 1866 to 1869.
Plymouth and South Kensington.

GRIMSHAW, HUGH, 1111.
Attended 1879 to 1882.
Macclesfield.

GROOME, ALICE, 131.
Attended 1877 to 1880.
Lambeth and South Kensington.

GULLAND, ELIZABETH, 1334.
Attended 1873 to 1877.
Edinburgh.

GURNER, H. T., 897.
Attended 1882 to 1884.
West London.

HADLEY, H. J., 354.
Attended ?
Worcester.

HADLEY, JAMES, 194, 195, 196.
Attended 1851 to 1862.
Worcester.

HADLEY, LOUIS, 356.
Attended 1881 to 1884.
Worcester.

HADLEY, T., 206.
Attended ?
School ?

HAITÉ, G. C., 527, 1065, 1069, 1258, 1265, 1273, 1276, 1278, 1306, 1311, 1317.
Attended 1873.
Croydon.

HALL, B. A., 780.
Attended ?
Coventry.

HALL, MRS., 437.
Attended ?
Lambeth.

HALL, PHILLIP, 58, 1451.
Attended 1876 to 1882, 1882 to 1884.
Durham and South Kensington.

HALLAM, JESSIE (Mrs. Hubbah), 1002, 1006, 1014.
Attended 1866 to 1878.
Exeter.

HAMMOND, C. M. D., 11.
Attended ?
Lambeth.

HAMMOND, EDWARD, 364, 372, 533, 1251, 1256.
Attended 1881 to 1884.
Lambeth and West London.

HAMMOND, THOMAS W., 958, 972, 973, 990.
Attended 1869 to 1878, 1881 to 1882.
Nottingham.

HANCOCK, ISABEL, 52.
Attended 1869 to 1876.
Bloomsbury.

HANCOCK, W. R. S., 959, 983.
Attended 1870 to 1876.
Nottingham.

HARDGRAVE, C., 536.
Attended 1869 to 1870.
South Kensington

HARDING, WILLIAM, 1003.
Attended?
Nottingham.

HARDING, MORTIMER, 1227.
Attended 1880 to 1884.
Salisbury.

HARDY, WILLIAM, 970, 971, 1036.
Attended 1878 to 1883.
Nottingham.

HODKINSON, H. P., 563, 600.
Attended 1866 to 1867 and 1872 to
1875.
Coventry.

HOGG, HERBERT W., 714.
Attended 1872 to 1881.
Derby.

HOGGINS, JAMES, 1076, 1118, 1120, 1121.
Attended 1875 to 1879, 1881 to 1884.
Coventry and Macclesfiold.

HOLGATE, J., 1214, 1263.
Attended 1866 to 1867.
Halifax.

HOLIDAY, THOS., 710.
Attended 1847 to 1854.
Edinburgh.

HOLLAND, MICHAEL, 960, 961.
Attended 1874 to 1876, 1879 to 1880.
Cork.

HOLLIS, BENJAMIN, 486.
Attended 1873 to 1874.
Dudley.

HOLLIS, ELIZABETH, 137.
Attended 1881 to 1884.
Lambeth.

HOLMES, GEORGE H., 1000.
Attended 1875, 1880 to 1884.
Nottingham.

HOLMES, MARY, 355.
Attended 1869 to 1884.
Great Yarmouth.

HOLT, MISS J. C., 835.
Attended ?
School of Art Wood Carving.

HOMAN, GERTRUDE, 46.
Attended 1880 to 1883.
West London.

HORNE, AGNES, 75.
Attended 1880 to 1883.
Lambeth.

HORSEFIELD, HENRY, 1015.
Attended 1872 to 1879.
Nottingham.

HORSMAN, FRANCIS, 821.
Attended ?
Leeds.

HOWARD, CHARLES T., 28.
Attended 1876 to 1884.
Boston.

HOWITT, MISS A., 839.
Attended 1881 to 1884.
Sheffield.

HUGHES, CATHERINE, 127.
Attended 1882, 1883.
Lambeth.

HUGHES, JOHN, 306, 307.
Attended 1875 to 1880.
Burslem.

HULME, F. EDWARD, 1454.
Attended 1857 to 1863.
South Kensington.

HUMPHRIES, C., 62.
Attended 1874 to 1875.
South Kensington.

HUSSEY, J. S., 1213.
Attended 1870 to 1883.
Kidderminster.

ILLSTON, G. A., 562, 573, 632, 861.
Attended 1851 to 1869, and 1858 to 1876.
Rotherham and Sheffield.

INGALL, J. SPENCE, 1045.
Attended 1874 to 1882.
Barnsley.

IRWIN, ELIZABETH, 1010, 1123.
Attended 1865 to 1876.
Dublin.

IRWIN, or URWIN, MISS M. L., 838.
Attended 1881.
School of Art Wood Carving.

IRWIN, MARCELLA, 1005, 10211, 129,
1208.
Attended 1865 to 1876.
Dublin.

JACKSON, FRANK G., 697, 698.
Attended 1848 to 1852, and 1854 to 1860.
Birmingham.

JACOB, ELLA, 175, 888.
Attended 1879 to 1884.
Salisbury.

JAMES, CHARLOTTE, 1340.
Attended 1860 to 1863.
Bloomsbury.

LAMBERT, GEORGE F., 234, 236, 237, 238, 239, 240, 337, 343, 348.
Attended 1864 to 1866, 1879 to 1882.
St. Martin's, W.C., and Derby.

LAMBERT, G. F., 349, 353
Attended 1874 to 1877.
Worcester.

LANE, JOHN QUILLER, 1115.
Attended 1871 to 1873, 1876 to 1877, 1879 to 1881 at Belfast, and 1873 to 1876 at South Kensington.

LANE, RICHARD, 949.
Attended?
Glasgow.

LANGLEY, LEONARD, 305.
Attended 1874 to 1878.
Burslem.

LARCHER, ULRIQUE A., 69.
Attended 7 years.
Lambeth.

LAWSON, W. A., 1202.
Attended 1870 to 1873.
Glasgow.

LAWSON, J., 575.
Attended 1874 to 1884.
Sheffield.

LEDWARD, RICHARD, A., 384, 385.
Attended 1871 to 1879.
Burslem and South Kensington.

LEE, FRANCIS E., 143.
Attended 1876 to 1880.
Lambeth.

LEE, HARRIETTE E., 108.
Attended 1877 to 1881.
Lambeth.

LEES, GEORGE, 968, 1231.
Attended 1862 to 1870, 1880 to 1884.
Kidderminster.

LEIGHTON, FREDERICK, 58, 340, 351, 387, 863, 1324, 1342.
Attended 1878 to 1883, and 1883 to 1884.
Coalbrookdale and South Kensington.

LEIGHTON, SIR FREDERICK, 1360, 1363.
Attended?
School?

LEISHMAN or LISHMAN, JAMES T., 1126.
Attended 1883.
Bradford.

LETHEREN, CHAS., 583 to 586, 614
Attended 1880 and 1877 to 1879 and 1882 to 1883.
Cheltenham, Christ Church, and St. Mark's.

LETHEREN, WM., (Senior), 559, 567, 629.
Attended 1865 to 1867.
Cheltenham.

LETHEREN, W. H., 571.
Attended 1877 to 1879 and 1880.
Christ Church and Cheltenham.

LEWIS, FLORENCE, 96, 100, 159, 434, 436.
Attended 1876 to 1880.
Lambeth.

LEWIS ISABEL, 68.
Attended 2 years.
Lambeth.

LEWIS, MARY AGNES, 1341.
Attended 1878 to 1883.
Lambeth.

LHUILLIER, V., 1394.
Attended?
School?

LILLIE, B. A., 1311.
Attended 1877.
West London.

LLEWELLYN, S. H., 35.
Attended?
South Kensington.

LLOYD, JULIANNA, 1257.
Attended 1878, 1880 to 1882.
West London.

LLOYD, MARY, 912.
Attended 1880 to 1884.
Dublin.

LOCK, EDWARD, 845.
Attended 1880.
Bath.

LOCK, MARY, C., 7.
Attended 1868 to 1873.
Dorchester.

LONDON, EMILY ALICE, 82.
Attended 1880 to 1884.
Lambeth.

LONG, NATHANIEL, 818.
Attended 1881 to 1884.
Cork.

LONGBOTTOM, SHELDON, 180, 182, 184,
185, 186, 187, 189.
Attended 1871 to 1878.
Darlington.

LONGDEN, H., 630, 631, 854.
Attended 1847 to 1849.
Sheffield.

LOVERING, IDA, MISS, 1401.
Attended 1873 to 1878.
Bloomsbury.

LUNN, RICHARD, 231, 232, 706, 715, 716,
748.
Attended 1857 to 1866, and 1866 to
1868.
Sheffield and South Kensington.

LUPTON, EDITH D., 758.
Attended 1875 to 1884.
Lambeth.

LYNDON, HERBERT, 1457.
Attended 1871 to 1876.
West London.

MACKENZIE, JOHN G., 737, 1018, 1033, 1044.
Attended 1877 to 1879, 1879 to 1881.
Belfast and South Kensington.

MADDOX, T. W., 593 to 597, 625.
Attended 1882 to 1884.
Birmingham.

MALTBY, CAROLINE, 1017.
Attended 1880 to 1883.
Bloomsbury.

MANLEY, ELEANOR, 1336.
Attended 1869 to 1873.
Bloomsbury.

MANNOCH, ALFRED, 1311.
Attended 1873 to 1874.
West London.

MANSELL, MARIANNE, 332, 519, 550, 789,
969, 1029.
Attended 1870 to 1873.
Lambeth.

MARSH, JAMES F., 229, 318, 319, 320, 321,
322.
Attended ?
Burslem and Stoke.

MARSHALL, FRANK, 622.
Attended 1871 to 1882.
Nottingham.

MARSHALL, WM., 718, 719, 949.
Attended 1869 to 1874, and 1862 to
1869.
South Kensington and Sheffield.

MARTIN, WM., 840.
Attended 1868 to 1883.
Edinburgh.

MASON, HERBERT, 603.
Attended 4 years.
Birmingham.

MASSEY, H. G., 2, 4.
Attended ?
South Kensington.

MAYEE, MARY A., 1117.
Attended ?
Dublin.

MAYSTON, J. H., 615.
Attended 1879 to 1882.
Yarmouth.

McARTHUR, BLANCHE, 1456.
Attended 1866 to 1877.
Bloomsbury.

McCORMICK, ARTHUR D., 864, 1327.
Attended 1877 to 1882 and 1882 to 1884.
Belfast and South Kensington.

McCULLOCH, JOHN, 620.
Attended 1877 to 1883.
Belfast.

McDONALD, J., (*See* "Old London," Sec. xxii.)
Attended ?
West London.

McFADDEN, FRANK, 1398.
Attended 1869 to 1873, 1873 to 1875.
Southampton and South Ken-
sington.

McGOWAN, WM., 747, 1031.
Attended 1876 to 1884.
Belfast.

McINROY, JOHN, 57.
Attended 1870 to 1875, 1878 to 1882.
Dundee.

McKENZIE, GEORGE, 754.
Attended 1872 to 1880.
Sheffield.

MEADE, ELIZA, 964.
Attended?
Ursuline Convent, Cork.

MELDRUM, THOMAS, 965.
Attended 1871 to 1881.
Nottingham.

MENZIES, JAMES, 723.
Attended 1870 to 1877.
Edinburgh.

MICKLEWRIGHT, J. FRED., 287.
Attended 1881 to 1884.
Hanley.

MIDGLEY, JOSEPH, 1125.
Attended 1882 to 1883.
Halifax and Bradford.

MILLER, ISABELLA, 126.
Attended 1875 to 1879.
Lambeth.

MILLSON, J. JOHN, 938.
Attended 1872 to 1873.
Manchester.

MILNE, E. P., 859, 860, 865, 867, 869, 892.
Attended 8 years.
Lancaster.

MILWAIN, W. J., 770.
Attended 3 years.
Glasgow.

MILWARD, E. J., 804, 1211.
Attended 1876 to 1878, 1880 to 1883.
Kendal.

MINNS, JAMES, 823.
Attended 8 years.
Norwich.

MITCHELL, EMILY, 331.
Attended 1878 to 1884.
West London.

MONTALBA, HENRIETTA, 794.
Attended 1868 to 1875.
South Kensington.

MONTALBA, HILDA, 795.
Attended 1868 to 1875.
South Kensington.

MONTFORD, HORACE L., 834.
Attended?
Royal Albert Hall, School of
Art Wood Carving.

MOODY, ELLWARD, 819.
Attended 1859 to 1865.
Huddersfield.

MOORCROFT, THOMAS, 216, 225, 227, 262,
267, 269, 275, 277, 288.
Attended 1869 to 1876.
Burslem.

MOORE, AMY GEORGINA, 157.
Attended 1881 to 1884.
Lambeth.

MOORE, E. MARY, 841.
Attended 1879 to 1884.
Southampton.

MOORE, GEORGE, 1344.
Attended?
Manchester.

MOORE, MARIAN, 1027.
Attended 1881 to 1884.
Dublin Metropolitan.

MOORE, MARY, 345, 316, 357.
Attended 1872 to 1881.
Preston.

MOORE, MISS, 1456.
Attended?
Bloomsbury.

MORGAN, ALFRED, 1286, 1292.
Attended 1849 to 1856.
South Kensington.

MORGAN, GEORGE, 932.
Attended 1866 to 1869.
Birmingham and South Ken-
sington.

MORGAN, GEORGE T., 781.
Attended 1860 to 1867, and 1867 to
1870.
Birmingham and South Ken-
sington.

MORGAN, WM. J,. 534.
Attended 1869 to 1870.
South Kensington.

MORRIS, R. J , 433, 944.
Attended 1865 to 1869.
Burslem and South Kensington.

MORRISON, P., 1152, 1160.
Attended 1862 to 1866, 1866 to 1870, 1881 to 1884.
Kidderminster and South Kensington.

MORRISON, W. W., 61.
Attended 1864 to 1865.
South Kensington.

MORROW, A. G., 45.
Attended?
South Kensington.

MORTON, GAVIN, 954.
Attended 1880 to 1884.
Kilmarnock.

MORTON, GEORGE, 16, 38, 39.
Attended?
South Kensington.

MORTON, W. SCOTT, 857, 578, 1206, 1247, 1280.
Attended 1856 to 1859 and 1862.
Glasgow and South Kensington.

MOSES, JOHN, 577.
Attended 1845 to 1848 and 1856 to 1859.
Somerset House and Coalbrookdale.

MOUNTFORD, FREDERICK, 1212, 1246.
Attended 1865 to 1882.
Kidderminster.

MUCKLEY, ANGELO F., 1136, 1338.
Attended 1875 to 1882.
Manchester.

MUCKLEY, W. J., 1136, 1269, 1338, 1344.
Attended 1848 to 1853.
Stourbridge, Birmingham, Somerset House, Marlborough House, and Manchester.

MUCKLEY, WILLIAM R., 1136, 1338.
Attended 1875 to 1882.
Manchester.

MULLIGAN, W. A., 9, 58.
Attended?
South Kensington.

MÜNTZER, FREDERICK, 862, 868, 870, 871.
Attended 1866 to 1868.
South Kensington.

MURRAY, CHARLES O., 1369, 1385, 1395, 1396, 1397.
Attended 1863 to 1869.
Edinburgh.

MURRAY, WILLIAM H., 1225.
Attended 1856 to 1869.
Dublin Metropolitan.

NAYLOR, ALBERT, 255.
Attended 1874 to 1882.
Stoke-on-Trent and Fenton.

NEEDHAM, ROBERT, 740.
Attended 1872 to 1882.
Sheffield.

NEWMAN, W. J., 616.
Attended 1871 to 1881.
South Kensington.

NEWNHAM, JOSEPHINE, 117.
Attended 1875 to 1877.
Lambeth.

NICHOLSON, J. O., 1076, 1120.
Attended 1856 to 1865.
Macclesfield.

NISBET, ETHEL CHAPMAN, 32, 793.
Attended 1879 to 1884.
Bloomsbury.

NOBLE, HENRY, 1262, 1277, 1311.
Attended 1873 to 1878.
West London.

NOBLE, JOHN S., 1394, 1395.
Attended 1870 to 1875,
West London.

NORRIS, FREDERICK C., 901.
Attended 1871 to 1873.
Bath.

NORTHWOOD, CHARLES, 513.
Attended 1880 to 1884.
Stourbridge.

NORTHWOOD, JOHN, 505, 507, 515.
Attended 1854 to 1864.
Stourbridge.

NORTHWOOD, WILLIAM, 510 to 512.
Attended 1871 to 1880.
Stourbridge.

NORTON, GEORGE, 713, 799.
Attended 1857 to 1860.
Sheffield.

NOWELL, A., 1216.
Attended 1878 to 1884.
Salisbury.

NUNN, WALTER, 84.
Attended 1859 to 1862, 1868 to 1869,
1869 to 1871, 1884.
Spitalfields, Charterhouse,
South Kensington, Lambeth.

OAKES, JANE, 215.
Attended 1884.
Burslem.

OGLEBY, J. T., 844.
Attended 1869 to 1872.
Sunderland.

ORCHARD, JOHN, 508, 509.
Attended 1868 to 1875 and 1883 to
1884.
Stourbridge.

OSCROFT, SAMUEL W., 952, 953.
Attended 1847 to 1870.
Nottingham.

OXER, JOHN JAMES, 797A.
Attended 1860 to 1867.
Lambeth.

PAGE, H. MAURICE, 1335.
Attended 4 years.
Croydon.

PAGE, JOHN W. E., 1248, 1255.
Attended 1879 to 1881 and 1881 to
1884.
Lambeth and South Ken-
sington.

PAGE, WM., 831, 838.
Attended 1882 to 1884.
South Kensington.

PALIN, WM. M., 1249.
Attended 1882 to 1884.
South Kensington.

PALMER, ALFRED, 5.
Attended 1876 to 1884.
York.

PARK, ALEXANDER, 1223, 1238.
Attended 1881 to 1884.
Glasgow.

PARK, JOHN H., 1153, 1163, 1229, 1243.
Attended 1870 to 1874.
Coventry.

PARKER, WILLIAM, 135.
Attended 1878 to 1882.
Lambeth.

PARKIN, GEORGE V., 598.
Attended 1858 to 1864.
Dudley.

PARNELL, ANNA, 43.
Attended 1866 to 1872.
Dublin.

PARR, JOSEPH, 310, 311, 312, 313, 314, 315,
317.
Attended 1869 to 1884.
Burslem.

PARRY, EDWARD, 256.
Attended 1881 to 1884.
Stoke-on-Trent and Fenton.

PATEY, WILLIAM, 179.
Attended 1870 to 1876.
Ryde.

PEACE, A. A., 750.
Attended 1875 to 1884.
Sheffield.

PEARCE, ARTHUR E., 8, 18.
Attended 1874 to 1884.
Lambeth.

PEARCE, HENRY, 708.
Attended 3 years.
Hull.

PEARCE, HENRY, 779.
Attended ?
Sheffield.

PEARSE, ALFRED, 1370, 1371, 1374, 1375,
1376.
Attended 1874 to 1876.
West London.

PENSON, F., 58.
Attended 1877 to 1883, 1883 to 1884.
Stoke-on-Trent and South
Kensington.

G

PERKINS, P. S., 610.
  Attended?
      Leicester.

PHILPOT, MISS, 438.
  Attended?
      Lambeth.

PILSBURY, W. H., 254, 432.
  Attended 1882 to 1884.
      Stoke-on-Trent and Fenton.

PLATT, WALTER, 907.
  Attended 1860 to 1864.
      Yarmouth.

PLATTS, JAMES, 230.
  Attended?
      Derby.

PONTIS, J. (*See* "Old London.")
  Attended?
      South Kensington.

POOLE, FREDERICK, 222, 223, 226, 261,
  265, 266, 273, 274.
  Attended 1878 to 1884.
      Burslem.

POOLE, J. O., 58, 328.
  Attended 1882 to 1884.
      South Kensington.

PORTER, FRANK, 1209, 1232, 1236, 1237.
  Attended 1877 to 1884.
      Stourbridge.

POYNTER, EDWARD JOHN, R.A., 1282 to
  1285.
  Attended 1849 or 1850.
      Somerset House.

POYNTON, HENRY, 579 to 581, 619.
  Attended 1858 to 1864 and 1877.
      Coventry.

PRICE, R., 721.
  Attended 1872 to 1873.
      Charterhouse.

PINCHES, RICHARD, 802, 803.
  Attended 1872 to 1879 and 1882 to
  1884.
      Lambeth and Chester.

PURCELL, ROBERT, 525.
  Attended 1882 to 1883.
      Manchester.

RAMSEY, ALLAN, 1311, 1312.
  Attended 3½ years.
      West London.

RANDALL, GEORGE, 1212.
  Attended 1877 to 1884.
      Kidderminster.

RANDALL, J., 1417 to 1429.
  Attended 1857 to 1866.
      South Kensington.

RANDALL, WILLIAM F., 743, 858, 872,
  873, 878, 882 to 885, 887, 893, 902 to 904.
  Attended 1863 to 1867 and 1867 to
  1869.
      Stroud and South Kensing-
      ton.

READ, GEORGE, 874.
  Attended 1864 to 1867.
      Leeds.

REASON, FLORENCE, 10, 13, 51, 1362.
  Attended 1872 to 1881.
      Bloomsbury.

REEKS, MISS M. E., 826, 827, 838.
  Attended 1871, 1877 to 1880, 1881 to
  1884.
      Royal Albert Hall School of
      Wood Carving and South
      Kensington.

RHEAD, GEORGE W., 23, 259.
  Attended 1847 to 1851, 1856 to 1863,
  1869 to 1871, 1878 to 1881.

RHIND, JOHN, 1252.
  Attended 1865 to 1874.
      Edinburgh.

RHIND, WILLIAM B., 917, 918, 922, 923,
  1453.
  Attended 1865 to 1874.
      Edinburgh.

RHODES, JEHOIADA A., 188, 699.
  Attended 1846 to 1848, 1854 to 1857,
  1878.
      Sheffield.

RHODES, R., 58, 929.
  Attended 1878 to 1882, 1882 to 1884.
      Newcastle-under-Lyme and
      South Kensington.

RICHARDSON, W. H., 501, 502.
  Attended 1862 to 1863.
      Stourbridge.

RICKATSON, R. O., 1268, 1305, 1311.
Attended 1872 to 1875.
West London.

RIDER, H., 58.
Attended ?
South Kensington.

RILEY, J. W., 1183 to 1185, 1204.
Attended 1869 to 1883.
Halifax.

RILEY, T., 1359.
Attended ?
South Kensington.

RISELEY, HERBERT, 1107.
Attended 1879 to 1884.
Macclesfield.

ROBERTS, CHAS., 1367.
Attended 1863 to 1868.
Lambeth and South Kensington.

ROBERTS, E. (? EMMA), 435.
Attended ?
Lambeth.

ROBERTS, EMMA, 71.
Attended 1877 to 1879, 1880 to 1884.
Lambeth and City and Guilds Institute.

ROBERTS, FLORENCE C., 101.
Attended 1875 to 1879, 1882 to 1884.
Lambeth.

ROBERTS, W., 299.
Attended ?
Stoke-on-Trent.

ROBERTSON, J. H., 54.
Attended 1876 to 1881.
Dundee.

ROBERTSON, ROBERT G., 879.
Attended 1868 to 1870.
Kilmarnock.

ROBINSON, HERBERT, 1145, 1156, 1161, 1164, 1176.
Attended 1865 to 1870.
Halifax.

ROBINSON, J. T., 1108.
Attended 1880 to 1884.
Macclesfield.

ROGERS, EDITH, 111, 891.
Attended 1879 to 1884.
Lambeth.

ROGERS, E. (EDITH), 333 (See 111).
Attended ?
Lambeth.

ROGERS, ISABEL M., 113.
Attended 1881 to 1884.
Lambeth.

ROGERS, KATE, 141.
Attended 1878 to 1881.
Lambeth.

ROGERS, MARK, 916, 920, 934.
Attended 1878 to 1881.
Lambeth.

ROGERS, MARTHA M., 89, 338, 342, 347.
Attended 1879 to 1884.
Lambeth and Westminster.

ROSSITER, HENRY, 535.
Attended 1869 to 1870.
Frome and South Kensington.

ROUSE, CHARLES, 230.
Attended ?
School ?

ROUSE, JAMES, Sen., 230.
Attended ?
School ?

ROWE, MISS ELEANOR, 826.
Attended 1870 to 1871, and 1883 to 1884.
West London and South Kensington (Secretary, Royal Albert Hall School of Wood Carving).

ROWLEY, JAMES, 908, 1138, 1175, 1199.
Attended 6 years.
West London.

RUDDOCK, SAMUEL, 942, 947.
Attended 1851 to 1856.
Somerset House and Marlborough House.

RUMBLE, E. L., 91.
Attended 1880 to 1882.
Lambeth.

G 2

RUMBOL, ELLEN, 114.
Attended 1880 to 1883.
Lambeth.

RUSSELL, LOUISA, 148.
Attended 1882 to 1884.
Lambeth.

RUXTON, MISS ANNA F., 1101.
Attended 1864 to 1874.
Dublin.

SAVAGE, WM., 523.
Attended 1876 to 1880.
Manchester.

SAVILL, EDITH, 15.
Attended ?
Lambeth.

SCHEIBNER, FRANCIS, 183.
Attended 1873 to 1878.
Stourbridge.

SCHEIBNER, FRANK, 506, 507.
Attended 1873 to 1878. .
Stourbridge.

SCHOOL OF ART WOOD CARVING, ROYAL ALBERT HALL, SOUTH KEN-SINGTON, THE STUDENTS OF THE, 824, 833, 837.

SCOTT, WALTER, 780, 787.
Attended 1864 to 1873.
Coventry.

SEADON, ROBERT, 295, 301.
Attended 1856.
Hanley.

SEDDING, J. W., 566.
Attended ?
School ?

SELOUS, EMILY, 582 (*See* Fennesy, Mrs.).
Bloomsbury.

SEWARD, EDWIN, R.C.A., 724, 1437, 1439, 1455.
Attended 1870 to 1876.
Cardiff.

SEWELL, ARTHUR J., 981.
Attended 1872 to 1888.
Nottingham.

SHELDON, FREDERICK, 1090 to 1094.
Attended 1870 to 1883.
Macclesfield.

SHELDON, GEORGE, 1037.
Attended 1869 to 1873.
Nottingham.

SHELDON, JOHN, 1077 to 1081.
Attended 1865 to 1872.
Macclesfield.

SHELTON, MISS CHARLOTTE, 1114.
Attended 1880 to 1883.
Cheltenham.

SHEPHERD, GEORGE W., 576, 940.
Attended 1871 to 1879, 1880, 1881 to 1882.
Coalbrookdale and South Kensington.

SHERLOCK, J. A., 751.
Attended 1869 to 1872, and 1872 to 1874.
Warrington and South Kensington.

SHETTLEWORTH, LIZZIE, 146.
Attended 1880 to 1881.
Lambeth.

SHORTER, ARTHUR P., 181.
Attended 1882 to 1884.
Middlesborough.

SILVER, ARTHUR, 1266, 1275, 1311.
Attended 1868 to 1872.
Reading.

SIMINDUCE, or SIMMANCE, ELIZA, 67.
Attended 1874 to 1884.
Lambeth.

SIMKIN, J., 1459.
Attended ?
Lambeth and West London.

SIMPSON, WILLIAM, 377.
Attended 1864 to 1867.
South Kensington.

SINGER, EDGAR R., & HERBERT W., 551, 561, 564, 565, 602, 628.
Attended 1871 to 1877.
Frome and South Kensington

SKIDMORE, MISS HARRIETT, 1431 to 1433.
Attended ?
Stourbridge and South Kensington.

SLATER, A., 379.
Attended 1858 to 1862.
Stoke-on-Trent.

SLATER, EMILY, 42.
Attended 1871 to 1884.
Gloucester.

SLOCOMBE, CHARLES P., 732, 733, 1384, 1387, 1389, 1390.
Attended 1847 and onwards.
Spitalfields and Somerset House.

SLOCOMBE, FREDERICK A., 63, 1386, 1388, 1391, 1392.
Attended 1861 to 1867.
South Kensington.

SMALL, ELIZABETH M., 152.
Attended 1876 to 1884.
Lambeth.

SMALL, MISS E., 58.
Attended 1874 to 1882.
Lambeth and South Kensington.

SMALLFIELD, KATHERINE B., 77.
Attended 1879 to 1880, 1883, 1884.
Kingsland and South Kensington.

SMART, THOS. C., 587 to 591.
Attended 1879 to 1884.
Dudley.

SMITH, CARRIE L., 244.
Attended 1874 to 1876, 1878 to 1880, 1882 to 1884.
Selby.

SMITH, ELLEN B., 156.
Attended 1881 to 1884.
Lambeth.

SMITH, F. GEORGE, 528, 1291.
Attended 1861 to 1863.
Lambeth and West London.

SMITH, FRANCIS, 472 to 476.
Attended 1876 to 1879.
Stourbridge.

SMITH, GERTRUDE, 138.
Attended 1859 to 1880.
Lambeth.

SMITH, H. J., 1452.
Attended ?
Nottingham.

SMITH, J. B., 1154, 1157.
Attended 1865 to 1869.
Halifax.

SMITH, J. MOYR, 428, 429, 430, 431, 542, 1379 to 1381, 1400, 1402.
Attended 1857 to 1860, 1869 to 1870.
Glasgow and South Kensington.

SMITH, MISS, 830, 836.
Attended ?
Royal Albert Hall School of Wood Carving, and Leeds.

SMITH, ROBERT, 842.
Attended ?
Inverness.

SMITH, THOS., 365, 744, 889, 1294.
Attended 1876 to 1884.
Coalbrookdale.

SOUTHALL, M., 1459.
Attended ?
Bishopsgate.

SPALL, THOS., 692 to 695, 734.
Attended 1869 to 1873.
Birmingham.

SPARKES, MRS. C. A., 371.
Attended 1859 to 1861, 1861 to 1866.
South Kensington and Lambeth.

SPOONER, WILLIAM J., 976, 982, 1008.
Attended 1878 to 1884.
Nottingham.

STAFFORD, GEORGE, 997.
Attended 1878 to 1883.
Nottingham.

STAPLETON, HARRY, 764A.
Attended 1871 to 1874.
St. Martin's, W.C.

STAYNES, F. J., 1034.
Attended 1879 to 1883.
Nottingham.

STORWER or STORMER, EMILY E., 150.
Attended 1875 to 1879.
Lambeth.

STORY, BLANCHE, 989.
Attended 1866 to 1884.
Nottingham.

STRATTON, AMY, 1242.
Attended 1869 to 1873.
Salisbury.

STUART, LOUISA, 81.
Attended 1883 to 1884.
Lambeth.

STURGEON, KATE, 107.
Attended ?
Lambeth.

SUDDARS, FRANK, 59, 60.
Attended ?
Bradford.

SUTHERS, WM., 1458.
Attended ?
. South Kensington.

SWAYNE, CHARLES, 504, 505.
Attended 1883 to 1884.
Stourbridge.

SYKES, GODFREY (the late), 943, 1355.
Attended 1843 to 1854.
Master of School, 1854 to 1863.
Sheffield.

SYMES, P. H., 909.
Attended 1878 to 1884.
Dublin.

TABOR, G. H., 58.
Attended ?
Lambeth.

TANNAHILL, WM., 1197, 1198.
Attended 1871 to 1878.
Kilmarnock.

TARVER, JANE, 1311.
Attended 1877 to 1879.
Northampton.

TATHAM, A. J., 848, 1272, 1311.
Attended 1878 to 1884.
West London.

TATLER, ALBERT, 208.
Attended 1882.
Burslem.

TAYLERSON, JOHN E., 933.
Attended 1880 to 1884.
Lambeth.

THATCHER, EUPHANIA, 151.
Attended 1878 to 1881.
Lambeth.

THATCHER, W. H., 1212.
Attended 1877 to 1884.
Kidderminster.

THICKETT, ERNEST, 720.
Attended 1874 to 1884.
Sheffield.

THOMAS, JAMES, 406, 756.
Attended 1880 to 1884.
Westminster   Architectural
Museum.

THOMAS, JOHN, 1178, 1182, 1186, 1192, 1195, 1196, 1241.
Attended 1873 to 1883.
Halifax.

THOMAS, T, 1103.
Attended ?
Dublin.

THOMPSON, EMILY G., 540.
Attended 1866 to 1870.
Manchester.

THOMPSON, E. L., 711.
Attended 1875 to 1877.
Sheffield.

THOMPSON, MINNIE G., 128.
Attended 1882 to 1884.
Lambeth.

THOMPSON, MISS SYDNEY, 607.
Attended 1871 to 1873.
Belfast.

THOMPSON, SAMUEL, 592.
Attended 1876, and 1882 to 1884.
Sheffield.

THORPE, STUART, 611, 741, 742.
Attended 1871 to 1874.
Sheffield.

TIDMARSH, HENRY, 745.
Attended 1878 to 1881.
West London.

TINWORTH, GEORGE, 162, 163, 164, 165, 166, 167, 168, 169, 170, 171.
Attended ?
Lambeth.

TITE, G., 805 to 807, 850.
Attended 1870 to 1872.
South Kensington.

TOMLINS, H. J., 58, 624, 633, 1316.
Attended 1872 to 1882, and 1882 to 1884.
Worcester and South Kensington.

TONKS, J. WILLIAM, 790 to 792, 760 to 768, 771.
Attended 1854 to 1863.
Birmingham.

TRAVELL, THOMAS F., 975.
Attended 1875, 1879 to 1880, 1882 to 1884.
Nottingham.

TREGO, JOHN, J., 20, 606, 788.
Attended 1866 to 1870, and 1875 to 1884.
Coventry.

TROWER, MISS CHARLOTTE G., 1020. 1030.
Attended 1882 to 1884.
East Herts.

TUCKER, G. E., 627, 749, 899, 900.
Attended 1874 to 1884.
West London.

TURNER, E. PAGE, 898, 1264, 1281, 1295, 1322.
Attended 1854 to 1863.
Sheffield.

TURNER, WM., 1252.
Attended 1880 to 1883.
Edinburgh.

TURTON, GEORGE F., 980.
Attended 1872.
Nottingham.

TWIGGE, MISS ANNE, 1011, 1035.
Attended 1871 to 1884.
Exeter.

TYZACK, HENRY, 924.
Attended 1870 to 1880.
Sheffield.

VARLEY, EMILY LUCY, 53, 1350.
Attended 1880 to 1884.
Bloomsbury.

WAHAB, MISS H. E., 828, 832.
Attended 1883 to 1884.
Royal Albert Hall School of Wood Carving, and South Kensington.

WAIN, LOUIS, 1361.
Attended 4 years.
West London.

WAKELY, LOUISA, 78.
Attended 1881 to 1884.
Lambeth.

WALKER, ROBERT, 877.
Attended 1875 to 1883.
Edinburgh.

WALTON, C. H., 829.
Attended ?
Reading, and Royal Albert Hall School of Wood Carving.

WALTON, WILLIAM R., 967.
Attended 1872 to 1882.
Nottingham.

WALLIS, GEORGE, 544.
Attended 1841, 1842 Student Exhibition, Somerset House.
1843 Head Master, Spitalfields.
1844, 1845, 1846, Head Master, Manchester.
1851 to 1858, Head Master, Birmingham.
1863 to 1884, Keeper of the Art Collections, South Kensington Museum.

WALLIS, MISS ROSA, 29, 543, 544, 698, 1399, 1434 to 1436.
Attended 1873 to 1874 and 1876 to 1878.
South Kensington.

WARD, GEORGE, 58.
Attended 1874 to 1881.
Devizes and South Kensington.

WARD, JAMES, 58, 1049, 1288, 12:7.
Attended 2 years.
Belfast and South Kensington.

WATERS, LIZZIE, 110.
Attended 1880 to 1882.
Lambeth.

WATERHOUSE, JOSEPH, 1133.
Attended 1850 to 1855.
Manchester.

WATKINS, JOHN, 734, 735, 1356, 1357, 1393.
Attended 1871 to 1872 and 1873 to 1875.
Birmingham and South Kensington.

WATSON, W. P., 24, 31, 34, 1446, 1447, 1448, 1450.
Attended ?
South Kensington.

WATSON, W. S., 895.
Attended ?
South Kensington.

WEATHERSTONE, ALFRED C., 880.
Attended 1879 to 1884.
West London.

WEBB, W. H., 19.
Attended 4 years.
West London.

WEBSTER, AGNES, 17.
Attended ?
South Kensington.

WEBSTER, W. H., 1181.
Attended 1870 to 1874.
Halifax.

WEST, MISS ALICE L., 797, 1343.
Attended 1863 to 1873.
Bloomsbury.

WEST, MAUD ASHLEY, 1339.
Attended 1874 to 1880.
Bloomsbury.

WHEATON, LOUISE, 1019.
Attended 1875 to 1884.
Exeter.

WHITE, W. F., 58.
Attended 1875 to 1879, 1879 to 1884.
Leeds and South Kensington.

WHITEHEAD, A., 930.
Attended ?
South Kensington.

WHITESIDE, H. J., 26.
Attended 1881 to 1884.
Birkenhead.

WILD, J. H., 1082 to 1086.
Attended 1868 to 1872.
Macclesfield.

WILLIAMS, HENRY, 233, 242.
Attended 1882 to 1884.
Coalbrookdale.

WILLIAMSON, J. J., 1403 to 1416.
Attended 1869 to 1871 and 1873.
South Kensington.

WILSON, GEORGE W., 941.
Attended 1883 to 1884.
Westminster.

WILSON, C. E., 613, 626.
Attended 1865 to 1880.
Sheffield.

WILSON, THOS., 522.
Attended 1865 to 1875.
Edinburgh.

WILSON, T. WALTER, 757, 758, 782, 783, 1430.
Attended 1868 to 1873.
South Kensington.

WINBURY, WILLIAM, 1159, 1162.
Attended 1870 to 1880.
Kidderminster.

WINDASS, MRS. M. A. S., 243.
Attended 1881 to 1884.
York.

WINTERBOTTOM, AUSTIN, 736, 905.
Attended 1873 to 1884.
Sheffield.

WISE, W. H., 1353.
Attended ?
School ?

WITTS or WILLS, ROBERT, 56.
Attended ?
Dundee.

WOOD, F., 211.
Attended ?
Burslem.

INDEX to the Exhibits from each School of Art contributing to the Art-Students Exhibition, 1884.

BARNSLEY.
Woven Damask in Linen and Cotton, 2

BARNSTAPLE.
Furniture and Wood Carving, 2

BATH.
Furniture and Wood Carving, 3

BELFAST.
Designs for Furniture, 1
Lace Fabrics, 3
Woven Damasks in Linen and Cotton, 7
Painted Decorations, 2
Designs for Ornamental Metal Work, 2
Designs for Loving Cups, 1

BIRKENHEAD.
Lace Fabrics, 1
School Studies in Stages of Instruction, 2

BIRMINGHAM.
Personal Ornaments, 12
Spade, Silver and Ivory, Enamelled and Parcel Gilt, 1
Gold and Silver Keys, 2
Jewellery, 1
Maces, 1
Seals, 1
Designs for Album Covers, 1
Designs for Stained Glass, 4
Cloisonné Enamels, 4
Champlevé Enamels, 1
Ornamental Metal Work, 14
Designs for Ornamental Work, 1
Silver and Gold Plate, Plated Wares and Electro Deposits, 62
Reduction of Panel in Silver, 1
Figure in Silver, 1
Plaques in Silver, 5
Vase, Silver and Gold, 1

BLOOMSBURY.
Fans, 1
Designs for Fans, 1
Plastic Decorations, 2
Lace Fabrics, 1
Lithographs, Chromo-lithographs, &c., 7
Drawings for Engravings, 1
Studies in Chalk, 1
Designs for Stained Glass, 1
Statuette in Bronze, 1
School Studies in Stages of Instruction, 1

BOSTON.
School Studies in Stages of Instruction, 1

BRADFORD.
School Studies in Stages of Instruction, 2

BRIGHTON.
Furniture and Wood Carving, 1

BROSELEY.
Ceramic Manufactures, 1

BURSLEM.
Ceramic Manufactures, 67

CARDIFF.
Architectural Drawings, 2
Book Binding, 1

CHELTENHAM.
Designs for Silk Fabrics, 1
Ornamental Metal Work, 7
Designs for Ornamental Metal Work, 4

CHESTER.
Furniture and Wood Carving, 1
Wood Mosaics, 1

CIRENCESTER.
Furniture and Wood Carving, 1
Blotting Books, Wooden, Painted, 2
Plastic Decorations, 1
Plaster Model of Shield, 1
Ceramic Manufactures, 16

COALBROOKDALE.
Designs for Furniture, 2
Plastic Decorations, 1
Painted Decorations, 4
Lithographs, Chromo-lithographs, &c., 1
Ornamental Metal Work, 5
Designs for Ornamental Metal Work, 1
Silver and Gold Plate, Plated good, and Electro deposits, 2
Designs for Plated Goods, 1
Ceramic Manufactures, 12
Ceramic Design, 5

CAMBRIDGE.
Wall Papers, 1

CORK.
Furniture and Wood Carving, 1
Lace Fabrics, 4

COVENTRY.
Jewellery. 1, 5
Silk Fabrics, 1
Carpets, 1
Designs for Carpets, 1, 1
Ornamental Metal Work, 1, 7, 1
Designs for Ornamental Metal Work, 1, 1, 2
School Studies in Stages of Instruction, 2

CROYDON.
Silk Fabrics, 2
Painted Decoration, 3
Wall Papers, 5
Lithographs, Chromo-lithographs, &c., 1

DARLINGTON.
Ceramic Manufactures, 3

DERBY.
Designs for Carpets, 1
Ornamental Metal Work, 3
Model for Rose Water Ewer, 1
Model for Plaque, 1
Ceramic Manufactures, 6
Ceramic Designs, 3

DORCHESTER.
School Studies in Stages of Instruction, 1

DOVER.
Lace Fabrics, 3

DUBLIN.
Designs for Inlaid Wood, 4
Lace Fabrics, 8
Woven Damasks in Linen & Cotton, 1
Silk Fabrics, 11
Designs for Silk Fabrics, 5
Designs for Muslins, 12
Designs for Carpets, 1
Designs for Wall Papers, 1
Designs for Diplomas, 1
School Studies in Stages of Instruction, 1
Ceramic Designs, 3

DUDLEY.
Glass, 12
Ornamental Metal Work, 13
Designs for Ornamental Metal Work, 1

DUNDEE.
School Studies in Stages of Instruction, 1

DURHAM.
Carpets, 2
Architectural Drawings, 1

EAST HERTS.
Lace Fabrics, 1, 1
Ceramic Manufactures, 1

EDINBURGH.
Personal Ornaments, 7
Furniture and Wood Carving, 3
Designs for Furniture, 4
Figures in Plaster, 6
Designs for Tapestries, 1
Painted Decorations, 4
Designs for Painted Decorations, 2
Designs for Wall Papers, 2
Lithographs, Chromo-lithographs, &c., 5
Drawings in Black and White, 2
Etchings, 3
Architectural Drawings, 1
Paintings on Glass, 2
Designs for Stained Glass, 4

EDINBURGH—continued.
Stained Glass, 1
Ornamental Metal Work, 1
Silver and Gold Plate, Plated Wares and Electro Deposits, 21
School Studies in Stages of Instruction, 21

EXETER.
Lace Fabrics, 8

FARNHAM.
Furniture and Wood Carving, 1

FEMALE CHROMO-LITHO-GRAPHIC STUDIO, RED LION SQUARE.
Chromo-lithographs, 2

FINSBURY.
Silver Vase
Testimonial in Silver

GLASGOW.
Personal Ornaments, 1
Curtains, 2
Designs for Carpets, 4

GLOUCESTER.
Designs for Fans, 1
Furniture and Wood Carving, 1
Plastic Decorations, 1
Designs for Centre Pieces, 4
School Studies in Stages of Instruction, 2

GREAT YARMOUTH.
Designs for Furniture, 1
Designs for Inlaid Wood, 2
Designs for Muslins, 14
Designs for Glass, 2
Designs for Ornamental Metal Work, 2
Designs for Silver Goods, 1
Designs for Silver Gilt Goods, 1

HALIFAX
Designs for Silk Fabrics, 5
Silk Fabrics, 3
Carpets, 10
Designs for Carpets, 2
Tapestries, 9
Curtains, 2
Designs for Wall Papers, 3
Wall Papers, 2

HANLEY.
Ceramic Manufactures, 10

HASTINGS AND ST. LEONARDS.
Architectural Drawings, 2

HUDDERSFIELD.
Furniture and Wood Carving, 1

INVERNESS.
Furniture and Wood Carving, 1

KENDAL.
Inlaid Wood, 1
Designs for Carpets, 1

SOUTH KENSINGTON.
Personal Ornaments, 2
Jewellery, 1
Designs for Jewellery, 1
Designs for Fans, 2
Furniture and Wood Carving, 5
Parqueterie, 1
Inlaid Wood, 1
Designs for Furniture, 17
Plastic Decorations, 2
Designs for Plastic Decorations, 10
Design for Silk Fabrics, 1
Designs for Printed Fabrics, 1
Carpets, 12
Designs for Carpets, 4
Painted Decorations, 4
Designs for Wall Papers, 1
Designs for Painted Decorations, 5
Designs for Certificates, 1
Title Pages of Books, 1
Ornamental Borders for Title Pages, 1
Engravings on Wood, 2
Drawings in Black and White, 2
Drawings for Engravings, 8
Etchings, 12
Engravings, 1
Pen and Ink Drawings, 1
Painted Photographs of Objects of Decorative Art, 33
Architectural Drawings, 9
Enamels on Metal, 4
Ornamental Metal Work, 36
Designs for Ornamental Metal Work, 9
Designs for Sculpture, 4
Designs for Terra Cotta, 1
Silver and Gold Plate, Plated Ware and Electro Deposits, 8
Model for Casket, 1
Model for Card Tray, 1
Shield, Repoussé Silver, 1
Design for Shield, 1
Design for Gold Casket, 2
School Studies in Stages of Instruction, 46
Ceramic Design, 16
Ceramic Manufactures, 40

SPITALFIELDS.
Silk Fabrics, 15

ST. MARTINS.
Painted Decorations, 1
Wall Papers, 2
Lithographs, Chromo-lithographs, &c., 1
Drawings for Engravings, 2
Drawings in Black and White, 2

STOKE-ON-TRENT.
Ornamental Metal Work, 1
Ceramic Manufactures, 30

STOURBRIDGE.
Printed Fabrics, 1
Designs for Carpets, 4
Glass, 95
Designs for Glass, 1

SUNDERLAND.
Furniture and Wood Carving, 1

TORQUAY.
Plastic Decorations, 1
School Studies in Stages of Instruction, 1
Ceramic Manufactures, 13

WEST LONDON.
Furniture and Wood Carving, 2
Designs for Furniture, 12
Plastic Decorations, 1
Printed Fabrics, 1
Carpets, 1
Tapestries, 1
Designs for Carpets, 1
Painted Decorations, 5
Designs for Painted Decorations, 12
Designs for Wall Papers, 12
Drawings in Black and White, 8
Etchings, 1
Designs for Stained Glass, 15
Stained Glass, 2
Designs for Ornamental Metal Work, 2
Design for Loving Cup, 1
School Studies in Stages of Instruction, 3
Ceramic Design, 4

WESTMINSTER.
Designs for Inlaid Wood, 1
Plastic Decorations, 1
Designs for Tapestries, 2
Designs for Carpets, 2
Painted Wall Decoration, 1
Designs for Ornamental Metal Work, 1

WEYMOUTH.
School Studies in Stages of Instruction, 1

WORCESTER.
Painted Decorations, 1
Designs for Ornamental Metal Work, 7
Ceramic Manufactures, 14
Ceramic Design, 9

YORK.
School Studies in Stages of Instruction, 1
Ceramic Manufactures, 1

YOUNG MEN'S CHRISTIAN INSTITUTE, LONG ACRE.
Ornamental Metal Work, 1

CIRCULAR *SENT TO CONTRIBUTORS WHOSE WORKS, OR SOME PORTION OF THEM, HAD TO BE RETURNED FOR WANT OF SUITABLE SPACE FOR THEIR EXHIBITION.*

SCIENCE AND ART DEPARTMENT
OF THE COMMITTEE OF COUNCIL ON EDUCATION,
SOUTH KENSINGTON.

EXHIBITION TO ILLUSTRATE THE OPERATIONS AND THE INFLUENCE OF SCHOOLS OF ART, 1884.

The response to the invitation to submit works for Exhibition from and through the various Schools of Art has been so general, and the works received have been so numerous, that the limited space placed at the disposal of this Department by the Executive Council of the Health Exhibition has unfortunately prevented the full representation of the objects sent up.

Whilst thanking all concerned for the hearty response to the request made, I am directed to inform you that the works and designs for which space has not been found will be forthwith returned free of cost.

I am,

Your obedient Servant,

J. F. D. DONNELLY,

Colonel R.E., Secretary.

INTERNATIONAL HEALTH EXHIBITION, 1884.

SCIENCE & ART DEPARTMENT OF THE COMMITTEE OF COUNCIL ON EDUCATION, SOUTH KENSINGTON.

EXHIBITION TO ILLUSTRATE THE OPERATIONS AND THE INFLUENCE OF SCHOOLS OF ART.

SCHOOL STUDIES—DRAWINGS, DESIGNS, AND MODELS.

WORKS OF ORNAMENTAL AND DECORATIVE ART PRODUCED FROM DESIGNS BY STUDENTS IN SCHOOLS OF ART.

WORKS OF ORNAMENTAL AND DECORATIVE ART, WOODCUTS, LITHOGRAPHS, AND ETCHINGS DESIGNED OR EXECUTED BY THOSE WHO HAVE BEEN STUDENTS IN SCHOOLS OF ART.

CLASSIFICATION.

Sect. I. School Studies in Stages of Instruction. Designs and Models executed by the Students in the Schools. (*The latter are classed with the Section to which they belong.*)

II. Ceramic Manufactures, Porcelain, Earthenware, Stoneware, Terra-Cotta, &c.

III. Glass—Cut, Engraved, Flashed, &c. Stained and Painted Glass in windows or panels, and designs.

IV. Enamels on Metal. Cloisonné. Champlevé, &c.

V. Ornamental Metal-work.—Bronze, Brass, Iron cast or wrought. Drawings and Photographs of such works as may have been executed.

VI. Silver and Gold Plate, Plated Wares, Electro Deposits, including models for silver and gold work. Drawings and Photographs of such works as may have been executed.

VII. Jewellery and Personal Ornaments.—Gold, Silver, Plated, or in any other suitable materials. Medals and Seals. Fans.

VIII. Furniture and Wood Carving. Inlaid Wood. Parqueterie. Papier Mâché Ware, &c.

IX. Decorative Carvings in Stone or Marble, and Plastic Decorations.

X. Lace.—Point, Pillow, and Machine-made Lace. Drawings and Photographs of such as may have been executed.

XI. Woven Damasks in Linen and Cotton, plain or in colours.

XII. Silks, Ribbons, Trimmings, &c., including Furniture and Dress Fabrics. Embroidery on Silk.

XIII. Mixed Woven Fabrics for Dresses, Shawls, Scarfs, &c.

XIV. Printed Fabrics.

XV. Carpets and Tapestry.—Curtains, Table Covers, &c.

XVI. Painted Decorations, Wall Papers, &c.

XVII. Lithographs, Chromolithographs, &c.

XVIII. Illuminations. Illuminated Addresses. Title Pages of Books. Bookbindings, &c.

XIX. Etchings, Engravings on Wood, and Drawings for Engraving.

XX. Painted Photographs of objects of Decorative Art.

XXI. Architectural Drawings, Designs, and Models of Buildings.

XXII. Miscellaneous. Works not included in any of the above divisions, but yet coming within the object of this Exhibition.

INTERNATIONAL HEALTH EXHIBITION, 8th MAY, 1884.

Private **Owners offering objects designed by Students of Schools of Art of the United Kingdom to the Science and Art Department Exhibition, to illustrate the operations and the influence of Schools of Art.**

HER MOST GRACIOUS MAJESTY THE QUEEN.
Chalk Drawing by Miss Ida Lovering. Queen Square School, Bloomsbury, W.C. "A Girl's Head."
Purchased and lent by Her Majesty the Queen. (From Osborne.)

HIS ROYAL HIGHNESS THE PRINCE OF WALES, K.G.
A Gold Key. Gothic Design. Presented to H.R.H. at Leicester, 1882.
Designed by J. W. Tonks, Birmingham.
Manufactured by Messrs. S. Blanckensee & Son, Birmingham.

HIS ROYAL HIGHNESS THE DUKE OF EDINBURGH, K.G., K.T.
Majolica Ware Dish. "De Morgan Lustre Ware."
Designed by James Gamble, Sheffield School.
Fired by Mr. De Morgan, Chelsea.

HER ROYAL HIGHNESS THE PRINCESS OF WALES.
A Gold Bouquet Holder. Presented at Swansea in 1881.
Designed by J. W. Tonks, Birmingham. School.
Manufactured by Messrs. T. & J. Bragg, Birmingham.
Gold Chatelaine. Presented at Swansea in 1881. Jewelled.
Designed by J. W. Tonks, Birmingham.
Manufactured by Messrs. T. & J. Bragg, Birmingham.
Silver Spade, with ivory handle, enamelled and gilt. Presented at Leicester in 1882.
Designed by J. W. Tonks, Birmingham School.
Manufactured by Messrs. S. Blanckensee and Son, Birmingham.

HER ROYAL AND IMPERIAL HIGHNESS THE DUCHESS OF EDINBURGH.
Study of Flower in Oils. "Azaleas."
Painted by Miss Isabel Hancock, Queen's Square School, Bloomsbury, W C.
Water Colour Drawing. "Head of a Sailor;" from life.
Painted by Miss Florence Reason, Queen's Square School, Bloomsbury, W.C.

HER ROYAL HIGHNESS THE PRINCESS CHRISTIAN.
Lace Dress.
Designed and worked by Mrs. Margaretta Clarke, Queen's Square School, Bloomsbury, W.C.

HER ROYAL HIGHNESS THE DUCHESS OF ALBANY.
Silk Fan. Pearl Mount.
Designed and painted by Mrs. Ethel C. Nisbet, Queen's Square School, Bloomsbury, W.C.

ALISON, GENERAL SIR ARCHIBALD, BART., K.C.B.
Sword of Honour. Presented at Glasgow.
Designed by W. J. Milwain, Glasgow School.
Manufactured by Messrs. G. Edwards & Sons, Glasgow.

ART UNION OF LONDON.
Bronze Statuette "Cimabue."
Designed by Miss Emily Selous (Mrs. Fennesy), Queen's Square School, Bloomsbury.
Executed by C. Delpech.

ASTLEY, SIR JOHN, BART.
Racing Plate. Silver Groups.
Designed by G. A. Carter, Lambeth School.
Manufactured by Messrs. Hunt & Roskell, Bond Street, W.

BAILEY, A. N., ESQ.,
Study of Roses.
Drawn by Miss A. M. Bailey (Mrs. T. Clack), South Kensington Schools.

BRIGHT, THE RIGHT HON. JOHN, M.P.
Silver Key. Gothic style, enamelled. Presented at Birmingham on opening the Cobden Coffee House, 1883.
Designed by J. W. Tonks, Birmingham School.
Manufactured by Messrs. T. & J. Bragg, Birmingham.

H

BRIGHTWYN, Mrs. Stanmore.
Study, "Chrysanthemums." Water Colour.
Drawn by Miss Ethel C. Nisbet, Queen's Square Schools, Bloomsbury, W.C.

FLETCHER, B. E., ESQ., Marlingford Hall, Norwich.
2 Carved Panels; Lime-wood.
Designed and Carved by James Minns, Norwich School.

HAWKSLEY, THOMAS, ESQ., C.E., F.R.S.
Silver Testimonial. Table Centre-piece. Two Dessert Stands. Salver.
Designed by J. Swaffield Brown, Finsbury School.
Manufactured by Messrs. Hunt & Roskell, Bond Street, W.

LAMBERT, MRS. ROWLEY, Hampton Court Palace.
Painted Decoration. Designs for Tapestry Curtains.
Drawn by W. Perry, Dublin Royal Society School.

LOMAX, JOHN, ESQ., Manchester.
Carved Oak Hall Seat.
Designed by T. Finchett, Manchester School.
Manufactured by Messrs. Kendal, Milne, & Co., Manchester.

OFFICERS COMMANDING FIRST BATTALION 4th KING'S OWN, ROYAL LANCASHIRE REGIMENT.
Trophy. The "Magdala." Silver and silver parcel gilt.
Designed by C. P. Slocomb, Spitalfields and Somerset House Schools.
Manufactured by Messrs. Elkington & Co., London and Birmingham.

OWEN, SIR PHILIP CUNLIFFE, K.C.M.G., C.B.
Painted Porcelain Panel, "Music."
Designed and made by R. A. Ledward, Burslem School.
Copper Gilt Flagon, with Cover.
Designed and executed by E. W. Clayton, Sheffield School.
Boudoir Mantel-piece Set, Porcelain Clock Case, Three Light Candlesticks, Two Flower Vases, Two Flower Pots.
Designed by R. Lunn, Sheffield School.
Manufactured by Messrs. McIntyre & Co., Burslem, and the Derby Crown Pottery Co., Derby.

OWEN, LADY CUNLIFFE.
Glass Bowl and Dish. Blue ground, "cut cameo" ornament.
Designed by T. Woodall, Stourbridge.
Manufactured by Messrs. T. Webb & Sons, Stourbridge.

PERKIN, Mrs, T. DIX, Harrow.
Gold Jewellery Set. Collarette, Bracelet and Earrings.
Designed by J. W. Tonks, Birmingham School.
Manufactured by Messrs. T. and J. Bragg, Birmingham.

POLSON, JOHN, ESQ., Paisley.
Silver Gilt Dessert Service.
Designed by Sir Noel Paton, R.S.A.
Modelled by Alexander Crichton, Edinburgh School.
Manufactured by Messrs. Mackay and Cunningham, Edinburgh.

PROPRIETORS OF THE "GRAPHIC" NEWSPAPER, London.
Portrait, "M. de Lesseps." Engraving.
Executed by Walter T. Wilson, South Kensington Schools.

SAMUDA, J. D'AGUILAR, ESQ., M.P.
Silver Testimonial. "King John signing Magna Charta."
Designed by G. A. Carter, Lambeth School.
Manufactured by Messrs. Hunt & Roskell, Bond Street, W.

SAMUEL, STUART, ESQ.
Cabinet, Wrought Iron.
Designed by H. Faulkes, Birmingham School.
Manufactured by A. Newman, Maddox Street, W.

SHEPHERD, R. H., ESQ.,
Time Study. "Daffodils."
Drawn by Miss Ethel Nisbet, Queen's Square School, Bloomsbury, W.C.

THE COUNCIL OF THE SOCIETY OF ANTIQUARIES OF LONDON.
Painted Photographs.
Executed by Miss Rosa Wallis, South Kensington School.

THE FINE ART SOCIETY, New Bond Street.
Etchings.
By Frederick A. Slocomb, South Kensington Schools.

THE MAYOR AND CORPORATION OF ROTHERHAM.
Gold Chain and Badge.
Designed by J. W. Tonks, Birmingham School.
Manufactured by Messrs. T. and J. Bragg, Birmingham.

THE **MAYOR AND CORPORATION**
OF **STOKE-UPON-TRENT.**
Gold Chain and Badge, 1875.
Designed by J. W. Tonks, Birmingham School.
Manufactured by Messrs. T. and J. Bragg, Birmingham.

THE **MAYOR AND CORPORATION**
OF **WEST BROMWICH.**
Gold Chain and Badge. Withdrawn.
Silver Mace.
Designed by J. W. Tonks, Birmingham School.
Manufactured by Messrs. T. and J. Bragg, Birmingham.

**WOLSELEY, GENERAL, THE
RIGHT HON. LORD, G.C.B.,
G.C.M.G.**
Silver Inkstand. Presented 1882.
Designed by G. M. Kertland, South Kensington Schools.
Manufactured by Messrs. R. & S. Garrard, Haymarket, W.

**WALLACE, SIR RICHARD, BART.,
M.P.**
Carved Wood Cabinet; 16th century style.
Designed by W. Allwright, West London School.
Manufactured by Messrs. Holland & Sons, Mount Street, W.

H 2

Index to Names of Students of Schools of Art, and of **Manufacturers**
offering objects to Science and Art Department Exhibition, to illustrate the Operations and the Influence of Schools of Art. **1884.**

ALPHABETICAL LIST.

ABRAHAM, FRANCIS X., West
London School, 1882-84.
  Tiles, in frame.   Sec. II.

ABRAHAM, F. X., South Kensington
Schools, 1883-84. Stoke - on - Trent
School, 1876-82. West London
School, 1883.
  Design. Earthenware Vase. Secs. I., II.

ABRAHAM, LILIAN, Queen Square
School, Bloomsbury, 1872-84.
  Sudy of Foliage.   Sec. I.

ACCRINGTON, THE BOROUGH OF.
  See TONKS, J. W.   Sec. VII.

ACKERMAN & CO., Regent Street,
London.
  See THOMSON, EMILY G.   Sec. XVII.

ADAM, PETER, Kidderminster School,
1868-76. South Kensington, 1876-77.
  (Tomkinson & Adam.)   Carpets.   6
  Rugs.   Sec. XV.

ADAMS, CHARLES JAMES, Leices-
ter School, 1877-84.
  Study.   Sec. I.
  Frieze Decoration.   Sec. XVI.
  (Wylie & Lockhead.) Wall Papers and
    Designs.   Sec. XVI.
  (Carlisle & Clegg.) Wall Papers.

ADAMS, EDWARD F., Kidderminster,
1872-78.
  (Barbour, Anderson, & Co.)   Silk
    Curtain.   Sec. XV.

ADAMS, FRANK E., Macclesfield Em-
broidery School.
  (J. O. Nicholson.) Collective exhibit.
    Silk Fabrics.   Secs. XII., XXII.
  See NICHOLSON, J. O.

ADAMS, FRANK E., Macclesfield
School, 1878-84.
  Design for Silk Hangings.
                               Secs. I., XII.
  Design for Furniture Silk.
                               Secs. I., XII.
  Designs for Wall Papers. Secs. I., XVI.

ADAMS, JAMES, Macclesfield. Coventry, 1845-49. Manchester, 1850.
  (Nicholson, J. O., Macclesfield.) Fabrics.
    Silks.   Sec. XII.

ADAMS, JAMES, Macclesfield Em-
broidery School.
  (J. O. Nicholson.) Collective exhibit.
    Silk Fabrics.   Sec. XII., XXII.
  See NICHOLSON, J. O.

ADAMS, MATILDA S., Lambeth
School, 1873-80.
  (Doulton & Co.) Keramics. Bowl.
                                    Sec. II.

ADAMS, ROBERT H., Allen Street
British Schools (Blackfriars), 1875-84.
  (Glanvill & Co.'s) Linoleum Floor-
    cloth.   See XXII.

ADAMSON, WILLIAM, Dundee
School, 1878-80.
  School Work. Machine Drawing Valves.
                                    Sec. I.

ADDEY, LOUISE, Londonderry
School, 1876-83.
  Door Panels (Personal).   Sec. XVI.
  Lithographs.   Sec. XVII.

ADEY, WILLIAM, Stourbridge School,
1858-65.
  (T. Webb & Sons.) Personal. Glass.
                                    Sec. III.

AGNEW, T., & SONS, London & Manchester.
  See ALCOCK, BEATRICE.   Sec. XXII.

AITKEN, MARGARET, Lambeth
School, 1875-77.
  (Doulton & Co.) Keramics. Vase.
                                    Sec. II.

ALBANY, H.R.H. THE DUCHESS
OF.
  See NISBET, ETHEL. Fan. Sec. XXII.

ARDING, HELEN ALICE, Lambeth School, 1874–78.
(Doulton & Co.) Keramics. Vase.
Sec. II.

ARDING, MARY M., Lambeth School, 1880–83.
(Doulton & Co.) Keramics. Jar.
Sec. II.

ARMITAGE, G. F., Macclesfield Embroidery School.
(J. O. Nicholson.) Collective exhibit.
Silk Fabrics. See XII.
See NICHOLSON, J. O.

ARMITAGE, IBBETSON & CO., Bradford.
See FRY, W. A. Sec. XVII.

ARNOTT, H. D., Great Yarmouth School, 1870–74. 1882–84.
Design. Sideboard. Secs. I., VIII.

ARTHUR, FREDERICK, Motcomb Street, S.W.
See RAMSEY, ALLAN. Secs. I., XVI.

ART UNION OF LONDON.
See SELOUS, MRS. Sec. V.

ARTISTIC STATIONERY CO., Dyers Buildings, Holborn.
Lithographs.
See SIBBITT, S. Sec. XVII.

ASCOTT, JOHN W., Widcombe Institute, Bath, 1881.
(Lock & Co.) Carved Wood Panel.
Sec. VIII.

ASTLEY, SIR JOHN, BART.
Racing Plate. Designed by G. A. Carter, Lambeth School. Sec. VI.
(Lent by Sir John Astley.)

ATKEY, CHARLES J., Nottingham School, 1873–80. 1884.
(M. Jacoby & Co.) Lace. Sec. X.
(T. B. Cutts). 4 Edgings.

ATKIN BROTHERS, Sheffield.
See STANNUS, HUGH. Sec. VI.

AUMONIER, LOUISA, St. Martin's School, W.C., 1860–64.
Designs. Chintz. Secs. XIV., XVI.
(Woollam's) Paperhangings. Sec. XVI.

AUSTIN, A., Derby School, 1879–84.
Metal Work, Models for. Sec. VI.

AYERS, ELLEN M., Great Yarmouth School, 1871–79.
Design. Glass Jug, mounted.
Secs. I., III., VI.

AYLING, ROBERT S., Westminster, 1880–83.
Royal Architectural Museum.
Design for Wrought Iron Gates.
Secs. I., V.

AYRE, MARY JANE, Queen Square School, Bloomsbury, 1882–84.
Studies. Stage 1a, 3b, 5b. Sec. I.

BACUP, THE BOROUGH OF, CORPORATION.
See TONKS, J. W. Sec. VII.

BAILEY, ALICE M., South Kensington Schools.
See CLACK, Mrs. T.

BAILEY, GEORGE, Derby Central School, 1870–81.
Collective Exhibit. Sec. XVIII.
See DERBY CENTRAL SCHOOL.

BAILEY, JOHN T., Newcastle-under-Lyme School, 1882–84.
Two Dessert Plates. Sec. II.
Keramics per Mintons, Voucher Reg. No. 3541, April 9, 1884.

BAILEY, A. N., ESQ.
Study of Roses. Drawn by Mrs. T. Clack, South Kensington Schools.
(Lent by A. N. Bailey, Esq.) Sec. I.

BAILY, ALICE, Dublin Metropolitan School, 1878–84.
Designs. Furniture Damasks. Lace.
Secs. I., X., XII.
Wall Decoration. Sec. XVI.

BAINBRIDGE, LOUISA, Cheltenham School, 1881–84.
Designs. Panels. Silk Hangings.
Secs. I., XII., XVI.

BAIN, LIZZIE, A., Kilmarnock School, 1878–84.
Copy of Oil Painting. Sec. I.

BAIRSTO, WILLIAM, Selby School, 1872–74. 1879–83.
School Work. Sec. I.

BAKER, ANNE, Cork, 1862–76.
Porcelain Tiles. Sec. II.
(Pym Brothers.) Poplins. Sec. XIII.

BAKER, THOMAS, Coventry School, 1864–69.
Studies. Sec. I.
(Rotherham & Sons.) Jewellery. Watchcases. Sec. VII.

BALFOUR, ANDREW, Glasgow School, 1880–84.
Design for a Church. Architecture.
Sec. XXII.

BALL, EDITH H., Lambeth School, 1880–84.
(Doulton & Co.) Keramics. Bowl.
Sec. II.

BALL, SUSAN, Dublin Metropolitan School, 1866–70.
Designs. Sec. I.
(Pym Brothers.) Damasks. Sec. XI.
(Bessborough Co.) Damasks.
Secs. XI., XII.
Lace. Sec. X.

BALLANTINE & SONS, Edinburgh.
See WILSON, THOMAS. Sec. III.

BALMENT, JAMES, Bristol School, 1880-84.
Studies. Anatomical Drawing. Sec. I.

BANGHAM, JOSEPH, Coalbrookdale, 1878-84.
(Maw & Co.) Keramics. Sec. II.

BANGOR, THE CITY OF, CORPORATION.
See TONKS, J. W. Sec. VII.

BANKS, JAMES, Stoke-on-Trent & Fenton School, 1881-84.
Two Flower-holders, 7s. 6d. each.
Sec. II.
Two Dessert Plates Sec. II.
Keramics, per Mintons, Voucher Reg. No. 3511, April 9, 1884.

BANKS, WILLIAM H., Rotherham, 1872-84.
Designs. Silver Work. Metal Work.
Secs. I., V., VI.
Wood Carving. Sec. VIII.

BARBOUR, ANDERSON, & CO., Glasgow.
See BROWN, JOHN. Sec. I..
LAWSON, W. A. Sec. XII.
ADAMS, EDWARD F. Sec. XII.
TANNAHILL, W. Sec. XV.

BARCLAY, FANNY, Dublin Metropolitan School, 1879-84.
Designs. Damasks. Secs. I., XI., XII.

BARDEN, GEORGINA, Dublin Metropolitan School, 1878-84.
Designs. Botanical Analysis. Sec. I.

BARKER, ALICE M., Lambeth School, 1881-84.
(Doulton & Co.) Keramics. Vase.
Sec. II.

BARKER, CLARA S., Lambeth School, 1876-78.
(Doulton & Co.) Keramics. Bottle.
Vase. Sec. II.

BARKER, GEORGE, Kidderminster School, 1870-73.
Technical Design. Carpets. Secs. I., XV.
(Assisted by William Tucker, Head Master.)

BARLOW, FLORENCE E., Lambeth School, 1873-81; & City & Guilds Institute.
(Doulton & Co.) Keramics. Flowerpot. Sec. II.

BARLOW, HANNAH B., Lambeth School, 1868-84, & City & Guilds Institute.
(Doulton & Co.) Keramics. Vase.
Sec. II.

BARLOW, LUCY A., Lambeth School, 1877-79. 1882-84; & City & Guilds Institute.
(Doulton & Co.) Keramics. Flowerpot. Sec. II.
N.B.—Ornament by Lucy A. Barlow; Animals in Panels by Hannah B. Barlow.

BARNARD, BISHOP, & BARNARDS, Norfolk Works, Norwich.
See BINNS, JAMES. Sec. VIII.

BARNFIELD, R. C., Gloucester, 1869-1882.
Illuminations. Sec. XVIII.

BARNEY, EMILY, Dublin Metropolitan School, 1880-84.
Designs. Embroidery, &c. Secs. I., XII.

BARON, WILLIAM, Lambeth, 6 months, & South Kensington Schools, 7 months.
(Doulton & Co.) Keramics. A Pot.
Sec. II.

BARRETT, THOMAS, Macclesfield School, 1879-84.
Design for Silk Hanging. Secs. I., XII.

BARTLETT, FLORENCE, Bristol School, 1878-84.
Studies. Drawings in Sepia from Cast.
Sec. I.

BARTLEY, ALICE, Coalbrookdale School, 1866-84.
(Maw & Co.) Tiles. Sec. II.

BARWELL, SONS, & CO., Birmingham.
See MADDOX, T. W. Sec. V.

BATCHELOR, MARY, Gosport School, 1875-80. 1882-84.
Design. Panels. Secs. I., II., IX.

BATCHELOR, M. H., Derby Central School, 1873-81.
Collective Exhibit. Sec. XVIII.
See DERBY CENTRAL SCHOOL.

BATE, EMILY, Plymouth School, 1877-80.
School Work. Oil Painting from Life.
Sec. I.

BATES, HENRY.
Photograph. A Carved Stone Panel.
Sec. IX.

BATEMAN, W. E., Sheffield, 1878-82.
(Pawson & Brailsford.) Lithographs, &c. Sec. XVII.

BATES, DAVID, & OTHERS, Worcester, 1856-64. 1872.
(Royal Porcelain Works.) Porcelain Jardinière.
Sec. II.

BATH, EMILY BRADFIELD, King's Lynn School, 3 years.
Studies for Wall Papers.   Sec. XVI.

BATH, WILLIAM BRADFIELD, King's Lynn School, 3 years.
Studies for Wall Papers.   Sec. XVI.

BATH, WILLIAM & EMILY, King's Lynn School.
Wall Papers.   Sec. XVI.
See BATH, EMILY B.   Sec. XVI.
    BATH, WILLIAM B.   Sec. XVI.

BATHGATE, GEORGE, Edinburgh, 1875-79.
School Work. Antique.   Sec. I.

BAUMGARTNER, MARY, Yarmouth School, 1879-84.
Studies. Muslins and Playing Cards.
Designs.   Secs. I., IX., XIV., XVII.

BAUMGARTNER, P., Great Yarmouth, 1881-83.
Design. Muslins.   Secs. I., XIV.

BAYLEY, A. W. C., South Kensington School.
Study of Flowers, Water Colour. Sec. I.

BAYNTON, HARRY, Coventry School, 1873-84.
Studies. Stages 3b, 5a, 5b, 8b1, 8b2, 10a, 15a, 22c, 23b, 23c, 23a.   Sec. I.
Designs for Watch Cases.   Sec. VII.

BEACALL, FRANK, Hanley School, 1881-84.
Two Dessert Plates.   Sec. II.
Keramics per Mintons, Voucher Reg. No. 3541, April 9, 1884.

BEAL, Royal Albert Hall, School of Wood Carving, W.
Wood carving. Gothic Panel. (Withdrawn.)   Sec. VIII.

BEATTIE, CHALLEN, Stoke-on-Trent, 1885. Birmingham School, 1859-60.
(Elkington & Co.) Bronze Work.
   Sec. V.
Silver Work.   Sec. VI.
(Tonks, W., & Sons. Pickering, J. W.)
Metal Work.   Sec. V.

BEATTIE, CHALLEN, Birmingham School, 1859-60.
(Elkington & Co.) Silver Cradle Centrepiece and Plate.   Sec. VI.

BEATTIE, H. W. (44 Richmond Gardens, Shepherd's Bush), South Kensington Schools; and Boston, U.S.A., School of Art, 7 months.
Model Design. Wall Tiles. Secs. I., II.

BEAUPRÉ, CHARLES J., West London School, 6 years. South Kensington, 1882-83.
(Liley & Wood.) Studies. Designs.
Furniture, &c.
   Secs. I., VIII., XVI., XVII.
(Furnival, T., & Sons.) Keramics.
Ewer and Basin.   Sec. II.
(Walton, F., & Co.) Decoration.
   Sec. XVI.

BECK, ACIDALIA, Lambeth School, 1881-84.
(Doulton & Co.) Keramics. Vase.
   Sec. II.

BECKHAM, J. T., York School, 1874-84.
Studies.   Sec. I.

BEDFORD, GEORGE, Torquay School.
(S. & A. Dept.) Photograph of Decoration.
Foliage in Plaster. Premiated 1874 by Plasterers' Company.   Sec. IX.
(Watcombe Terra-Cotta Co.) Terra-Cottas, Architectural Details.
   Sec. II., XXI.

BEDFORD, GEORGE, Torquay School, 1866-77.
Decoration. Plaster.   Sec. IX.
(Watcombe Terra-Cotta Co.) Terra-Cotta.
   Sec. II.

BEECH, DANIEL, Stourbridge, 1872-1875.
(Stevens & Williams.) Ornamental Glass.   Sec. III.

BELL, EMILY M., Bristol School, 1876-81.
Study. Oil Painting. Fruit.   Sec. I.

BENNETT, REUBEN, Manchester School, 1869-70.
(Woollams.) Decoration.   Sec. XVI.

BENSON & SON, Ludgate Hill.
Gold and Jewelled Casket.   Sec. VI.
H.I.M. the Emperor of Russia.

BENZIE, JAMES, Kilmarnock School, 1875-79.
School Work.   Sec. I.

BERGIN, ISABELLA C., Dublin Metropolitan School, 1868-81.
Designs. Muslin and Damask. Silk.
   Secs. I., XIII.
Design for Inlaid Border.
   Secs. VIII., XIV.

BERKS, EDWARD, Stoke-upon-Trent School.
(Mintons.) Ornamental Tiles. Sec. II.

BESBOROUGH CO., Newry.
Damasks.
See BALL, SUSAN.   Secs. I., XII.

BEST, GEORGE, Salisbury School, 1880-84.
Designs. Damask, Linen. Secs. I., XI.

BETTS, JESSIE, Weymouth School, 1877-78. 1881-84.
Designs. School Studies. Sec. I.

BILLOWS, EMMA C., West London School, 1876-79. 1880-82.
Study. Sec. I., II.

BILTON, LOUIS, Stoke - on - Trent & Fenton School, 1873-84.
Two Jars, 75s. each. (Bowls.) Sec. II.
Two Vases, 52s. 6d. each. Sec. II.
Two Tiles, 6 + 6, 12s. each. Sec. II.
Two Vases, 18 guineas each. Soc. II.
Two Vases, 15 guineas each. Sec. II.
Keramics per Mintons.

BINDON, GEORGE, Lambeth School.
Study of a Head from Life (Terra Cotta). Sec. II.

BINNS, ALBERT, Worcester School, 1879-82.
Designs. Tea Cups. Secs. I., II.

BIRAM, JANE, Sheffield School, 1858-1884.
Madonna and Child. Wood carving. Sec. VIII.

BIRCHENOUGH, JOHN, & SONS, Macclesfield.
Collective Exhibit.
See SHELDON, J. Sec. XII.
SHELDON, F. Sec. XII.
CARTWRIGHT, A. Sec. XII.
WILD, J. Sec. XII.
DORAN, THOMAS. Sec. XII.
KERR, THOMAS. Sec. XII.

BIRCH, BESSIE, Dublin Metropolitan School, 1872-75.
Designs. Tea Service. Secs. I., II.

BIRCUMSHAW, LOUIS, Nottingham School, 1877-84.
Lace Set. Designs. Secs. I., X., XVI.

BIRKS, EDWARD, Stoke-on-Trent & Fenton School, 1875-84.
One Tile, 6 + 6, 6s. each. Sec. II.
Keramics, per Mintons.

BISHOP, ROBERT H., Nottingham School, 1869.
Designs for Lace Curtains. Secs. I., X.

BLACK, J. J., Manchester School, 1844-51.
(Cowlishaw, Nicol, & Co.) Tapestry. 3 pieces.
Carpets. Secs. XII. & XV.

BLACK, WILLIAM S., Edinburgh School, 1870-79.
(Constable, T. A., & Co.) Ornamental Stationery. Sec. XVII.
Menu Cards. Sec. XVII.
Engravings. Sec. XIX.
(Waterston, G., & Sons.) Chromo-Lithographs. Sec. XVII.

BLAIR, J., Edinburgh, 1865-73.
(Grant, R., & Son.) Personal.
Illuminations. Sec. XVIII.
School Work. Sec. I.

BLANCKENSEE & SON, Birmingham.
Jewellery. Gold Key. Silver Spade.
See TONKS, JOSEPH W. Secs. VI., VII.

BOARDMAN, W., Burslem School, 1884.
(Doulton & Co.) Keramics. Plate. Sec. II.

BODLEY, E. J. D., & CO., Hill & Crown Works, Burslem.
See MICKLEWRIGHT, FREDERICK. Sec. II.
WRIGHT, WILLIAM. Sec. II.
CAPEY, A. J. Sec. II.
CARTWRIGHT, H. Sec. II.
HARTLEY, S. Sec. II.
HOSBAND, H. Sec. II.
MOORCROFT, T. Sec. II.
POOLE, F. Sec. II.

BOGUE, DAVID, London.
Engravings for "Dramatic Notes."
See WILSON, WALTER T. Sec. XIX.

BOOLE, ALICIA, West London School, 1882-84.
Studies. Sec I.

BONCHETTE, MARTIN E., Spitalfields School, 1879-80. Islington, 1875-76. Finsbury Park, 1872-73.
Lamp. Design. Sec. IV.
Panel. Design. Sec. I.

BONE, HERBERT, Lambeth School, 1870-76.
Oil Painting. Study. Sec. I.
Decoration. Sec. XVI.

BONNER, ETHEL, M., Sleaford School, 1879-82.
School Studies. Sec. I.

BONTWOOD, CHARLES, Plymouth School, 1877-80.
School Work. Sec. I.

BOOTH, JAMES, Sheffield School, 1869-81.
Copper Panel. Sec. V.
(Meeson, J.) Silver Work. Sec. VI.
Silver Box. Sec. VI.

BOOTH, JOHN, Macclesfield School, 1877-84.
Design for Embroidered Silk Cover. Sec. XII.

BREADON & SONS, Plymouth.
Lithographs.
See HAWKINS, JOHN.   Sec. XVII.

BREDIN, MARY, Dublin Metropolitan
School, 1863-72.
Designs. Carpets.   Secs. I., XV.

BRETT, FRANCES, Dublin Metro-
politan School, 1869-73.
Wall Papers.   Sec. XVI.
Designs. Damasks. Porcelain.
                  Secs. I., II., XI., XII.

BRETT, MARY, Dublin Metropolitan
School.
(Wedgwood & Sons). Design. Plates.
Keramics.   Sec. II.

BRIDGWATER, H. S., Dudley, 1881-
1884.
Studies. Wrought Ironwork.
                           Secs. I., V.

BRIGGS, JOHN, Edinburgh School,
1874-84.
School Work. Stage 22a.   Sec. I.
Wood Panelling.   Sec. VIII.
Design for Tiles.   Sec. II.

BRIGHT, RIGHT HON. JOHN, M.P.
Silver Key.
See TONKS, J. W.   Sec. VII.

BRIGHTWYN, Mrs., The Grove, Stanmore.
See NISBET, ETHEL CHAPMAN.   Sec. I.

BRINDLEY, CHARLES A., Kidder-
minster, 1873-74. South Kensington,
1874-77.
Carpets.   Sec. XV.
Studies.   Sec. I.
Printed Cretonne and Chintz. Sec. XIV.
Designs.   Sec. I.
Printed Fabrics.   Sec. XIV.

BROAD, WILLIAM, Stoke-on-Trent
and other Schools, 1867-72. Worcester, 1874-76. South Kensington, 1876-
1879.
Architectural Designs.   Sec. XXI.
Wall Decoration.   Sec. XXI.

BROADHEAD, GEORGE, Nottingham School, 1866-70.
(Broadhead, G.) 2 Lace Curtains.
                            Sec. X.

BROADHEAD GEORGE, Players'
Factory, Nottingham.
See BROADHEAD, GEORGE.   Sec. X.

BROAD, JOHN, Lambeth School,
1874-80.
(Doulton & Co.) Dancing Figure, low
relief. Terra Cotta Plaque. Sec. II.
(Doulton Pavilion.)

BROOKE, JOHN, Sheffield School,
1858-76.
Designs. Metalwork. Stoves.
                           Secs. I., V.

BROWN, GERTRUDE L., Great Yarmouth School, 1872-76. 1878-84.
4 Designs. Muslins.   Sec. I., XIV.

BROWN, JOHN, Glasgow School,
1878-1884.
(Barbour, Anderson & Co.) Silk Curtains.   Sec. XV.

BROWN, JOHN, & OTHERS, Glas-
gow School, 1878-84.
School Work. Collective. Premiated
Designs and Studies. Carpets. De-
coration. Renna'ssance Panel.
                  Sec. I., XV., XVI.
See also FLETCHER, JAMES.
        PARK, ALEXANDER.
        FERRIS, RICHARD.

BROWN, JEMIMA E. A., Cirencester
1860-66.
3 Plates.   Sec. II.
Woodcarving. Table. Bookcovers.
                           Sec. VIII.
Carpet.   Sec. XV.
Carved Wood Furniture.   Sec. VIII.

BROWN, T. SWAFFIELD, Finsbury
School, 1855-56.
(Hunt & Roskell). Silver Vases. Sec. VI.
Hawksley Testimonial.   Sec. VI.

BROWN, W. & F., & CO., Chester.
See PINCHES, R.   Sec. VIII.

BROWN, W. KELLOCK, West London School, 1881-84.
Studies. Designs for door furniture, &c.
                           Sec. I., V.

BROWN, WILLIAM L., Salisbury
School, 1879-84.
Design. Silk Hangings, &c.
                           Secs. I., XII.

BROWN, WILMOT, Hanley School,
1882-84.
(Doulton & Co.) Four Vases. Porcelain.   Sec. II.
Assisted by Mr. John Slater.

BROWNHILL POTTERY CO. (THE),
Tunstall.
See FORD, R.   Sec. II.
       HUGHES, J.   Sec. II.
       PARR, JOSHUA   Secs. II., V.
       PARR, JOSEPH.   Sec. II., V.

BROWNING, MARION, Salisbury
School, 1878-83.
Design for Lace Handkerchief.
                           Secs. I., X.

BROWNSWORD, J. J., Derby School, 1876-84.
Damasks.   Carpets.   Sec. XV.

BRUCE, LIZZIE, Perth School, 1880, 1882-84.
Studies.   Sec. I.

BRUCKMAN, F., Munich.   ·
Christmas Cards.
See DUNDAS, JAMES.   Sec. XVII.

BUCKNALE, WILLIAM, Nottingham School, 1874-81.
Designs for Lace Curtains.   Sec. I., X.

BUDD, HENRY A. J., Lambeth School, 1870-73.
Designs. Wallpapers and Carpets.
                             Sec. I.

BUDDEN, ALICE E., Lambeth School, 1878-84.
(Doulton & Co.) Keramics. Flowerpot.   Sec. II.

BULLAS, WALTER, Sheffield, 1882-1884.
(Longdon & Co.) Metal Work. Sec. V.
See FIDLER, F.
     LONGDON, H.

BURFIELD, FRANCES, Hastings & St. Leonards, 1876-81.
School Work. Watercolour. Stage 16.
                             Sec. I.

BURGESS, ROSETTA C., Great Yarmouth School, 1874-84.
Designs. Muslins.   Secs. I. XIV.
Architecture.   Sec. XXI.
Cups and Saucers.   Secs. II.

BURGH, CATHERINE, Cheltenham School, 1875-1884.
Designs. Silks.   Secs. I., XII.

BURLTON, ALICE LOUISA, Lambeth School, 1877-78.
(Doulton & Co.) Keramics. Vase.
                             Sec. II.

BURNETT, THOMAS STUART, Edinburgh School, 1866-76.
Statuettes.   Sec. I. IX.

BURR, GEORGINA D., Lambeth School, 1878-84.
(Doulton & Co.) Keramics. Vase.
                             Sec. II.

BUSH, JOHN G. W., Bath, 1867-69.
Woodcarving. Panel.   Sec. VIII.

BUTLER, CLEHOROW CAROLINE, West London School, 1881-83.
Study. "Hercules."   Sec. I.

BUTLER, FRANK A., Lambeth School, 1874-84.
(Doulton & Co.) Keramics. Vases,
                                 Sec. II.
Doulton Pavilion.   Sec. II.

BUTLER, JAMES, Nottingham School, 1875-83.
Designs for Lace Curtains. Secs. I., X.

BUTTERS, MARY, Lambeth School, 1881-84.
(Doulton & Co.) Keramics. Vase.
                             Sec. II.

BUTTERTON, MARY, Lambeth School, 1874-84.
(Doulton & Co.) Keramics. Amphora.
                                 Sec. II.
Designs for Cambrics.   Sec. I., XIII.
Flower Studies.   Sec. I.
Design. Tiles for Dados. Secs. I., II.

BUXTON, S., Stoke-on-Trent School, 1847-49.
(Minton Hollins.) Keramics. Panel of
Painted Tiles.   Sec. II.
Keramics. Tile Panel.   Sec. II.

CALLOWHILL, CLARENCE, Worcester School.
Keramics. Vase.   Sec. II.
Assisted by CALLOWHILL, JAMES.

CALLOWHILL, JAMES, Worcester.
(Royal Porcelain Works,) Keramics.
Plates, Dessert and other, Vases.
                                 Sec. II.
Design for Panel.   Sec. XVI.

CALLOWHILL, JAMES, & OTHERS, Worcester, 1851-60. 1869.
(Royal Porcelain Works.) Porcelain.
See HADLEY, JAMES.
     BRADLEY, JAMES.
     BATES, DAVID.
     BOTT, JOHN.   Sec. II.
     CALLOWHILL, JAMES.

CALLOWHILL, JAMES CLARENCE, Worcester School, 1878-84.
(Royal Porcelain Works.) Designs.
Keramics.   Secs. I., II.

CALLOWHILL, SIDNEY, Worcester School, 1878-84.
Designs. Keramics. Vases. Plates.
                                 Secs. I., II.
Plaque. Keramic.   Sec. II.
Assisted by CALLOWHILL, JAMES.

CAMBRIDGE SCHOOL OF ART (THE).
(H. W. Ellis.) Wall Papers. Sec. XVI.

CAMERON, HENRY, St. Martin's School, W.C. 2 years.
Designs for Frames.   Secs. I., XXII.

CAMERON, MARY, Dublin Metropolitan School, 1881-84.
Studies. Furniture Damask.
Secs. I., XII.

CAMM, THOMAS W., Birmingham & Sponham Branch Schools, 1855-60.
(Camm, T. W.) Designs for domestic stained glass Windows. Secs. I., III.

CAMM, THOMAS W., Cambridge Street, Birmingham.
Stained Glass Windows. Designs.
Secs. I., III.
(Assisted by Henry Reynolds, Birmingham and South Kensington Schools, and Thomas William Camm, Birmingham School.)

CAMPBELL, ALICE, Lambeth School, 1883-84.
(Doulton & Co.) Keramics. Faience jug. Sec. II.

CAMPBELL, CHARLES, Lambeth School; & SMITH, FREDERICK GEORGE, West London School.
Collective. Designs for Church Decorations and Stained Glass Windows.
Secs. I., III., XVI.

CAMPBELL, CHARLES, Lambeth, 1860-64; & West London Schools, 1866-69.
Designs for stained glass and Decorations. Secs. I., III., XVI., XIX.
Tiles. Sec. II.
See also CAMPBELL, SMITH, & CAMPBELL.

CAMPBELL, DAVID, Halifax, 1880-1884. Glasgow, 1879.
(Ward, J. W. & Co.) Fabrics, Carpets.
Sec. XV.

CAMPBELL, DUNCAN, Glasgow, 1847-52.
(Ward, J. W. & Co.) Fabrics. Sec. XV.

CAMPBELL, SMITH & CAMPBELL, 75 Newman Street, W.
Designs. Sec. I.
See CAMPBELL, CHARLES.
SMITH, FREDERICK GEORGE.
HAMMOND, EDWARD. Sec. III.
OLD LONDON.

CAMPBELL, J. E., Lambeth, and West London School.
See OLD LONDON.

CANDLER, ARTHUR, West London School, 2½ years.
Design. Panel, wood. Secs. I., VIII.

CANE, HERBERT C., West London School, 1½ years.
Design. Mirror frame. Secs. I., V.

CANTON, SUSAN R., Bloomsbury School, 1871-78.
Designs. Plaster Spandril 23e.
Secs. IX.
Spandril, Mudie design. Sec. I.

CANTRELL, JOHN, Kidderminster.
Technical Drawings. Carpet Design.
(Assisted by William Tucker, Head Master.) Sec. XV.

CANTY, LUCY M., Lambeth School, 1883-84.
(Doulton & Co.) Keramics. Flower Vase. Sec. II.

CAPES, MARY, Lambeth School, 1874-84.
(Doulton & Co.) Keramics. Vase.
Sec. II.

CAPES, MAY, Lambeth School, 1878, 1879, 1881.
(Doulton & Co.) Keramics. Vase.
Sec. II.

CAPEY, ARTHUR J., Burslem School, 1879-84.
(Bodley & Co.) Keramic. Dessert Plates. Sec. II.

CARDER, FREDERICK, Stourbridge School, 1879-84.
(Stevens & Williams.) Personal. Glass.
Sec. III.

CAREY & SONS, Nottingham.
Lace Curtains.
See DRAKE, GEORGE E. Sec. X.

CARLISLE & CLEGG, Queen Victoria Street, E.C.
Wall Papers.
See ADAMS, C. J. Sec. XVI.

CARMICHAEL, ALEXANDER, Worcester School, 1877-84.
School Study. Sec. I.

CARNEGIE, IDA F., Dublin Metropolitan School, 1878-84.
Designs. Studies. Sec. I.

CARPENTER, ALFRED, West London School, 1882-84.
Study. Decoration. Sideboard. Mantels.
Secs. I., VIII., XVI.

CARR, JOHN M., Nottingham School, 1876-78.
Designs, Lace Curtains. Secs. I., X.

CARR, MABEL, Cork School, 1880-84.
(Meade, Eliza.) Personal. Lace.
Sec. X.

CARTER, C. J., Kidderminster School, 1873-84.
Technical Designs. Studies. Carpets.
(Assisted by William Tucker, Head Master.) Secs. I., XV.

CARTER, G. A., Lambeth School, 1863-66.
(Hunt & Roskell.) Silver group.
Sec. VI.
(Hunt & Roskell.) Silver group.
Sec. VI.
(Hunt & Roskell.) Silver group.
Sec. VI.
(Lent by Sir John Astley.)
(Hunt & Roskell.) Gold Belt.
Sec. VII.

CARTER, MARY E., Queen Square School, Bloomsbury, 1876-82.
School Study in Sepia. Sec. I.

CARTWRIGHT, ARTHUR, Maccles-field School, 1875-84.
Design for Furniture Silk.
Secs. I., XII.
(Birchenough & Co.) Carpets. Sec. XII.

CARTWRIGHT, HERBERT, Burslem School, 1870-72. 1873-76. 1877-79.
(Bodley & Co.) Keramics. Plates.
Sec. II.

CASH, J. & J., Coventry.
See GREEN, J. S. Sec. XII.

CASTLE, THOMAS C. H., Birkenhead, 1875-82.
Study in monochrome. Horse's Head.
Sec. I.

CATCHPOOL, HERBERT, West London School, 2½ years.
Study. Still Life. Sec. I.

CANTRELL, JOHN, Kidderminster School, 1873-81.
Designs. Carpets. Secs. I., XV.

CHADBOURNE, STEPHEN L., Nottingham School, 1875. 1880-84.
Designs, Wall Papers. Secs. I., XVI.

CHALLIS, MARGARET, Lambeth School, 1875-77.
(Doulton & Co.) Keramics. Vase.
Sec. II.

CHAMBERS, J. H., Halifax, 1874-83.
(Ward, J. W., & Co.) Personal. Carpets.
Sec. XV.

CHAMBERS, MICAH, Durham School, 1854-59.
(Henderson & Co) Carpets. Sec. XV.

CHANCE, JANE, West London School, 1876-84.
Designs. Embroidery. Studies, &c.
Sec. I., XII.

CHANDLER, EMILY, Lambeth School, 1879-84; & City & Guilds Institute.
(Doulton & Co.) Keramics. Flower Pot. Sec. II.

CHAPLIN, WALTER H., Coventry School, 1874-84.
Studies. Sec. I.

CHATTAWAY, HERBERT, Coventry School, 1869-76.
Studies. Iron Screens. Sec. I. V.

CHESTERTON, WALTER, Walsall School of Art, 1875-77.
Design. Metal Work. Sec. V.

CHILDE, ANDREW, Coalbrookdale, 1879-84.
(Maw & Co.) Keramics. Tiles. Sec. II.

CHISHOLM, D., Royal Albert Hall School; South Kensington School, 1869 or 1870.
Wood Carving. Oak Frame, £6 6s.
Sec. VIII.

CHIVERS, CEDRIC, Bath, 1876-77.
Bindings. Sec. XVIII.
Photographs. Sec. XX.

CHRIPPES, WALTER, West London School, 6 years.
Designs. Tapestry, Carpets, Papers.
Secs. I., XV., XVI.

CHRISTIAN, H.R.H. PRINCESS,
A Lace Veil.
See CLARKE, MARGARETTA. Sec. X.

CHURCHER, G. P., South Kensington School, 1859.
(Woollams.) Decorations. Sec. XVI.

CLACK, MRS. T., South Kensington Schools, 1863-65.
Study. Flower Group in water colour.
Sec. I.

CLAPHAM, MARY, West London School.
Designs. Studies. Architecture. Cups and Saucers. Secs. I., II., XXI.

CLULOW, WILLIAM JAMES, Macclesfield School, 1875-83.
Design for Silk Handkerchief.
Secs. I., XII.
Designs for Furniture Silk, Damasks and Hangings. Secs. I., XII.

CLARK, ROBERT, Edinburgh School, 1875-77.
(Morton, W., Scott, & Co.) Tile Painting. Sec. II.

CLARKE, J., Gloucester School, 1861-1872.
Drawings. Sec. I.
Carved stone. Sec. IX.

CLARKE, JAMES, South Kensington School.
Four School Studies. Sec. I.
Study in Chalk, from cast. Sec. I.

CLARKE, MARGARETTA, Queen Square School, Bloomsbury, 1858-62.
(Mrs. Clarke) Lace Veil. Sec. X.
Lent by H.R.H. The Princess Christian.
(WITHDRAWN.)

CLAY, SONS, & TAYLOR, Bread Street Hill, E.C.
See COWARD, W. G. Sec. XIX.

CLAYTON, E. W., Sheffield School, 27 Allen Terrace, Beaufort House, Chelsea.
Electrotype Goods. Sec. VI.
A Flagon. Bouquet Holders.
(Voucher is, Agenda, No. 1539a. 16 April, 1884.)

CLEWS, JOHN, Nottingham School, 1875-82.
Designs, Wall Papers and Lace Curtains. Secs. I., X.

CLISSOLD, C. W., St. Martin's, W.C., 1877. Draycott Street, S.W., 1877, 1879. South Kensington, 1879-82.
Silver Work. Sec. VI.

CLOW, JOHN J., Exeter School, 1879.
Wood Carving. 2 Panels. Sec. VIII.

COALBROOKDALE IRON CO. (THE).
See KERSHAW, J. Sec. V.
MOSES, J. Sec. V.
SHEPHERD, G. W. Sec. V.
MORTON, W. SCOTT. Sec. V.

COATES, WILLIAM, Nottingham School, 1870-78.
(Heymann & Co.) 5 Lace Curtains. Bedcover. Sec. X.

COBELY, WILLIAM H., West London School, 3 years.
Designs. Chalk Study. Sec. I.

COCKRILL, W. B., Great Yarmouth School, 1867-77.
Studies. Ornament. Sec. I.
Design for Inlaid Work. Sec. VIII.

COLE, EDWIN, Shrewsbury, 1873-84.
Decorations. Personal. Sec. XVI.

COLEMAN, EDITH M., Lambeth School, 1881-84.
(Doulton & Co.) Keramics. Vases. Sec. II.

COLLIS, JANE J., Salisbury School, 1874-83.
Designs. Carpet, Muslin, Fabrics, Glass. Secs. I., III., XIII., XV.

COMLEY, JAMES W., Coventry School, 1876-84.
Studies. Sec. I.

CONAN, JEANIE C., Dublin Metropolitan School, 1880-84.
Study. Sec. I.

CONNOLLY, ARTHUR, Stoke-on-Trent & Fenton School, 1882-84.
2 Dessert Plates. Sec. II.
Keramics, per Mintons.

CONNOLLY, WILLIAM, Dublin Metropolitan School, 1881-84.
Study. Sec. I.

CONSTABLE, T. & A., & CO., Edinburgh.
See BLACK, W. S.
Secs. XVII., XIX.
GULLAND, ELIZABETH. Sec. XXII.

CONWAY, JAMES, Hastings & St. Leonards, 1877-83.
School Work. Sec. I.

COOK, EMILY ANNIE, West London School, 1873-78. 1878-82.
School Studies. Sec. I.

COOK, FANNY L., West London School, 4 years.
Study in Oil. Sec. I.

COOK, LUCY E. M., Sheffield School, 1881-84.
Wood Carving. Panel. Sec. VIII.

COOKE, ERNEST O., Nottingham School, 1879-84.
Studies in Oil. Sec. I.

COOPER, WILLIAM, Hastings & St. Leonards School, 1876-84.
Architecture. Sec. XXI.

COPE, J., Stoke-on-Trent. Hanley School, 1869. South Kensington, 1870-71.
(Cope, J.) Keramics. Toilet Service. Slabs inlaid. Slabs for cabinets. Sec. II.
(Cope, J.) Keramics. Enamelled Slabs. Toilet Ware. Spill, paste sur pate. 2 plates. Sec. II.

COPE, J., Cliff Bank, Stoke-on-Trent.
See COPE, J. Sec. II.

COPPING, HAROLD, West London School, 1877-82.
Studies. Sec. I.

CORBITT, W. & CO., Rotherham.
See ILLSTON, G. A. Sec. V.

CORPORATION (THE), West Bromwich.
Gold Chain and Badge of: (Withdrawn.)
Silver Mace of:
See TONKS, JOSEPH W. Secs. VI., VII.

CORPORATION (THE), Stoke-on-Trent.
Gold Chain and Badge of:
See TONKS, JOSEPH W. Sec. VII.

CORPORATION (THE), Rotherham.
Gold Chain and Badge of:
See TONKS, JOSEPH W. Sec. VII.'

CORPORATION (THE), of Bangor, North Wales.
See TONKS, JOSEPH W. Sec. XXII.

CUMMING, J. FORRESTER S., Leicester School, 1881-84.
Design Carpet.　　　　Secs. I., XV.

CUNDALL, FLORENCE J., Bristol School, 1879-84.
Studies.　Botanical; Models in Sepia.
　　　　　　　　　　　Sec. I.

CUNNINGTON, MARY M., Dorchester School, 1870-74.
School Work.　　　　Sec. I.

CURTIS, LILIAN, Lambeth School, 1881-83.
(Doulton & Co.)　Keramics.　Flower Pot.　　　　　　Sec. II.

CUTHBERT, MINNIE, Hastings & St. Leonards, 1879, for 4¾ years.
School Work.　　　　Sec. I.

CUTTS, JOHN, Nottingham School, 1870-72.
(M. Jacoby & Co.)　Lace Curtains.
Nine Edgings.　　　　Sec. X.

CUTTS, THOMAS B., Nottingham.
Lace Edgings.　　　　Sec. X.
See STAYNES, F.

DADD, STEPHEN T., West London School, 1879-82.　1884.
Christmas Cards.　　Sec. XVII.

DALGLEISH, THEODORE J., Coventry School, 1870-74.
Studies.　　　　　　Sec. I.
Designs for Iron Gates, &c.　Sec. V.

DALTON, JOSEPH, Hanley School, 1874-84.
Two Registered Plaques (Painted Views), 63s. each.　　　　Sec. II.
Two Registered Plaques (Painted Views), 80s. each.　　　　Sec. II.
Keramics per Mintons.　Voucher Reg. No. 3541, 9th April, 1884.

DANCEY, H. A., Gloucester School, 1874-81.
Architectural Drawings.　Secs. I., XXI.

DANIELS, GEORGE, Spitalfields School, 1866-79.
Designs.　Metal Work.　Illuminations, &c.　　　　Secs. I., V., XVIII.

D'ARCY, LOUISA, Dublin Metropolitan School, 1878-84.
Studies.　　　　　　Sec. I.

D'ARCY, MARIANNE A., Dublin Metropolitan School, 1878-84.
Studies.　　　　　　Sec. I.

DARTON, WILLIAM, Plymouth School, 1876-84.
School Work.　　　　Sec. I.

DAVENPORT, MESSRS., Longton.
Porcelain and Pottery.
See MARSH, J. F.　　　Sec. II.

DAVEY, ARTHUR JAMES, Torquay School, 1873-84.
(Watcombe Terra Cotta Co.)　Keramic Ware.　Terra Cotta.　Panel.
　　　　　　　　　Secs. II., IX.

DAVIES, MINNIE M., West London School, 2 years.
Studies.　　　　　　Sec. I.

DAVIS, HARRY ALBERT, Dudley School, 1877.
(Webb, T., & Sons.)　Glass Vase.
　　　　　　　　　Sec. III.

DAVIS, HARRY A., Dudley School.
(T. Webb & Sons.)　Glass Ware.
　　　　　　　　　Sec. III.

DAVIS, LOUIS, South Kensington Schools, 1876-84.
Painted Decoration.　Frieze.　Sec. XVI.

DAVIS, LOUISA J., Lambeth School, 1876-78.
(Doulton & Co.)　Keramics.　Jardinière.
　　　　　　　　　Sec. II.

DAVIS, MARY Lambeth School, 3 years.
(Doulton & Co.)　Keramics.　Vase.
　　　　　　　　　Sec. II.

DAVIS, OWEN, West London School, 1862-63.
(Woollam's) Paperhangings.　Sec. XVI.
Decoration.　　　　Sec. XVI.

DAVIS, W. H., Birmingham, 1874-80.
Engine Model.　　　Sec. XXII.

DAVIS, WILLIAM, Cardiff School, 4 years.
(W. Davis & Son.)　Decorations.　Painted.
　　　　　　　　　Sec. XVI.

DAVIS, WILLIAM, Coalbrookdale School, 1879-84.
School Work.　Designs, Tazza, &c.
　　　　　　　　　Secs. I., II.
(Craven, Dunnill, & Co.)　Tiles. Sec. II.

DAVIS, W., & SON, Queen Street, Cardiff.
Painted Decoration.
See DAVIS, WILLIAM.　　Sec. XVI.

DAWE, LAURA, Plymouth School, 1876-82.
School Work.　Studies.　　Sec. I.

I

DAWSON, CHARLES F., The Salt
Schools, Shipley, 1882–84. Bingley,
1877–82.
Decorations.   Sec. XVI.

DAWSON, JAMES E., Macclesfield
School, 1877–82.
Design for Silk Handkerchief.
Secs. I., XII.

DEAN, EDWIN, Stoke-on-Trent &
Fenton School, 1878–80.
Two Bottles, 26s. 6d. each.   Sec. II.
Keramics per Mintons. Voucher Reg.
No. 3541, 9th April, 1884.

DEAN, THOMAS, Hanley School,
1869–81.
Two Tiles, 8 in. by 8 in. 12s. each.
Sec. II.
Keramics per Mintons. Voucher Reg.
No. 3541, 9th April, 1884.

DE LA RUE & CO., Bunhill Row, E.C.
See WEST, ALICE L.   Sec. XVII.
See THOMSON, EMILY G.   Sec. XVII.

DENLEY, MARY, Lambeth School,
1876–84. Westminster (S. Mary's).
(Doulton & Co.) Keramics.   Vases.
Plaques.   Sec. II.
Designs. Carpet, Tiles, China, &c.
Sec. I., II., XV.

DENNIS, ADA, Lambeth School, 1880–
84, and City and Guilds Institute, 1
year.
Design. Wood Inlay.   Sec. I., VIII.
(Doulton & Co.) Keramics. Vase.
Sec. II.

**DEPARTMENT OF SCIENCE &
ART (THE).**
See SCIENCE AND ART DEPARTMENT.
SOUTH KENSINGTON SCHOOLS.

**DERBY CROWN PORCELAIN COM-
PANY**, Derby.
Keramics.   Sec. II.
See LAMBERT, GEORGE F.
LUNN, RICHARD.   Secs. II., VI.

**DERBY CENTRAL SCHOOL OF
ART**, Derby.
Collective Exhibit by Students. Illu-
minated Address.   Sec. XVIII.
See BAILEY, GEORGE.
MARPLES, THOMAS.
TURNER, F. E.
BATCHELOR, M. II.
HOLTZENDORF, COUNT.
JOSEPH, ADA M.
GOODWIN, ADA.
WARD, GEORGE.
HOAG, HERBERT.
WALE, J.

DE SATOR, EDMUND, C.B., Dublin
Metropolitan School, 1856–74.
Study. "Laocoön."   Sec. I.

DEWSBERY, DAVID, Burslem School,
1870–77.
(Doulton & Co.) Vases, Porcelain, and
Sets.   Sec. II.
Assisted by Mr. John Slater.

DEWSBERY, GEORGE, Burslem
School, 1872–77.
(Doulton & Co.) Vases, Porcelain.
Assisted by Mr. John Slater. Sec. II.

DEWSON, THOMAS, Manchester
School, 1854–59.
(Goodall, E., & Co.) Furniture.
Sec. VIII.

DICK, MATTHEW, Kilmarnock
School, 1877–81.
School Work. Machine Drawing.
Sec. I.

DICKIE, JOHN E., Kilmarnock
School, 1869–72.
School Work. Decoration. Secs. I., XVI.

DICKISON, AGNES J., Dover School,
1872–75. 1878–84.
4 Designs. Lace.   Secs. I., X.
Designs. Lace-set.

DICKSON, H. J., & SONS, Kidderminster.
See COTTON, ALFRED.   Sec. XV.

DILWORTH, SAMUEL, Halifax
School, 1875–83.
(Ward, J. W., & Co.) Hangings.
Sec. XV.

DIXON, W. H., Broseley School, 1858–
1860.
(Mintons.) Keramics. Panels. Sec. II.
(Minton, Hollins.) Keramics. 2 Panels
Painted Tiles.   Sec. II.

DIXON, H. J., & SONS, Kidder-
minster.
Carpots.
See KINGMAN, GEO.   Sec. XV.

DOBBS, FREDERICK H., Nottingham
School, 1871–77.
Designs, Lace Curtains.   Secs. I., X.

DODD, C. T., South Kensington Schools,
1879–84.
Design. Clock Case.   Secs. I., V.
Drinking Cup, Silver.
Secs. I., VI.

DONOHUE, THOMAS J., Macclesfield
School, 1878–84.
Design for Furniture. Silk.
Secs. I., XII.
Design for Embroidered Silk Cover.
Secs. I., XII.

DORAN, THOMAS E., Macclesfield
School, 1879-84.
Design for Silk Hanging. Secs. I., XII.
Design for Silk Handkerchief.
Secs. I., XII.
(Birchenough & Co.) Satin Damask
Dress. Silk Handkerchief. Sec. XII.

DORMAN, ANNIE LOUISE, Hastings
and St. Leonards, 1879-84.
School Work. · Sec. I.

DOUGHTY, EDWIN, Nottingham
School, 1867-69.
Designs, Lace Shawl. Secs. I., X.

DOUGLAS, HILDA, Dublin Metro-
politan School, 1879-84.
Designs. Inlaid Border. Secs. I., VIII.
Study. Anatomical. Sec. I.

DOUGLAS, ROBERT S., Dundee
School, 1876-81. 1883-84.
School Work. Engineering Drawing.
Bridge. Secs. I., XXI.

DOULTON & CO., Burslem and Lambeth.
Pavilion. Decorative exhibit of Doulton
ware applied to architecture and orna-
mentation. The details designed by
about 130 Students of Lambeth and
Burslem Schools of Art. Sec. II.

DOULTON & CO., Nile Street, Bur-
slem.
Porcelain Ware, &c. Sec. II.
See ALLEN, ROBERT. Sec. II.
BROWN, WILMOT. Sec. II.
DEWSBERY, DAVID. Sec. II.
DEWSBERY, GEORGE. Sec. II.
ELLIS, SAMUEL. Sec. II.
HANCOCK, FREDERICK. Sec. II.
JOHNSON, WILLIAM. Sec. II.
LANGLEY, LEONARD. Sec. II.
ROBERTS, JOSEPH. Sec. II.
SEADON, ROBERT. Sec. II.
WORTON, JAMES. Sec. II.
WRIGHT, ALBERT. Sec. II.
SLATER, JOHN.
BOARDMAN, W. Sec. II.
BRATT, J. W. Sec. II.
KELSALL, A. R. Sec. II.
LEDWARD, RICHARD A. Sec. II.
OAKES, JANE. Sec. II.
TATLER, ALBERT. Sec. II.
WOOD, FREDERICK. Sec. II.

DOULTON & CO., Lambeth Art Pot-
tery Works, Lambeth, S.
Keramics, &c. Sec. II.
See ADAMS, MATILDA S.
ALLEN, F. J. ·
AITKEN, MARGARET.
ARDING, HELEN, A.
ARDING, MARY M. ·
BALL, EDITH H.
BARKER, CLARA S.

BARKER, ALICE M.
BARLOW, HANNAH B.
BARLOW, LUCY A.
BARLOW, FLORENCE E.
BARON, WILLIAM.
BECK, ACIDALIA.
BOWEN, ELIZA F.
BROAD, JOHN.
BUDDEN, ALICE F.
BUTLER, FRANK A.
BUTTERS, MARY.
BUTTERTON, MARY.
BURR, GEORGINA D.
BURLTON, ALICE L.
CAMPBELL, ALICE.
CANTY, LUCY M.
CAPES, MARY.
CAPES, MAY.
CHALLIS, MARGARET.
CHANDLER, EMILY.
COLEMAN, EDITH M.
CRAWLEY, MINNA.
CRUIKSHANK, JAMES R.
CURTIS, LILIAN.
DAVIS, LOUISA J.
DAVIS, MARY.
DENLEY, MARY.
DENNIS, ADA.
DURTNALL, BEATRICE M.
DURTNALL, JOSEPHINE A.
DURTNALL, LULU EMOGENE.
ECKENSTEIN, ALICE.
EDWARDS, LOUISA E.
ELLIOTT, AMY.
EMERTON, ELIZABETH.
EVANS, BERTHA.
EYRE, J.
FISHER, ELIZABETH.
FORCEY, EMILY.
FRENCH, ELIZABETH.
GANDY, JESSIE.
GATHERCOLE, ELLEN.
GARRETT, NELLIE.
GOLDSACK, LILIAN.
GREEN, ALBERTA.
GROOM, ALICE.
HAREY, SARAH M.
HAUGHTON, LIZZIE.
HAWKSLEY. EMILY.
HAYS, ANNA.
HIERAPATH, ALICE M.
HINCHLIFF, JESSIE.
HOLLIS, ELIZA.
HORNE, AGNES.
HUGHES, CATHERINE M.
KEEN, ROSA.
KING, HENRY JAMES.
LARCHEN, ULRIQUE A.
LEE, FRANCES.
LEE, HARRIET.
LEWIS, FLORENCE.
LEWIS, ISABEL.
LEWIS, MARY AGNES.
LILLEY, ELIZABETH A.
LUPTON, EDITH B.
LONDON, EMILY A.
McLELLAN, J. H.

I 2

MILLER, ISABEL.
MOORE, AMY G.
NETTLEWORTH, LIZZIE.
NEWNHAM, JOSEPHINE.
NUNN, J. W.
PARKER, WILLIAM.
PEARCE, A. E.
ROBERTS, EMMA.
ROBERTS, FLORENCE.
ROGERS, EDITH.
ROGERS, ISABEL.
ROGERS, KATE.
ROGERS, MARTHA M.
RUMBLE, E. L.
RUMBOL, ELLEN.
RUSSELL, LOUIE.
SIMMANCE, ELIZA.
SMALL, ELIZABETH M.
SMALLFIELD, KATHARINE.
SMITH, ELLEN B.
SMITH, GERTRUDE.
STORMER, EMILY EDITH.
STUART, LOUISA.
THATCHER, EUPHEMIA.
THOMPSON, MINNIE.
VARGAS, MISS.
WAKELY, LOUISA.
WATERS, LIZZIE.
YOUATT, BESSIE J.

D'OUSELEY, SOPHIE, Bath School, 1882-83.
School Study.   Sec. I.

DOWLING, RICHARD, Dublin Metropolitan School, 1869-73.
Studies. Architecture.   Secs. I., XXI.

DOWNES, ANNABEL, South Kensington Schools, 1877-84.
Studies from Life.   Sec. I.

DRAKE, GEORGE E., Halifax School, 1865-69.
(D. Walters & Sons). Designs. Silk Fabrics.   Sec. XII.
(Carey & Sons.) 2 Lace Curtains.   Sec. X.
Tapestry.   Sec. XV.
(Scott, Cuthbertson & Co.) Wall Papers.   Sec. XVI.

DUBLIN MUSEUM OF SCIENCE AND ART.
Specimens of Irish Lace.   Sec. X.

DUCK, DANIEL, Kidderminster. 1868-73, Coventry School.
(Harrison, C.; Naylor, T. & A.; Shaw, E., & Co.; Whittall, M., & Co.; Worth, T. B.) Fabrics. Woollen.   Sec. XV.
See also PARK, J. H. Carpets, &c.   Sec. XV.

DUFF & CO., Edinburgh.
Wall Papers.   Sec. XVI.
See HAY, THOMAS W.

DUFFIELD, E., Birmingham School, 1868-84.
(Elkington & Co.) Enamels, Metal.   Sec. IV.

DUFFY, JAMES, Dublin.
See PERRY, WILLIAM.   Sec. XVII.

DUMET, MONS., Paris.
Silk.   Secs. XII., XVI.
See HAY, THOMAS W.

DUNDAS, JAMES, Dundee School, 1855-59. South Kensington, 1859-1864.
(Bruckman, F., Munich; Schipper, J. F., & Co.; Eyre & Spottiswoode; Hildesheimer & Fulkner.) Personal. Christmas Cards.   Sec. XVII.

DUNLOP, MORTON J., Kilmarnock School, 1875-82.
School Work. Wall Papers.   Secs. I., XVI.

DUNTHORNE, R., Vigo Street, Regent Street, W.
Etchings.
See SLOCOMBE, CHARLES P. Sec. XIX.
SLOCOMBE, FREDERICK A. Sec. XIX.

DURTNALL, BEATRICE, Lambeth School, 1875-84.
(Doulton & Co.) Keramics. Vase.   Sec. II.

DURTNALL, JOSEPHINE, Lambeth School, 1882-84.
(Doulton & Co.) Keramics. Vase.   Sec. II.

DURTNALL, LULU I., Lambeth School, 1882-84.
(Doulton & Co.) Keramics. Jug.   Sec. II.

DUTTON, THOMAS, Nottingham School, 1879-81. 1884.
Designs, Lace Fabrics. Curtains.   Secs. I., X.

DYSON, CHARLES H., Macclesfield School, 1880-84.
Design for Silk Handkerchief.   Secs. I., XII.

EASSIE, MRS., Gloucester, 1863-78.
Fan. Illuminations. Dessert Plates.
Designs.   Secs. I., II., VII., XVIII.

EASTLAKE, ELIZABETH, Plymouth School, 1880-84.
School Work.   Sec. I.

EASTWOOD, H., & CO., Netherton.
See THOMAS, JOHN.   Sec. XV.

ECCLESTON, GEORGE, Stoke-on-Trent & Fenton School, 1880-84.
Two Dessert Plates. Sec. II.
Keramics per Mintons. Voucher Reg. No. 3541, 9th April, 1884.

ECKENSTEIN, ALICE, Lambeth School, 1880-84.
(Doulton & Co.) Keramics. Bottle Vase. Sec. II.

EDMUNDSON & SON, R. B., Manchester.
See JENKINSON, THOMAS. Sec. III.
PURCELL, ROBERT. Sec. III.
SAVAGE, WILLIAM. Sec. III.

EDWARDS, CHARLES G., West London School, 3 years.
Design. Wall Papers. Secs. I., XVI.

EDWARDS, ERNEST H., Manchester School, 1882-84.
(Falkner, G., & Sons.) Decoration. Sec. XVIII.

EDWARDS, G., & SONS, Glasgow.
See MILWAIN, W. J. Sec. VI.

EDWARDS, T. G., Sheffield School, 1871-79.
Designs. Staircase. Secs. I., VIII.

EDWARDS, LOUISA, E., Lambeth School, 1876-83.
(Doulton & Co.) Keramics. Vase. Sec. II.

EDINBURGH, HIS ROYAL HIGHNESS THE DUKE OF, K.G., K.T.
Majolica Ware Dish.
See GAMBLE, JAMES. Sec. II.

EDINBURGH, HER ROYAL AND IMPERIAL HIGHNESS THE DUCHESS OF.
Studies of Flowers in Oils.
See HANCOCK, ISABEL. Sec. I.

ELKINGTON & CO., Birmingham & London.
See ALLEN, GEORGE. Sec. VI.
BEATTIE, CHALLEN. Secs. V., VI.
DUFFIELD, E. Sec. IV.
FELLOWS, H. Sec. VI.
HARPER, F. Sec. V.
JACKSON, F. Sec. VI.
SPALL, T. Secs. V., VI.
WATKINS, JOHN. Sec. V.

ELLIOTT, FANNY, Lambeth School, 1875-79.
(Doulton & Co.) Keramics. Vase. Sec. II.

ELLIOTT, JOHN W., Preston School, 1878-81.
School Work. Sec. I.

ELLIOTT, J. W., Manchester School, 1881-83.
School Work. Panel Decoration. Secs. I., XVI.

ELLIS, H., Lambeth School.
Doulton Ware. Doulton Pavilion. Sec. II.

ELLIS, H. W., Cambridge School, 1867-70.
Wall Papers. Sec. XVI.
Wall Papers. (Woollam's.) Sec. XVI.

ELLIS, JOHN, Hanley School.
(S. & A. Dept.) Photograph. Design for a Bracket in Plaster. Decoration. Premiated 1875 by Plasterers' Company. Sec. XVI.

ELLIS, SAMUEL, Hanley School.
(Doulton & Co.) Two Plaques. Landscapes. Porcelain. Sec. II.
Assisted by Mr. John Slater.

ELLIS, T. S., MRS., Gloucester, 1861-66.
Drawings. Sec. I.

ELSWORTHY, HENRI C., Hastings & S. Leonards, 1878-81.
Architecture. Sec. XXI.

ELWOOD, MARION L., Nottingham School, 1876-84.
Designs. Lace Fabrics, Curtains. Secs. I., X.

EMERTON, ELIZABETH, Lambeth School, 1 year and 5 months.
(Doulton & Co.) Keramics. Vase. Sec. II.

EMERY, T. Stoke-on-Trent School.
(Minton, Hollins, and Co.) Keramics. Tiles. Sec. II.

EMERY, ALBERT J., Bristol School, 1878-84.
Study. Chalk Drawing from Antique. Sec. I.

EMMS, JOHN, Yarmouth School. South Kensington Schools, 1865-66.
Study. Tempera Painting from Nature. Sec. I.

ERRINGTON, C., Coventry, 1865-73.
(Rotherham & Sons.) Watch Cases. Sec. VII.

EVANS, BERTHA, Lambeth School, 1877-81. 1884.
(Doulton & Co.) Keramics. Biscuit Box. Sec. II.

EVANS, J. A., Gloucester, 1878-83.
School Work. Design for a Truss. Secs. I., IX.

EVANS, MISS, South Kensington School.
Study in Oil from Life. Sec. I.

FINE ART SOCIETY, 148 New Bond
Street, W.
Etchings. Sec. XIX.
See SLOCOMBE, FREDERICK A.

FINNEY, VIRGINIA L., South Ken-
sington Schools, 1882–83.
Study. Copy of an Oil Painting by
Velasquez. Sec. I.

FINNIGAN, THOMAS, Dublin Metropolitan School, 1870–72.
Studies. Secs. I., XIX.

FISHER, A., Gosport School. (Halifax,
1863–65. 1873–79.)
Tapestry Design. Sec. XV.
Decoration. Sec. XVI.
Architecture. Sec. XXI.

FISHER, ALEXANDER, Torquay
School, 5 years (1879–84).
(Torquay Terra Cotta Works.) Keramics.
Jardinière. Sec. II.
Studies. Sec. I.
Studies from Nature. Sec. I.
Terra Cotta Plaque. Sec. II.
(Torquay Terra Cotta Works.) Terra
Cotta. Sec. II.
Keramics. Terra Cotta. Sec. II.

FISHER, ELIZABETH, Lambeth
School, 1874–77.
(Doulton & Co.) Keramics. Jug.
Sec. II.

FISHER, JOHN, Sheffield, 1875–83.
South Kensington Schools, 7 months.
Designs for Iron Panels. Secs. I., V.
Designs. Metal Work for Grates.
Secs. I., V.
Design for Plaster Panel. Sect. IX.

FITZGERALD, MICHAEL, Dublin
Metropolitan School, 1868–71.
Study. Sec. I.

FLAVELLE, JULIA, Dublin Metropolitan School, 1879–84.
Design. Tiles. Secs. I., II.

FLEMING, J., & CO., Leicester.
Lithographers.
See LEWITT, B. M. Sec. XVII.

FLEMING, W. R., Dundee School,
1874–80.
School Work. Machine Drawing.
Sec. I.

FLETCHER, B. E., Martingford Hall,
Norwich.
Wood Carving. Sec. VIII.
See MINNS, JAMES.

FLETCHER, BENJAMIN J., Coalbrookdale School, 1877–84.
(Maw & Co.) Tiles. Sec. II.

FLETCHER, JAMES, Glasgow School,
1881–84.
Premiated Designs. Secs. I., XV.
Carpets. Sec. XV.
Decoration. Sec. XVI.
Rennaissance Panel. Sec. IX.
See BROWN, JOHN.
PARK, ALEXANDER.
FERRIS, RICHARD.

FLETCHER, JOHN H., Nottingham
School, 1873–84.
Cards, &c. Designs for Book Covers
Secs. I., XVII. XVIII

FLINT, WILLIAM, Devonport School,
1879–84.
Studies. Sec. I.

FOLLIOTT, WILLIAM, Spitalfields
School, 1851–57.
(D. Walters & Sons.) Furniture Silks
and Brocades, 15 pieces. Curtains.
Sec. XII.

FORCEY, EMILY A., Lambeth
School, 1881–84.
(Doulton & Co.) Keramics. Vase.
Sec. II.

FORD, ALFRED, Bath, 1883–84.
Wood Carving. Sec. VIII.

FORD, RICHARD, Burslem School,
1878–81.
(Brownhill Pottery Co.) Keramics. Biscuit Box and Cruet. Vases. Sec. II.

FORD, THOMAS, & CO., Birmingham.
See MADDOX, T. W. Sec. V.

FOSTER, ARTHUR, Nottingham
School, 1874–78.
(Thornley & Clarke.) Lace, 24 pieces.
Sec. X.

FOSTER, FREDERICK, Worcester
School, 1879–84.
Studies. Secs. I., II.

FOSTER, JONATHAN, Halifax, 1877.
Bradford Technical College Schools,
1883.
Designs. Mixed Fabrics. Secs. I., XIII.

FOSTER, WILLIAM, Salisbury School,
1879–84.
Design. School Work. Floor Cloth.
Secs. I., XV.

FOSTER, W. G., Leeds School, 1877–84.
School Work. Freehand Drawings.
Sec. I.
Christmas Cards. Sec. XVII.

FOWLER, WILLIAM THOMAS,
Macclesfield School, 1876–83.
Design for Silk Hanging. Secs. I. XII

FOX, EDWIN, Birmingham School, 1855, & South Kensington School, 1865-66.
Metal Frame.   Sec. V.
Lacquered Brass.
(Attendant South Kensington Museum.)

FRAMPTON, EDWARD, West London School, 1865-68, 82 Buckingham Palace Road, S.W.
(E. Frampton.) Panels of Stained Glass. Subjects: "Romeo and Juliet," "Taming of the Shrew," Renaissance Ornament.   Sec. III.
Cartoons. Designs. Stained Glass.
     Secs. I., III.
Designs for Painted Windows, Domestic and Ecclesiastical.   Secs. I., III.
Designs for Mural Paintings and Mosaic Work.   Secs. I., III., XVI.
Stained Glass. Designs, various.

FRAMPTON, GEORGE J., Lambeth School, 1881-84.
Portrait Bust.   Sec. II.

FREEMAN, THOMAS L., Manchester School, 1874-77.
Silver Ware. Metal Work. Domestic.
     Sec. V., VI.

FREEMAN & COLLIER, Princess Street, Manchester.
Metal Work.
See FREEMAN, THOMAS.   Sec. V.

FRENCH, ELIZABETH, Lambeth School, 1879-82.
(Doulton & Co.) Keramics. Vase.
     Sec. II.

FRENCH, THOMAS, Dublin Metropolitan School, 1878-84.
Study. Bust.   Sec. I.

FRIDAY, JAMES, Coventry School, 1863-75.
Studies. Designs for Watch Cases.
     Sec. I., VII.
(Rotherham & Sons.) Engraved Watch Cases.   Sec. VII.
School Work.   Sec. I.

FIRTH [or FRITH], WILLIAM S., Lambeth School; also at Gloucester and Worcester.
Designs, 2.   Secs. I., IX.
Photographs.   Sec. XXII.

FRITH, HENRY, Gloucester, 1861-1863.
Plaster Casts.   Sec. IX.
Wood Carving.   Sec. VIII.

FROST, JOHN, Coventry School, 1862-1869. 1870-73.
Studies. Design for Watch Cases.
     Sec. I., VII.

FRY & CO., Westmoreland Street, Dublin.
See BOYLE, JAMES.   Secs. XI., I.
KAVANAGH, JOSEPH.   Secs. XI., I.
KILPATRICK, W. J.   Sec. XI.
RUXTON, ANNA F.   Sec. XI.
THOMAS, HENRY F.   Secs., XI., I.
WALSH, EDWARD.   Sec. XI.

FRY, PRISCILLA A., Bristol School, 1866-84.
Studies. Designs for Fans, Tiles, Linoleum, &c.   Secs. I., II., XXII.

FRY, WILLIAM A., The Salt Schools, Shipley, 1880-84.
(Armitage, Ibbotson, & Co.) Lithographs.
     Sec. XVII.

FURNIVAL, THOMAS, & SONS, Colridge, Stafford.
See BEAUPRÉ, C. J.   Sec. II.

GALLOWAY, JAMES, Dundee School, 1877-83.
School Work. Machine Drawing. Sec. I.

GAMBLE, JAMES, Rich Terrace, South Kensington; Sheffield School, 1852-60.
Terra Cotta Decorations from Technical City and Guilds of London College, South Kensington.   Secs. II., XXI.
Three Panels. Achievements of Worshipful Companies — Fishmongers, Armourers and Braziers, Goldsmiths. Manufactured by Messrs. Gibbs & Canning, Tamworth.
Majolica Ware Garden Stool, from Bethnal Green Branch Museum.   Sec. II.
Majolica Ware Dish, lent by H.R.H. the Duke of Edinburgh, K.G., K.T.
     Sec. II.
(S. & A. Dept.) Design for Certificate.
(Lithograph, &c., Mateaux.)
     Sec. XIX.

GAMESON, ETHEL, Plymouth School, 1883-84.
(Brannam, H. C.) Keramics. Sec. II.

GANDY, HERBERT, Lambeth School. Engravings on Wood.   Sec. XIX.

GANDY, JESSIE, Lambeth School, 1881-84.
(Doulton & Co.) Keramics. Vase.
     Sec. II.

GANDY, WALTER, Lambeth School, 1872-73. 1875-77.
Designs. Panel Tiles, Wall Papers.
     Secs. I., II., XVI.

GARBETT, NELLIE, Lambeth School, 1877-80.
(Doulton & Co.) Keramics. Vase.
     Sec. II.

GARBUTT, MATTHEW, West London School, 18 months.
Design. Iron Gates. Secs. I., V.

GARDNER, ANNIE ELIZABETH, Leicester School, 1880-84; Nottingham, 1878-79.
Study. Flowers. Sec. I.

GARDNER, JOHN, Coventry School, 1874-78.
Studies. School Work. Sec. I.

GARDNER, WILLIAM, Sheffield, 1872-75.
(Pawson and Brailsford.) Engraving.
Sec. XIX.

GARLAND, MARY, Gloucester School, 1871-84.
Oil Painting. Sec. I.

GARRARD, R. & S., Haymarket, S.W.
See KERTLAND, GEORGE M. Sec. VI.

GARRINGTON, ARTHUR W., Bristol School, 1880-84.
Study. Shading from Cast. Sec. I.

GATER, J., South Kensington Schools, 1882-84. Newcastle-under-Lyme School, 1878-82.
Design. Silver Vase. Secs. I., VI.
Grill, wrought-iron. Secs. I., V.

GATHERCOLE, ELLEN, Lambeth School, 1882-84.
(Doulton & Co.) Keramics. Vase. Sec. II.

GIBB, WILLIAM O., Edinburgh School, 1858-61.
(Watherston, G., & Sons.) Lithographs. Sec. XVII.

GIBB, WILLIAM, & ANDERSON, ELIZABETH F., Edinburgh School.
(Watherston, G., & Sons.) Lithographs. Sec. XVII.

GIBBONS, FRANCIS, Coalbrookdale, 1881-82. South Kensington, 1879-81. Cirencester, 1869-79.
(Allen, B., Broseley.) Keramics. Platter. Plaques. Sec. II.
(S. & A. Dept.) Photograph. Design for Frieze in Plaster. Decoration. Premiated 1879 by the Plasterers' Company. Secs. IX., XVI.
(S. & A. Dept.) Photograph. Design for part of a Frieze in Plaster. Decoration. Premiated 1876 by the Plasterers' Company. Secs. IX., XVI.

GIBBONS, OWEN, Cirencester School, 1860-67. South Kensington, 1867-73.
(Maw & Co.) Keramics. Sec. II.
Model Design for Shield. Sec. I., VI.
(B. Allen.) Vase. Sec. II.

GIBBS & CANNING, Tamworth.
Terra Cotta.
See GAMBLE, JAMES. Sec. II.

GIBBS, JAMES C., Worcester School, 1874-84.
Design. Encaustic Tiles, &c. Secs. I., II.

GIBSON, EDWARD, Dublin Metropolitan School, 1867-77.
Copies. Figures. Secs. I., VI.

GIBSON, HENRY, South Kensington Schools.
Designs for Cretonnes. Sec. XIV.

GILBERT, HENRY, East Herts, Hertford, 1883-84.
Inlaid Table Tops. Sec. VIII.
Carved Wood Plate. Sec. VIII.
Carved Oak Alms Dish. Sec. VIII.
Inlaid Wood Alms Dish. Sec. VIII.
Inlaid Wood Cabinet. Sec. VIII.

GILLOW & CO., 406 Oxford Street, W.
See NOBLE, HENRY. Sec. XVI.
MORTON, W. SCOTT. Sec. XVI.
HAY, THOMAS W. Sec. XVI.

GINN, GERTRUDE M., Bloomsbury, Queen's Square School, 1879-84, and now at East Herts School.
Design. Sec. I.
Tiles. Sec. VIII.
Cups & Saucers. Sec. II.

GIRADOT, LUCY S., Farnham, 1880-1883.
Wood Carvings. Sec. VIII.

GLANVILL, G., & CO., Crown Works, Blackfriars.
See ADAMS, ROBERT II. Sec. XXII.

GLASGOW SCHOOL (SIMMONDS, T. C., Master). Voucher Reg. No. 4882. (No names given).
School Work. Sec. I.

GLASSBY, ROBERT, Sheffield.
Stone Carving. Sec. IX.

GOLDSACK, LILIAN, Lambeth School, 1883-84.
(Doulton & Co.) Keramics. Vase. Sec. II.

GOOCH, ANNIE G. S., Bristol School, 1881-84.
School Work. Drawings from Casts. Sec. I.

GOODALL, E., & CO., Manchester.
See DEWSON, THOMAS. Sec. VIII.
FIGGINS, ELIZABETH. Sec. XVIII.

GOODFELLOW, ANNIE, Dorchester School, 1880-84.
School Work. Sec. I.

GOODWIN, ADA, Derby Central School, 1875–81.
Collective Exhibit. Sec. XVIII.
See DERBY CENTRAL SCHOOL.

GOODYEAR, E., Dudley School, 1878–1884.
(Webb, T., & Sons.) Glass. Sec. III.

GOODYER, MARY HELEN, Nottingham School, 1875–84.
Designs. Lace Curtains. Secs. I., X.

GRAHAM, DELIA, Dublin Metropolitan School, 1881–84.
Study. Flowers. Sec. I.

GRANDISON, WILLIAM BAIRD, Perth School, 1884.
(Shields, Perth.) Damask Fabrics. Sec. XI.
Design. Cotton Hangings. Sec. XIV.

GRANT, MARIA LOUISA, Queen Square School, Bloomsbury, 1881–84.
Perspective Study. Sec. I.

GRANT, R., & SONS, 107 Princes Street, Edinburgh.
See BLAIR, JOHN. Sec. XVIII.
TAYLOR, MARGARET. Sec. XVIII.

GRAYSON, W., West London School, 1869–72.
Studies. Cupid and Psyche. Sec. I.

GREEN, ALBERTA L., Lambeth School, 1879–83.
(Doulton & Co.) Keramics. Vase. Sec. II.

GREEN, J. S., Coventry School, 1850–1852. 1860–63.
(Cash, J. and J.) Fabrics. Silk. Sec. XII.

GREEN, W., & SONS, Kidderminster.
See MORRISON, P. Sec. XV.

GREGORY, THOMSON, & CO., Kilmarnock.
See THOMSON, JOHN. Sec. XV.
See TANNAHILL, W. Sec. XV.

GREY, JANE WILLIS, St. Martin's School, 3 years.
(Hildesheimer and Falkner.) Christmas Cards. Sec. XVII.

GRIBBLE, HERBERT A., South Kensington, 1866–69 ; & Plymouth Schools, 1862–66, 10 Sydney Street, Fulham Road, S.W.
Architecture. Four Drawings of the new Roman Catholic Church, The Oratory, Brompton. Design for a Roman Catholic Cathedral. Sec. XXI.

GRIGGS, W., Elm House, Hanover Street, Peckham, London, S.E.
Chromo-lithographs.
See VARLEY, EMILY L. Sec. XVII.
YOUNG, LILIAN. Sec. XVII.

GRIMSHAW, HUGH, Macclesfield School, 1879–82.
2 Designs for Silk Handkerchief. Secs. I., XII.

GROOME, ALICE, Lambeth School, 1877–80 ; & South Kensington.
(Doulton & Co) Keramics. Jug. Sec. II.

GRUBB, ALEXANDER G., Dundee School, 1868–72. 1875–81.
School Work. Architecture. Secs. I., XXI.

GUEST, Agnes Winifrede, Queen Square School, Bloomsbury, 1881–83.
Study from Nature. Sec. I.

GULLAND, ELIZABETH, Edinburgh School, 1873–77.
School Work. Study of Head. Sec. I.
Book Covers, &c. Sec. XVI.
(Constable, T. A., & Co.) Ornamental Stationery. Sec. XXII.

GUMMER, OAKLEY, Salisbury School, 1873–75.
School Studies. Secs. I., II.

GURNER, H. THORNTON, West London School, 1882–84.
Designs. Decoration and Furniture. Secs. I., VIII., XVI.

HADDON, ARTHUR F., Dublin Metropolitan School, 1882–83.
Study. "Ajax." Sec. I.

HADFIELD, JOHN JAMES, Macclesfield School, 1879–84.
Design for Silk Hanging. Secs. I., XII.

HADLEY, HOWARD, Worcester School, 1879–84.
Designs. Panels, Plates, &c. Keramics. Secs. I., II.

HADLEY, JAMES (& OTHERS), Worcester, 1851–62.
(Royal Porcelain Works.) Porcelain. Sec. II.

HADLEY, LOUIS, Worcester School, 1881–84.
Designs. Vases. Sec. I.

HAGUE, T., & CO., Sheffield.
See THOMSON, SAMUEL. Sec. V.

HAITÉ, GEORGE C., Croydon, 1873. (Cowlishaw, Nicol, & Co.) Satin Damask.
Sec. XII.
(Woollams) Paperhangings. Sec. XVI.
Wall Paper. Stained Glass, Decorations, Illuminations. Engravings.
Secs. III., XVI., XVIII., XIX.

HALIDAY, THOMAS, Edinburgh School.
See HOLIDAY, THOMAS. Sec. VI.

HALL, MARY, West London School, 1881-84.
Studies. Sec. I.

HALL, MRS., Lambeth School.
(Doulton & Co.) Decorative Tiles. "Lilies." Sec. II.

HALL, THOMAS, JUNR., Edinburgh School, 1871-74.
(Woollams) Paperhangings. Sec. XVI.

HALL, P., South Kensington Schools, 1882-84. Durham School, 1876-82.
Design. Inlaid Table Top, wood.
Secs. I., VIII.
Clock Case. Sec. VI.
Architectural Drawing. Sec. XXI.

HALLAM, JESSIE (MRS. HUBBAH), Exeter School, 1866-78.
Lace, Designs for. Secs. I., X.
See HUBBAH, MRS.

HALLAM, RICHARD, Newcastle, 1881-84.
Floorcloth. Sec. XIV.

HALLORAN, HARRIETT, Plymouth School, 1883-84.
(Brannam, H. C.) Keramics. Sec. II.

HAM, ADA, Queen Square School, Bloomsbury, 1877-84.
Study from the flat. Sec. I.

HAMEL & WRIGHT, Nottingham.
See JENNINGS ARTHUR. Sec. X.

HAMILTON, CRICHTON, & CO., Edinburgh.
Design. Silver Work. Salver.
See MENZIES, JAMES.

HAMILTON, HILL, & CO., Linen Hall Street, Belfast.
Damasks. Sec. XI.
See MACKENZIE, J. G.

HAMMOND, EDWARD, West London School, 1881-84.
Studies and Designs, various.
Secs. I., II., III., XVI.

HAMMOND, EDWARD, West London School, 1881-84.
(Campbell, Smith, and Campbell.) Designs for Glass Windows. Sec. III.

HAMMOND, ELI, Stourbridge School, 1883-84.
(Stevens & Williams.) Personal. Glass. Sec. III.

HAMMOND, C. M. D., Lambeth School.
Chalk Studies. "Heads." Sec. I.

HAMMOND, MARIA THEKLA, Queen Square School, Bloomsbury, 1881-84.
Study. Sciography. Stage E. 1. Sec. I.

HAMMOND, THOMAS W., Nottingham School, 1869-78. 1881-82.
Three Designs, Lace Curtains and Shawl.
Sec. I.
Two Designs, Lace Curtains. Sec. X.
(M. Jacoby & Co.) Lace curtains, machine made. Sec. X.

HANCOCK, FREDERICK, Burslem School, 1879.
(Doulton & Co.) Table Sets, Porcelain. Assisted by Mr. John Slater. Sec. II.

HANCOCK, ISABEL, Queen Square School, Bloomsbury, 1869-76.
Study, flowers, in oils Sec. I.
(Lent by the Duchess of Edinburgh.)

HANCOCK, W. R. S., Nottingham School, 1870-76.
Designs. Lace Curtains. Secs. I., X.
(M. Jacoby & Co.) Lace Curtains, Machine made. Sec. X.

HANLON, HARETTA, Dublin Metropolitan School, 1869-74.
Studies. Carpets. Metal Work, &c.
Secs. I., V., XI., XV.

HARDGRAVE, C., York School, and South Kensington Schools, 1869-70.
Design for Stained Glass Window.
Secs. I., III.

HARDING, MORTIMER, Salisbury School, 1880-84.
Designs. Carpets. Lace. Damasks. Iron Gates. Secs. I., V., X., XI., XV.

HARDY, WILLIAM, Nottingham School, 1878-83.
Two Designs. Lace Curtains.
Secs. I., X.
Design, Lace Set. Sec. X.

HARE, GEORGE., Limerick School, 1875-77. South Kensington, 1877-1884.
School Study from Life. Sec. I.

HAREY, SARAH M., Lambeth School, 1878-81.
(Doulton & Co.) Keramics. Vase.
Sec. II.

HARMAN, ALBERT, Hastings & St Leonards, 1882-84.
Architecture. Sec. XXI.

HARPER, FREDERICK, Birmingham School, 1879-82.
(Elkington & Co.) Silver and Electro Metal Work. Sec. VI.

HARRIS, GEORGE, Kidderminster School, 1882-84.
Designs. Carpets, Technical Designs for. (Assisted by William Tucker, Head Master.) Secs. I., XV.

HARRIS, HENRY C., Cardiff School, 1866-75.
Architectural Designs. Sec. XXI.

HARRISON, C., Stourport.
See PARK, J. H., Kidderminster.
Sec. XV.
DUCK, D., Kidderminster. Sec. XV.

HARRISON, JOSEPH, Nottingham School, 1867-69.
Designs. Silk. Secs. I., XII.
Designs. Chintzes. Secs. I., XII.

HARSMAN, FRANCIS, Leeds School, 1870-74.
Designs. Decorations. Secs. I., XVI.
Screen. Sec. VIII.

HART, HARRY, The Salt Schools, Shipley, 1882-84.
(Bradford Art Needlework Society.)
Tapestries. Sec. XV.

HARTLEY, STEPHEN, Burslem School, 1882-84.
(Bodley & Co.) Keramics. Sec. II.
Coffee and Tea Pot. Biscuit Box.

HARTSHORN, JAMES E., Coalbrook-dale School, 1859.
(Allen, B., Broseley.) Keramic Enamels.
Sec. II.

HARVEY, HENRY, South Kensington School, 1876-79.
Model Design for an Alms Dish.
Secs. I., VI.
(*Premiated by Goldsmiths' Company,* 1880.)

HARVEY, J. K., Kidderminster, and Somerset House School, London.
(Morton & Sons.) Personal. Carpets.
Sec. XV.

HAUGHTON, LIZZIE, Lambeth School, 1877-80.
(Doulton & Co.) Keramics. Vase, Impasto ware. Sec. II.

HAWARD, JAMES AUGUSTUS, Northgate, Darlington.
See HAWARD, SIDNEY. Sec. VIII.

HAWARD, SIDNEY, South Kensington School, 1875.
(J. A. Haward.) Cabinet. Sec. VIII.

HAWKINS, JOHN, Plymouth School, 1876-81.
(St. Louis, America) Lithographs. Executed for W. Spence Bate, F.R.S.
(Breadon & Sons, Plymouth).
Sec. XVII.

HAWKSLEY, EMILY, Lambeth School, 1879-84.
(Doulton & Co.) Keramics. Vase.
Sec. II.

HAWTHORNE, RICHARD, York, 1883-84.
Stained Glass. St. George and Dragon.
Sec. III.

HAY, THOMAS WALLACE, Edinburgh School, 1857-59.
(Gillow & Co.) Panels and Frieze, Decoration. Sec. XVI.
(Cowlishaw, Nicol, & Co.)} Silk Damask.
(Dumet, M., Paris.) } Sec. XII.
(Duff & Co.) } Wall Papers.
(Gillow & Co.) } Sec. XVI.
(Woollams) } Wall Papers.
(Dumet, Paris)} Sec. XVI.

HAYS, ANNA, Lambeth, 1 year; & St. Martin's Schools, 3 months.
(Doulton & Co.) Keramics. Tobacco Jar. Sec. II.

HAYES, ELLEN, Cork, Ursuline Convent Industrial School.
(Meade, Eliza.) 2 Designs and 3 Specimens ; Irish Crochet. Sec. X.

HAYLEY, JANET M. B., West London School, 1879-84.
Studies. Oil Colour Group. Sec. I.

HEALD, FRANCIS, Nottingham School, 1869-71.
Designs. Lace Curtains. Secs. I., X.

HEARE, GERTRUDE.
See ELLIS, MRS. T. S. Sec. I.

HEATH, ERNEST D., West London School, 1880-84.
Studies. Chalk Study. Sec. I.

HEATH, MARGARET A., Gloucester, 1877-83.
School Work. Architecture.
Secs. I., X.

HEISE, EMILY S., Birkenhead, 1877-1881 ; Tranmere, 1881-84.
Designs. Lace. Flounces. Secs. I., X.
Studies. Sec. I.

HELBRONNER, R., Oxford Street, W.
See ROWLEY, J. Sec. XII.

HENDERSON & CO., Durham.
See CHAMBERS, MICAH. Sec. XV.

HENDERSON, JAMES, Dundee
School, 1876–81.
School Work. Engineering Drawing.
Tunnel 23A. Sec. I.

HENK, JOHN, Stoke-on-Trent and
Fenton School, 1863–74.
Flower Holder (Stand), £11. Sec. II.
Japanese Boat, £6. 6s. Sec. II.
Vase, 37s. 6d. Sec. II.
Two Cupids and Shells, 26s. 6d. each.
Sec. II.
One Majolica Jardinière, £8 14. Sec. II.
Keramics per Minton's Reg. Voucher, No.
3541, 9 April, 1884.

HENN, MARION RYDER, Queen
Square School, Bloomsbury, 1880–84.
Design. Oil Cloth. Secs. I., XXII.

HENNEY, G. F., South Kensington
Schools, 1883-84. Birmingham
School, 1879–83.
Designs. Various. Sec. I.
Vase in Earthenware. Secs. I., II.
Terra Cotta Column. Secs. I., II.
Grill, wrought-iron. Secs. I., V.
Gates, wrought-iron. Secs. I., V.
Electric Light Pendant. Secs. I., V.

HENTON, GEORGE M., Leicester
School, 1872–84.
Landscapes. Sec. I.
Designs. Secs. I., II.

HEPBURN, ISABELLA, West London
School, 1870–72.
Studies. Botanical. Sec. I.

HEPBURN, MARY, West London
School, 1873–77.
Studies. Botanical. Sec. I.

HER MAJESTY THE QUEEN.
Chalk Drawing. Head from Life. Lent
by Her Majesty.
See LOVERING, IDA. Sec. I.

HER ROYAL HIGHNESS THE
PRINCESS OF WALES.
Jewelled Bouquet Holder.
Jewelled Chatelaine.
Silver Spade, ivory-mounted handle.
See TONKS, JOSEPH W. Secs. VI., VII.

HERON, JAMES, Edinburgh School,
1861-65. 1872–76.
School Work. Design. Chimney Mantel.
Secs. I., VIII.

HEWITT, A. E., South Kensington
Schools, 1883 - 84. Birmingham
School, 1871–83.
Design. Clock Case. Secs. I., V.

HEWITT, J. P., Stoke-on-Trent School,
1872–73.
(Mintons) Keramics. Panel. Sec. II.
(Minton Hollins) Keramics. Tile Panel.
Sec. II.
Tile Panel. Sec. II.
Keramics. Panel of Tiles. Sec. II.

HEYMANN & ALEXANDER, Not-
tingham.
See COATES WILLIAM. Sec. X
JONES, LOUIS. Sec. X.
OSCROFT, SAMUEL. Sec. X.

HERAPATH, ALICE M., Lambeth
School, 1880–84.
(Doulton & Co.) Keramics. Vase.
Sec. II.

HIGHET, KATE, Kilmarnock School,
1881–84.
School Work. Landscape. Oil. Sec. I.

HILDESHEIMER & FAULKNER,
Jewin Street, E.C.
See DUNDAS, JAMES. Sec. XVII.
GREY, JANE W. Sec. XVII.
PAGE, HALL. Sec. XVII.
PAGE, H. M. Sec. XVII.

HILDESHEIMER & FAULKNER,
Jewin Street, E.C.
See MANLY, ELEANOR. Sec. XVII.
MUCKLEY, W. J. } Collective,
MUCKLEY, W. R. } Sec. XVII.
MUCKLEY, A. FAIRFAX }

HILL, E., Sheffield School, 1852–60.
Silver Work. Sec. VI

HILL, GEORGE L., Bristol School,
1879–84.
School Work. Drawing from Antique.
Sec. I.

HILL, HENRY, Boston School, 1865–
1875.
Designs. Porcelain. Sec. I., II.

HILL, JAMES, Stourbridge, 1864–81.
(Stevens & Williams.) Glass. Sec. III.
3 Designs. Lace. Sec. X.

HILL, MARGARET M., Cork, 1860–73.
Porcelain Tiles. Panel. Sec. II.

HILL, WILLIAM, Stourbridge School,
1868–69.
(Webb & Sons.) Glass Ware. Sec. III.

HILLS, MARY ANN, West London
School, 1876–84.
Studies. Funs. Secs. I., VII.

HINCHCLIFFE, JAMES E., Coventry
School, 1880–84.
Studies. Sec. I.

HOLMES, RHODA CARLETON, Queen Square School, Bloomsbury, 1874-78.
Study. Head in Chalk. Sec. I.

HOLT, MISS J. C., Royal Albert Hall School.
Wood Carving. Sec. VIII.

HOLTZENDORF, COUNT, Derby Central School, 1876-81.
Collective Exhibit. Sec. XVIII.
See DERBY CENTRAL SCHOOL.

HOMAN, GERTRUDE, West London School, 1880-83.
Studies. Group in Oil. Monochrome.
Sec. I.

HOOD, HENRY, Nottingham School, 1859-75.
Design, Lace Shawl. Secs. I., X.
(Zuber & Co.) Wall Papers. ? Design.
Sec. XVI.

HORNE, AGNES, Lambeth School, 1880-83.
(Doulton & Co.) Keramics. Bowl.
Sec. II.

HORSFIELD, HENRY, Nottingham School, 1872-79.
Design, Lace Shawl. Secs. I., X.

HORSMAN, FRANCIS, Leeds School.
Four-fold Wood Screen. Painted Tapestry. Sec. VIII.
(Made by himself.)

HOSBAND, HENRY, Burslem School, 1874-84.
(Bodley & Co.) Keramics. Sec. II.

HOSKYN, MARY, West London School, 1876-78.
Studies. Ornament. Sec. I.

HOUSEHAM, J., Sleaford School, 1876-77.
Study. Botanical Outline. Sec. I.

HOW, ALICE, Dorchester School, 1875-84.
School Work. Flowers. Still Life.
Sec. I.

HOWARD, CHARLES T., Boston School, 1876-84.
Studies, water-colour. Sec. I.

HOWARD & SONS, Newman Street, London, W.C.
See RANDALL, W. F. Sec. VIII.

HOWELL, WILLIAM, Cardiff School, 1880-84.
(Owen, Daniel, & Co.) Chromolithos.
Sec. XVII.

HOWITT, AGNES, Sheffield School, 1881-84.
Carved Wood Box. Sec. VIII.

HOYLE, THOMAS, & SONS, Manchester.
Printed Cotton Fabrics.
See WATERHOUSE, JOSEPH. Sec. XIV.

H.R.H. THE DUKE OF EDINBURGH, K.G. K.I.
Majolica Ware Dish.
See GAMBLE, JAMES. Sec. II.

HUBBAH, MRS., Exeter School, 1866-1878.
Design. Lace, Honiton. Secs. I., X.

HUDDERSFIELD TECHNICAL SCHOOL AND MECHANICS' INSTITUTE.
See MOODY, EDWARD. Sec. VIII.

HUGHES, KATHARINE M., Lambeth School, 1882-83.
(Doulton & Co.) Keramics. Vase.
Sec. II.

HUGHES, HELEN, Dublin Metropolitan School, 1880-84.
Designs. Tiles. Secs. I., II.

HUGHES, ELLEN, Ursuline Convent, Cork.
Irish Crochet. 2 designs, 3 Specimens.
Sec. X.

HUGHES, JOHN, Dublin Metropolitan School, 1876-84.
Studies. Casts. Sec. I.

HUGHES, JOHN, Burslem, 1875-80.
(Brownhill Pottery Co.) Keramics.
Tea Set and Tray Mounts of Silver.
Salad Bowl. Sec. II.

HULME, F. EDWARD, South Kensington School, 1857-63.
16 Books. Guides to Art. Sec. XXII.

HUMPHRIES, C., South Kensington Schools, 1874-75.
Study. Tempera Painting, from Nature.
Sec. I.

HUNT & ROSKELL, New Bond Street, London.
Silver Ornamental Table Plate.
See CARTER, G. A. Secs. V., VI.
BROWN, T. SWAFFIELD. Sec. VI.
CRACKNELL, ELLEN K.
Secs. I., III., VI.

HUNTER, DAVID, Kilmarnock School, 1879-84.
School Work. Outline, &c. Sec. I.

HUNTER, JAMES B., Edinburgh
School, 1872-73. 1876-84.
Scliool Work. Still Life. Water-colour.
Sec. I.

HUNTSMAN, ALICE M.,West London
School, 1874-82. 1883-84.
Studies. Ornament.   Sec. I.

HUNTSMAN, FLORENCE S., West
London School, 1874-84.
Studies.   Sec. I.

HUSSEY, J. S., Kidderminster School,
1870-1883.
Designs. Carpets.   Secs. I., XV.

HUTH, FREDERICK, Edinburgh
School, 1877-83.
Lithographs.   Sec. XVII.

HUTTON, J. S. P., Sleaford School,
1876-80.
Drawing. Horseradish.   Sec. I.

HYDES, ROBERT, Sheffield, 1875-78.
(Pawson & Brailsford) Etchings, &c.
Sec. XIX.

HYTCHE, KEZIA, West London
School, 1878-84.
Study.   Sec. I.

ILLSTON, G. A., Rotherham, 1858-76.
(Corbitt, W., & Co.) Metal Work.
Sec. V.

ILLSTON, G., Sheffield School, 1851-
1869.
Design. Furniture. Metal Work.
Secs. I., V., VIII.

INCHBOLD, EDWARD S., West London School, 1882-84.
Studies.   Sec. I.

INGALL, J. S., Barnsley, 1874-82.
(Richardson & Co.) Damasks.   Sec. XI.

INGOLDBY, MARY E., Sleaford
School, 1878-81.
Drawing. Outline.   Sec. I.

IRELIVING, SAMUEL, Devonport
School, 1875-84.
Studies. Groups. Sepia.   Sec. I.

IRWIN, ELIZABETH, Dublin Metro-
politan School, 1865-76.
Designs. Damasks, Lace, Carpets. Fur-
niture Fabrics.
Secs. X., XI., XII., XV.
Study.   Sec. I.

IRWIN, MARCELLA, Dublin Metro-
politan School, 1865-76.
Designs.   Damasks, Muslin, Carpets,
Lace.   Secs. I., X., XI., XIV.
Study. Still Life Group.   Sec. I.

IRWIN, MARIA L.
See Unwin.

JACKSON, FRANCES, Bristol School,
1880-84.
Studies, from casts, in Sepia.   Sec. I.

JACKSON, FRANK G., Birmingham
School, 1848-52. 1854-60.
(Elkington & Co.) Electro Silver Plate.
Sec. VI.
Enamels.   Sec. VI.

JACOB, ALICE, Dublin Metropolitan
School, 1879-84.
Studies. Head, in chalk.   Sec. I.

JACOB, ELLA, Salisbury School,
1879-84.
Keramics. Salisbury Ware.   Sec. II.
Design. Table Top.   Sec. VIII.
(Designed and manufactured by herself.)

JACOBY, M., & CO., Nottingham.
See Hammond, T. W.   Sec. X.
Hancock, W. R. S.   Sec. X.
Staynes, F. J.   Sec. X.
Cutts, John.   Sec. X.
Atkey, C. I.   Sec. X.

JAMES, CHARLOTTE, Queen Square
School, Bloomsbury, 1860-63.
(Tuck, R., & Sons.)
Christmas Cards.   Sec. XVII.
Designs, Wall Papers.   Sec. XVI.
Design, Frieze.   Secs. I., XVI.

JAQUES, LILIAN A., Leeds School,
1881-84.
Design. Group, in water colour. Sec. I.

JARRATT, EDWIN, Coalbrookdale
School, 1876-84.
Designs. Silver Work.   Secs. I., VI.
Tile Panel, &c. Mosaic.   Sec. II.

JEFFREY & CO., Essex Road, N.
See Noble, Henry.   Sec. XVI.
Ramsey, Allan.   Sec. XVI.
Tracey, Agnes.   Sec. XVI.
Morton, J. Scott.   Sec. XVI.
Hay, Thomas W.   Sec. XVI.
Muckley, W. J.   Sec. XVI.

JEFFREY, JOHN G., Coalbrookdale
School, 1881-84.
Design. Tile Panel.   Secs. I., II.

JENKINSON, THOMAS, Manchester
School, 1868-70.
(Edmundson, R. B., & Son.) Stained
Glass.   Sec. III.

JENNINGS, ARTHUR, Nottingham School, 1874-78.
(Hamel & Wright.) 2 Lace Curtains. Sec. X.

JEROME, CHARLES, Gosport School, 1875-1877. 1880-84.
School Work. Decoration. Secs. I., XVI.

JESSOP, CHARLES H., Sheffield, 8¼ years, and Derby School, 7¼ years.
Metal Work. Sec. V.
Decorative Panels. Cast Iron, Cast Brass, and Pewter. (Designed and executed by C. H. Jessop.) Sec. V.

JESSOP, F. C., Rotherham School, 1873-84.
Designs. Wrought-iron Gates. Secs. I., V.
(Perrot & Habershon.) Stoves, etc. Sec. V.

JOCKEL, CHARLES A., Edinburgh School, 1861-69.
(Jockel & Co.) Hangings. Sec. XV.
Decoration. Sec. XVI.

JOCKEL, CHRISTIAN, & CO., Edinburgh.
See JOCKEL, CHARLES A. Secs. XV., XVI.

JOHNSON, HERBERT, St. Martin's School, W.C., 2½ years.
Drawings for Woodcuts and Etchings for "Graphic." Sec. XIX.

JOHNSON, WILLIAM, Stoke-on-Trent School, 1876-78.
(Doulton & Co.) Vases. Porcelain. Assisted by Mr. John Slater. Sec. II.

JOHNSTON, MATILDA, Dublin Metropolitan School, 1881-84.
Design. Inlay Work. Secs. I., VIII.

JOHNSTONE, WILLIAM, Edinburgh, Coachbuilder.
See JOHNSTONE, WILLIAM. Sec. XXII.

JOHNSTONE, WILLIAM, Stirling School (The High School), 1872-73.
(W. Johnstone) Photograph of a Hansom Cab. Sec. XXII.

JONES, HELEN P., Gloucester School, 1882-84.
Painting on Silk, for fan. Secs. I., VII.

JONES, H. OVERTON, South Kensington Schools, 1876-1878.
(Jones, G., & Sons) Keramics. Table Ware. Sec. II.

JONES, G., & SONS, Trent Pottery, Stoke-on-Trent.
(G. Jones & Sons.) Keramics. Table Ware. Ewers and Basins, Cups, Saucers, and Plates, and the like.
See JONES, H. O. Sec. II.

JONES, JANE G., Dublin Metropolitan School, 1873-78.
Design. School Work. Sec. L

JONES, JEANNIE, Dublin Metropolitan School, 1873-77.
Study. Oil Painting. Sec. I.

JONES, LOUIS, Nottingham School, 1878-84.
(Heymann & Alexander.) Window Blinds and Curtains. Lace. Sec. X.

JONES, WILLIAM, Manchester School, 1858-76.
(Oliver & Atcherley.) Damask. Sec. XI.
Decoration. Sec. XVI.
(Cowlishaw, Nicol, & Co.) Carpets, Tapestry. Sec. XV.

JOSEPH, ADA M., Derby Central School, 1875-81.
Collective Exhibit. Sec. XVIII.
See DERBY CENTRAL SCHOOL.

JORDAN, FRANCES LYDIA, Dublin Metropolitan School, 1867-81.
Four designs. Muslins. Sec. XIV.
(Pym Brothers.) Damasks. Sec. XI.
Designs. Lace Flounce. Secs. I., X.

JOYCE, MARY, Dover School, 1872-1884.
2 Designs. Honiton Lace. Secs. I., X.

JULIAN, MARY, Plymouth School, 1883-84.
(Brannam, H. C.) Keramics. Sec. II.

JUNCK, OSCAR A., West London School, 1870-76.
Studies. Modelling. Secs. I., V., IX.

JUPP, G., St. Martin's School, W.C., 5 or 6 years. .
Design. Plaster Frieze. Secs. I., XXI.
Casts so broken; withdrawn. Per J. Parker, Master, St. Martin School.

KAVANAGH, JOSEPH, Dublin Metropolitan School, 1869-77.
Design. Sec. L
(Fry & Co.) Damasks and Tapestry. Secs. XI., XII.

KEEN, ROSA, Lambeth School, 1877-1880.
Imposto Ware.
(Doulton & Co.) Keramics. Vase. Sec. II.

KEEVIL, FRANK, Bath, 1871-72.
Wood Carving. Sec. VIII.

KELLETT, ANNA, Dublin Metropolitan School, 1869-75.
Design. Decoration. Secs. I., XVI.

K

KELLY, SAMUEL, Torquay School, 1876-79. 1881-84.
Study of Drapery. Oil.   Sec. I.

KELSALL, A. R., Burslem School, 1882-84.
(Doulton & Co.) Keramics. Plates.
        Sec. II.

KENDAL, MILNE, & CO., Manchester.
See FINCHETT, THOMAS.   Sec. VIII.

KENNAWAY, CHARLES G., JUN., Dundee School, 1881-84.
School Work. Machine Drawing.
        Sec. I.

KERR, ELEANOR, Dublin Metropolitan School, 1880-84.
Designs. Decoration, Muslin, &c.
        Secs. I., XIV., XVI.

KERR, THOMAS, Macclesfield School, 1877-84.
Design for Silk Handkerchief.
        Secs. I., XII.
(Birchenough & Co.) Brocaded Silk.
        Sec. XII.

KERSHAW, JOSEPH, Coalbrookdale, 1856-59.
(Coalbrookdale Iron Co.) Metal Work.
        Sec. V.

KERTLAND, GEORGE M., Birmingham, 1864-74.
(Garrard, R. & S.) Silver Work.
        Sec. VI.

KILPATRICK, W. J., Dublin Metropolitan School, 1865-73.
(Fry & Co.) Damasks.   Sec. XI.

KING, ADELINE, Salisbury School, 1871-84.
Designs. Lace.   .   Secs. I., X.

KING, DUNCAN, Edinburgh School, 1875-83.
(Morton, W., Scott, & Co.) Drawing of an actual Sideboard.   Sec. XXII.

KING, HARRY, Nottingham School, 1878-84.
Designs. Wall Papers. Secs. I., XVI.

KING, HENRY J., Lambeth School, 1883-84.
Decoration Panel.   Sec. XVI.

KING, LYDIA BACON, Queen Square School, Bloomsbury, 1881-84.
Fan—Silk, per Rimmel.   Sec. VII.
Study of Roses, &c.   Sec. I.

KINGDON, MAUD J., Exeter School. 1875-84.
Lace, Designs for Collars. Secs. I., X.

KINGMAN, GEORGE, Kidderminster, 1868-70. South Kensington, 1866-1868. Bath, 1858-66.
(Dixon, H. J., & Sons.) Carpets.
        Sec. XV.

KINGSTON, THOMAS, Bristol School, 1880-84.
Studies. Botanical and others. Sec. I.

KINGSTON, W. J., Leeds School, 1871-1883.
Design. Wall Papers. Secs. I., XVI.
A Fan   .   Sec. VII.

KIRBY, CORNELIUS M., West London School, 1881-84.
Design, Cabinet. Secs. I., VIII.
Decoration.   Sec. XVI.

KIRK, THOMAS L., Nottingham School, 1877-80.
Design. Lace Curtains. Secs. I., X.

KIRKMAN, KATE, Lambeth School, 1879-84.
Designs.   Sec. II.
Keramic Plaques.   Sec. II.

KIRKWOOD, HENRY B., Edinburgh School, 1867-1870.
(Kirkwood, } Silver Work. Sec. VII.
R. & H. B.) } Silver Plate. Sec. VI.

KIRKWOOD, R. & H. B., Edinburgh.
See KIRKWOOD, H. B. Secs. VI., VII.

KITTRIDGE, JOHN, Newcastle-under-Lyme School, 1881-84.
Flower Holder. 9s.   Sec. II.
Keramics, per Mintons. Voucher, Reg. No. 3541, 9th April, 1884.

KNIGHT, JOHN, Nottingham School, 1872-82.
Design for Furniture. Secs. I., VIII.

KNOWLES, DAVIDSON, West London School, 1872-81.
Architectural and other Drawings.
Engravings. Secs. XIX., XXI.

KNOWLSON, W. L., York School, 1880-84.
Reg. letter 4019, 21.iv.'84. (Cancelled.)

KNY, THEODORE, Stourbridge School, 1877-78. 1883.
(Webb & Sons.) Glass Bowls, &c.
        Sec. III.

KOERT, CORNELIUS VAN, West London School, 1880-84.
Studies. Chalk, Antique. Sec. I.
See VAN KOERT.

LAMB, JOHN, West London School, 1870-71.
Decoration.   Sec. XVI.

LAMBERT, GEORGE F., Derby
School, 1879–82. St. Martin's, W.C.,
1864–66.
(The Derby Crown Porcelain Co., Derby.)
Plates, &c. Keramic Ware. Flower
Vase. Sec. II.
Designs. Wall Papers. Keramics.
Porcelain. Secs. I., II., XVI.

LAMBERT, G. F., Worcester School,
1874–77.
Designs. Porcelain. Secs. I., II.

LAMBERT, ISABELLA, Dublin Metropolitan School, 1864–73.
Studies. Head. Oil, Chalk. Sec. I.

LAMBERT, MRS. ROWLEY, Hamp-
ton Court Palace.
Painted Decoration. Sec. XVI.
Design for Window Curtain of Silk.
(Withdrawn) Sec. XII.
See PERRY, W. Sec. I.

LANE, FREDERICK W., West London School, 1880–81.
Architecture. Sec. XXI.

LANE, JOHN QUILLER, Belfast
School, 1871–73. 1876–77. 1879–81;
also South Kensington, 1873–76.
Designs for Fabrics, various.
Secs. I., II., XVI., XXII.
Damasks (Ferguson & Co.)
Secs. XI., XII.

LANE, R. P,, Glasgow School.
(S. & A. Dept.) Photograph. Decorative Panel in Plaster. Premiated 1874
by Plasterers' Company. Sec. XVI.

LANGLEY, LEONARD, Burslem
School, 1874–78.
(Doulton & Co.) Bowl. Porcelain.
Sec. II.
Assisted by Mr. John Slater.

LARCHER, ULRIQUE A., Lambeth
School, 7 years.
(Doulton & Co.) Keramics. Vase.
Sec. II.

LAWRIE, JANE, Kilmarnock School,
1878–84.
School Work. Oil Painting. Sec. I.

LAWSON, J. Sheffield School, 1874–
1884.
(Watson, Moorwood, & Co.) Metal
Work. Sec. V.

LAWSON, W. A., Glasgow, 1870–73.
(Barbour, Anderson, & Co.) Two Silk
Curtains. Secs. XII., XV.

LEDWARD, RICHARD A., Burslem
and South Kensington, 1871–79.
(Craven, Dunnill, & Co.) Tiles.
Sec. II
(Malkin, Edge & Co.) Keramics. Tiles.
Sec. II.
(Doulton & Co.) Plaque.

LEE, ALICE, Dublin Metropolitan
School, 1870–73.
Study. Head, in Chalk. Sec. I.

LEE, FRANCES E., Lambeth School,
1876–80.
(Doulton & Co.) Keramics. Vase
Sec. II.

LEE, HARRIETTE E., Lambeth
School, 1877–81.
(Doulton & Co.) Keramics. Vase.
Sec. II.

LEES, GEORGE. Kidderminster
School, 1862–70. 1880–84.
Two Designs. Lace. Carpets.
Secs. X., XV.

LEGGETT, WILLIAM J., Ipswich
School, 1874–84.
Glass Decoration, Sec. III.
Painted Decoration. Sec. XVI.

LEIGHTON, F., South Kensington
Schools, 1883–84. Coalbrookdale
School, 1878–83.
Design. Grill, in wrought-iron.
Secs. I., V.
Design. Vitreous Mosaics. Secs. I., III.
Tiles. Sec. II.
Design. Decoration.
Secs. I., XVI., XIX.
Designs. Christmas Cards. Sec. XVII.
Sideboard. Sec. VIII.

LEIGHTON, SIR FREDERICK,
P.R.A.
Engraving. "Industrial Art applied to
War." From the cartoon in South
K. Museum.
Type of Beauty, No. 6.
(Engraved on wood, C. Roberts.)
Sec. XIX.

LETHEREN, C., Cheltenham, 1860.
Christ Church, 1877–79. St. Marks,
1882–83.
Ornamental Cast and Wrought Iron
Work. Sec. V.

LETHEREN, W. H., Cheltenham, 1860.
Christ Church, 1877–79.
Iron Work. Sec. V.

LETHEREN, W., Cheltenham, 1865–
1867.
Iron Work. Sec. V.

LETHEREN, W., & Sons, Cheltenham.
Ornamental Metal Work. Sec. V.
See LETHEREN, C.
LETHEREN, W. H.
LETHEREN, W.

LEVIN, VICTORIA, West London
School, 1880–84.
Studies. Group. Sepia. Sec. I.

K 2

LEWIS, FLORENCE, Lambeth School,
1876-80.
　(Doulton & Co.)　Keramics.　Vase.
　　　　　　　　　　　　　　Sec. II.

LEWIS, ISABEL, Lambeth School, 2
years.
　(Doulton & Co.)　Keramics.　Vase.
　　　　　　　　　　　　　　Sec. II.

LEWIS, MARY AGNES, Lambeth
School, 1878-83.
　Designs.　Christmas Cards.
　　　　　　　　　　　Secs. I., XVII.

LEWIS, E., Lambeth School.
　Doulton Ware.　Doulton's Pavilion.
　　　　　　　　　　　　　　Sec. II.

LEWITT, BENJAMIN M., Leicester
School, 1877-84.
　(Fleming, J., & Co.)　Designs.　Calendar.
　　　　　　　　　　　Secs. I., XVII.
　Lithographs.　　　　　Sec. XVII.

LEWTY, RICHARD, Stoke-on-Trent
and Fenton School, 1880-84.
　Two Dessert Plates.　　Sec. II.
　Keramics per Mintons.　Voucher, Reg.
　No. 3541.　9th April, 1884.

LIBERTY, OCTAVIA R. H., Nottingham School, 1875-81.
　Designs.　Hangings.　Secs. I., XII.

LILEY, HENRY G., West London
School, 1870-77.
　Studies.　Linoleum and Decoration.
　　　　　　　　Secs. I., XVI., XXII.

LILEY & WOOD, Radnor House,
Gloucester Square, W.
　See BEAUPRÉ, C. J.　　　　Sec. I.

LILLEY, ELIZABETH A., Lambeth
School, 1878-84.
　Studies.　Drawing from Life.　Sec. I.

LILLIE, B. A., West London School,
1877.
　(Woollams.)　Paperhangings.　Sec. XVI.

LINNELL, THOMAS, Leicester
School, 1881-84.
　Design, Wall Papers.　Secs. I., XVI.
　Design, Tapestry.　　Sec. I., XV.

LINTHORPE POTTERY (J. HARRI-
SON), Middlesboro'.
　See WORTH, LUCY.　　　Sec. II.
　　　PATEY, R. W.　　　Sec. II.
　　　LONGBOTTOM, S.　　Sec. II.

LISHMAN, JAMES T., Bradford
Technical College School, 1883.
　Designs.　Mixed Fabrics.　Sec. XIII.

LITTLER, JOSEPH, Stoke-on-Trent
and Fenton School, 1882-84.
　Three Dessert Plates.　Sec. II.
　Keramics, per Mintons.

LLEWELLYN, S. H., South Kensington School.
　Group in Oil Colour.　Sec. I.

LLOYD, JULIANNA, West London
School, 1878.　1880-82.
　Studies.　Decorations.　Designs.
　　　　　　　Secs. I., II., VIII., XVI.

LLOYD, MARY, Dublin Metropolitan
School, 1880-84.
　Designs.　Furniture Stuffs.　Inlay
　Work.　　　　Secs. I., VIII., XII.

LLOYD, MARY J., Bristol School,
1872-84.
　Studies.　Drawings in Sepia and in
　chalk.　　　　　　　　Sec. I.

LOCK, EDWARD, Bath, 1880.
　Circular Panel.　Wood Carving.
　　　　　　　　　　　　　Sec. VIII.

LOCK, MARY, Dorchester, 1868-73.
　School Work.　Study in Chalk from Cast.
　　　　　　　　　　　　　Sec. I.

LOCK, MESSRS., Cabinet Works,
Bristol Road, Bath.
　See ASCOTT, JOHN W.　　Sec. VIII.

LODGE, E. D., Royal Albert Hall
School.
　Wood Carving.　　　Sec. VIII.

LOMAX, JOHN, Esq., Manchester.
　Carved Oak Hall Seat.
　See FINCHETT, T.　　　Sec. VIII.

LONDON, EMILY ALICE, Lambeth
School, 1880-84.
　(Doulton & Co.)　Keramics.　Vase.
　　　　　　　　　　　　　Sec. II.

LONG, NAT., Cork, 1881-84.
　Carved Wood.　Side-board.　Sec. VIII.

LONGBOTTOM, S., Darlington, 1871-
1878.
　(Linthorpe Pottery Co.)
　Keramics.　Vases.　　Sec. II.

LONGDON, HENRY, Sheffield School,
1847-49.
　(Longdon & Co.)　Metal Work.　Sec. V.
　Carved wood Mantelpiece　Sec. VIII.
　See BULLAS, W.
　　　FIDLER, F.　　　　Sec. V.

LONGDON & CO., Phœnix Foundry,
Sheffield.
　Metal Work.　　　　　Sec. V.
　See BULLAS, W.　　　　Sec. V.
　　　FIDLER, F.　　　　Sec. V.
　　　LONGDON, H.　　　Sec. V.
　　　SEDDING, J. D.　　Sec. V.

LONGMAN, THOMAS, Stoke-on-
Trent and Fenton School, 1864-75.
　One Pedestal.　23 guineas.　Sec. II.
　One Jardinière.　12 guineas.　Sec. II.
　One Ewer.　94s. 6d.　　Sec. II.
　Keramics, per Mintons.　Voucher, Reg.
　No. 3541.　9th April, 1884.

LOVERING, IDA, Queen Square School, Bloomsbury, 1873-78.
Chalk Study. Secs. I., XIX.
(Purchased by Her Majesty tho Queen, aud lent by Her Majesty.)

LOW, MARIE A., Bloomsbury School, 1871.
Lithographs. Christmas and other Cards. Sec. XVII.

LOXLEY, RICHARD, Sheffield, 1878-1884.
(Pawson & Brailsford.) Engravings.
Sec. XIX.

LUNN, RICHARD, Sheffield School, 1857-66. (South Kensington, 1866-1868.) (Assisted by J. Platts, C. Rouse, and J. Rouse.)
(Derby Crown Porcelain & Pottery Co.)
Keramic Ware, silver mounted.
Tankards and Cups. Secs. II., VI.
Dessert Service, W. E. G., 1883. Sec. II.
(Derby Crown Porcelain Co., Rhodes & Barber.) Dinner Plates and Dishes.
Designs. Porcelain. Silver Plate.
Secs. I., II., VI.
Boudoir Mantel-set ; Porcelain Clock, Candlesticks, 4 Flower Vases. Sec. II.
Lent by Sir P. C. Owen, K.C.M.G., C.B., C.I.E.

LUPTON, E. D., MISS, Lambeth School, 1875-84.
Design. Tiles for Dado. Secs. I., II.
(Doulton & Co.) Keramics. Vase.
Sec. II.

LYNDON, HERBERT, West London School, 1871-76.
Studies. Playing-card Backs.
Secs. I., XVII.
Six Specimens Playing Card Backs.
Sec. XXII.

McALPINE, JOHN, Edinburgh School, 1880-83.
(Morton, W. Scott, & Co.) Drawing, Copy of Design for a Cabinet.
Sec. XXII.

MACARTHUR, BLANCHE, Queen Square School, Bloomsbury, W.C., 1866-87.
Figure Painting in Water Colours. 16 plates. Sec. XXII.

MACCLESFIELD EMBROIDERY SCHOOL (NICHOLSON, J. O., Secretary).
See NICHOLSON, J. O. Sec. XII.
HOGGINS, JAMES.
ADAMS, F. E.
ADAMS, JAMES.

MACCLESFIELD SCHOOL OF ART.
See CLULOW, W. J.
ADAMS, F. E.
DONOHUE, T. J.
DORAN, T. E.

HADFIELD. J.
RISELEY, H.
KERR, T.
DAWSON, J. E.
BOOTH, JOHN.
STARR, J. B.
CARTWRIGHT, A.
THOMPSON, WILLIAM.
GRIMSHAW, HUGH.
ROBINSON, J. T.
FOWLER, W. T.
Designs for Silk Fabrics. Sec. I.

McCORMICK, ARTHUR D., Belfast School, 1877-82; South Kensington, 1882-84.
Designs. Sideboard. Carved Wood Panel. A Frieze. Secs. I., VIII., XVI.

McCREA & CO., Halifax.
See RILEY, J. W. Sec. XV.

McCULLOUGH, WILLIAM JOHN, Belfast School, 1877-83.
(Musgrave & Co.) Design. Iron gates.
Secs. I., V.

McDONALD, J., West London School.
See "Old London."

McFADDEN, FRANK, Southampton, 1869-73; South Kensington, 1873-75.
Personal. Etchings. Sec. XIX.

McFADDEN, ROWLAND, Southampton, 1864-66. 1879-84.
Etchings. Sec. XIX.

McGEE, MARIANNE, Dublin Metropolitan School, 1866-78.
Designs. Muslin Curtains.
Secs. I., XIII.
Designs. Furniture Damasks.
Secs. I., XII.

McGILL, DAVID M., Kilmarnock School, 1877-84.
School Work. Monochrome. Sec. I.

MacGOUN, JANET, Edinburgh School, 1872-81.
Decoration. Sec. XVI.
School Work. Study : Still Life. Sec. I.

McGOWAN, WILLIAM, Belfast School, 1876-84.
Designs. Cup. Damasks. Lace.
Secs. I., VI., X., XI.

McINROY, JOHN, Dundee School, 1870-75. 1878-82.
School Work. Engineering Drawing.
Girders, Tay Bridge. Secs. I.

MACKAY & CHISHOLM, Edinburgh.
See HOLIDAY, THOMAS. Sec. VI.
CRICHTON, JOHN. Sec. VI.

MACKAY & CUNNINGHAM, Edinburgh.
See CRICHTON ALEXANDER. Sec. VI.

McKENZIE, GEORGE, Sheffield
School, 1872-80.
  Designs. Scissors.　　Secs. I., VI.

MACKENZIE, JOHN GUTHRIE,
Belfast School, 1877-79; South Ken-
sington, 1879-81.
  (Hamilton, Hill & Co.) Damask Table
    Cloths, Lace Curtain.　Secs. X., XI.
  School Studies. 22D, 23 c.　　Sec. I.
  Design for Silver Candlestick.　Sec. VI.

McLAREN, THOMAS, Stirling School,
1877-79.
  Lithographs.　　　　　Sec. XVII.

McLATCHY, FREDERICK M., Kilmarnock School, 1878-79.
  School Work. Machine Drawing. Stu-
    dies.　　　　　　Sec. I.

McLATCHY, KATE C., Kilmarnock
School, 1879-81.
  School Work. Flowers (Water-colour).
    Sec. I.

McLELLAN, J. H.
  (Doulton & Co.)
  Faience. Tile Panels & Doulton Ware.
  (Doulton Pavilion).　　Sec. II.

McMILLAN, EMELINE S., Lambeth
School, 1875-84.
  Studies.　　　　　Sec. I.

MADDOX, T. W., Birmingham School,
1882-84.
  Designs. Lamp and Light Fittings.
    Sec. I., V.
  (Barwell, Sons, & Co.; Crofts & Assin-
    der; Ford, Thomas, & Co.; White-
    house, W. & Co.) Metal Work.
    Sec. V.

MAFFETT, ISABELLA, Dublin Metropolitan School, 1868-73.
  Design for Plate.　Sec. I., II., VI.

MAGEE, T. H., & CO., Belfast.
  See WARD, JAMES.　　Sec. XV.

MAHONY, MINNIE, Dublin Metropolitan School, 1868-73.
  Design. Furniture Damask.
    Sec. I., XII.

MAIN, L., West London School.
  Drawing in black and white. Sec. XIX.

MALKIN, EDGE, & CO., Encaustic
Tile Works, Burslem.
  Keramics.
  ee LEDWARD, R.A.　　Sec. II.

MALTBY, CAROLINE, Queen
Square School, Bloomsbury, 1880-83.
  Design for lace fan.　Secs. I., X.

MANLY, ELEANOR, Queen Square
School, Bloomsbury, 1869-73.
  (Hildesheimer & Faulkner.) Christmas
    Cards.　　　　Sec. XVII.

MANNOOCH, ALFRED, West London
School, 1873-74.
  (Woollams.) Wallpapers.　Sec. XVI.

MANSELL, CARRY.
  See WATSON, MRS.

MANSELL, MARIANNE, Lambeth
School, 1870-73.
  Designs. Enamelled Casket.　Sec. IV.
    Glass.　　　　Sec. III.
    Three, Lace.　　Sec. X.
    Jewellery.　　Sec. VII.
    Porcelain.　　Sec. II.

MAPPIN & WEBB, Sheffield; &
Queen Victoria Street, London, E.C.
  See MASON, HERBERT.　　Sec. V.
  and MASON, HERBERT, & Co., Bir-
    mingham.

MARKS, FLORENCE, West London
School, 1880-84.
  Keramics.　　　　Sec. II.

MARPLES, THOMAS, Derby Central
School, 1870-78.
  Collective Exhibit.　Sec. XVIII.
  See DERBY CENTRAL SCHOOL.

MARSH, ARTHUR H., Manchester
School, 1866-70.
  (Falkner, G., & Sons.) Decorations.
    Sec. XVII.

MARSHALL, ARTHUR, Nottingham
School, 1873-79.
  Architectural Designs.　Sec. XXI.

MARSH, JAMES F., Burslem School.
  (Davenport, Messrs.) Keramics. Fruit
    Dish.　　　　Sec. II.
  Ewers and Basins, Jugs, &c.　Sec. II.

MARSHALL, JAMES F., Nottingham
School, 1871-82.
  Design. Iron gates.　Secs. I., V.

MARSHALL, WILLIAM, Sheffield,
1862-69; South Kensington, 1869-74.
  Silver Work, Models for.　Sec. VI.

MARSHALL, W., South Kensington
Schools.
  (S. & A. Dept.) Photograph. Design
    for a Doorway. Plaster Decorations.
    Premiated 1875 by Plasterers' Com-
    pany.　　　Secs. IX., XVI.

MARTIN, ANNE O., Perth School,
1880-84.
  Studies. Shading.　　Sec. I.

MARTIN, WILLIAM, Edinburgh
School, 1868-83.
  Wood Carving. Two Panels, &c.
    Sec. VIII.

MASON, HERBERT, & CO., Birmingham.
Ornaments in Metal and Brass Work.
See MASON, HERBERT. Sec. V.

MASON, HERBERT, Birmingham School, 4 years.
(Lent by Mappin & Webb.) Ornamental Metal Work. Brass Work. Clock Cases, Lamps, Inkstands.
Sec. V.

MASON, ROBERT, Newcastle-under-Lyme School, 1881-84.
2 Dessert Plates. Sec. II.
Keramics per Mintons, Voucher Ref., No. 3541, 9th April 1884.

MASSEY, H. G., South Kensington School.
Geometrical Studies. Sec. I.
Study in Sepia. Sec. I.

MATHERS, SAMUEL, Dublin Metropolitan School, 1882-84.
Study. Bust. Sec. I.

MAW & CO., Benthal, Broseley, Salop.
See BANGHAM, JOSEPH. Sec. II.
BRADBURN, J. W. Sec. II.
CHILDE, ANDREW. Sec. II.
BARTLEY, ALICE. Sec. II.
FLETCHER, B. J. Sec. II.
GIBBONS, OWEN. Tiles. Sec. II.
FIDLER, J. B. Sec. II.

MAXWELL, BLANDINA, Edinburgh School, 1881-83.
School Work. Studies. 23 c. Sec. I.

MAY, SAMUEL F., West London School, 1876-84.
Studies. Group. Head. Oil. Sec. I.

MAYSTON, J. H., Great Yarmouth School, 1879-82.
Designs. Wrought Iron Gate. Silver Salts. Sec. I., V., VI.

MEADE, ELIZA, Cork—Ursulin Convent.
Irish Crochet. 2 Designs. 3 Specimens.
See CARR, MABEL. Sec. X.
HAYES, ELLEN. Sec. X.
PERRY, LIZZIE. Sec. X.

MEAR, ALBERT, Hanley School, 1882-84.
2 Dessert Plates. Sec. II.
Keramics, per Mintons, Voucher Reg., No. 3541. 9 April, 1884.

MEESON, JAMES, Sheffield.
See BOOTH, JAMES. Sec. VI.

MELDRUM, THOMAS, Nottingham School, 1871-81.
Design. Lace Curtains. Secs. I., X.

MENZIES, JAMES, Edinburgh School, 1870-77.
Silver Work. Waiter. Sec. VI.
Silver Work. Plates. Sec. VI.
(Hamilton, Crichton & Co.) Presentation Salver in Silver: Plaster reverse of.
Secs. I., VI.

MERRITT, W. J., South Kensington Schools.
(S. & A. Dept.) Photograph. Design for Capital of a Pilaster. Decoration. Premiated 1876 by the Plasterers' Company. Sec. XVI.

MICKLEWRIGHT, FRED., Hanley, 1881-84.
(Bodley, E. J. D., & Co.) Keramics. Plates. Sec. II.

MIDDLETON, ALONZO, Nottingham School, 1877-82.
Design. Wall Paper. Sec. I., XVI.

MIDGLEY, JOSEPH, Halifax, 1882-1883, and Bradford Technical College, 1883.
Designs. Mixed Fabrics. Sec. XIII.

MILLBURN, G.W., York School, 1857-1865; Leeds, 1869; Chester, 1870.
Modelling. Sec. I.

MILLER, ISABEL, Lambeth School, 1875-79.
(Doulton & Co.) Keramics. Tobacco Jar. Sec. II.

MILLIGAN, W. A., South Kensington School, 1881-84. Walsall School, 1875-81.
Design. Clock Case. Secs. I., V.
Drinking Cup, silver.
Secs. I., VI.

MILLSON, JOHN J., Manchester School, 1872-73.
Stone Carvings. Two Subjects. Sec. IX.

MILNE, E. P., Lancaster, 8 years.
(Milne & Sons, Lancaster.) Furniture. Cabinet. Sec. VIII.
(Appleyard & Sons, Sheffield.) Coloured Photograph. Oak Cabinet. Sec. VIII.

MILWAIN, W. J., Glasgow, 3 years at School.
(Edwards, G., & Son.) Sword of Honour. (Lent by General Sir A. Alison, Bart., K.C.B.) Sec. VII.

MILWARD, E. J., Kendal, 1876-78. 1880-83.
Designs. Wallpapers. Carpets. Curtains. Inlaid Wood.
Secs. I., VIII., XV., XVI.

MINNS, JOHN, Norwich School, 4 years.
(J. Minns.) Carved Wood Panel.
Sec. VIII.

MINNS, JAMES, Norwich Schools,
8 years.
  (Fletcher, B. E.) Wood Carving.
                                Sec. VIII.
  Carved Wood Panels.   Sec. VIII.

MINNS, JOHN, Norwich.
  See MINNS, JOHN.   Sec. VIII.
  MINNS, JAMES.   Sec. VIII.

MINTONS, Limited, Stoke-on-Trent.
  (Minton & Co.) Keramic Wares. Por-
    celain and Pottery.   Sec. II.
  See BILTON, LOUIS.
    BIRKS, EDWARD.
    BOULTON, ARTHUR.
    BANKS, JAMES.
    CONNOLLY, ARTHUR.
    CRAWFORD, GEORGE.
    DEAN, EDWIN.
    ECCLESTONE, GEORGE.
    HODGKINSON, WILLIAM.
    LEWTY, RICHARD.
    LITTLER, JOSEPH.
    MURRELL, FREDERICK.
    NAYLOR, ALBERT.
    PARRY, EDWARD.
    PENSON, HENRY.
    PILSBURY, W. H.
    PENSON, FREDERICK.
    SNOW, JAMES.
    HENK, JOHN.
    LONGMON, THOMAS.
    FERRYHOUGH, GEORGE.
    KILTRIDGE, JOHN.
    MASON, ROBERT.
    STUBBS, THOMAS.
    WHITTAKER, GEORGE.
    BEACALL, FRANK.
    DALTON, JOSEPH.
    DEAN, THOMAS.
    MEAR, ALBERT.
    SLATER, WALTER.
    TAYLOR, ELIJAH.

MINTON, HOLLINS, & SONS., Tile
  Works, Stoke-on-Trent.
  See BRADLEY, SARAH A.
    BUXTON, S.
    DIXON, W. H.
    HEWETT, J. P.
    SLATER, A.
    WRIGHT, A.
    SIMPSON, W.

MITCHELL, ANNA, Dublin Metropolitan School, 1869–82.
  Studies.   Sec. I.

MITCHELL, EMILY, West London
  School, 1878–84.
  Studies, Keramics.   Secs. I., II.
  Engravings.   Sec. XIX.
  China Plate.   Sec. II.

MITCHELL, MARY, Lambeth School,
  1874–84.
  Studies. St. John.   Sec. I.

MITCHELL, WILLIAM, Bath, 1866–
  1867. 1878–79.
  Table Top. Inlay.   Sec. VIII.
  Wood Carving.   Sec. VIII.

MITCHELL, WILLIAM, West London School, 1882–84.
  Studies. Chalk.   Sec. I.

MONTALBA, HENRIETTA, South
  Kensington Schools, 1868–75.
  A Fan. Vellum. "The Feast."
                                Sec. VII.

MONTALBA, HILDA, South Kensington Schools, 1868–75.
  A Fan. Vellum. "La Grace."
                                Sec. VII.

MONTFORD, H. L., Royal Albert Hall
  School.
  Wood Carving.   Sec. VIII.

MONTGOMERY, MISS, Dublin Metropolitan School, 1870–73.
  Designs. Damasks.   Secs. I., XI.

MOODY, ELLWARD, Huddersfield
  School, 1859–65.
  Wood Carving. Oak Chair. Sec. VIII.

MOODY, JESSE, Bath, 1873.
  Wood Carving.   Sec. VIII.

MOOR, GEORGE, Manchester School.
  Collective Exhibit. Chromolithograph.
  A Vase, drawn by Muckley, W. G.
                                Sec. XVII.

MOORCROFT, THOMAS, Burslem,
  1869–76.
  (Bodley & Co.) Keramics. Plates.
                                Sec. II.

MOORE, AMY G., Lambeth School,
  1881–84.
  (Doulton & Co.) Keramics. Bowl.
                                Sec. II.

MOORE, ESTHER MARY, Southampton, 1879–84.
  Wood Carving. Panel.   Sec. VIII.

MOORE, H. W., Oxford School, 1873–
  1874; Bristol, 1870–71.
  Architectural Designs.   Sec. XXI.
  Title-pages.   Sec. XVIII.

MOORE, JENNIE, Queen Square
  School, Bloomsbury, W.C., 1870–74.
  Drawing from the Antique. Sec. XXII.

MOORE, MARGARET M., Leicester
  School, 1870–84.
  Study, still life.   Sec. I.

MOORE, MARION, Dublin Metropolitan School, 1881–84.
  Design. Lace Flounce.   Secs. I., X.

MUCKLEY, W. J., Stourbridge and other Schools, **1848-53.**
  (Hildesheimer & Faulkner) Christmas and Easter Cards. Sec. XVII.
  Collective with Muckley, W. R.; Muckley, A. Fairfax.
  Chromolithographs. Collective with Geo. Moore. (J. J. Sale & Sons, Manchester.) Sec. XVII.
  (Potter & Co.) Printed Dress Fabrics.
                          Soc. XIV.
  (Jeffrys & Co.) Wall Papers. Sec. XVI.

MUCKLEY, WILLIAM R.; MUCKLEY, ANGELO F., Manchester School, **1875-82.**
  Collective with Muckley, W. J., Stourbridge. Sec. XIV.

MULLETT, ALFRED, Bath, **1879-84.**
  School Study. Sec. I.

MULLIGAN, W. A., South Kensington School.
  Study in Chalk, from Cast. Sec. I.
  Design. Silver Cup. Sec. VI.

MUNTZER, FREDERICK, South Kensington, **1866-68.**
  Embossed Velvet. Sec. XII.
  Decoration. Sec. XXI.
  Furniture. Sec. VIII.

MURRAY, C. O., Edinburgh, **1863-69.**
  Illuminations. Sec. XVIII.
  Engraving and Etchings. Sec. XIX.
  Drawings in Black and White.
                          Sec. XIX.

MURRAY, DAVID S., Dundee School, **1877-84.**
  School Work. Machine Drawing.
                          Sec. I.

MURRAY, WILLIAM H., Dublin Metropolitan School, **1856-69.**
  Designs. Damasks. Secs. I., XII.
  Carpets. Sec. XV.

MUSGRAVE & CO., Ann Street, Belfast.
  Ironwork. *See* McCullough, W. J.
                          Sec. I.

MUTLOW, GEORGE, Worcester School, **1881-84.**
  Studies. Ornament. Sec. I.

NATIONAL ART TRAINING SCHOOLS, South Kensington.
  See Science & Art Department.
  South Kensington Schools.

NAYLOR, ALBERT, Stoke-on-Trent & Fenton School, **1874-82.**
  One Oval Tray, 10s. 6d. each Sec. II.
  Two Octagon Trays, 10s. 6d. each.
                          Sec. II.
  One Oval Tray, 13s. 6d. each. Sec. II.
  Keramics per Mintons, Voucher Reg. No. 3541. 9 April, 1884.

NAYLOR, T. & A., Kidderminster.
  See Park, J. H. Sec. XV.
  Duck, O. Sec. XV.

NEEDHAM, R., JUNR., Sheffield School, **1872-82.**
  Designs. Silver Ware. Sec. VI.
  (Pawson & Brailsford.) Designs. Illuminations. Sec. XVII

NETTLEWORTH, or **SHETTLEWORTH, LIZZIE,** Lambeth School, **1880-81.**
  (Doulton & Co.) Keramics. Vase.
                          Sec. II.

NEWMAN, ALFRED, 19 Maddox Street, W.
  Silver Work for a Cabinet. Sec. VI.
  See Faulks, H. Sec. VI.

NEWMAN, W. J., South Kensington, **1871-81.**
  Metal Work. Sec. V.
  Electro-Plate. Sec. VI.

NEWNHAM, JOSEPHINE E., Lambeth School, **1875-77.**
  (Doulton & Co.) Keramics. Vase.
                          Sec. II.

NICHOLSON, J. O., Macclesfield.
  See Hoggins, James. Secs. XII., XXII.
  Adams, F. E. Secs. XII., XXII.
  Adams, James. Sec. XII.
  Armitage, G. F. Sec. XII.
  Morris, Wm. Sec. XII.

NICHOLSON, J. O., Hope Mills, Macclesfield, at Macclesfield School from **1856-65.**
  Silk and Embroidery.
  See Macclesfield Embroidery School.
  Also *See* Adams, Frank E.
    Adams, James.
    Armitage, G. F.
    Hoggins, James.
    Morris, William.
    Nicholson, J. O. Sec. XII.
  Silk Embroidery ; Colouring. Sec. XII.

NISBET, ETHEL CHAPMAN, Queen Square School, Bloomsbury, **1879-84.**
  A Fan, silk. Design. Sec. VII.
  Purchased by H.M. The Queen; lent by H.R.H. Duchess of Albany.
  (Rimmel.) A Fan, silk. Sec. VII.
  Studies. "Chrysanthemums." Water Color. Lent by Mrs. Brightwyn, The Grove, Stanmore.
  Time Study, "Daffodils." (Lent by R. H. Shepherd, Esq.) (Withdrawn.)
                          Sec. I.

PAWSON AND BRAILSFORD, Sheffield.
See PRYOR, C. W.
NEEDHAM, R. Sec. XVII.
BATEMAN, W. E.
PEACE, W. Sec. XIX.
PEACE, ALFRED.
GARDNER, W.
HYDES, R.
LOXLEY, R.

PEACE, WALTER, Sheffield, 1870-83; & PEACE, ALFRED, Sheffield, 1875-1884.
(Pawson & Brailsford.) Etchings. Sec. XIX.

PEACE, A. A., Sheffield School, 1875-1884.
Design. Silver Salts. Secs. I., VI.

PEARCE, ARTHUR E., Lambeth School, 1874-84.
Study in chalk from life. Sec. I.
Stained glass. Sec. III.
(Doulton & Co.) Mosaics. Keramic.
Doulton ware. Sec II.
(Doulton Pavilion.) Sec. II.

PEARCE, HENRY, Hull School, 3 years.
Silver Table Ware. Sec. VI.
(Made by H. Pearce, Huddersfield.)
Gold Key; mounted Fob and Seal. Sec. VII.
(Executed by J. Mackenzie, Huddersfield School.)

PEARCE, J., South Kensington Schools, 1882-84. Bristol School, 1876-82.
Design. Clock Case. Secs. I., V.

PEARSE, ALFRED, West London School, 1874-76. 1878-81.
Engravings, &c. Sec. XIX.

PEARSON, F., South Kensington Schools, 1883-84. Stoke-on-Trent School, 1877-83.
Design. Brussels Carpet. Secs. I, XV.

PECKITT, THOMAS, West London School, 1881-84.
Studies. Antique. Sec. I.

PEGG, WILLIAM H., Nottingham School, 1879-84.
Elementary Design. Sec. I.

PEGRAM, HENRY A., West London School, 1876-84.
Studies. "Satyr" in plaster. Sec. IX.
Design for Church Decorations. Sec. XVI.

PENSON, F., South Kensington Schools, 1883-84. Stoke-on-Trent School, 1877-83.
Design. Brussels Carpet. Secs. I,. XV.

PENSON, FREDERICK, Stoke-on-Trent & Fenton School, 1877-84.
Two Plaques, 30s. each. Sec. II.
Two Oval Trays, 8s. 3d. each. Sec. II.
Keramics, per Mintons, Voucher Reg. No. 3541. 9 April, 1884.

PENSON, HENRY, Stoke-on-Trent Fenton School, 1880-84.
One Oblong Slab, painted view, 15s. Sec. II.
One Dessert Plate. Sec. II.
Keramics, per Mintons.

PERKIN, MRS. T. DIX, Harrow.
Jewellery: Collarette, Bracelet, and Earrings. Gold.
See TONKS, JOSEPH W. Sec. VII.

PERKINS, P. S., Leicester School.
Metal Work. Design for Iron Screen. Sec. V.

PERROT AND HABERSHON, Rotherham.
See JESSOP, F. C. Sec. V.

PERRY, LIZZIE, Cork, 1874-84.
(Meade, Eliza.) Lace. Sec. X.

PERRY, WILLIAM, Dublin Royal Society School, 1858-62. 1869.
(Lambert, Mrs. Rowley.) Designs. Sec. I., XII., XVI.
(Weldon, W. H.) Decorations. Sec. XVI.
(Duffy, James, & Co.) Drawings for Lithographs. Sec. XVII.
W. Lipscombe, The Square, Isleworth.

PHILLIP, CHARLES G. L., Dundee School, 1880-83.
School Work. Machine Drawing. Sec. I.

PHILLIPS, JAMES, Gosport School, 2 years.
Design for Painted Panel. Secs. I., XVI.

PHILLIPS, MIRIAM, Dublin Metropolitan School, 1880-84.
Design for Border Inlay. Secs. I., VIII.

PHILLIPS, THOMAS, Belfast School, 3 years. South Kensington, 2 years.
Designs—Damask Table Linen. Secs. I., XI.

PHILLIPSON, JULIA, Dublin Metropolitan School, 1878-82.
Design for Embroidery. Secs. I., XII.

PHILPOT, MISS, Lambeth School.
(Doulton & Co.) Tiles. Female Heads. Sec. II.

PICK, S. PERKINS, Leicester School, 1874-78.
Architectural Studies. Sec XXI.
Design—Chancel Screen. Secs. I., XXI.

PICKERING, J. W.
See BEATTIE, CHALLEN. Sec. V.

PILSBURY, W. H., Stoke-on-Trent & Fenton School, 1882-84.
Two Oval Trays, 13s. 6d. each.   Sec. II.
Two Tiles, 6 by 6, 6s. 6d. each.   Sec. II.
Two Tiles, 8 by 8, 8s. 3d. each.   Sec. II.
Keramics per Mintons, Voucher Reg. No. 3541.   9 April, 1884.

PINCHES, R., Chester, 1882-84. Lambeth School, 1872-1879.
(Brown, W. F. & Co.) Wood Carving, &c. Side-board.   Sec. VIII.

PLATT, WALTER, Yarmouth School, 1860-84.
School Work. Designs, Tiles, Muslin, Decoration, Oak Carving.
Secs. I., II., XIII., VIII.

POLSON, JOHN, Esq., Paisley.
Silver Gilt Dessert Service. Modelled by Alexander Crichton, Edinburgh School.   Sec. VI.
(Lent by John Polson, Esq.)

POMEROY, FREDERICK, Lambeth School, and City and Guilds Institute, 1874-78.
Statue.   Sec. II.

POOLE, FREDERICK, Burslem, 1878-1884.
(Bodley & Co.) Keramics. Plates.   Sec. II.

POOLE, J. O., South Kensington Schools, 1882-84.
Design. Table Top (Inlaid Wood.)   Secs. I., VIII.
Design. Porcelain.   Sec. II.

POOLE, WILLIAM, West London, 1862-64.
Studies.   Sec. I.
Design for Arabesque Pilaster.   Sec. XXII.

POPE, MARIE J., Bristol School, 1878-1884.
Study. Chalk Drawing from cast.   Sec. I.

PORTER, FRANK, Stourbridge School, 1877-84.
Designs for Carpets.   Secs. I., XV.

POTTER, E. C., & CO., Manchester.
See MUCKLEY, W. R. } Painted Fabrics.
MUCKLEY, A. F. }   Sec. XIV.

POWELL, WILLIAM, Worcester School, 1871-76. 1884.
School Work. Cast.   Sec. I.

POYNTER, EDWARD JOHN, R.A., 28 Albert Gate, S.W. Somerset House School, 1849 or 1850.
Four Frames. Ceiling Decorations. Billiard Room at Wortley Hall, near Sheffield. Design. Decoration for Soffit of Arch of Lecture Theatre, South Kensington Museum. Three Designs for Wall Tile Decoration of

the Grill Refreshment Room, South Kensington Museum. Subjects, "January," "February," "March." Painted Decorations.   Sec. XVI.

POYNTON, HENRY, Coventry, 1858-1864. 1877.
(Richardson, Elson, & Co.) Iron Gates. Brass work.   Sec. V.

PRATT, RALPH, Leeds School, 1870-1881. 1883-84.
Study. "Discobolus."   Sec. I.

PRICE, RICHARD B., Charterhouse School, 1872-73.
Bas-relief. Silver Panel.   Sec. VI.

PROCOPIDES, CONSTANTINE, Manchester School, 1881-82. 1884.
School Work.   Sec. I.
Design for Surface Decoration.   Sec. XVI.

PROPRIETORS OF THE "GRAPHIC" NEWSPAPER."
Engravings by Wilson, Walter T.
See WILSON, W. T.   Sec. XIX.

PROWETT, JAMES C., Stirling School, 1878-79. 1882-83.
Architectural Drawing.   Sec. XXI.

PRYOR, W., Sheffield, 1875-78.
(Pawson & Brailsford.) Lithographs.   Sec. XVII.
See also BATEMAN, W. E.

PURCELL, ROBERT, Manchester School, 1882-83.
(Edmundson, R. B. & Son.) Stained Glass.   Sec. III.

PYM BROTHERS, Dublin.
See BALL, SUSAN.   Sec. XI.
JORDAN, FRANCES L.   Secs. I., XI.
BAKER, ANNE.   Sec. XIII.

QUEEN, HER MAJESTY THE.
Head in Chalk from Life. Lent by Her Majesty.
See LOVERING, IDA.   Sec. I.

RAILTON, JAMES, Kilmarnock School, 1875-84.
School Work. Perspective Architecture.   Secs. I., XXI.

RAILTON, ISABELLA, Kilmarnock School, 1875-77.
School Work. Flowers, Water Colour.   Sec. I.

RAMSEY, ALLAN, West London School, 3½ years.
(Arthur, F., & Co.) Design.   Sec. I.
(Jeffreys & Co.) Wall Papers. Sec. XVI.
(Wollams & Co.) Wall Papers.   Sec. XVI.

RANDALL, GEORGE, Kidderminster School, 1877-84.
Technical Designs for Carpets. Technical.   Secs. I., XV.
(Assisted by William Tucker, Head Master.)

L

SCHOOL OF ART, WOOD CARVING,
Albert Hall.
　Wood Carving.　　　　　Sec. VIII.
　See WOOD CARVING SCHOOL.

SCIENCE & ART DEPARTMENT,
South Kensington, W.
　Students' Works:—
　See ANDREW, P. W.　　　　Sec. XIX.
　　BEDFORD, GEORGE.　　　Sec. XVI.
　　ELLIS, J.　　　　　　　Sec. XVI.
　　GAMBLE, J.　　　　　　Sec. XIX.
　　GIBBONS, F.　　　　　　Sec. XVI.
　　LANE, R. P.　　　　　　Sec. XVI.
　　MARSHALL, W.　　　　　Sec. XVI.
　　MERRITT, W. J.　　　　Sec. XVI.
　　MORRIS, R. J.　　　　　Sec. II.
　　RANDALL, J.　　　　　　Sec. XX.
　　RANDALL, W. F.　　　　Sec. VI.
　　SKIDMORE, HARRIET.　　Sec. XX.
　　SYKES, GODFREY.　　　Sec. II.
　　TOWNROE, R.　　　　　Sec. XIX.
　　WALLIS, ROSA.　　　　Sec. XX.
　　WILLIAMSON, J. J.　　Sec. XX.
　　WILSON, WALTER.
　　　　　　　　Secs. VII., XIX., XX.
　　WATKINS, J.　　　　　Sec. XIX.
　　WISE, W.　　　　　　　Sec. XIX.
　Painted or Plain Photographs, Designs
　and Drawings, of Art Objects, South
　Kensington Museum.

SCOTT, CUTHBERTSON, & CO.,
Paper Stainers, Chelsea.
　Paper Hangings.
　See DRAKE, G. E.　　　　Sec. XVI.

SCOTT, WALTER, Coventry, 1864–73.
　(Rotherham & Sons.) Jewellery. Watch
　Cases. Designs.　　　Secs. I., VII.
　Studies. Stages.　　　　Sec. I.

SCRIVEN, JAMES, West London
School, 9 months.
　Marble Bust.　The Young Augustus.
　Study.　　　　　　　Secs. I., IX.

SEADON, ROBERT, Hanley School,
1856.
　(Doulton & Co.) Vases and Bowls.
　Porcelain.　　　　　　Sec. II.
　Assisted by Mr. JOHN SLATER.

SEARLE, EMMA E., St. Martin's
School, W.C., 1 year.
　Glass. Stained Glass. Mirror Frame.
　　　　　　　　　　　　Sec. III.

SEAWARD, S. C., Andover, 1869–77.
　(Staines Linoleum Co.) Personal. De-
　sign. Linoleum Floor Cloth.
　　　　　　　　　　　Secs. I., XXII.

SEDDING, J. D.
　(Longdon & Co.) Metal Work. Wrought-
　iron Balustrade.　　　　Sec. V.

SELONS, or SELOUS, EMILY (MRS.
FENNESSEY), Queen Square School,
Bloomsbury, 1868–73.
　Model for Bronze "Cimabue" Statuette.
　　　　　　　　　　　　Sec. V.
　(Lent by Art Union of London.)

SEWARD, EDWIN, Cardiff School,
1870–76.
　Photo Gold Key.　　　　Sec. VI.
　Photo Stone Carvings.　　Sec. IX.
　Architectural Drawings.　Sec. XXI.
　A Catalogue (Bookbinding).
　　　　　　　　　　　Sec. XVIII.

SEWELL, ARTHUR J., Nottingham
School, 1872–81.
　Design. Lace Curtains.　Sec. X.

SHARP, THOMAS WILLIAM, South
Kensington, 1868–72.
　(Toleman, J. & Co.)　Paperhangings.
　　　　　　　　　　　Sec. XVI.

SHAW, E. & CO., Kidderminster.
　See PARK, J. H.　　　　Sec. XV.
　　DUCK, D.　　　　　　Sec. XV.
　　COTTON, A.　　　　　Sec. XV.

SHAW, MARY, Dublin Metropolitan
School, 1879–84.
　Study. "Apollo."　　　Sec. I.
　Mantel-board Embroidery　Sec. XII.

SHELDON, GEORGE, Nottingham
School, 1869–73.
　Designs. Lace Shawl.　Secs. I., X.

SHELDON, JOHN, Macclesfield. 1865–
1872.
　(Birchenough & Co.)　Silk Brocades for
　Hangings and Garments, Cashmeres,
　Silk and Satin Mufflers.　Sec. XII.
　Designs for Lace.　　　Sec. X.

SHELDON, FREDERICK W., Macclesfield, 1870–83.
　(Birchenough & Co.) Silk Brocades,
　Satin Damasks, Silk and Satin Hand-
　kerchiefs and Mufflers.　Sec. XII.

SHELTON, CHARLOTTE F., Cheltenham School, 1880–83.
　Designs. Silk Hangings and Mantel-
　boards.　　　　　　　Sec. I., XII.

SHEPHERD, GEORGE W., Coalbrook-
dale, 1871–79. 1881–82. South Ken-
sington, 1880.
　Design. Iron Gates and Fireplace.
　　　　　　　　　　　Secs. I., IX.
　Per School. Design. Iron Panels. Sec. I.
　Per Coalbrookdale Iron Co. Metal
　Work.　　　　　　　　Sec. V.
　Design for Bay.　　　　Sec. IX.

SHEPHERD, R. H.
　See NISBET, ETHEL CHAPMAN.　Sec. I.

SHEPPARD, PHILIP H. S., Preston,
Avenham School, 5 years.
　Architectural Drawing.　Sec. XXI.

L 2

SMITH, THOMAS, or FRANK, Dublin Metropolitan School, 1868-76.
Silver Chasings. Sec. VI.

SNOW, JAMES, Stoke-on-Trent & Fenton School, 1877-80.
One Oval Tray. 13s. 6d. each Sec. II.
One Heart Tray. 4s. 6d. each. Sec. II.
Keramics, per Mintons, Voucher Reg. No. 3541. 9th April, 1884.

SOCIETY OF ANTIQUARIES OF LONDON (The Council).
See WALLIS, ROSA.
Secs. XVII., XIX., XX.

SOCKL & NATHAN, Jewin Crescent, E.C.
See WATSON, ADA. Sec. XVII.
SWAN, ALICE C. Sec. XVII.

SOPER, WILLIAM, Brighton School, 1862-63. South Kensington, 1875.
Enamel Painting. Sec. IV.

SOUTH KENSINGTON NATIONAL ART TRAINING SCHOOLS.—(The Students).
Twenty-five Frames. Painted Photographs. Sec. XXII.
Four Frames. Designs for Silver Plate. Sec. VI.
Thirteen Frames. Models in Terra Cotta, and Photographs of the same. Sec. II.
Three Imperial Frames. Photo-plastic Decoration. Sec. IX.
Twenty Frames. Etchings and Engravings. Sec. XIX.
See also DAVIS, LOUIS. See. XVI.
PAGE, JOHN W. E. Sec. XVI.
PALIN, MAINWARING. Sec. XV.
SCIENCE & ART DEPARTMENT.

SOUTH KENSINGTON NATIONAL ART TRAINING SCHOOLS.
Present Students, 1884—
ABRAHAMS, F. X. Secs. I., II.
BRADBURN, J. W. Secs. I., II., III., V., VI., XV.
DODD, C. T. Secs. I., V., VI.
HALL, P. Secs. I., VIII.
HENNEY, G. F. Sec. I., II., V.
HEWITT, A. E. Secs. I., V.
GATER, J. Secs. I., V., VI.
PEARCE, J. Secs. I., V.
POOLE, J. O. Secs. I., VIII.
MULLIGAN, W. A. Secs. I., V., VI.
LEIGHTON, F. Secs. I., III.
PENSON, F. Secs. I., XV.
SPENCER, A. Secs. I., V.
RIDER, H. Secs. I., V., VI.
RHODES, R. Secs. I., II., XV.
TOMLINS, H. J. Secs. I., II., VI., XV.
WARD, G. Secs. I., VI., VIII.
WHITE, W. F. Secs. I., VIII.

SMALL, MISS E. Secs. I., II., VIII.
BUTTERTON, MISS M. Secs. I., II.
LUPTON, MISS E. B. Secs. I., II.
WILSON, E. W. Secs. I., II.

SPALL, THOMAS, Birmingham School, 1869-73.
(Elkington & Co.) Ornamental Metal Work. Silver. Sec. V.
Electro Plate. Sec. VI.

SPARKES, CATHERINE A., MRS., South Kensington Schools, 1859-61. Lambeth School, 1861-66.
Frame. Photographs of Ornamental Tiles, painted by herself. Keramics. Sec. II.
Subjects: Scene from "Comus." "King Lear."

SPENCER, A., South Kensington Schools, 1880-84.
Design. Clock Case. Secs. I., V.

SPICER, MISS, South Kensington Schools; Royal Albert Hall School.
Wood Carving. Gothic Panel. (Withdrawn.) Sec. VIII.

SPILLER, MARY ETHEL, Queen Square School, Bloomsbury, 1875-84.
Silk Fan. Sec. VII.

SPOONER, WILLIAM J., Nottingham School, 1878-84.
Design. Lace Fabrics. Curtains. Secs. I., X.

STAFFORD, GEORGE, Nottingham School, 1878-83.
Designs, Wall Paper, and Lace Curtains. Secs. I., X., XVI.

STAINES LINOLEUM MANUFACTURING CO. (THE).
See SEAWARD, SAMUEL C. Sec. I.

STANIFORTH, JOSEPH, Cardiff School, 1870-84.
(Owen, D., & Co.) Lithographs. Sec. XVII.

STANNUS, HUGH, Sheffield School, 1853-63.
(Atkin Brothers) Cup. Silver Plate. (Withdrawn.) Sec. VI.

STANTON, ROSE EMILY, Stroud School, 1862-72.
School Work. Sec. I.

STAPLETON, HARRY, St. Martin's School, 1871-74.
Jewellery. Sec. VII.

STAPLETON & SON, Poland Street, W.C.
See STAPLETON, HARRY Sec. VII.

STARR, JOSEPH B., Macclesfield School, 1878-84.
Design for Silk Hanging. Secs. I., XII.

STAYNES, FREDERICK J., Nottingham School, 1879-83.
(M. Jacoby & Co.) Lace Curtains.
(Woodward, F., & Co.) 6 Edgings.
(T. B. Cutts.) Lace Edging. Sec. X.

STAYNES, GEORGE, Manchester School, 1883-84. Nottingham, 16 years.
Lithographs. Sec. XVII.

STEANE, ISAAC, Coventry, 1861-63.
Architecture. Sec. XXI.

STEELE, HARRIETTE, MRS., Plymouth School, 1883-84.
(Brannam, H. C.) Keramics. Sec. II.

STEER, AMY BEATRICE, Maidstone, 1881-82.
Keramic. Sec. II.

STEVENS & WILLIAMS, Stourbridge & Brierley Hill.
See BEECH, D. Sec. III.
CARDER, F. Sec. III.
HAMMOND, E. Sec. III.
HILL, J. Sec. III.
NORTHWOOD, WILLIAM. Secs. III., XIX.
NORTHWOOD, J. Sec. III.
ORCHARD, J. Sec. III.
SCHEIBNER, F. Sec. III.
SWAYNE, C. Sec. III

STEVENSON, DAVID W., Edinburgh School, 1859-67.
Terra Cotta Statuette. Sec. II.
Model, Platt Memorial, Oldham.
Design for Byron Memorial. Sec. XXII.

STEVENSON, W. G., Edinburgh School, 1864-75.
School Work. Machine Drawing. Sec. I.

STIRLING, JAMES, Dundee School, 1880-83.
School Work. Machine Drawing. Sec. I.

STOKE-UPON-TRENT, THE CORPORATION OF.
See CORPORATION, or TONKS, J. W. Sec. VII.

STOKOE, J. D., Leeds School, 1873-81.
Trade Cards. Sec. XVII.

STORMER, EMILY E., Lambeth School, 1875-79.
(Doulton & Co.) Keramics. Pâte sur Pain. Sec. II.

STORY, BLANCHE, Nottingham School, 1866-84.
Design. Lace Curtains. Secs. I., X.

STRANGE, W. E., Manchester School, 1880-84.
Design. Ornament. Decoration. Secs. I., XVI.

STRATTON, AMY, Salisbury, 1869-73.
(Yates & Co.) Carpets. Sec. XV.

STRODE & CO., St. Paul's Churchyard, E.C.
See TUCKER, G. E. Secs. V., XIX.

STUART, LOUISA, Lambeth School, 1883-84.
(Doulton & Co.) Keramics. Vase. Sec. II.

STUBBS, THOMAS, Newcastle-under-Lyme School, 1873-79.
One Dessert Plate. £4. Sec. II.
Keramics per Mintons, Voucher Reg. No. 3541. 9th April, 1884.

STURGEON, KATE, Lambeth School.
(Doulton & Co.) Plaque. Sec. II.

SUDDARS, FRANK, Bradford School (Grammar), 1881.
Study from Still Life. Water-colour. Stage 15B. Sec. I.

SURENNE, MARY H., Edinburgh School, 1864. 1869-82.
School Work. Chalk and Water Colour Drawings. Sec. I.

SUTHERS, WILLIAM, South Kensington School.
Study. Flowers. Sec. XXII.

SWAN, ALICE C., Cork, 1875-82.
(Sockl & Nathan.) Personal. Christmas Cards. Sec. XVII.

SWAYNE, CHARLES, Stourbridge School, 1883-84.
(Stevens & Williams.) Glass. Cut Decanter. Sec. III.
Hock Glass, orange.
Designed by F. Calder and John Northwood. Executed by C. Swayne.

SYKES, GODFREY (THE LATE), Sheffield School, 1843-54. Master of School, 1854-63.
(S. & A. Dept.) Drawings. Designs for Keramic Alphabetical Letters. Sec. XVIII.
Photographs of Terra Cotta Columns, designed by him. Sec. II., IX.

SYMES, PENELLA, Dublin Metropolitan School, 1878-84.
Design for Border Inlay. Secs. I., VIII.

TABOR, G. H., Lambeth School.
Designs. Painted Wall Tiles. Sec. I.
TANNAHILL, WILLIAM, Kilmarnock, 1871-78.
(Gregory, Thomson, & Co.) Carpets.
Sec. XV.
(Barbour, Anderson, & Co.) Curtains.
Sec. XV.
TARVER, JANE, Northampton School, 1877-79.
(Woollams.) Paperhangings. Sec. XVI.
TATE, EDWIN, York School, 1875-78. 1882-84.
School Work. Architecture. Rennaissance. Secs. I., XXI.
TATHAM, A. J., West London School, 1878-84.
Wood Inlay. Girondoles and Panel.
Sec. VIII.
Design. Frieze in Italian Style.
Sec. XXI.
Studies, Ornament. Sec. I.
(Woollams & Co.) Paperhangings.
Sec. XVI.
TATLER, ALBERT, Burslem School, 1882.
(Doulton & Co.) Keramics. Two Vases.
Sec. II.
TAYLERSON, JOHN E., Lambeth School, 1880-84.
Designs. Panel. Sec. I.
Panel in plaster. Sec. IX.
TAYLOR, EDWARD J., West London School, 3 years.
Study. Life Study. Sec. I.
TAYLOR, ELIJAH, Hanley School, 1881-84.
Two Flower Holders, 7s. 6d. Sec. II.
Keramics per Mintons, Voucher Reg. No. 3541, April 9, 1884. Sec. II.
TAYLOR, JOHN, Edinburgh School, 1869. 1872-75.
Studies. Antique; and from the round.
Sec. I.
TAYLOR, MARGARET, Edinburgh School, 1859-63.
(R. Grant & Sons.) Illuminations.
Sec. XVIII.
THATCHER, EUPHEMIA, Lambeth School, 1878-81.
(Doulton & Co.) Keramics. Vase.
Sec. II.
THATCHER, W. H., Kidderminster School, 1877-84.
Technical Designs for Carpets.
Secs. I., XV.
(Assisted by William Tucker, Head Master.)
THICKETT, ERNEST, Sheffield School, 1865. 1874-84.
Ornamental Wood-carved Mantle-piece.
Sec. VIII.
Designs for Silver Cup. Secs. I., VI.

THOMAS, GEORGE, Cardiff School, 1867-75.
Photographs. Architectural Buildings.
Sec. XXI.
THOMAS, HENRY PHELIX, Dublin Metropolitan School, 1863-68.
Designs. Sec. I.
(Fry & Co.) Damasks. Sec. XII.
THOMAS, JAMES, Westminster, Royal Architectural Museum, 1880-84.
Design for Mosaic Pavement.
Secs. I., II.
Design. Silver Salad Bowl. Sec. VI.
THOMAS, JOHN, Halifax School, 1873-83.
(Eastwood, H., & Co.) Tapestry. Curtains, &c. Sec. XV.
(Ward & Co.) Hanging Tapestry.
(Thomas, J.) Tapestries. Sec. XV.
Axminster Carpet Design. Secs. I., XV.
THOMPSON, E. L., Sheffield School, 1875-77.
Silver Work. Sec. VI.
THOMPSON, MINNIE G., Lambeth School, 1882-84.
(Doulton & Co.) Keramics. Mug.
Sec. II.
THOMPSON (MISS) SYDNEY M., Belfast School, 1871-83.
Design for Iron Work. Secs. I., V.
THOMPSON, SAMUEL, Sheffield, 1876. 1882-84.
(Hague & Co.) Fenders, etc. Sec. V.
THOMPSON, WILLIAM, Macclesfield School, 1876-82.
Design for Furniture Silk. Secs. I., XII.
THOMSON, EMILY G., Manchester School, 1866-70.
(Ackerman & Co.) ⎧ Christmas Cards.
⎨ Sec. XVII.
(De la Rue & Co.) ⎩
(Falkner, G., & Sons.)
Design for Stained Glass. Sec. III.
THOMSON, JOHN, Kilmarnock School, 1877-84.
School Work. Foliage. Sec. I.
Design for Hangings. Sec. XV.
(Gregory, Thomson, & Co.) Carpets.
Sec. XV.
THOMSON, R. R., Perth School, 1879-1883. Sydney Street, S.W.
Study. Stage 12a. Sec. I.
THORNLEY & CLARKE, Nottingham.
See FOSTER, A. Sec. X.

THORPE, STUART, Sheffield School, 1871–84.
Design.   Cast-iron Balustrade.   Fire
Dogs.   Secs. I., V.
Gold and Silver Communion
Plate.   . Sec. VI.

THURSTON, JAMES H., Wolver-
hampton, 1875–82.
Personal. School Work. Architecture.
Sec. XXI.

TIDMARSH, HENRY E., West Lon-
don School, 1878–84.
Design for Shield.   Secs. I., VI.
Plaques.   . Sec. II.
Ceiling.   Sec. XVI.

TINWORTH, GEORGE, Lambeth.
(Doulton & Co.) Panels and Groups.
Terra Cotta.   Sec. II.

TITE, G., Kilburn.   South Kensington
Schools, 1870–72.
Wood Carving. Tea Caddy, Table,
Cabinet, Sideboard.   Sec. VIII.

TOLEMAN, JAMES, 17 Goswell Road,
E.C.
See SHARP, T. W.   Sec. XVI.

TOMKINSON & ADAM, Kidderminster.
See ADAM, PETER.   Sec. XV.

TOMLINS, HENRY J., Worcester
School, 1872–82. South Kensington,
1882–84.
Designs.   Sec. I.
    „   for Coal Boxes.   Sec. VIII.
Umbrella Stands.   Sec. V.
Wall Papers.   Sec. XVI.
Iron Trays.   Sec. V.
Design. Silver Vase.   Secs. I., VI.
Design. Earthenware Vase. Secs. I., II.
Design. Brussels Carpet. Secs. I., XV.

TONKS, JOSEPH WILLIAM, Bir-
mingham School, 1854–63.
(Bragg, T. & J.) Jewellery. Personal
Ornaments. Jewelled Bouquet Holder.
Chatelaine. Presented to H.R.H. the
Princess of Wales at Swansea, 1881.
Sec. VII.
Lent by H.R.H. the Princess of
Wales.
(Blanckensee & Son.)   Silver Spade.
Ivory Handle, enamelled and gilt.
Presented to H.R.H. the Princess of
Wales at Leicester, 1882.   Sec. VII.
Lent by H.R.H. the Princess of
Wales.
(Blanckensee & Son.) Gold Key. Gothic
Design.   Presented to H.R.H. the
Prince of Wales, K.G., at Leicester,
1882.   Sec. VII.
Lent by H.R.H. the Prince of
Wales, K.G.

(Bragg, T. & J.) Suit of Jewellery:—
Collarette, Bracelet, Ear-rings (gold).
Property of Mrs. T. Dix Perkin.
Harrow.   Sec. VII.
Lent by Mrs. T. Dix Perkin.
(Bragg, T. & J.) Gold Chain and Badge.
Corporation of West Bromwich. Gift
of Earl of Dartmouth.   Sec. VII.
Silver Mace. Corporation of West
Bromwich. Gift of Alderman R Farley.
Sec. VII.
Lent by the Corporation of West
Bromwich.
(Bragg, T. & J.)   Gold Chain and
Badge, Corporation of Stoke-upon-
Trent. Gift of Colin Minton Camp-
bell, 1875.   Sec. VII.
Lent by Corporation of Stoke-on-
Trent.
(Bragg, T. & J.) Photographs. The
Corporation Regalia of Stockport,
Accrington, Neath, Swansea, Kidder-
minster, Walsall and Rochester. De-
sign for an Album Cover.
(Bragg, T. & J.)   Gold Chain and
Badge. Corporation of Rotherham.
Sec. VII.
Lent by Corporation of Rotherham.
(Bragg, T. & J.) Silver Key, presented
to John Bright, Esq., M.P., 1883, at
Birmingham.   Sec. VII.
Lent by John Bright, Esq., M.P.
Seals.   Corporation Seals for City of
Bangor and Boroughs of Accrington
and Bacup. Impressions of the seals.
Sec. VII.

TONKS, WILLIAM, & SONS, Birmingham.
See BEATTIE, CHALLEN.   Sec. V.

TOOLEY, H., Great Yarmouth School,
1881–84.
Studies, Ornament.   Sec. I.
Illumination.   Sec. XVII.

TORQUAY TERRA COTTA WORKS,
Torquay (T. BENTLEY, Manager).
See FISHER, ALEXANDER.   Sec. II.

TOWNROE, R., Sheffield School,
1848–58.
(S. & A. Dept.) Design for a Certificate.
Sec. XVIII.

TRACEY, AGNES, Ipswich School,
1868–83.
(Jeffreys & Co.) Wall Papers, &c.
Sec. XVI.

TRAVELL, THOMAS F., Nottingham
School, 1875. 1879–80. 1882–84.
Design. Lace.   Secs. I., X.

TREGO, JOHN J., Coventry School,
1866–70. 1875–84.
School Studies. Stages 3ᵇ, 5ᵃ, 5ᵇ, 8ᵇⁱ,
8ᵇ², 15ᵃ, 22ᵃ, 23ᵇ, 23ᶜ, 23ᵈ.   Sec. I.
Designs, Metalwork.   Sec. V.
    „   Watch Cases.   Sec. VII..

TRELOAR AND SONS, Ludgate Hill, E.C.
Durham Axminster Carpets. Designed by Micah Chambers, Durham School.
Sec. XV.
(Lent by Messrs. Treloar & Sons.)

TREW, ANTHONY F., Bristol School, 1874-80.
Studies. Architectural Drawings.
Secs. I., XXI.

TREW, JOHN F., Bristol School, 1882-1884.
Studies. 'Designs for Stone and Iron Screens.' Secs. I., XXI.

TROWER, CHARLOTTE GEORGINA, East Herts School, 1882-84.
Designs. Lace. Secs. I., X.

TUCK, RAPHAEL, & SONS, London.
Christmas and Birthday Cards.
See JAMES, CHARLOTTE. Sec. XVII.

TUCKER, GEORGE EDWARD, West London School, 1874-84.
(Strode & Co.) Metal Work & other objects. Secs. I., V., XIX.
Carved Woodwork. Sec. VIII.
Painted Panels. Sec. XVI.
Painted Frieze. Sec. XVI.
Design for Silver Work. Sec. VI.

TUCKER, WILLIAM, Head Master, Kidderminster School.
Drawings illustrating a technical course for carpet designers, developed by himself.
See CANTRELL, JOHN.
HARRISS, GEORGE.
MOUNTFORD, FREDERICK.
BARKER, GEORGE.
CARTER, C. J.
RANDALL, GEORGE.
THATCHER, W. H.

TURNER, EDWARD J., West London School, 1875.
Design. Painted Panel. Sec. I., XVI.

TURNER, E. PAGE, Sheffield, 1854-63.
Tiles. Wood Mantel. Sec. II., VIII.
Decorations. Sec. XVI.

TURNER, F. E., Derby Central School, 1870-81.
Collective Exhibit. Sec. XVIII.
See DERBY CENTRAL SCHOOL.

TURNER, WILLIAM, & RHIND, JOHN, Edinburgh School.
(Morton, Scott & Co.) Tapestry.
Sec. XV.
Frieze. Sec. XVI.

TURNER, WILLIAM, Edinburgh School, 1880-82.
(Morton, W., Scott, & Co.) Drawing of Actual Tiles. Sec. II.
Grate with Tiles. Sec. V.

TURTON, GEORGE F., Nottingham School, 1872.
Design. Lace Curtain. Sec. I., X.

TYZACK, HENRY, Sheffield School, 1870-80.
Study. Bas-relief. Plaster Panel.
Secs. I., IX.

TYSON, JAMES, JUNIOR, Preston.
Avenham School, 7 years.
School Work. Drawing in Chalk. Fruit.
Sec. I.

TYSON, JAMES, SENIOR, Preston.
Avenham School, 7 years.
Study in Plaster. Cornice. Sec. I.

TWEMLOW, MARY, Dublin Metropolitan School, 1881-84.
Design. Sec. I.
Embroidery. Sec. XII.

TWIGGE, ANNE L., Exeter School, 1871-84.
Designs. Honiton Lace. Secs. I., X.

ULLATHORNE, THOMAS S., Selby School, 1871-84.
Architectural Drawings. Sec. XXI.

URIE, ALLIE, Kilmarnock School, 1878-1884.
Water Colour. Fruit from Nature.
Drapery. Oil Colour from Nature.
Sec. I.

URSULIN CONVENT, Cork.
See MEADE, ELIZA. Sec. X.
Irish Lace.

URWIN or IRWIN, MARIA L., Royal Albert Hall School, Lambeth School, 1881.
Wood Carving. Sec. VIII.

VANKOERT, CORNELIUS, West London School, 1880-84.
Studies. Chalk. Antique. Sec. I.

VARGAS, MISS, Lambeth School.
(Doulton and Co.) Faience, Tiles and Doulton Ware. (Doulton Pavilion.)
Sec. II.

VARIAN, AGNES, Dublin Metropolitan School, 1879-83.
Study. Apples. Water Colour. Sec. I.

VARLEY, EMILY LUCY, Queen Square School, Bloomsbury, 1880-1884.
(Rimmel.) A Fan. Silk. Sec. VII.
(Griggs.) Chromolithograph. Sunflower.
Sec. XVII.
School Studies. Sec. I.

VINCE, J. M., Yarmouth School, 1871-1874. 1878-84.
School Work. Sec. I.
Wrought Iron Panels. Sec. V.

WAHAB, HENRIETTA E., Royal Albert Hall; South Kensington School, 1883-84.
Wood Carving. Bellows. Sec. VIII.

WARD, J. W. & C., Halifax.
See CHAMBERS, J. H. Sec. XV.
CROSSLEY, FREDERICK. Sec. XV.
SMITH, J. B. Sec. XV.
DILWORTH, SAMUEL. Sec. XV.
WEBSTER, W. H. Sec. XV.
CAMPBELL, DAVID. Sec. XV.
CAMPBELL, DUNCAN. See XV.

WARD, G., South Kensington Schools, 1881–84. Devizes School, 1878–81.
Design. Table Top. Inlaid Wood. Sec. I.
Design. Drinking Cup. Silver. Sec. I.

WATCOMBE TERRA COTTA CO., Torquay, S. Mary Church.
See BEDFORD, GEORGE. Sec. II.
DAVEY, ARTHUR JAMES. Sec. II.

WATERHOUSE, JOSEPH, Manchester School, 1850–55.
Fabrics. (Printed Cotton.) Sec. XIV

WATERS, LIZZIE, Lambeth School, 1880–82.
(Doulton & Co.) Keramics. Bottle. Vase. See II.

WATERSTON, GEORGE, & SONS. Edinburgh.
See ANDERSON, ELIZABETH F. Sec. XVIII.
BRAMAH, THOMAS. Sec. XXII.
BLACK, W. S. Sec. XVIII.
GIBB, WILLIAM. Sec. XVII.
GIBB, W. Sec. XVII.
ANDERSON, ELIZABETH F. Sec. XVIII.

WATKINS, JOHN, Birmingham, 1871–1872; & South Kensington Schools, 1873–75.
(Elkington & Co.) Metal Work. A Shield. (Chased by T. Spall.) Sec. VI.
The Design for the Shield. Sec. VI.
J. Watkins is now in Paris. Ateliers Merson, Rue Notre Dame des Champs.
2 Title Pages. Sec. XVIII.
(Lithograph. Petit.)
Twenty Engravings for "L'Art." Sec. XVIII.
(S. & A. Dept.) Eleven Pen-and-Ink Drawings. Interiors of S. K. M.
(S. & A. Dept.) One Pen-and-Ink Drawing. Interior of Bethnal Green Branch Museum.
(S. & A. Dept.) One Pen-and-Ink Drawing. Library of late John Foster. Sec. XIX.

ATKINS, JOSEPH, Dublin Metropolitan School, 1863–71.
Busts. Sec. I., XXII.

ATSON, ADA, Cambridge School, 1878–80.
(Sockl & Nathan.) Lithographs. Sec. XVII.

WATSON, MRS., Gloucester, 1861–66.
School Work. Chalk Drawing, Scroll. Sec. I.

WATSON, MOORWOOD & CO., Sheffield.
Metal Work. Grate. Sec. V.
See LAWSON, J.

WATSON, W. P., South Kensington School.
Water-colour Study from Nature. Sec. I.
Five Architectural Drawings. Sec. XXI.

WATSON, W. S., South Kensington Schools.
Design. Carved Wood Panel. Sec. VIII.

WEATHERSTONE, ALFRED C., West London School, 1879–84.
Design. Oak Chimney Piece. Wall Papers. Sec. I., VIII., XVI.

WEBB, FREDERICK T., Wolverhampton, 1871–77.
School Work. Decoration. Sec. XVI.

WEBB, THOMAS & SONS, Stourbridge.
See FACER, JABEZ. Sec. III.
HILL, WILLIAM. Sec. III.
RICHARDSON, W. HENRY Sec. III.
SMITH, FRANCIS. Sec. III.
WOODALL, GEORGE. Sec. III.
WOODALL, THOMAS. Sec. III.
GOODYEAR, E. Sec. III.
DAVIS, HARRY A. Sec. III.
FEREDAY, JOHN T. Sec. III.
ADEY, WILLIAM. Sec. III.
HODGETTS, JOSHUA. Sec. III.
KING, THEODORE. Sec. III.
DAVIS, HARRY A. Sec. III.
FEREDAY, J. T. Sec. III.
HOLLIS, B. Sec. III.

WEBB, WALTER H., West London School, 4 years.
School Work. Outlines. Bust. Heads in Chalk. Sec. I.
Study in Sepia. Sec. I.

WEBSTER, AGNES, South Kensington School.
Two School Sketches. Sec. I.

WEDGWOOD & SONS, Worcester.
See BRETT, MARY. Sec. II.

WEBSTER, W. H., Halifax, 1870–74.
(Ward, J. W. & C.) Hangings. Sec. XV.

WEEKS, CONSTANCE E., West London School, 2½ years.
Design. Plaque. Secs. I., II.

WELDON, W. H., College of Arms, Queen Victoria Street, E.C.
See PERRY, W. Secs. I., XVI.

WELLAND, WILHELMINA, West London School, 5 years.
School Work. Still Life and group. Oil. Sec. I.

WELLS, AUGUSTA, Queen Square School, Bloomsbury, 1856–61.
Study of Fruit. Sec. I.

WEST, ALICE L., Bloomsbury School, 1868–73.
A Fan. Sec. VII.
(De la Rue & Co.) Lithographs. Sec. XVII.

WEST BROMWICH, THE CORPORATION OF.
See CORPORATION OF WEST BROMWICH.

WEST, MAUD ASHLEY, Queen Square School, Bloomsbury, 1874–80.
(De la Rue & Co.) Christmas Cards. Designs. Sec. XVII.

WESTCOTT, MINNIE H., Leeds School, 1878–84.
School Work. Drapery Study. Sec. I.

WESTWOOD, FREDERICK, Birmingham Schools, 4 years.
(Parkes & Westwood, F.) Jewellery. Sec. VII.
St. Paul's Day School; Frederick Street Middle Class School; Howard Street Institute; schools.
Jewellery and Personal Ornaments.

WHEATON, LOUISE, Exeter School, 1875–84.
Designs. Honiton Lace. Sec. I., X.

WHEELERSMITH, OLIVE, West London School, 1880–83.
School Work. Still Life. Sec. I.

WHITEHOUSE, WILLIAM, & CO., Birmingham.
See MADDOX, T. W. Sec. V.

WHITESIDE, H. J., Birkenhead, 1881–1884.
Studies. Stages 14ᵃ, 5ᵃ, 5ᵇ, 3ᵇ. Sec. I.

WHITE, EDWARD, 20 Cockspur Street, S.W.
See SLOCOMBE, CHARLES E. Secs. I., IV.
Hall or Table Striking Clock; Metal Gilt Case. Student's Design.

WHITE, WILLIAM H., Bristol School, 1882–84.
Architectural Drawings. Sec. XXI.

WHITE, W. F., South Kensington Schools, 1879–84. Leeds School, 1875–1879.
Design. Table Top. Inlaid Wood. Sec. I.

WHITEHEAD, A., South Kensington.
Design. Doorway. Secs. I., IX.

WHITTAKER, GEORGE, Newcastle-under-Lyme School, 1880–84.
One Dessert Plate. Sec. II.
Two Tazzas on feet, 12s. 6d. each. Sec. II.
Keramics per Mintons, Voucher Ref. No. 3541, April 9, 1884. Sec. II.

WHITTALL, M., & CO., Kidderminster.
See PARK, J. H.
DUCK, D.

WIGG, B. H. G., Great Yarmouth School, 1880–84.
Designs. Painted Tiles. Secs. I., II

WIGG, MARGARETTE, Yarmouth School, 1880–84.
Studies. Designs for Muslin. Secs. I., XII

WILD, JAMES, Macclesfield, 1868–7
(Birchenough & Co.) Figured Sat Dress. Design. Piece of Figured Sil Moyen Age. Silk Mufflers. Sec. XI

WILKINSON, H., & CO., Sheffield.
See PARR, JOSEPH, Metal Work. Secs. II.,

WILLIAMSON, J. J., South Kensington Schools, 1869–71. 1873.
(S. & A. Dept.) 14 Coloured Photograp Original Objects in the South Ke sington Museum. From H.R.H. T Prince of Wales' Indian Collecti Sir Richard Wallace, Bt., Collecti late John Jones' Collection. Sec.

WILLIAMS, HENRY, Coalbrookda 1882–84.
(Allen, B. Broseley.) Keramics. Pla Vase, Etruscan. Sec

WILLIAMS, MISS C., Royal Alb Hall School. Bloomsbury Scho 1881.
Wood Carving. Sec.

WILSON, ARBAR, Edinburgh Scho 1881–83.
Architecture. Sec.

WILSON, C. E., Sheffield School, 16 1880.
Designs. Cast-iron Lamp. Band S &c. Sec. I., V.,
Metal Work. Se

WILSON, E. W., Lambeth Sch 1880–83.
Design. Tiles for Dado. Secs.

WILSON, GEORGE WILLI Westminster School, 1883–84.
Design. Frieze for a Chimney Pie Secs. I.

WILSON, H. & SONS, Kilmarnock.
See YOUNG, R. Sec. XV.

WILSON, THOMAS, Edinburgh
School, 1865-75.
(Ballantine & Sons.) Painting on Glass.
Sec. III

WILSON, T. WALTER, South Ken-
sington Schools, 1868-73.
Six Frames. Drawings for Engravings:
for "Graphic" and "Dramatic Notes."
(Bogue) (Proprietors of "Graphic")
Sec. XIX.
One Frame. Designs. Jewellery; pre-
sentation and personal.
Sec. VI.
(Benson & Son.) Casket, gold and
jewelled. (Presented to H.I.M. The
Emperor of Russia. Sec. VI.
(Garrards.) Two Necklaces with Pen-
dants. Casket. For H.R.H. The Prince
of Wales, K.G. Sec. VII.
(S. & A. Dept.) Coloured Photograph.
Limoges Enamel Dish; in the Col-
lection of Sir Richard Wallace, Bart.
Sec. IV.
Study. Tempera Painting, from Nature.
Sec. I.

WILSON, WILLIAM, Dundee School,
1872-80.
School Work. Power Loom. Machine
Drawings. Sec..I.

WINBURY, ALFRED, Kidderminster,
1873-83.
(Morton & Sons.) Carpets Sec XV.

WINBURY, WILLIAM, Kidderminster, 1870-80.
(Morton & Sons.) Carpets. Sec. XV.

WINDASS, JOHN, York, 1866-70.
Selby, Thirsk, York Institute, Schools.
School Studies. Sec. I.
Designs. Damasks. Plate, Cup and
Saucer. Secs. I., II.

WINDASS, MRS., M.A.S, York School,
1881-84.
Painting on China.. Tea Service.
Sec. II.

WINTERBOTTOM, A., Sheffield
School, 1873-84.
Designs. Bronze Doors. Sec. I., V.
Silver Candelabrum. Sec. VI.
Porcelain. Sec. II.
Doorway, Wood. Sec. VIII.

WISE, ALICE, Kilmarnock School.
School Work. Sec. I

WISE, W., South Kensington School.
(S. & A. Dept.) Design for Certificate.
(Lithograph, H. Harrel.) Sec. XVIII.

WITTS or WILLS, ROBERT, Dundee
School, 1879-82.
School Work. Machine Drawing. Crane.
Sec. I.

WOOD CARVING SCHOOL OF ART,
Royal Albert Hall.
See CHISHOLM, B. Sec. VIII.
ROWE, ELEANOR. Sec. VIII.
REEKS, MARIA. Sec. VIII.
PAIGE, W. Sec. VIII.
URWIN, MARIA. Sec. VIII.
WAHAB, HENRIETTA. Sec. VIII.
YOUNG, MAGGIE. Sec. VIII.
WILLIAMS, MISS. Sec. VIII.
SMITH, Miss. Sec. VIII.
MONTFORD, H. L. Sec. VIII.
WALTON, C. H. Sec. VIII.
HOLT, Miss J. C. Sec. VIII

WOOD, JOHN W., Nottingham School,
1872-80.
Design. Lace Curtains. Secs. I., X.

WOOD, MILLY, Leeds School, 1878-
1884.
School Work. Figure Study. Sec. I.

WOODALL, AMY E., West London
School, 4½ years.
School Work. Chalk Studies. Sec. I.

WOODALL, GEORGE, Stourbridge
School, 1867-68.
(Webb & Sons) Glass Ware. Sec. III.

WOODALL, THOMAS, Stourbridge
School, 1863-81.
(Webb & Sons.) Glass Ware. Sec. III.
(Thomas Webb & Sons) Stourbridge.
Glass Bowl and Plate. Sec. III.

WOODALL, WILLIAM H., West
London School, 4½ years.
School Work. Head, Chalk Drawing.
Sec. I.
Designs. Floor and Wall Tiles.
Sec. II.

WOOD, FREDERICK, Burslem School,
1881-84.
(Doulton & Co.) Keramics. 2 plates.
Sec. II.

WOODHOUSE, F. W., South Kensing-
ton Schools.
Architecture. Design for a Collegiate
School. Sec. XXI.

WOODWARD, F., Broad Street, Not-
tingham.
Lace Curtains.
See STAYNES, W. J. Sec. X.

WOODWARD, GROSVENOR, & CO.,
Kidderminster.
See COTTON, ALFRED. Sec. XV.

WOOLLAMS, WILLIAM & CO., High Street, Marylebone, W.

See BENNETT, R.	Sec. XVI.
AUMONIER, LOUISA.	Sec. XVI.
CHURCHER, G. P.	Sec. XVI.
DAVIS, OWEN W.	Sec. XVI.
ELLIS, HENRY W.	Sec. XVI.
HAITÉ, G. C.	Sec. XVI.
HAY, T. W.	Sec. XVI.
LILIE, B. A.	Sec. XVI.
MANNOOCH, ALFRED.	Sec. XVI.
NOBLE, H.	Sec. XVI.
RICKATSON, R. O.	Sec. XVI.
SILVER, A.	Sec. XVI.
TATHAM, A. J.	Sec. XVI.
TARVER, JANE.	Sec. XVI.
HALL, THOMAS, Jun.	Sec. XVI.
MORRIS, P. WILSON.	Sec. XVI.
RAMSEY, ALLEN.	Sec. XVI.

(Wall Papers.)

WOOLLATT, GEORGE, Nottingham School, 1867-78.
Design. Lace Curtain. Secs. I., X.

WOON, ANNIE K., Edinburgh School, 1874-83.
School Work. Studies. Head in Chalk.
Design, stage 12*. Sec. I.

WOOTON, JAMES, Burslem School, 1870-72.
(Doulton & Co.) Tankards, &c. Porcelain. Sec. II.
(Assisted by Mr. John Slater.)

WORTH, LUCY, Nottingham School, 1862-72.
(Linthorpe Pottery Co.) Keramics. Dessert Plates. Sec. II.

WORTH, T. B., Stourport.
See PARK, J. H., Kidderminster. Sec. XV.
DUCK, D., Kidderminster.

WRIGHT, A., Stoke-on-Trent School, 1864-67.
(Mintons.) Keramics. Two Panels. Sec. II.
(Hollins Minton.) Keramics. Two Panels of Tiles. Colours. Sec. II.

WRIGHT, ALBERT, Hanley School, 1872-82.
(Doulton & Co.) Vases. Porcelain.
(Assisted by Mr. John Slater.) Sec. II.

WRIGHT, JOHN E., Nottingham School, 1869-72.
Design. Lace Curtain. Secs. I., X.

WRIGHT, J. R., Selby School, 1878-1884. 1876-79 at Leeds School.
School Work. Still life. Water Colour. Sec. I.

WRIGHT, WILLIAM, Hanley, 1863-1872.
(Bodley, E. J. D. & Co.)
Keramics. Sec. II.
Ewer and Basin. Plates. Biscuit Box.

WYBURD, LEONARD, West London School, 2 years.
Design. Tiles. Secs. I, II.
School Work. Studies. Sec. I., XV.
Decorative Designs. Sec. XVI.

WYLIE & LOCKHEAD, Glasgow.
Wall Papers. Secs. XVI., L
See ADAMS, C. J., Leicester School.

YATES & CO., Wilton, Salisbury.
See NOYLE, W. A. Sec. XV.
STRATTON, AMY. Sec. XV.

YATES, PARDOE, Wilton Branch School, Salisbury, 1871-73.
Carpets. Sec. XV

YEATES, GEORGE G., Dublin Metropolitan School, 1869-84.
Study. Life Studies. Sec. I

YOUATT, BESSIE J., Lambeth School, 1878-84.
(Doulton & Co.) Keramics. Jug. Sec. II

YOUNG, MISS, Royal Albert Hall School, Bloomsbury School, 1879.
Wood Carving. Sec. VIII

YOUNG, ROBERT, Kilmarnock, 1866-1867.
(Wilson, H. & Sons.) Carpets. Sec. XV

YOUNG, LILIAN, Queen Square School, Bloomsbury, 1876-84.
(Griggs.) Chromo-lithograph.
Fox Glove. Sec. XVII
Designs for Lithographic Work. Sec. XVII
Design. Tapestry. Secs. I., XV

ZINK, GEORGE FREDERICK, West London School, 6 years.
School Work. Study of Antique. Sec.

ZUBER & CO., Rixheim, Alsace.
See HOOD, HENRY. Sec. XV

H. S.

Schools of Art offering objects to Science and Art Department
Exhibition, to illustrate the Operations and the Influence
of Schools of Art, 1884.

ALPHABETICAL LIST.

ABERDEEN, MECHANICS' INSTI-
TUTION.—J. P. Fraser, Master. Sec. VI.

ALLEN STREET BRITISH SCHOOL,
Blackfriars.—(See METROPOLIS.)

ANDOVER.—Samuel Seaward, Master.
Sec. I.

AVENHAM INSTITUTE. (See PRESTON.)
W. B. Barton, Master. Secs. I., XXI,

BARNSLEY.—J. B. Taylor and J. S. Ingall,
Masters. Sec. XI.

BARNSTAPLE.—Joseph Kennedy, Master.
Sec. VIII.

BATH.—C. M. Hodges, Master.
Secs. I., VIII., XVIII.

BELFAST.—G. Trowbridge and J. Sumner,
Masters. Sec. XV.

BIRKENHEAD.—John Bentley, Master.
Sec. I.

BIRMINGHAM.—E. R. Taylor and others,
Masters. Secs. I., V., VI., XIX., XXII.

BLOOMSBURY. (See METROPOLIS.)—
Louisa Gann, Mistress.
Secs. I., II., III., VIII., XVII., XXII.

BOSTON.—Vernon Howard, Head Master.
Sec. I.

BRADFORD TECHNICAL COL-
LEGE. Sec. XIII.

BRIGHTON.—Alexander Fisher, Master.
Secs. IV., VIII.

BRISTOL.—J. N. Smith, Master.
Secs. I., II., XV., XVI., XVIII., XX., XXI.

BROSELEY.—J. P. Bacon, Master. Sec. II.

BURSLEM.—George Theaker, Head Master
Sec. II.

CAMBRIDGE.—Daniel Wood, Master.
Secs. XVI., XVII., XIX.

CARDIFF.—J. Bush, Master.
Secs. V., IX.., XVI., XVII., XXI., XXII.

CHARTERHOUSE. (See METROPOLIS.)—
F. Black, Master. Sec. V.

CHELTENHAM.—C. S. Millard, Master.
Sec. V.

CHESTER.—W. Craister, Master.
Sec. VIII.

CIRENCESTER.—James Miller and J. W.
Taylor, Masters. Secs. II., VIII., XV.

CITY AND SPITALFIELDS.—(See
METROPOLIS.) Secs. IX., X.

COALBROOKDALE.—Owen Gibbons and
F. Gibbons, Masters. Sec. I., II., V.

CORK.—James Brenan, Master.
Secs. II., VIII. X., XIII., XVII.

COVENTRY.—John Anderson, Master.
Secs. I., V., VII., XII., XXI.

CROYDON.—W. Wallis, Master, and Mary
Hackford, Mistress.
Secs. III., XII., XVI., XVII., XVIII., XIX.

DARLINGTON.—Samuel Ellton, Master.
Sec. II.

DERBY. — A. A. Bradbury and others.
Masters. Secs. I., V., VI., XV, XVIII.

DERBY CENTRAL SCHOOL OF
ART, Derby.—T. Simmonds, Past Master.
Sec. XVIII.

DEVONPORT.—H. R. Babb, Master.
Sec. I.

DORCHESTER.—Thomas Baker, Master.
Sec. I.

DOVER.—W. H. East, Master. Sec. I.

DUBLIN METROPOLITAN SCHOOL.
(See METROPOLITAN.) R. E. Lyne, Master.
Secs. I., VI, X., XI.

DUBLIN ROYAL SOCIETY. (See
ROYAL.) R. E. Lyne, Master.
Secs. I., XVI., XVII.

DUDLEY.—David Jones, Master.
Secs. I., III , V.

DUNDEE.—W. M. Grubb, P. W. Lawder, and others, Masters.　　Sec. I.

DURHAM.—F. Thompson, Master.
Sec. XV.

EAST HERTS.—G. A Wood, Master.
Secs. I., XIII., XXI., XXII.

EDINBURGH.—E. W. Marshall, Master, or Charles W. Hodder, Head Master; Alex. W. Inglis, Secretary.—Rosa E. Woon, Mistress.
Secs. I., II., III., VI., VII., VIII., IX., XII., XV., XVI., XVII., XVIII., XIX., XXII.

EXETER.—James B. Birkmyer, Master.
Secs. I., VIII., X.

FARNHAM.—Joseph Hill, Master.
Sec. VIII

FEMALE CHROMOLITHO-GRAPHIC STUDIO, 33 Red Lion Square, W.C.—B. Faustin, Director. Per Queen's Square School, Bloomsbury, W.C. (*See* METROPOLIS.)　　Sec. XVII.

FEMALE CHROMOLITHO-GRAPHIC STUDIO, Royal Albert Hall, Kensington, W.—B. Faustin, Director. Per National Art Training School, South Kensington, W. (*See* METROPOLIS.)
Sec. XVII.

FENTON.—(*See* STOKE-UPON-TRENT.

FINSBURY.—(*See* METROPOLIS.)

FROME, SOMERSET.—W. G. H. Collins, Master.　　Sec. V.

GLASGOW.—Thomas S. Simmonds, Head Master.
Secs. I., V., VI., VIII., IX., XII., XV.

GLOUCESTER.—John Kemp, Head Master.
Secs. I., IX., XVIII.

GOSPORT.—A. Fisher, Head Master.
Secs. I., XV., XVI., XXI.

GREAT YARMOUTH. (*See* YARMOUTH.)
J. F. Ryan, Master.　　Secs. I., III., VI.

HALIFAX.—W. H. Stopford, Master.
Secs. I., X., XV., XVI.

HANLEY.—S. J. Cartlidge, Master. Sec. II.

HASTINGS AND ST. LEONARDS.—
M. Sullivan, Head Master.　　Secs. I., XXI.

HUDDERSFIELD.—H. Burrows, Master.
Sec. VIII.

HUDDERSFIELD TECHNICAL SCHOOL & MECHANICS INSTITUTE. — Austin Keon, Secretary.
Sec. VIII

HULL.—John Menzies and Maria Menzies Master and Mistress.　　Sec. VI

INVERNESS.—Peter H. Smart, Master.
Sec. VIII

IPSWICH.—W. F. Griffiths, Master.
Secs. III., XVI

KENDAL.—G. Turner, Master.　　Sec.

KIDDERMINSTER.—W. Tucker, Master
Secs. XIII., XV

KILMARNOCK.—Charles B. Millar and R. P. McHowell, Masters.
Secs. I., III., VIII., XV., XVI

KING'S LYNN.—E. T. Bearcroft, Master
Sec. XV

LAMBETH, MILLER'S LANE. (*See* METROPOLIS.)—H. J. Dennis and I. Nightingale, Masters.　　Secs. I., II., XVI

LANCASTER.—Herbert Gilbert, Master.
Sec. VII

LEEDS.—A. Stevenson and T. Ramsden Masters.　　Secs. I., VIII., XVII., XXI

LEICESTER.—Joseph Harrison, Master.
Secs. I., XVI., XVII., XX

LONDONDERRY. — Joseph P. Addey Master.　　Secs. I., XVI., XVI

LONDON SCHOOLS OF ART. (*See* METROPOLIS.)

LONG ACRE. (*See* METROPOLIS.)—John Parker, Master.　　Sec.

MACCLESFIELD. — W. Scott, Master Vouchers on Reg. Paper No. 3763, 16 April 1884.　　Secs. I., XII., XX

MACCLESFIELD SCHOOL OF ART —W. Scott, Master. Vouchers on Reg. Paper No. 3763, 16 April, 1884.　　Sec.

MACCLESFIELD EMBROIDERY SCHOOL. — J. O. Nicholson, Secretary. Vouchers on Reg. Paper No. 4045, 22 April 1884.　　Secs. XII., XX

MAIDSTONE.—　　　　　　　Sec.

MANCHESTER.—R. H. Willis, Z. Prichard, J. H. Farran, W. E. Crowther and others, Masters.
Secs. I., III., VIII., XI., XIV., XV XVII., XVIII., XX

MANSFIELD.—F. Sherwood, Master.
Sec. X

METROPOLIS.—
ALLEN STREET (British School). Sec. XV

BLOOMSBURY, W.C. (See QUEEN'S SQUARE.) Louisa Gann, Mistress.

CHARTERHOUSE, E.C.—F. Black, Master.
Sec. V.

CHROMOLITHOGRAPHIC SCHOOLS. (*See* FEMALE CHROMOLITHOGRAPHIC STUDIO, Red Lion Square, W.C.; and Royal Albert Hall, W.)

CITY AND SPITALFIELDS, E.C. Secs. I., X.

FINSBURY (now closed). Sec. VI.

LAMBETH (MILLER'S LANE).—H. J. Dennis and L. C. Nightingale. Secs. I., XVII.

LONG ACRE, W.C.—John Parker, Master.
Sec. V.

MARLBOROUGH HOUSE, S.W., now SOUTH KEN-SINGTON. Sec. XIX.

NATIONAL ART TRAINING SCHOOL, South Kensington, W. (*See* SOUTH KENSINGTON.)

SOMERSET HOUSE, W.C.; now SOUTH KEN-SINGTON. Secs. XV., XVI.

ST. MARTIN'S, W.C.—John Parker and A. Mason, Masters. Secs. XVI., XVII.

QUEEN'S SQUARE, W.C.— Louisa Gann, Mistress. Secs. I., III., VIII., XVII., XXII.

WEST LONDON, N.W.—J. S. Rawle, Head Master.
Secs. I., II., V., XII., XIV., XV., XVI., XVII., XIX., XXII.

WESTMINSTER ROYAL ARCHITECTURAL MU-SEUM.—F. Brown, Master. Sec. XVI.

ETROPOLITAN SCHOOL, DUB-LIN.—R. E. Lyne, Master.
Secs. I., VI., X., XI.

IDDLESBORO'.—J. W. Watson, Master.
Sec. II.

ATIONAL ART TRAINING SCHOOL, South Kensington, S.W.—(*See* SOUTH KENSINGTON.)

EWCASTLE-UNDER-LYME.—T. J. Bacon, Master. Sec. II.

EWCASTLE - ON - TYNE. — Joseph Moore, W. C. Way, J. Watson, and others, Masters. Sec. XIV.

ORTHAMPTON.—H. Hill, Master.
Sec. XVI.

ORWICH.—R. Cochrane, Master.
Sec. VIII.

OTTINGHAM.—T. J. Dalgleish, Master.
Secs. I., II.

OXFORD.—Alexander Macdonald and H. B. Price, Masters. Sec. XXI.

PERTH.—F. M. Black, Master. Secs. I., XI.

PLYMOUTH.—H. R. Babb and G. H. Evans, Masters. Secs. I., II.

PRESTON. (*See* also AVENHAM.) W. B. Barton, Master. Sec. I.

QUEEN'S SQUARE. (*See* METROPOLIS.) Louisa Gann, Mistress.

READING.—Charles R. Havill, Master.
Sec. XVI.

ROTHERHAM.—George A. Illston, Master.
Secs. I., V.

ROYAL DUBLIN SOCIETY.—R. E. Lyne, Master. Secs. I., XVI., XVII.

RYDE, ISLE OF WIGHT.—Wm. Cox, Master. Sec. II.

SALISBURY.—Joseph Harris, Master.
Secs. I., II., XV., XVI.

SCHOOL OF ART, WOOD CARV-ING, SOUTH KENSINGTON. (*See* WOOD.)—Eleanor Rowe, Secretary.
Sec. VIII.

SELBY.—John Windass, Master.
Secs. I., III., XXI.

SHEFFIELD.—Thomas Cook, Master.
Secs. I., II., V., VI., VIII., IX., XVI., XVII., XIX.

SHIPLEY, THE SALT SCHOOLS.—Edward Renard, Head Master.
Secs. XV., XVI., XVII.

SHREWSBURY. — Charles Cortissos, Master. Sec. XVI.

SLEAFORD.—Mary Wedd, Mistress.
Sec. I.

SOMERSET HOUSE. (*See* METROPOLIS.)

SOUTHAMPTON.—T. C. Charbonier and A. W. F. Langman, Masters.
Secs. VIII., XIX.

SOUTH KENSINGTON. — J. C. L. Sparkes, Principal, and others.
Secs. II., V., VI., VIII., XII., XVI., XVII. XXI., XXII

ST. MARTIN'S. (*See* METROPOLIS.) John Parker and others, Masters.

STIRLING.—Leonard Baker, Master.
Secs. XVII., XXI.

STOKE-ON-TRENT AND FENTON. —J. P. Bacon, Master. Secs. II., V., XXI.

M

STOURBRIDGE.—E. J. Simms, Master.
Secs. I., II., III., XIX.

STROUD, GLOUCESTER.—W. H. C.
Fisher, Secretary. W. Broad, Master.
Secs. I., VIII.

SUNDERLAND.—W. C. Way and J. W.
Stubbs, Masters.   Sec. VIII.

TORQUAY.—George Bedford, Head Master.
Secs. I., II.

WALSALL.—C. Gregory, Master.   Sec. I.

WARRINGTON.—J. C. Thompson, Master.
Secs. I., II., V., VI.

WEST LONDON. (*See* METROPOLIS.) J.
S. Rawle, Head Master.

WESTMINSTER.—(*See* METROPOLIS.) F.
Brown, Master.   Sec. XVI.

WEYMOUTH.—T. Baker, Master.   Sec. I.

WOLVERHAMPTON.—A. Gunn, Master.
Secs. XVI., XXI.

WOOD CARVING, SCHOOL OF ART, ROYAL ALBERT HALL, SOUTH KENSINGTON. — Eleanor
Rowe, Secretary.   Sec. VIII.

WORCESTER. — Albert Hodder, Head
Master.   Secs. I., II.

YARMOUTH.—J. F. Ryan, Head Master.
(*See* GREAT YARMOUTH.)   Secs. I., III., VI.

YORK.—J. A. Kean and J. Windass, Masters,
Secs. I., III., XVIII., XXI.

YOUNG MEN'S CHRISTIAN INSTITUTE, Long Acre, W.
Sec. V.

MANUFACTURERS offering objects designed by Students of Schools of Art of the United Kingdom to the Science and Art Department Exhibition, to illustrate the operations and the influence of Schools of Art. 1884.

ALPHABETICAL LIST OF FIRMS.

ACKERMAN & CO., Regent Street, W.
Chromo-lithographs. Sec. XVII.

AGNEW, THOMAS, & SONS, Manchester; & London.
Gilt Picture Frame. Sec. XXII.

ALDERTON, H., Brighton.
Furniture. Sec. VIII.

ALLEN, W., Coalbrookdale, or ALLEN, B., Broseley.
Keramic Ware. Sec. 11.

APPLEYARD, MESSRS. & SONS, Sheffield.
Furniture. Sec. VIII.

ARMITAGE & IBBETSON, Bradford.
Lithographs. Sec. XVII.

ARTISTIC STATIONARY CO., Holborn, W.C.
Lithographs. Sec. XVII.

BAILEY, G., & CO., Derby.
Illuminations. Sec. XVIII.

BALLANTINE & SONS, Edinburgh.
Glass. Sec. III.

BARBOUR, ANDERSON & CO., Glasgow.
Dress Fabrics. Carpets. Secs. XII., XV.

BARTON, W., & CO., Boston, Lincolnshire.
Keramic Ware. Sec. II.

BARWELL, J., & CO., Birmingham.
Metal Work. Sec. V.

BENSON & SON, Ludgate Hill.
Gold and Jewelled Casket. Sec. VI.

BESSBOROUGH CO., Newry, Ireland.
Damasks. Sec. XI.

BIRCHENOUGH, J., & SONS, Macclesfield.
Furniture and Dress Fabrics. Silk. Sec. XII.

BLANCKENSEE & SONS, Birmingham.
Gold Key. Silver Spade. Sec. VII.

BODLEY, E. J. D., Burslem.
Keramic Ware. Sec. II.

BOGUE, DAVID, London.
Engravings. Sec. XIX.

BRADFORD ART NEEDLEWORK SOCIETY.
Curtains. Sec. XV.

BRAGG, T. & J., Birmingham.
Jewellery and Plate. Secs. VI., VII.

BRANNAM, C. H., Barnstaple.
Keramic Ware. Sec. II.

BRAY, NICHOLAS, Sheffield.
Silver and Plated Ware. Sec. VI.

BRENDON & SONS, Plymouth.
Lithographs. Sec. XVII.

BROADHEAD, GEORGE, Nottingham.
Lace. Sec. X.

BROWNHILL POTTERY CO., Tunstall.
Keramic Ware. Sec. II.

BROWN, W. & F., & CO., Chester.
Furniture. Sec. VIII.

BRUCKMAN, F., Munich.
Lithographs. Sec. XVII.

CAMM, BROTHERS, Smethwick.
Glass. Sec. III.

CAMPBELL, SMITH, & CAMPBELL, Oxford Street, W.C.
Stained Glass. Sec. III.

M 2

CAREY & SONS, Nottingham.
Lace. Sec. X.

CARLISLE & CLEGG, Queen Victoria Street, E.C.
Wall Papers. Sec. XVI.

CASH, J. & J., Coventry.
Trimmings. Sec. XII.

CLAY, SONS, & TAYLOR, Bread Street Hill, E.C.
Engravings. Sec. XIX.

COALBROOKDALE IRON CO., Shropshire.
Iron and Metal Work. Sec. V.

CONSTABLE, T. A., & CO., Edinburgh.
Ornamental Stationery. Sec. XXII.

COPE, J., Stoke-on-Trent.
Keramic Ware. Sec. II.

CORBITT, W., & CO., Rotherham.
Metal Work. Sec. V.

COWLISHAW, NICOL, & CO., Manchester.
Furniture and Carpet Fabrics. Secs. XII., XV.

COWTAN & SONS, London.
Furniture. Sec. VIII.

CRAVEN, DUNNILL & CO., Jackfield, Shropshire.
Tiles. Sec. II.

CROFTS & ASSINDER, Birmingham.
Metal Work. Sec. V.

CROSSLEY, J., & CO., Halifax.
Carpets. Sec. XV.

CUTTS, THOMAS B., Nottingham.
Lace Edgings. Sec. X.

DALZIEL BROTHERS, London.
Lithographed Certificate. Sec. XVIII.

DAVENPORT, MESSRS., Longton.
Porcelain and Pottery. Sec. II.

DAVIS, W., & SONS, Cardiff.
Wall Papers. Sec. XVI.

DE LA RUE & CO., Bunhill Row, E.C.
Lithographs. Sec. XVII.

DERBY CROWN PORCELAIN CO., Derby.
Porcelain. Sec. II.

DIXON, H. J., & SONS, Kidderminster.
Carpets. Sec. XV.

DOULTON & CO., High Street, Lambeth; and Nile Street, Burslem.
Pottery and Porcelain. Sec. II.

DUFF & CO., Edinburgh.
Wall Papers. Sec. XVI.

DUFFY, JAMES, Dublin.
Lithographs. Sec. XVII.

DUMET, M. M., Paris.
Wall Papers. Sec. XVI.

DUNTHORNE, R., Vigo Street, W.
Engravings. Sec. XIX.

EASTWOOD, H., & CO., Huddersfield.
Carpets. Sec. XV.

EDMUNDSON, R. B., & SON, Manchester.
Glass. Sec. III.

EDWARDS, G., & SON, Glasgow.
Plate. Sec. VI.

ELKINGTON & CO., Regent Street, W.
Ornamental Metal Work and Plate. Secs. IV., V., VI.

EYRE & SPOTTISWOODE, Great New Street, W.C.
Lithographs. Sec. XVII.

FALKNER, G. & SONS, Manchester.
Lithographs. Sec. XVII.

FERGUSON, T., & CO., Bainbridge, Ireland.
Damasks. Sec. XI.

FINE ART SOCIETY, New Bond Street, W.
Etchings. Sec. XIX.

FLEMING, J., & CO., Leicester.
Lithographs. Sec. XVII.

FORD, T. & CO., Birmingham.
Metal Work. Sec. V.

FRAMPTON, E., Buckingham Palace Road, S.W.
Stained Glass. Sec. III.

FREEMAN & COLLIER, Manchester.
Metal Work. Sec. V.
Silver Plate. Sec. VI.

FRY & CO., Dublin.
Damasks. Sec. XI.
Furniture. Sec. VIII.

FURNIVAL, T., & SON, Stafford.
Pottery. Sec. II.

GARRARD, R. & S., Haymarket, W.
Silver Cups and Plate. Sec. VI.

GIBBS & CANNING, Tamworth.
Terra Cotta. Sec. II.

GILLOW & CO., Oxford Street, W.
Furniture.   Sec. VIII.
Wall Papers.   Sec. XVI.

GLANVILL & CO., Blackfriars, S.E.
Linoleum.   Sec. XXII.

GOODALL, E. & CO., Manchester.
Furniture.   Sec. VIII.
Decoration.   Sec. XVI.

GRANT, R., & SON, Edinburgh.
Illuminations.   Sec. XVIII.

GREEN, W., & SONS, Kidderminster.
Carpets.   Sec. XV.

GREGORY, THOMPSON, & CO., Kilmarnock.
Carpets.   Sec. XV.

GRIGGS, W., Peckham.
Chromo-lithographs.   Sec. XVII.

HAGUE & CO., Sheffield.
Fenders and Metal Work.   Sec. V.

HAMEL & WRIGHT, Nottingham.
Lace.   Sec. X.

HAMILTON, CRICHTON, & CO., Edinburgh.
Presentation Salver.   Sec. VI.

HAMILTON, HILL, & CO., Belfast.
Damasks.   Sec. XI.

HARRISON, C., Stourport.
Carpets.   Sec. XV.

HAYWARD, J. A., Darlington.
Furniture.   Sec. VIII.

HELBRONNER, R., Oxford Street, W.
Embroidery.   Sec. XII.
Carpets.   Sec. XV.

HENDERSON & CO., Durham.
Carpets.   Sec. XV.

HEYMAN & ALEXANDER, Nottingham.
Lace.   Sec. X.

HILDESHEIMER & FALKNER, Jewin Street, E.C.
Lithographic Work.   Sec. XVII.

HODKINSON, H. P., Art Metal Works, Coventry.
Metal Work.   Sec. V.

HOLLAND & SONS., Mount Street, W.
Furniture.   Sec. VIII.

HOLLINS MINTON.
See MINTON HOLLINS.

HOWARD & SONS, Newman Street, W.C.
Furniture.   Sec. VIII.

HOYLE, THOMAS, & SONS, Manchester.
Printed Cotton Fabrics.   Sec. XIV.

HUNT & ROSKELL, New Bond Street, W.
Silver Plate.   Sec. VI.

JACOBY, M., & CO., Nottingham.
Lace.   Sec. X.

JEFFREY & CO., Essex Road, N.
Wall Papers.   Sec. XVI.

JESSOP, C. H., Sheffield.
Metal Work.   Sec. V.

JOCKEL, C., & CO., Edinburgh.
Hangings and Decorations.   Sec. XV.

JOHNSTONE, W., Edinburgh.
Photograph of a Cab.   Sec. XXII.

JONES, H. O., Stoke-on-Trent.
Pottery and Porcelain.   Sec. II.

KENDAL, MILNE, & CO., Manchester.
Furniture.   Sec. VIII.

KIRKWOOD, R. & H. B., Edinburgh.
Silver Metal Work, &c.   Secs. VI., VII.

LETHERAN, W., & SONS, Cheltenham.
Metal Work.   Sec. V.

LILEY & WOOD, Radnor House, Gloucester Square, W.
Furniture.   Sec. VIII.

LINTHORPE POTTERY CO., Middlesborough.
Pottery and Porcelain.   Sec. II.

LOCK & CO., Bristol Road, Bath.
Carved Wood Panel.   Sec. VIII.

LONGDEN & CO., Sheffield.
Metal Work.   Sec. V.
Furniture.   Sec. VIII.

McCREA & CO., Halifax.
Carpets and Hangings.   Sec. XV.

McINTYRE, Burslem.
Porcelain Clockcase.   ⎫
Candlesticks.   ⎬ Sec. II.
Vases.   ⎭

MACKAY & CHISHOLM, Edinburgh.
Silver Plate.   Sec. VI.

MACKAY & CUNNINGHAM, Edinburgh.
Silver Plate.   Sec. VI.

MAGEE & CO., Belfast.
Decoration.   Sec. XVI.
Damasks.   Sec. XI.

MALKIN, EDGE, & CO., Burslem.
Tiles.   Sec. II.

MASON, HERBERT, & CO., Birmingham.
Metal Work.   Sec. V.

MAW & CO., Benthall, Broseley.
Tiles, &c.   Sec. II.

MEESON, JAMES, Sheffield.
Silver Work.   Sec. VI.

MILNE & SON, Lancaster.
Furniture.   Sec. VIII.

MILLWARD, A. J., Kendal.
Furniture.   Sec. VIII.

MINNS, JOHN, Norwich.
Furniture.   Sec. VIII.

MINTON, HOLLINS, & SONS, Stoke-
on-Trent.
Pottery and Porcelain.   Sec. II.

MINTONS, LIMITED, Stoke-on-Trent.
Pottery and Porcelain.   Sec. II.

MORTON & CO., Darwell.
Lace Curtain.   Sec. X.

MORTON, W., SCOTT, & CO., Edinburgh.
Secs. II., VI., VIII., XII., XV., XVI., XXII.

MORTON & SONS, Kidderminster.
Carpets.   Sec. XV.

MUSGRAVE & CO., Belfast.
Design. Iron Gates.   Sec. V.

NAYLOR, T. & A., Kidderminster.
Carpets.   Sec. XV.

NEWMAN, A., Maddox Street, W.C.
Silver Mounts for Furniture. Sec. VIII.

NICHOLSON, J. O., Macclesfield.
Embroidery. Silks.   Sec. XII.

NORTHWOOD, J. & J., Stourbridge.
Glass.   Sec. III.

NORTON, GEORGE, Sheffield.
Silver Plate.   Sec. VI.

OLIVER & ATCHERLEY, Manchester.
Damasks.   Sec. XI.

PARKES & WESTWOOD, Birmingham.
Silver Ornaments.   Sec. VI.

PAWSON & BRAILSFORD, Sheffield.
Illuminations, &c.   Secs. XVIII., XIX.

PEARCE, HENRY, 4 New Street,
Huddersfield.
Silver Plate. Goldsmith's Work.
                                    Sec. VI.
Jewellery.   Sec. VII.

PERROT & HABERZHON, Rotherham.
Metal Work.   Sec. V.

POTTER, E. O., & CO., Manchester.
Fabrics, Prints.   Sec. XIV.

PYM BROTHERS, Dublin.
Silk Fabrics.   Sec. XII.

RHIND, JOHN, Edinburgh.
Carpets.   Sec. XV.

RHIND, WILLIAM BERNIE, Edinburgh.
Statue Models.   Sec. XXII.

RHODES & BARBER, Sheffield.
Silver Work.   Sec. VI.

RHODES, JEHOIADA, Sheffield.
Silver Plate.   Sec. VI.

RICHARDSON & CO., Barnsley.
Damasks.   Sec. XI.

RICHARDSON, ELLSON, & CO., Coventry.
Metal Work.   Sec. V.

RIMMEL, E., Strand, W.C.
Fans.   Sec. VII.

ROBB, WILLIAM, Aberdeen.
Silver Work.   Secs. VI., VII.

ROBERTSON, R. C., & SONS, Kilmarnock.
Furniture Ware.   Secs. III., VIII.

ROODHOUSE & SONS, Leeds.
Photo: Furniture.   Sec. XXII.

ROTHERHAM & SONS, Coventry.
Engraved Watch Cases, Gold and Silver.
                                    Sec. VI.

SALE, J. J., & SONS, Manchester.
Chromo-lithographs.   Sec. XVI.

SCHIPPER, T. F., & Co., King Street,
W.C.
Chromo-lithographs.   Sec. XVI.

SCOTT, CUTHBERTSON, & CO.,
Chelsea.
Wall Papers.   Sec. XVI.

SHAW, E., & Co., Kidderminster.
Carpets.   Sec. XV.

SHRIGLEY & HUNT, John Street,
W.C.
Tiles.   Sec. II.
Glass.   Sec. III.

SHIELDS, Wallace Works, Perth.
Damasks. Sec. XI.

SIBBALD & SONS, Edinburgh.
Chimney-piece. Secs. I., XXI.

SINGER, JOHN W., & SONS, Frome.
Art Metal Work. Sec. V.

SMALE, W., & SONS, Macclesfield.
Silk Goods. Sec. XII.

SMART, THOMAS, Dudley.
Metal Work. Sec. V.

SMITH, R., & SONS, Kidderminster.
Carpets. Sec. XV.

SOCKL & NATHAN, Jewin Crescent, E.C.
Chromo-lithographs. Sec. XVII.

STAINES LINOLEUM CO., Staines.
Patterns for Linoleum. Secs. I., XXII.

STAPLETON & SON, Poland Street, W.
Jewellery. Sec. VII.

STEVENS & WILLIAMS, Brierly Hill, Stourbridge.
Glass. Sec. III.

STRODE & CO., St. Paul's Churchyard, E.C.
Metal Work. Sec. V.

THOMAS, JOHN, Halifax.
Tapestry Hangings. Sec. XV.

THOMPSON, E. L., Sheffield.
Silver Work. Sec. VI.

TOLMAN, JAMES, Goswell Road, N.
Wall Papers. Sec. XVI.

TOMKINSON & ADAM, Kidderminster.
Carpets. Sec. XV.

THORNLEY & CLARKE, Nottingham.
Lace. Sec. X.

TORQUAY TERRA COTTA CO., Torquay.
Terra Cotta. Sec. II.

TUCK, RAPHAEL, & SONS, London.
Christmas and Birthday Cards. Sec. XVII.

TONKS, WILLIAM, & SONS, Birmingham.
Metal Work. Sec. V.

WALTON, F. & CO., Berners Street, W.C.
" Walton Decorations." Sec. XVI.

WALTERS, D., & SON, Newgate Street, E.C.
Silks, &c. Sec. XII.

WARD, J. W., & CO., Halifax.
Carpets. Sec. XV.

WATCOMBE TERRA COTTO CO., Torquay.
Terra Cotta. Sec. II.

WATERSTON, G., & SONS, Edinburgh.
Illuminations, &c. Sec. XVIII.
Chromolithographs. Sec. XVII.

WATSON, MOORWOOD & CO., Sheffield.
Metal Work. Sec. V.

WEBB, THOMAS, & SONS, Stourbridge.
Glass. Sec. III.

WEDGWOOD & SONS, Worcester.
Porcelain. Sec. II.

WESTWOOD, FREDERICK, Sheffield.
Jewellery. Sec. VII.

WHITEHOUSE, W., & CO., Birmingham.
Metal Work. Sec. V.

WHITTALL & CO., Kidderminster.
Carpets, Sec. XV.

WHITE, EDWARD, Cockspur Street, W.
Gilt Metal Clock. Sec. VI.

WILEY & LOCKHEAD, Glasgow.
Wall Papers. Sec. XVI.

WILSON, H. & SONS, Kilmarnock.
Carpets. Sec. XV.

WOODWARD, FRANK, Nottingham.
Lace. Sec. X.

WOOLLAMS, WILLIAM, & CO., High Street, Marylebone.
Wall Papers. Sec. XVI.

WORCESTER ROYAL PORCELAIN WORKS.
Pottery and Porcelain. Sec. II.

WORTH, T. B. Stourport.
Carpets. Sec. XV.

YATES & CO., Wilton, Salisbury.
Carpets. Sec. XV.

YATES, PARDOE, Wilton, Salisbury.
Carpets. Sec. XV.

ZUBER & CO., Rixheim, Alsace.
Wall Papers. Sec. XVI.

INTERNATIONAL HEALTH AND EDUCATION EXHIBITION, 1884.

SCHOOLS OF ART EXHIBITION.

No. of Schools offering	118
No. of Schools exhibiting	78
No. of Students exhibiting	724
No. of Manufacturers offering	176
No. of Objects exhibited	1782

TRAINING CLASS AND NATIONAL SCHOLARSHIPS,

CENTRAL SCHOOL, SOUTH KENSINGTON.

ESTABLISHED BY THE DEPARTMENT OF SCIENCE AND ART.

As a supplementary record of the operations and the influence of Schools of Art, the following lists of Students who have passed through the National Art Training Class, and of those who have had the advantage of the National Scholarships, are appended.

The Training Class for Masters was established in 1853 at Marlborough House, and continued at South Kensington in 1857. The Students were selected from the various schools throughout the country, on passing a satisfactory examination, and executing certain prescribed works. A weekly stipend was allowed as maintenance allowance, according to ability and industry.

The National Scholarships were established in 1863 with a view to train designers for art manufactures, &c. These were tenable for two years, renewable for a third in cases of great proficiency, and the maintenance allowance varied from 20s. to 40s. a week.

LIST OF
STUDENTS IN TRAINING CLASS.

CENTRAL SCHOOL,
MARLBOROUGH HOUSE AND SOUTH KENSINGTON.
COMMENCING 1853.

LIST OF STUDENTS IN TRAINING FROM 1853.

Came.	Name.	Whence.	Appointed to.	Left.
November 1853	Allan, James B.	Metropolitan	Retired	March 1856
October 1853	Arthur, Thomas	Metropolitan	Retired	February 1857
October 1853	Anderson, Henry T.	Metropolitan	Birmingham	January 1855
January 1856	Anderson, Henry T.	Metropolitan	Truro	July 1857
January 1860	Anderson, Henry T.	Metropolitan	Retired	December 1860
March 1855	Atkinson, George M.	Cork	Birmingham	January 1857
April 1857	Atkinson, George M.		Retired	February 1859
March 1854	Ashworth, Susan A.	Metropolitan	Dublin	April 1855
March 1858	Ashworth, Susan A.	Metropolitan	Edinburgh	Sept. 1858
October 1855	Andrew, Frederick W.	Metropolitan	Employed S. K. Museum	
March 1858	Anderson, John	Stoke	Halifax	July 1860
March 1861	Anderson, John		Coventry	February 1863
February 1853	Bustin, R. B.	Metropolitan	Hereford	February 1854
December 1853	Van Bever, Anthony	Unconnected	Dismissed	July 1854
June 1853	Brook, Alfred Newton	Manchester	Glasgow	December 1853
February 1854	Brook, Alfred Newton	Manchester	Carlisle	Sept. 1854
November 1856	Brook, Alfred Newton	Manchester	Retired	July 1857
November 1858	Brook, Alfred Newton	Manchester	Cheltenham	January 1859
October 1854	Bacon, Joseph	Manchester	Potteries	October 1856
October 1853	Baker, William John	Unconnected	Southampton	April 1855
October 1853	Bowen, William P.	Worcester	Worcester	March 1854
October 1853	Baker, Leonard	Metropolitan	Dunfermline	March 1854
			Retired	1856
December 1853	Burkinshaw, Samuel	Birmingham	Liverpool	April 1855
October 1854	Bently, John	Macclesfield	Swansea	February 1857
June 1857	Bently, John	Macclesfield	Toronto	Nov. 1857
July 1859	Bently, John	Macclesfield	Birkenhead	January 1861
March 1855	Brenan, James	Dublin	Birmingham	April 1857
April 1858	Brenan, James	Dublin	Yarmouth	April 1860
June 1860	Brenan, James	Dublin	Cork	August 1860
October 1855	Blizard, Edward	Metropolitan	Birmingham	March 1860
October 1855	Bale, Edwin	Metropolitan	Retired	January 1863
March 1856	Broom, Edward	Metropolitan	Retired	December 1857
March 1854	Belinaye, Laura de la	Metropolitan	Retired, afterwards Queen's Square	December 1857
November 1856	Brophy, Patrick	Dublin	Great Yarmouth	December 1861
November 1865	Brophy, Patrick	Dublin	Dead.	February 1866
October 1855	Baines, Catherine	Metropolitan	Retired	February 1859
March 1857	Brophy, Nicholas A.	Dublin	Limerick	October 1859
March 1857	Banner, Alexander	Liverpool	Glasgow	July 1861
October 1857	Birtles, Thomas	Warrington	Dismissed	April 1858
October 1857	Birkmeyer, James B.	Liverpool	Exeter	January 1861
March 1860	Boon, William	Hanley	Canterbury	January 1865
May 1854	Clark, Thomas	Coventry	Limerick	October 1855
October 1859	Clark, Thomas	Coventry	Charter House	March 1861
June 1852	Croome, John D.	Unconnected	Waterford	July 1852
February 1854	Croome, John D.	Unconnected	Belfast	January 1856
November 1852	Collier, Thomas F.	Dublin	Cork	March 1853
			Marlboro' House	March 1855
January 1853	Cochrane, Robert	Unconnected	Dudley	March 1853

Came.	Name.	Whence.	Appointed to.	Lett.
October 1859	Cochrane, Robert	Unconnected	Norwich	January 1860
February 1853	Casey, William L.	Cork	Limerick	December 1853
April 1855	Casey, William L.	Cork	Lambeth	October 1855
June 6, 1853	Collinson, Robert	Manchester	Warrington	June 18, 1853
			Marlboro' House	October 1855
Oct. 17, 1853	McCloy, Samuel	Belfast	Waterford	Nov. 1853
October 1853	Cole, Archibald	Unconnected	York	October 1854
			Afterwards Madras	October 1855
February 1854	Cahill, Richard S.	Unconnected	Dunfermline	July 1856
October 1857	Cahill, Richard S.	Unconnected	Removed	February 1858
December 1853	Chevalier, Thomas Wm.	Metropolitan	Tavistock	Sept. 1854
October 1855	Chevalier, Thomas Wm.	Metropolitan	Yarmouth	July 1857
October 1854	Cotchett, Thomas	Metropolitan	Retired	February 1856
March 1855	Clark, Charles Macdonald	Manchester	South Kensington	October 1859
March 1856	Carter, James	Metropolitan	Burnley	April 1859
April 1861	Carter, James	Metropolitan	Hanley	October 1861
February 1854	Collins, Florence	Metropolitan	South Kensington	October 1855
March 1855	Channon, Mary E.	Metropolitan	South Kensington	December 1857
April 1856	Cosbie, William S.	Liverpool	Bristol	August 1860
March 1858	Cameron, Duncan	Dundee	Dismissed	January 1859
October 1858	Chandler, Edwin	Plymouth	Hull	October 1864
October 1859	Campbell, John A.	Metropolitan	No record	February 1865
December 1861	Collins, Emma	Metropolitan	Freemason's School, Clapham	April 1866
November 1852	Drummond, John G.	Cork	Llanelly	July 1853
September 1854	Drummond, John G.	Cork	Bath	April 1857
January 1853	Davies, James	Metropolitan	Carmarthen	June 1854
May 1857	Davies, James	Metropolitan	Bridgwater	January 1860
March 1854	Doidge, Sarah	Metropolitan	District Schools, London	January 1859
February 1860	Dundas, James	Dundee	Greenwich Hospital School	October 1864
October 1860	Dominy, John	Devonport	Yarmouth	October 1865
March 1861	Duncan, William	No record	Dismissed	March 1863
April 1853	Elton, Samuel	Metropolitan	Norwich	Sept. 1854
October 1856	Elton, Samuel	Metropolitan	Darlington	Nov. 1857
October 1855	Edgley, Sarah Jane	Metropolitan	Retired	July 1860
March 1858	Edwards, Maria	Metropolitan	Employed by Owen Jones	April 1864
March 1857	Edwards, John	Dumfirmlie	Stirling	Nov. 1858
October 1857	Elliott, Rebecca	Metropolitan	Retired	February 1862
October 1853	Finnie, John	Newcastle	Liverpool	July 1855
October 1854	Foster, William	Manchester	Birkenhead	July 1855
April 1855	Ford, William	Spitalfields	Retired	July 1857
April 1856	Fraser, A. Edward	Dublin	Clonmel	April 1860
November 1856	Ford, James	Penzance	Leeds	April 1861
October 1855	Freed, Mary A.	Metropolitan	No record	February 1858
March 1859	Freed, Mary A.	Metropolitan	No record	February 1861
October 1858	Fussell, Arthur	St. Martins	Retired	October 1859
October 1861	Fraser, John P.	Aberdeen	Salisbury	March 1867
April 1853	Gilbert, Herbert	Metropolitan	Bath	March 1854
September 1854	Gilbert, Herbert	Metropolitan	Lancaster	Sept. 1856
April 1853	Geofroi, H. M.	Metropolitan	Penzance	Sept. 1853
June 1853	Gill, George R.	No record	Truro	Sept. 1854
November 1853	Griffiths, William T.	No record	Yarmouth	Sept. 1854
October 1856	Griffiths, William T.	No record	Ipswich	July 1858
November 1853	Girling, Richard	No record	Retired	March 1856
October 1855	Gray, George	Potteries	Retired	July 1857
March 1856	Griffiths, John	Metropolitan	Employed by Department as modeller	October 1864
October 1855	Greene, Archibald	No record	Burnley	March 1858
April 1859	Greene, Archibald	No record	Taunton	October 1859

Came.	Name.	Whence.	Appointed to.	Left.
May 1856	Gallimore, Samuel	Potteries	Dismissed	July 1858
October 1859	Gallimore, Samuel	Potteries	Retired	July 1860
Dec. 29, 1855	Gibbs, Charlotte J.	Metropolitan	Retired	January 1861
June 1857	Griffiths, Richard	Carnarvon	Truro	March 1860
March 1858	Glass, Alexander	No record	Dismissed	July 1858
October 1858	Godwin, Mary	Dublin Lace School	Retired	Dec. 1863
December 1858	Geddes, William	Glasgow	Retired	February 1859
October 1859	Glenny, William Joseph	St. Martins	King's College	January 1865
October 1860	Gray, Thomas	No record	Dismissed	Sept. 1863
October 1861	Gillo, Robert	Bath	Retired (illness)	Sept. 1863
January 1853	Healy, James	Dublin	Clonmel	Sept. 1854
October 1853	Hagreen, Henry B.	No record	Appd. Marlboro' House	October 1855
February 1854	Holmes, Thomas	Dublin	Dublin	Nov. 1854
October 1859	Holmes, Thomas	Dublin	Devonport	October 1861
October 1854	Hodder, Charles D.	Metropolitan	Hanley	July 1856
October 1854	Hale, Robert	Manchester	Belfast	July 1856
March 1868	Hale, Robert	Manchester	No record	October 1869
October 1854	Hosford, Frederick F.	Cork	Carmarthen	May 1857
October 1854	Heazle, William	Cork	Retired	February 1858
March 1855	Harley, Robert	No record	Cambridge	October 1858
March 1854	Hipwood, Sarah	Metropolitan	Retired	February 1858
October 1855	Hill, John	Warrington	Bath	Nov. 1859
October 1855	Howard, Vernon	Metropolitan	Boston, Lincolnshire	January, 1861
November 1856	Hone, Alfred	No record	Dismissed	December 1859
October 1855	Harden, Maria	Metropolitan	Retired	July 1860
October 1856	Hodgetts, Thomas	Metropolitan	Retired	March 1857
September 1855	Hunt, Jane	Metropolitan	Retired	February 1858
February 1858	Hale, Henry Owen	Metropolitan	Retired	March 1858
March 1858	Harold, Henry	Finsbury	Retired	May 1858
October 1858	Hill, Henry	Birmingham	Retired	March 1860
October 1859	Hulme, Frederick E.	Metropolitan	Resigned	October 1864
March 1858	Hill, Joseph	Metropolitan	Dismissed	February 1861
October 1860	Hulme, Robert C.	Metropolitan	Retired	July 1863
October 1861	Haydon, Edward	Warrington	Retired	February 1863
March 1854	Jackson, William	No record	Retired	February 1855
November 1856	Jewsbury, Thomas	Metropolitan	Retired	February 1857
March 1858	Julyan, Mary	Metropolitan	No record	No record
March 1858	James, Charlotte	Metropolitan	Retired	October 1860
April 1858	Inskep, Janet	Metropolitan	No record	February 1864
February 1853	Kinnebrook, William A.	No record	Retired	January 1855
February 1854	Kemp, John	Cork	No record	January 1855
October 1858	Kemp, John	Cork	Gloucester	April 1860
October 1854	Kennedy, John	Dublin	Dundee	February 1856
March 1858	Kennedy, Joseph	Dundee	Kidderminster	February 1862
March 1860	Kelley, Edwin J.	Macclesfield	Lavers and Co., Glassworks.	October 1863
February 1854	Lanchenick, John Claude	Metropolitan	Retired	August 1854
December 1861	Lanchenick, John Claude	Metropolitan	Dismissed	Sept. 1862
January 1854	Lyne, Robert Edward	No record	Paisley	October 1854
October 1855	Lyne, Robert Edward	No record	Glasgow	October 1856
April 1854	Longshaw, Alfred B.	Macclesfield	Dismissed	July 1855
March 1855	Legge, Lionel	Metropolitan	Lancashire	July 1857
October 1857	Legge, Lionel	Metropolitan	Sheffield	October 1859
March 1854	Lord, John	Dublin	Newcastle	Sept. 1857
March 1854	Lees, Herbert	Metropolitan	Carlisle	January 1858
March 1855	Lamprey, Joshua	Dublin	Retired	July 1856
October 1855	Lock, Henry H.	Metropolitan	St. Helen's Gasworks	July 1856
October 1858	Lock, Henry H.	Metropolitan	Westminster ; left for India	Nov. 1863

Came.	Name.	Whence.	Appointed to.	Left.
October 1852	Muckley, William Jabez	Birmingham	Burslem	April 1853
March 1855	Mulligan, James A.	No record	Coalbrookdale	October 1856
February 1854	Mills, Eliza	Female School	Retired; Teacher Whiteland's College	April 1857
October 1855	Morley, William Arthur	Metropolitan	Edinburgh	October 1858
October 1855	Midwood, William H.	Huddersfield	Retired	May 1856
October 1855	Mattcaux, Clarina.	Female School	Retired	July 1860
January 1858	Mills, Samuel F.	Metropolitan	Spitalfields	Nov. 1863
April 1858	Miller, James	Aberdeen	Gloucestershire	March 1860
March 1859	Macdonald, Alexander	Dundee	No record	October 1864
October 1859	Mulready, Augustus E.	Metropolitan	No record	No record
March 1860	Morrogh, John J.	Cork	Retired	July 1860
October 1860	Menzies, John	Aberdeen	Appd. Charterhouse	April 1866
October 1855	Nichols, Alfred P.	Metropolitan	Bristol	October 1863
March 1858	Noyes, Henry J.	No record	Retired	July 1858
April 1854	Offord, John J.	No record	Plymouth	July 1856
April 1853	Pozzie, William E.	Metropolitan	Retired	Nov. 1853
May 1854	Pozzie, William E.	Metropolitan	Carlisle	August 1856
July 1857	Pozzie, William E.	Metropolitan	Tavistock	May 1858
January 1860	Pozzie, William E.	Metropolitan	Hull	July 1861
November 1856	Peal, Samuel E.	Metropolitan	Finsbury	March 1859
March 1858	Pilsbury, Richard	No record	Dismissed	July 1858
March 1859	Parker, John B.	Birmingham	Mauritius	February 1862
October 1865	Parker, John B.	Birmingham	Charterhouse; afterwards St. Martin's	October 1867
October 1859	Pilsbury, Wilmot	Birmingham	Marylebone	October 1864
October 1859	Puckett, Robert C.	Metropolitan	Brighton	October 1861
December 1861	Puckett, Robert C.	Metropolitan	Bath	January 1865
November 1853	Rafter, Henry	No record	Coventry	March 1854
March 1854	Riley, Benjamin	Manchester	Retired	January 1856
April 1854	Ryles, George	Potteries	Potteries	August 1854
October 1856	Ryles, George	Potteries	Basingstoke	December 1857
January 1853	Rowland, John C.	No record	Carnarvon	June 1853
December 1854	Rowe, John	Penzance	Manchester	April 1857
October 1865	Rowe, John	Penzance	Taunton	Dec. 1866
October 1854	Ryan, Charles	Dublin	Leeds	Nov. 1856
March 1855	Randall, John	Metropolitan	Employed by Department, Designer to Jackson & James	June 1865
March 1857	Robjohn, Francis R.	Tavistock	Nottingham	February 1861
October 1857	Raimbach, David	No record	Birmingham	February 1858
March 1858	Rawle, John Samuel	No record	Nottingham and West London 1880	October 1864
March 1857	Rees, Mary	Metropolitan	No record	July 1865
October 1860	Richards, Charles	Birmingham	Dismissed	July 1861
February 1853	Swallow, John C.	Metropolitan	Leeds	Sept. 1854
October 1870	Swallow, John C.	Metropolitan	Ryde	August 1872
November 1873	Swallow, John C.	Metropolitan	Pro. tem. Glasgow	April 1874
October 1853	Swinstead, Charles	Metropolitan	Marlboro' House	March 1855
November 1853	Sturtevant, Charles T.	No record	York	Sept. 1855
	Sturtevant, Charles T.	No record	Birmingham	February 1858
April 1853	Stanton, G. Clark	Birmingham	Retired	July 1853
March 1855	Sheil, Edward	No record	Cork	January 1856
May 1854	Slocombe, Charles P.	Metropolitan	South Kensington, and invalided 1882	October 1855
November 1852	Stannus, Anthony	Belfast	Merthyr Tydvil Bath	June 1853 Sept. 1854

Came.	Name.	Whence.	Appointed to.	Left.
March 1855	Sparkes, John	No record	Lambeth, & Principal N.A.T.S. 1882	March 1859
October 1855	Smith, Walter	Metropolitan	St. Martin's and Charterhouse	May 1857
July 1859	Smith, Walter	Metropolitan	Leeds	January 1860
October 1855	Sonnes, William H.	Metropolitan	Birmingham	April 1857
October 1855	Sylvester, Henry	Metropolitan	Aberdeen	July 1858
November 1856	Swallow, Jane F.	Metropolitan	Retired	February 1861
October 1857	Stevenson, Andrew	Dundee	Leeds	July 1858
October 1860	Stevenson, Andrew	Dundee	No record	March 1861
November 1857	Smyth, Walter E.	Dublin	Dublin	February 1858
March 1858	Sawkins, Isabel	Metropolitan	No record	July 1867
March 1859	Short, John T.	Bath	Andover	Sept. 1864
September 1861	Soden, Susannah	Metropolitan	No record	April 1865
October 1859	Smith, John A.	Dundee	Oxford	October 1864
October 1860	Stopford, William H.	Cork	St. Martin's	Sept. 1863
December 1853	Tucker, Raymond	No record	Tavistock	October 1855
June 1858	Tucker, Raymond	No record	Wellington College	May 1859
December 1853	Thompson, J. C.	No record	Warrington	October 1855
October 1858	Taylor, Edward R.	Burslem	Wolverhampton	October 1859
November 1860	Taylor, Edward R.	Burslem	Lincoln	February 1863
October 1854	Urie, Daniel	Paisley	Paisley	July 1855
July 1853	Walker, James W.	Norwich	Birmingham	April 1854
November 1853	White, John	No record	Leeds	July 1856
January 1854	Wigzel, Montague	Metropolitan	Exeter	Nov. 1854
January 1861	Wood, Daniel	Metropolitan	Cambridge	October 1862
April 1853	Williamson, James B.	Belfast	Newcastle	August 1853
September 1854	Williamson, James B.	Belfast	Taunton	May 1856
June 1859	Williamson, James B.	Belfast	Female School, Gower Street	October 1859
October 1854	Whitaker, Charles H.	Metropolitan	Dismissed; afterwards Birmingham	Dec. 1855
April 1857	Whitaker, Charles H.	Metropolitan	Struck off pay list	October 1857
October 1855	Waite, James	Newcastle	Newcastle	July 1856
November 1854	Wilson, Catherine	Metropolitan	South Kensington	October 1855
October 1855	Wardle, George	Macclesfield	Devonport	January 1859
October 1861	Wardle, George	Macclesfield	Dismissed	June 1863
March 1856	Way, Charles Jones	Metropolitan	Canada	Nov. 1858
March 1856	Wright, Henry William	No record	Retired	February 1858
April 1856	Woolner, Henry	No record	Coalbrookdale	March 1861
November 1856	Way, William Casens	Metropolitan	Wolverhampton	July 1858
June 1859	Way, William Casens	Metropolitan	Newcastle	Dec. 1861
November 1856	Walsh, Nicholas	Dublin	Retired	March 1857
November 1856	Wheeler, Sarah Ann	No information	Retired	February 186
October 1857	Wrigley, William	Aberdeen	Died.	March 1859
October 1857	Wilson, Helena	Metropolitan	Queen's Square	Sept. 1861
October 1860	Waite, Robert Thorn	Cheltenham	Retired	Nov. 1863
July 1853	Yeats, George P.	No record	Stourbridge	April 1854
September 1854	Young, William Allen	Dublin	Dismissed	February 1856
October 1853	Nottingham, John Wm.	Metropolitan	Dismissed	July 1855
March 1861	Kennedy, James	Dublin	Retired	July 1863
March 1862	Fisher, Alexander	Dudley	Lewes	May 1868
March 1862	Goepel, James S.	Liverpool	Frome	May 1867
March 1862	Stevenson, Rea J.	Halifax	Perth	Sept. 1869
October 1862	McGill, Murdoch W.	Dudley	Cape of Good Hope	October 1868
November 1862	Jones, David	Carmarthen	Dudley	January 1868
March 1862	Thomas, Stephen G.	Penzance	No record	October 1866
March 1868	Thomas, Stephen G.	Penzance	Dismissed	July 1868
March 1862	Sturgeon, William	Leeds	Leeds	April 1868
March 1862	Pritchard, Zachariah	Macclesfield	Grammar School, Manchester	January 1869

N

Came.	Name.	Wnence.	Appointed to.	Left.
March 1861	Sadler, Alfred	Metropolitan	Retired	Sept. 1863
March 1863	Ryan, Francis James,	Metropolitan	Employed by Captain Fowke, R.E.	February 186
February 1863	Black, Amy Eliza	Metropolitan	Became National Scholar	June 1868
March 1862	Horncastle, Jane A.	Metropolitan	No record	July 1867
October 1863	Larking, Mary	Metropolitan	Private School	January 186
March 1867	Larking, Mary	Metropolitan	Painting tiles for department	June 1868
November 1864	Duckett, William	Preston	Retired	October 186
March 1870	Duckett, William	Preston	Dover	July 1870
November 1864	Sullivan, Michael	Metropolitan	Kendall, afterwards Hastings	July 1870
June 1865	Bradbury, Alfred	Leeds	Hanley	May 1870
April 1865	Craister, Walter	York	Chester	February 186
March 1865	Spragge, Catherine	Metropolitan	Retired; Dr. Dresser	Dec. 1866
February 1865	Ryder, Emily	Dublin	No record	February 186
April 1866	Childe, Ellen Eliza	Metropolitan	Philadelphia; returned to S. K. 1875	October 186
January 1867	Tucker, William	Taunton	Kidderminster	February 18
April 1867	Theaker, George	Sheffield	Burslem	October 1869
March 1867	Grubb, William	Dundee	No record	October 186
March 1867	McCarty, William	Cork	Retired	October 187
March 1867	Lyons, Thomas	Cork	Monmouth	February 18
March 1867	Cox, William	Metropolitan	Sheffield	April 1869
March 1867	Hall, Julia Georgina	Metropolitan	No record	February 18
October 1867	Catley, William	Boston	Preston, since dead	May 1872
October 1867	Roberts, William	Southampton	Oxford	January 186
October 1870	Roberts, William	Southampton	Stroud	August 187
October 1867	Robinson, Thomas W. H.	Leeds	Lewes	August 187
October 1867	Lindsay, Thomas	Liverpool and Cape Town	Belfast Rugby College	July 1870 July 1880
October 1867	Lowne, Joseph J.	Metropolitan	Struck off pay list	January 187
October 1867	Dickenson, Henry D.	Newcastle-on-Tyne	Broomsgrove	August 187
October 1867	Smith, Isabella F.	Queen's Square	No record	February 18
March 1868	Barry, Sarah	Cork	No record	February 18
March 1868	Home, Emily	Bristol	No record	February 18
March 1868	Nesbitt, Sidney	Boston	Bath and Chippenham; afterwards to Frome	Dec. 1869
April 1868	Rawson, William	Leeds	Keighley	January 187
November 1868	Charbonnier, Theodore	Bristol	Ryde, since Southampton 1882	March 1874
October 1868	McMinn, Jane K.	Metropolitan	No record	February 18
October 1868	Croasdale, Elizabeth	Metropolitan	Appd. S. America, retired	May 1869
March 1869	Harbutt, William	Metropolitan	Bath	Nov. 1874
March 1869	Jones, William	Carmarthen	Barnsley	Sept. 1874
March 1869	Pratt, Robert	Dundee	Inverness	October 186
April 1869	Baker, Thomas	Coventry	Bridport	April 1873
March 1869	Bunker, Joseph	Oxford	Stroud, afterwards Wakefield	October 187
March 1869	Teasdale, John	Newcastle-on-Tyne	Belfast pro. tem.	October 18
March 1869	Underhill, Edward S.	Metropolitan	Died	February 1
October 1869	Cortissos, Charles	Rotherhithe	Shrewsbury	Sept. 1874
October 1869	Pryce, Henry E.	Metropolitan	Died	October 18
October 1869	McGregor, Sarah E.	Queen's Square	No record	February 1
October 1869	Ayres, Helena	Bristol	No record	February 1
October 1869	Woon, Rosa E.	Metropolitan	No record	Sept. 1873

Came.	Name.	Whence.	Appointed to.	Left.
March 1870	Blair, David	Birkenhead	Resigned	February 1872
October 1870	Broad, William	Tavistock	Stroud	Dec. 1875
March 1870	Hodder, Albert	Bridport	Tavistock	Nov. 1873
January 1875	Hodder, Albert	Bridport	Worcester	Sept. 1875
March 1, 1870	Ireland, Samuel J.	Metropolitan	Barrow-in-Furness	Sept. 1874
March 1, 1870	Turner, George	Metropolitan	Kendal	January 1875
March 1870	Watson, Thomas	Leeds	Dollar	Nov. 1875 .
March 1870	Williamson, James J.	Metropolitan	Rossell College, Lancashire	January 1872
January 1873	Williamson, James J.	Metropolitan	No record	Nov. 1873
March 1870	Twynam, Elizabeth	Metropolitan	No record	February 1872
March 1870	Watson, Lizzie	No record	No record	February 1872
October 1870	Steel, Margaret	Dundee	No record	Sept. 1872
April 1871	Brown, Frederick	Metropolitan	Royal Architectural Museum, Westminster	February 1877
April 1871	Gear, Arthur Handel	Metropolitan	Retired	October 1874
April 1871	Miller, Annie Dupuy	Newcastle-on-Tyne	No record	February 1873
April 1871	Park, John	Newcastle-on-Tyne	Resigned	February 1878
April 1871	Parkinson, Amelia	Metropolitan	No record	February 1873
April 1871	Tunmer Harris, John	Metropolitan	Southampton	January 1874
April 1871	Webster, Alfred George	Metropolitan	Lincoln	May 1877
October 1871	Hodges, Charles Martin	Bristol	Bath	October 1879
October 1871	Payne, George	Metropolitan	Resigned	April 1873
March 1872	Hepworth, Walter	Leicester	Resigned	April 1873
March 1872	Merritt, William J.	Gloucester	Retired,afterwards Isle of Man	Nov. 1880
March 1872	Murcott, Theophilus	South Kensington	Resigned	May 1877
March 1872	Elgood, George S.	Leicester	Resigned	February 1874
March 1872	Hill, Joseph	Hanley	Manchester	Dec. 1877
March 1872	Jobbins, William Henry	Leicester	Nottingham	Dec. 1876
March 1872	Carter, Grace	South Kensington	Resigned	March 1874
March 1872	Carter, Mary	South Kensington	No record	Sept. 1873
March, 1872	Gibbons, Edward	Cirencester	Edinburgh	May 1876
October 1872	Addey, Joseph Poole	Cork	Londonderry	March 1875
October 1872	Took, Frederick A.	South Kensington	Retired	January 1875
January 1873	Luke, Frederick	Tavistock	Dublin (Royal Society)	Nov. 1877
March 1873	Morton, George	Newcastle-on-Tyne	Assistant Master, South Kensington	Sept. 1878
March 1873	Scott, Walter	Coventry	Macclesfield	October 1879
March 1873	Hammond, Ellen G.	Macclesfield	Time expired, drowned going to Bombay	March 1877
May 1873	Harley, George William	Windsor	Second Master, Belfast	February 1880
May 1873	Millar, Charles B.	Kilmarnock	Kilmarnock	Dec. 1877
October 1873	McNaught, Alexander	Kilmarnock	Preston	February 1876
October 1873	East, W. H.	Metropolitan	Dover	Sept. 1877
October 1873	Hill, H.	Cardiff	Northampton	January 1875
October 1873	Gill, E. Rowland	Leeds	Bridport	Sept. 1877
October 1873	Taylor, J. B.	Metropolitan	Cheltenham	Sept. 1878
October 1873	Marsh, Isabella	Metropolitan	No record	February 1877
March 1874	Langman, A. W. F.	Metropolitan	Manchester Grammar School	Sept. 1875
October 1878	Langman, A. W. F.	Metropolitan	Hartley Institute	February 1881
March 1874	Dalgleish, T. J.	Coventry	Nottingham	Sept. 1880

N 2

Came.	Name.	Whence.	Appointed to.	Left.
April 1874	Riley, Thomas	Kendal	With Mr. Poynter, R.A.	Sept. 1881
March 1874	Jefford, J. A.	Bridport	No record	Feb. 1878
April 1874	Thompson, F.	Darlington	Durham	Dec. 1877
April 1874	Fish, Evelyn	Metropolitan	Retired	Sept. 1875
October 1874	Cartlidge, S. J.	Burslem	Hanley	Feb. 1881
October 1874	Moffat, Miss F. J.	Metropolitan	Retired	June 1877
March 1875	Thorne, R. C.	Gravesend	Cheltenham	Sept. 1880
March 1875	Wallis, W.	Birmingham	Croydon	Sept. 1879
March 1875	Trowbridge, G.	Birmingham	Belfast	April 1880
April 1875	Kean, J. A.	Aberdeen	Doncaster	Sept. 1878
March 1875	Collier, Bernard C.	Metropolitan	Off list, since York, Canterbury	Sept. 1880
October 1875	Kemp, Minna	Metropolitan	Time expired, afterwards South Africa	Feb. 1879
April 1876	Farncombe, Henry	Brighton	Rose Hill Training College	Dec. 1881
April 1876	Anderson, David	Dundee	Glasgow	Sept. 1881
April 1876	Watson, William P.	Metropolitan	Time expired, afterwards South Kensington	April 1881
November 1875	Wade, George	Metropolitan	Resigned	May 1876
December 1876	Greenwood, Edwin	Kidderminster	Bombay	June 1882
March 1877	Millard, Charles S.	Metropolitan	Off list, afterwards Cheltenham	January 1881
March 1877	Wood, George A.	Metropolitan	Hertford	Sept. 1882fi
March 1877	Willis, Richard H. A.	Cork	Manchester	March 1883
March 1877	Broad, Sophia	Metropolitan	Resigned	July 1879
March 1877	Walford, Amy T.	Metropolitan	Became N. Scholar	Sept. 1878
April 1877	Lewis, Alfred	Leicester	Weston - super - Mare	Sept. 1882
March 1877	Geffroi, Frederick	Penzance	Died	Sept. 1877
April 1877	Hare, George	Limerick	Off list, afterwards South Kensington	January 1884
November 1877	Barkas, Henry D.	Bath		
November 1877	Perkin, Emil S.	Barrow - in - Furness	Tiverton	Sept. 1882
November 1877	Spain, John H.	Dover	Tavistock	Sept. 1882
March 1878	Baldry, Alfred L.	Metropolitan	Resigned	February 187!
March 1878	Bate, Henry F.	Metropolitan	Resigned	Feb. 1879
June 1878	Wright, Peter	No record	No record	July 1878
April 1878	Gill, Henry P.	Brighton	Adelaide, South Australia	Sept. 1882
March 1878	Clarke, James	Metropolitan	Artist	Sept. 1880
April 1878	Barton, William B.	Leicester	Preston	Oct. 1882
October 1878	Black, Francis	Nottingham	Charter House	May 1882
November 1878	Norris, William	Gloucester	South Kensington	March 1883
March 1879	Llewellyn, S. H. W.	Cirencester	South Kensington, since Lambeth 1884	.
November 1878	Whitehead, Arthur	Leamington	South Kensington	March 1884
November 1878	Renard, Edwin	Hastings	Shipley	October 1881
October 1878	Hackford, Mary	Metropolitan	Retired	J|nuary 1884
March 1879	Fisher, Amy	Metropolitan	Time expired	February 188!
November 1879	Lowenthal, Dora	Bristol	Time expired	Sept. 1882
November 1879	White, William	Leeds		
November 1879	Somerscales, John	Hull	Manchester	Sept. 1883
November 1879	Schröder, Walter	Brighton	Chester	June 1884
October 1879	Sharpe, Herbert	Metropolitan	Off list	D.c. 1882
October 1879	Elton, Edgar	Metropolitan		
April 1880	Bebb, Isabel L.	Bath	Time expired	March 1883
April 1880	Raimbach, Lewis	Metropolitan	Retired	April 1882

Came.	Name.	Whence.	Appointed to.	Left.
April 1880	Havell, Ernest B.	Reading	Madras	Nov. 1883
April 1881	Lloyd, J. A.	Metropolitan	Marlboro' College	May 1883
April 1881	Mulligan, Walter	Wallsall		
April 1881	Ward, George	Devizes		
April 1881	Busk, William	Metropolitan		
October 1881	Earles, Frederick R.	Metropolitan		
October 1881	Spencer, Augustus	Metropolitan		
October 1881	Randerson Pauline	Metropolitan		
January 1882	Newbury, F. H.	Metropolitan		
March 1882	Caston, Alice	Metropolitan	Time expired	March 1884
March 1882	Dodd, Charles T.	Metropolitan		
October 1882	Pearce, Joseph A.	Bristol		
April 1883	Woodhouse, F. W.	Metropolitan		
October 1882	Cole, Thomas W.	Metropolitan	South Kensington	March 1884
October 1882	Hall, Philip	Cirencester		
October 1882	Hudson, Henry	Metropolitan		
October 1882	Dunlop, James M.	Kilmarnock		
October 1882	Heath, Alice M.	Gloucester		
April 1883	Craigmile, William	Hull		
March 1883	Hunter, Annie	Metropolitan		
April 1883	Hewitt, Alfred E.	Birmingham		
April 1883	Rider, Haywood	York		
April 1883	Lee, John	Darlington		
November 1883	Reily, Francis	Birmingham		
October 1883	Poole, John O.	South Kensington		
October 1883	Wilkinson, Alfred	South Kensington		

LIST OF
NATIONAL SCHOLARS.

CENTRAL SCHOOL,

SOUTH KENSINGTON.

COMMENCING 1863.

Names.	Dates.	Age.	Previous Occupation.	Where from.	Employment on leaving School.
s, Luke	1863 to 1865	19	Designer for Textiles	Warrington	Designer and Draughtsman (afterwards A.R.A.)
is, Joseph (ow Master at icester)	1863 to 1865 1870 to 1871	18	.. ..	Nottingham	Left on account of ill health. Designer for Lace and Embroidery. Appointed to Salisbury
hy, Andrew	1863 to 1865	20	.. ..	Dublin	Engagement with Messrs. Trollope
, James	Jan. 1864 to July 1864	26	A.M., Leeds School	Leeds	Appointed to Macclesfield
mbe, Fred.	1864 to 1867	17	.. ..	Metropolitan	Designer to a Cabinet Maker
ly, Robert	Nov. 1864 to Jan. 1865	17	..	Metropolitan	Engaged as Draughtsman at Northampton
l, Henry	1865 to 1867	18	.. ..	Warrington	Draughtsman on "Graphic" (now A R.A.)
is, Rowland	1865 to 1871	24	..	Burslem	Employed as Modeller to Wedgwood, Burslem
;nt, Wm.	1865 to 1868	21	.. ..	Burslem	Modeller to Messrs. Blashfield, Stamford
)man, John	1865 to 1867	18	.. ..	Metropolitan	Employed by Department Modelling for Building
'ison, Walter m.	1865 to 1866	21		Training School	Employed by Department under Godfrey Sykes, Modelling
)ons, Albert	1865 to 1868	20	.. ..	Gloucester	Drowned in Serpentine
1s, John	1865 to 1867	21	Local Scholar.	Great Yarmouth	Ecclesiastical Decorator, afterwards Animal Painter
rtnall, Edird	1865 to 1867	19	Apprentice Cotton Manufacturer	Warrington	Draughtsman on Wood
) William	1866 to 1868	21	.. ..	Training School	Employed by Messrs. Minton on Departmental Decoration
nleighton, ward	1866 to 1868	24	.. ..	Training School.	Engaged by Messrs. Trollope
), Richard	1866 to 1868	26	..	Sheffield.	Engagement in Draughtsman's Office, afterwards Master at Sheffield
son, William ge	1866 to 1868	21	.. ..	Metropolitan	No record
nan, George	1866 to 1868	21		Bath.	Designer to Messrs. Benton & Lewis, Kidderminster
'ns, Owen	1866 to 1869	19	..	Cirencester.	Employed by Department as Decorative Painter and Modeller
), James	1866 to 1867	25	.. ..	Stoke	Appointed Potteries as Designer and Modeller
n, George	1866 to 1868	21	Die Sinker	Birmingham	Engaged as Die Sinker by Messrs. Wyon, afterwards at Washington Mint
ness, Wil-	1867 to 1869	18	..	Training School	Designer to Messrs. Morris & Co.

Names.	Dates.	Age.	Previous Occupation.	Where from.	Employment on leaving School
Sharpe, Thomas	1867 to 1869	24	..	Charterhouse	Designer to Messrs. Morri
Morrison, Peter	1867 to 1869	29	..	Kidderminster	Engaged as Designer at K derminster
Randall, Wm.	1867 to 1869	21		Stroud	Designer to Messrs. Hartl & Co., Westminster
Beesley, James	1867 to 1869	22		Birmingham	Engaged as Designer at B mingham
Rushworth, Geo.	1867 to 1869	22	..	Halifax	Designer to Messrs. Cross Halifax
Brooke, John	1867 to 1869	31	Draughtsman for an iron foundry	Sheffield	Employed by Rowland M ris as Modeller
Mason, Herbert	1867 to 1868	21	Designer and Modeller	Birmingham	Designer and Modeller Birmingham
Galli, Luigi	1868 to 1872	24	Student, R.A.	Preston	Appointed Preston, 5th A 1872
Cox, Thomas	Mar. 1868 to Oct. 1868	21	Architectural Draughtsman	Birmingham	Designer to Messrs. Hart&
Eyre, John	1868 to 1870	20	Porcelain Painter	Stoke-on-Trent	Messrs. Morris, Quee Square. Tile painting
Perks, Benjamin	1868 to 1871	27	Designer for Carpets	Kidderminster	Designer
Kirkman, Wm.	Oct. 1868 to Dec. 1868	25	Student	S. Kensington	Died
Turner, John	1868 to 1870	36	Cabinet Maker & Designer	Sheffield	Engaged by Messrs. Wall Cabinet Makers
Frost, John	Oct. 1868 to Nov. 1868	18	Architect's assistant	Coventry	Dismissed. Mad
Black, Amy Eliza	1868 to 1869	21	S. in Training	Metropolitan	Engaged by Departm Painting Tiles
Walker, Susannah	1868 to 1869	22	S. in Training	South Kensington.	Engaged by Departm Painting Tiles
Arnold, W. Henry	1869 to 1871	24	S. S. Kensington	Metropolitan	Engaged by Messrs Min
Foster, Herbert W.	1869 to 1871	21	Student	Nottingham	Engaged by Department Decorative Painter
Hardgrave, Charles	1869 to 1871	21	Glass Stainer	York	Designer, Whitefriars Gl Works
Marshall, Wm.	1869 to 1871	22	Modeller and Designer.	Sheffield	Modeller
Morgan, Walter Jenks	1869 to 1871	21	Lithographer	Birmingham	Designer, Stained Glass
Nunn, Walter J.	1869 to 1871	28	China Painter	Charterhouse	Engaged by Messrs. Bu and Sons, Fleet Street
Smith, John Bates	1869 to 1871	18	Carpet Designer	Halifax	Carpet Designer, Crossb Co., Halifax
Rossiter, Henry	1869 to 1871	22	Glass Painter.	Frome	Glass Painter, Me O'Connor, Berners St Oxford Street
Wilson, Thos. W.	1869 to 1871	17	Student, South Kensington	S. Kensington	Drawing on Wood and Ge ral Designor
Golding, Thos. A.	1869 to 1871	16	Student	S. Kensington	Glass Painter at Me Heaton, Butler & Bain
Morton, Chas. J.	1869 to 1871	21	Designer and Modeller	Birmingham	Designer to Messrs. Mitc Vane, & Co., New Yor
Fourness, Wm.	1869 to 1871	26	Decorator	Charterhouse	Engaged by Messrs. Trol
Drake, George E.	186. to 1871	21	Carpet Designor	Halifax	Designer to Messrs. McC Halifax. Carpet desi on his own account
Rhodes, Wm. P.	1869 to 1871	20	China Painter	Newcastle	Dead
Marklew, Wm.	Mar. 1870 to Sept. 1870	21	Embosser	Birmingham	Resigned
Cope, James	1870 to 1872	24	Stone Carver and Modeller	Hanley	Employed in the Potter
Rowley, James	1870 to 1872	22	Designer for Lace	West London	Employed by Messrs. B bruner, Regent Street

Names.	Dates.	Age	Previous Occupation.	Where from.	Employment on leaving School.
eeves, Thomas	1870 to 1872	22	Engraver	Birmingham	Employed by Messrs. Dee, of Sherwood
auson, Wm.	1870 to 1872	20	Decorative Artist	S. Kensington	Engaged by Messrs. Trollope
yne, George	1871 to 1873	17	Student and Designer	South Kensington	Designer to Messrs. Akroyd & Sons, Halifax
aw, John J.	1871 to 1873	21	Art Student and Designer	South Kensington	Engaged by Messrs. Aitchison, Architects
mpson, George	1871 to 1873	20	.. ..	South Kensington	Art Master
ler, James W.	1871 to 1872	23	.. ..	South Kensington	Resigned.
dges, George H.	1871 to 1873	24	Carver and Designer for Furniture	Spitalfields	S. Royal Academy
rrison, Joseph	1871 to 1873	25	.. ..	Nottingham	Engaged at Sheffield
ger, Walter H.	1871 to 1873	18	Designer for Ironwork	Frome	Designer at Frome
nery, Charles E.	1871 to 1873	21	.. ..	Birmingham	Drowned in Thames trying to save life
ulson, Matthew	1871 to 1873	22	.. ..	Newcastle-on-Tyne	Engaged by Messrs. Trollope
bbons, Edward	March 1872 to Oct. 1872	28	Plasterer	Cirencester	Appointed student in training. 2nd Master Edinburgh S. of Art
ummond, Geo. D.	1872 to 1874	25	Student	South Kensington	Engaged by Mr. Heyman, Lace Manufacturer, Nottingham
ntgomery, Wm.	1872 to 1874	21	Glass painter	Newcastle-on-Tyne	Engaged by Messrs. Clayton and Bell.
raham, Robert	1872 to 1874	20	Flower Painter on Porcelain	Stoke - on - Trent	Employed at Potteries
rrie, Sidney D.	1872 to 1874	20	Brass Founders' Pattern Maker	Birmingham	Working on his own account
omas, James H.	1872 to 1874	18	Marble Carver and Modeller	Bristol	Sculptor on own account
ly, Edward	1872 to 1874	24	Shoemaker	Salisbury	Carpet Designer, own account
tkins, John	1873 to 1875	18	Lithographic Draughtsman	Birmingham	Engaged by Department as an Etcher
ae, John Q.	1873 to 1875	20	Designer for Damask	Belfast	Designer
enck, Fred.	1873 to 1875	24	Modeller	Hanley	Art Master, Hanley.
gley, Walter	1873 to 1875	21	Lithographer	Birmingham	Member of Institute Painters in Water Colours
usen, George	1873 to 1875	21	Decorative Designer	South Kensington	Working on his own account
rlock, John	1873 to 1875	22	House Decorator	Warrington	Employed at Simpson's, Decorator
mphries, rles	1874 to 1876	22	Student	South Kensington	Dead
rd, James	1874 to 1876	22	House Decorator	Belfast	Employed by Department on Sir Frederick Leighton's Cartoon and Art Teacher
dley, Charles	1874 to 1875	27	Designer. Tile Work	Coalbrookdale	Retired, Art Director in Pottery Works
rick, William	1874 to 1876	22	Marble Carver	Bristol	Employed, School of Art, Bristol
ndley, Charles	1874 to 1876	23	Carpet Designer	Kidderminster	Designer for Textiles, on own account
marsh, Hy. E.	1874 to 1876	19	Art Decorator	S. Kensington	Working on own account

Names.	Dates.	Age.	Prevous Occupation.	Where from.	Employment on leaving School
Edelstein (Miss), A. J.	1874 to 1876	30	Teacher and Illuminator	Warrington	No record
Jameson, Benjamin	1875 to 1877	20	Bricklayer	Warrington	Employed at Templeton Glasgow
Collins, Charles Edward	1875 to 1877	22	Designer for Iron Work	Birmingham	Designer for Iron Wo Birmingham
Bloor, Daniel	1875 to 1878	21	Modeller	Hanley	Employed with Mr. Bro Sculptor
Bell, Thomas F.	1875 to 1878	25	Linen Trade	Belfast	Designer for Damask, on o account
Reynolds, Henry	1875 to 1878	23	Lithographer	Birmingham	Glass Painter and Desig at Birmipgham
Harvey, Henry	1875 to 1878	26	Plasterer	South Kensington	Modeller, on own account
Broad, William	1876 to 1878	24	Pottery Painter	Worcester	Jackson's, designing dec tions
Holgate, Joseph	1876 to 1879	22	Carpet Designer	Halifax	Teaching at Westminster Designer, own account
Phillips, Thomas	1876 to 1878	21	Clerk in Linen Trade	Belfast	Master, School of Art, S ney. Since dead
Singer, Edgar Ratcliffe	1876 to 1879	18	Designer for Iron-work	Frome	Designer, own account
Cresswell, C. F. E. (Miss)	1876 to 1878	27	Student	Bristol	Decorative Designer Rooms and Windows
Rhead, George W.	1877 to 1879	22	Pottery Painter	Stoke-on-Trent	Pottery Painting
Benson, John Marsh	1877 to 1879	27	Draughtsman	Sheffield.	Designer for Silver Pottery
Kennington, Thomas	1877 to 1879	21	House Decorator	Liverpool	Artist
McKenzie, Wm.	1878 to 1880	20	Damask Designer	Belfast	Damask Designer
Ascough, Edward W.	1878 to 1880	17	.. ..	Birmingham.	Modelling Master, Dublin
Bladen, Thomas W.	1878 to 1880	19	Pottery Painter	Newcastle.	Designer, Cards, Glass, &c
Nicholas, Arthur	1878 to 1880	20	Tile Painter	Coalbrookdale	Designing on own accoun
Rhead, Louis J.	1878 to 1880	19	Pottery Painter.	Newcastle	Designer for a book f Brooklyn, U.S.
Walford, Amy Isabella, Miss	1878 to 1880	26	Student	South Kensington	Teaching Technical Sch Kennington
Ledward, Richd. A.	1879 to 1882	21	Modeller	Burslem	Appointed Assistant-Mast South Kensington
Marriott, Fredk.	1879 to 1882	18	Tile Painting	Coalbrook-dale	Designer, Marcus War Co.
Hayes Michael	1879 to 1881	22	Decorative Artist	Limerick	Designer, Messrs. Trollo[
Proctor, Joseph	1879 to 1882	22	Draughtsman and Designer	Burslem	Teacher of Design at Cha house School of Art
McKenzie, John	1879 to 1881	23	Damask Designer	Belfast	Damask Designer, own count
Drury, Alfred	1879 to 1881	22	Stone Carver and Designer	South Kensington	With Monsieur Dalou, Sc tor, Paris
Riley, Arthur D.	1879 to 1881	19	Decorator	South Kensington	Master, Art School, Syd
Pratt, Wm. B.	1880 to 1882	27	Draughtsman and Designer	Cirencester	Designer for Ecclesias Furniture
Bowcher, Alfred W.	1881 to 1883	19	Student	South Kensington	Terra-cotta Works, Cans Cornwall. T. S. Steve
Gibbons, Francis	April 1881 to Dec. 1881	28	Plasterer, Decorator, and Designer	Cirencester	Engaged Bethnal Po Works
Morrow, Albert J.	1881 to 1883	17	Designer, House Decorator	Belfast	Art Society, Bond Stree

Names.	Dates.	Age.	Previous Occupation.	Where from.	Employment on leaving School.
Albert A.	1881 to 1883	19	Modeller	Newcastle	Designer on own account
ell, Charles	1881 to 1883	21	Designer (Metal Work)	Birmingham	Designing Stained Glass at Birmingham (now working for Department)
i, Louis	1881 to 1883	21	Student	South Kensington	Designer, House Decorations, Stained Glass
, John W. E.	1881 to 1883	19	Draughtsman (Doulton's)	Lambeth	Working for Director for Department
ias, W. G.	1881 to 1883	23	Designer	Westminster	Designing Master, Manchester School of Art
', John	1882	24	Tailor	Newcastle-under-Lyne	Monitor to N. S. in N. T. S. Designer on his own account
, Wm. M.	1882 to 1883	19	Figure Painter on China	Burslem	Employed by Department in Italy
es, Roland	1882	17	Modeller and Stone Carver	Newcastle-under-Lyne	
ins, Henry	1882	22	Designer and Ornamental Draughtsman	Worcester	Designer, Patent Office, Chancery Lane
iy, Frank	1882 to 1883	19	Designer (Silver Work)	Birmingham	Designer, silver work
iurn, John	1882	22	Draughtsman (Tile Works)	Coalbrookdale	
s, John A.	1882	28	Art Teacher	Gloucester	
ts, Ellis W.	1882	22	Figure Painter on China	Stoke-on-Trent	
rinick, Ar-r D.	1883	22	Clerk	Belfast	
ey, Geo. F.	1883	20	Draughtsman	Birmingham	
iam, Francis	1883	24	Designer and Decorator for Pottery.	West London	
n, Henry	1883	33	Calico Printers' Designer	Preston	
n, Fredk. T.	1883	17	China Painter	Stoke-on-Trent	
iton, Fredk.	1883	21	Tile Painter and Designer	Coalbrookdale	
pton, Edw.	1883	27	Student	S. Kensington	
, Wm. H.	1883	27	Modeller and Designer	S. Kensington	
r, John	1883	22	Designer and Modeller	Sheffield	

www.ingramcontent.com/pod-product-compliance
Lightning Source LLC
Chambersburg PA
CBHW031057280326
41928CB00049B/964